The Diplomacy of the Crucial Decade

The Diplomacy of the Crucial Decade

American Foreign Relations During the 1960s

Diane B. Kunz, Editor

NEW YORK   COLUMBIA UNIVERSITY

Columbia University Press
New York   Chichester, West Sussex
Copyright © 1994 Columbia University Press
All rights reserved

Library of Congress Cataloging-in-Publication Data

The diplomacy of the crucial decade: American foreign relations
    during the 1960s / Diane B. Kunz, editor.
        p.   cm.
    Includes bibliographical references and index.
    ISBN 0–231–08176–6 (cl: acid-free paper). – ISBN 0–231–08177–4
    (pa: acid-free paper)
        1. United States—Foreign relations—1961–1963. 2. United States—
    Foreign relations—1963–1969.   I. Kunz, Diane B., 1952–   .
E841.D46   1994
327.73—dc20   93–37995

⊗   CIP
Casebound editions of Columbia University Press books are printed on
permanent and durable acid-free paper.

Printed in the United States of America
c 10 9 8 7 6 5 4 3 2 1

Contents

•

About the Contributors

•

David Kaiser is Professor in the Strategy Department of the Naval War College, Newport, Rhode Island. He received his B.A. and Ph.D from Harvard and is the author of *Economic Diplomacy and War: European Conflict from Philip II to Hitler*, as well as numerous articles and reviews on American foreign policy.

Diane B. Kunz is Associate Professor of History at Yale University and author of *The Economic Diplomacy of the Suez Crisis*. A former corporate lawyer, she is at work on a history of American economic diplomacy during the Cold War.

Douglas Little is Associate Professor of History at Clark University, where he has taught since 1978. His articles on U.S. policy toward the Middle East since 1945 have appeared in the *Journal of American History*, the *Middle East Journal*, and the *International Journal of Middle East Studies*.

Thomas A. Schwartz is Associate Professor of History at Vanderbilt University in Nashville, Tennessee. He is the author of *America's Germany: John J. McCloy and the Federal Republic of Germany*.

Michael Schaller is Professor of History at the University of Arizona. He is the author of several books on the history of American-East Asian relations including The American Occupation of Japan: the Origins of the Cold War in Asia.

Robert D. Schulzinger is Professor of History at the University of Colorado at Boulder, where he has taught since 1977. He is the author of numerous books on the history of U.S. foreign relations including *American Diplomacy in the Twentieth Century* (1994) and *Henry Kissinger: Doctor of Diplomacy* (1989).

Gerald Thomas (Ph.D., Yale 1973) is a retired Rear Admiral, U.S. Navy, and a former U.S. Ambassador to Guyana and Kenya. He is a Lecturer in History and African and Afro-American Studies and also serves as Master of Davenport College at Yale University.

William O. Walker III, Professor of History at Ohio Wesleyan University, is the author of *Drug Control in the Americas* and *Opium and Foreign Policy: The Anglo-American Search for Order in Asia, 1912–1954*, as well as numerous articles concerning international drug control policy. The recipient of a Social Science-Research Council-John D. and Catherine T. Macarthur Foundation Fellowship in International Peace and Security, Walker is also a senior research associate at the North-South Center of the University of Miami.

Arthur Waldron is a Harvard-trained China specialist who teaches strategy at the U.S. Naval War College and East Asian Studies at Brown University. He is the author of *The Great Wall of China: From History to Myth*.

Vladislav M. Zubok, graduate of Moscow State University, is a Russian historian of the Cold War. His chapter is written with the help of a grant from the John D. and Catherine T. Macarthur Foundation and a grant from the U.S. Institute of Peace.

The Diplomacy of the Crucial Decade

"The idea of a fundamental conflict between our international commitments and the strength of our economy is seldom borne out; it is a question of our willingness to pay, not our ability."

PAUL M. VOLCKER, SECRETARY OF THE TREASURY

Introduction: The Crucial Decade

•

A new president has taken office. One of the youngest ever, he had run on a campaign platform pledged to get the country out of the torpor that had gripped it during years of Republican rule—Republicans who also represented a different generation. While this description fits William Jefferson Clinton, the man Americans elected to lead the United States toward the twenty-first century, it also depicts his role model and inspiration, John F. Kennedy. During Kennedy's administration and that of his Democratic successor, Lyndon B. Johnson, the United States embarked on a new domestic journey. Civil rights, the women's movement, Medicare, the war on poverty: these transforming developments all began in the last Democratic-run decade. But to Kennedy, domestic affairs took second place to the world stage. He had campaigned on a platform that stressed the growing power of America's opponent in the bipolar contest in which we were then embroiled: the Soviet Union. Both Kennedy and Johnson waged the Cold War mightily: their diplomatic successes and failures form the subject of this book.

From 1948, when the Cold War's grip irrevocably constricted geopolitical realities, a bipartisan consensus on foreign affairs took hold in American political life. Both mainstream Democrats and Republicans accepted the realities of the Cold War and embraced the policy of containment. This doctrine, framed and named by master diplomat George Kennan, held that "the main element of any United States policy toward the Soviet Union must be that of a long-term patient but firm and vigilant containment of Russian expansive tendencies."[1] Under its aegis the United States for the first time created a national security apparatus that embraced a defense establishment, a large standing army, and the Central Intelligence Agency. The battle lines became clear: the United States would not attempt to alter the existing lines of demarcation between East and West but would oppose any advance by Communist forces by overt or covert means.

During the Republican administration of Dwight D. Eisenhower, president from 1953 until 1961, the boundaries of containment hardened. Washington sponsored coups in Iran and Guatemala and landed Marines on the shores of Lebanon. American support flowed generously to authoritarian regimes whose leaders were invited to join the plethora of security pacts Secretary of State John Foster Dulles had assembled. Yet, in 1956, when Soviet tanks brutally crushed the Hungarian anti-Communist revolt, the administration offered only rhetorical support. Geographical facts, Soviet conventional military superiority and the dangers of nuclear war combined to make any other response unthinkable.

Because Eisenhower had embraced the Democratic foreign policy in essence although not in name, rivals for the 1960 Democratic presidential nomination had been given no other choice during the late 1950s than to attack Eisenhower from the right. Exacerbating these tendencies was the specter of McCarthyism, an ideology to which the Republican senator from Wisconsin had given his name. It had unleashed a domestic witch hunt and created the realistic fear that anyone who deviated from a relentless anti-Communist stance would instantly be labeled a Communist sympathizer. Therefore, men like Hubert Humphrey of Minnesota, Stuart Symington of Missouri, and John Kennedy of Massachusetts, all Senate Democratic liberals, constantly urged the Eisenhower administration to take a stronger line against the Soviet Union.

By 1960 this drive manifested itself most strongly in the so-called missile gap issue: the continual reiteration by Kennedy that the Soviet Union's production of missiles had begun to exceed that of the United States. Both Kennedy and Richard Nixon (Eisenhower's Vice-President) placed their harsh Cold War rhetoric at the center of the race for the presidency. Kennedy used the missile gap issue against Nixon during their four televised debates while Nixon hinted that Kennedy would be soft on Communism. The territory of acceptable discussion on foreign policy issues had never been more narrow.

Kennedy squeaked into office with the smallest popular vote margin on record. He was the first president of the television age and on that still young medium Kennedy's youth and vigor contrasted sharply with the seventy-year-old Eisenhower's bearing. That Kennedy in reality was a sickly person who depended on frequent cortisone shots for his chronic Addison's Disease had been carefully concealed. Equally hidden was the President's constant marital infidelities, which gave the lie to the picture of family harmony repeatedly projected by the White

House. Yet despite these and other revelations, many Americans who remember the Kennedy years continue to hold Kennedy in a special light. His tragic death is in part responsible. Moreover, Kennedy's wit, charm and quick intelligence captivated his advisers then and affect historians today. Kennedy also represented to many Americans a particular optimistic view about this country—one that the dilemmas and dissent of the Vietnam war destroyed.

On that icy January morning in 1961, after Kennedy took the oath of office, he proclaimed that the United States would pay any price and bear any burden in defense of liberty. Generational factors partly account for this activist rhetoric. Just as important was the generally held belief that the United States was losing the Cold War. When Soviet premier Nikita Khrushchev pledged that "we will bury you," he expressed the fear prevalent in American society that developed nations and as well as the crowd of newly emergent countries would succumb to the embrace of a world communist movement that seemed on the march. Ironies abound. As we now know, the 1960s were the last decade in which the Soviet Union retained the ability to challenge the United States economically. Furthermore, for the United States that decade would become the most prosperous of the Cold War decades.

These realizations come with hindsight. For Kennedy and his advisers the Cold War ranked as their first priority. International realities partly determined Kennedy's continual interest in foreign policy; the president's own predilections also accounted for his emphasis on this issue. Like more recent presidents, Kennedy found both the global issues and nitty-gritty of international questions more to his taste than the humdrum details of domestic policy. In his state of the union message, Kennedy proclaimed a bevy of new programs, including a food for peace foreign aid plan and the Peace Corps, which would send American college graduates to help less developed nations. On March 13, 1961, before assembled Latin American diplomats, Kennedy announced the Alliance for Progress. But surreptitiously another Latin American initiative occupied the attention of the President and his team: the Bay of Pigs invasion. Kennedy had found himself trapped in the Eisenhower's administration's covert operation against Fidel Castro's Cuban government and to his bitter embarrassment had no choice but to take public responsibility for the Cuban exiles' failed attempt.

As it recovered from the Bay of Pigs debacle the Kennedy administration found it had little respite from foreign policy problems. Indeed, from Laos to the Vienna summit, from the Cuban Missile Crisis to Vietnam, the thousand days of the Kennedy administration resonated with the constant sound of alarm bells. How Kennedy dealt with these issues at a time of growing fears with regard to the decreasing American economic strength that buttressed our defense effort and that of our allies is revealed in the various chapters that follow. Implicit in some contributions, explicit in others, is the unanswerable question: What would have happened had Kennedy not been assassinated in Dallas, Texas on November 22, 1963?

Vice President Lyndon Johnson, who took the oath of office aboard Air Force One on that tragic day could not have been more different from his predecessor: born poor where Kennedy had been fabulously wealthy, homely rather than handsome, awkward rather than charming. Only their drive for power seemed similar. Like Kennedy, Johnson had been a senator. But while Kennedy had been regarded as a dilettante playboy, Johnson became a major powerhouse, rising to Senate Majority leader. Throughout his time in that position, from 1955 to 1961, Johnson had fully backed Eisenhower's foreign policy. He maintained the same loyalty during his years in virtual limbo as vice president.

Unexpectedly thrust into office, Johnson immediately confronted the issue of Vietnam. The growing war in that small, relatively insignificant country ever more steadily dominated Johnson's administration. Unlike his predecessor, Johnson relished focusing on domestic issues. While he avoided a declaration of war against North Vietnam, he did launch a war against poverty. Programs like medical insurance for the elderly and Head Start education for children grabbed his attention just as they had that of his mentor, Franklin D. Roosevelt. Johnson's domestic accomplishments measured up to his goals. Yet the Vietnam incubus steadily destroyed Johnson's standing until, admitting defeat, he announced on March 31, 1968 that he would neither seek nor accept another term in office. The image of Johnson that lingers is that of the prisoner of the rose garden—unable to leave the While House for fear of angry demonstrations against the Vietnam war, unable to comprehend how he could be excoriated for having pursued containment to its logical conclusion.

The chapters in this volume explore different areas of American foreign policy during the Kennedy and Johnson administrations. (The inauguration of Richard Nixon as president on January 20, 1969 marked the end of the 1960s, both in terms of government policy and for the purposes of this book.) That each contributor stresses the importance of the Cold War should not come as a surprise because this confrontation, suddenly now solely of historical interest, dominated all discussions of American foreign policy during the 1960s. Another theme is America's eroding relative economic position. While the United States through-out the 1960s remained economically superior to all other nations, the surging economies of Western European and Asian nations during this period began to affect American foreign policy decisions. The third common thread in the articles is the pattern of similarities and differences between the two Democratic administrations. Every author shows contradictory examples of change and continuity between the Kennedy and Johnson years, providing in the process new evidence, should any be needed, of the pivotal importance each president plays in the shaping of his administration and his era.

American diplomatic endeavors during the Kennedy years proved wide ranging. Although Latin America was the scene of the most intensive confrontation, relations with Khrushchev occupied much White House time. Concurrently Washington paid significant attention to Western Europe and Southeast Asia. By contrast, during the Johnson administration events in Vietnam not only sucked energy and initiative away from the domestic agenda but also eroded the president's interest in other areas of foreign policy. At the highest level relations with the Soviet Union remained virtually on hold while simultaneously American diplomats attempted to preserve the status quo in Western Europe. During the Johnson years State Department officials and other advisers evolved their policies out of Kennedy-era ideas. The significant shifts in American policies toward specific countries generally came during crises such as the Dominican invasion or the Six Day War between Israel and Egypt. In the absence of sheer necessity Johnson rarely developed or delegated new foreign policy initiatives. David Kaiser, in his article on the men and policies of the 1960s, illuminates the distinctions between the two administrations.

The Cold War dominated the 1960s. Not surprisingly Soviet-American relations are at the center of this study. The last year of the Eisenhower administration had opened on an optimistic note. The question of the status of Berlin, which had been raised by Khrushchev in 1958, was quietly returned to the back burner. As the two superpowers, the United States and the Soviet Union, joined by Britain and France, prepared for a summit conference in May 1960, both Khrushchev and Eisenhower, the latter looking now not at present events but at his place in history, held high hopes for a productive meeting. The Soviet military's successful attack on an American U-2 spy plane over Russia on the eve of the summit demolished any chance for a superpower détente. As Vladislav Zubok makes clear in his article, Khrushchev understood

Kennedy's dilemma: the "young" president, untested as a leader, faced tremendous domestic pressure to take a hard line against the Soviet Union, particularly after the Bay of Pigs fiasco. The Vienna summit of June 1961 further exacerbated the situation; only after the near catastrophe of the Cuban Missile Crisis in October 1962 did the superpowers begin to adopt more pacific positions. The resulting reevaluation in both Moscow and Washington produced in August 1963 the Limited Test Ban Treaty which forbade nuclear testing in the atmosphere. While the agreement, signed only by the United States, Britain, and the Soviet Union, was narrow in scope and reach, it remained a first step, which taken together with the Non- Proliferation Treaty of 1967 (an attempt to limit the spread of nuclear missiles), represented a major evolution from the strident rhetoric of 1961.

Zubok's successful excavation in the newly available Soviet archives makes his article especially valuable. During the entire Cold War period American scholars of Soviet foreign policy (known as Kremlinologists) had no choice but to practice their trade virtually without documents. The end of the Soviet Union also ended the documentary vacuum. Among other things, Zubok shows that the Soviet Union's relations with the Communist "satellite" states of Eastern Europe were every bit as complex and multidimensional as were American ties with its allies.

American relations with the major nations of Western Europe, Great Britain, West Germany, and France, are the subject of two articles. In "Cold War Dollar Diplomacy" Diane Kunz focuses on foreign economic diplomacy while Thomas Schwartz concentrates on the security nexus among these countries. Historians have long debated the "special" nature of the Anglo-American relationship. What clearly emerges from the record of 1960s diplomacy is the way in which Britain, discarding its empire but blocked from joining the European Economic Community (also known as the Common Market or EEC) by France, clung ever more tightly to its ties with the United States. The three circles of British interest (Empire, European, and Anglo-American), which had been alluded to often by British leaders in the immediate postwar period, now, fifteen years later, seemed to be collapsing into one. Both economic and diplomatic factors compelled this result: the British government's decision to cling ever more desperately to an overvalued currency forced it to rely on American-organized loans to prop up the pound sterling while the diminishing size of the Empire increased British reliance on its superpower ally. Yet this dependency had its limits: despite American pressure, Britain neither sent a brigade to Vietnam nor retained a commitment to a military presence East of Suez.

American relations with Federal Republic of Germany (West Germany) during the decade displayed a different sort of dependency. While American officials reliably reiterated that the Rhine was America's Cold War frontier, West German leaders did not have the luxury of debating whether their nation would be at the center of any European conflict. This reality and the proximity of hundreds of thousands of Soviet troops across the border meant that West Germany needed American forces to protect its very existence. The Berlin crisis of 1961 in retrospect proved to be a defensive Communist maneuver but at the time it highlighted West German vulnerability. While Chancellor Konrad Adenauer from 1961 to 1963 cemented his warm relationship with French President Charles de Gaulle, Adenauer and his successors never departed from a recognition of the centrality of West German relations with the United States.

By contrast, American relations with France, led throughout this period by President Charles de Gaulle, could never be described as warm. De Gaulle deserves credit for many things: for never succumbing to the lure of Nazi collaboration during World War II but instead leading the Free French forces to fight the German army at the side of British and American troops, for forcing his wartime allies to treat France as a great power, for reunifying a France that in 1958, when de Gaulle assumed the presidency, was rent by civil disorder, and for recognizing that French control of Algeria had become a dream that needed to be discarded. In its place de Gaulle constructed a new idealized France, a nation which through past glory, sound finance, skillful diplomacy, and independent military might could dominate European diplomacy. Measured from the nadir of virtual anarchy that enveloped France in 1958, de Gaulle succeeded to a remarkable extent. He nurtured the French-German rapprochement, something that would have seemed incomprehensible a decade earlier. The EEC, the economic union of France, West Germany, Italy, the Netherlands, Belgium, and Luxembourg, gave de Gaulle a personal vehicle for expanding France's role on the world stage. By dominating the EEC while blocking any attempt to dilute the power of any individual state, the French President magnified French influence in Western Europe. The independent French nuclear force gave de Gaulle another card to play as did NATO (the North Atlantic Treaty Organization), the American-Western European defensive alliance formed in 1949. By expelling NATO institutions from French soil in 1966 de Gaulle asserted French independence and strength in a risk-free manner: he knew that NATO headquarters would only move across the border to Belgium. De Gaulle's attitude and actions tormented American officials throughout the decade but they realized that the state of tension and discontent between the United States and France suited de Gaulle very well indeed.

Vietnam proved one of the most difficult subjects for discussions between Paris and Washington. Knowing that French forces had been definitively defeated in Vietnam in 1954 convinced de Gaulle that the American effort would never prevail. Neither the Kennedy nor Johnson administrations would ever heed this advice, as Robert Schulzinger explains. The Vietnam conflict formed the fulcrum that tested the limits of the policy of containment. When the American war effort proved ineffective, it shattered the postwar American foreign policy consensus. In the debate between the "hawks," who wanted to expand the limited war, and the "doves," who sought an American troop pull-out from Vietnam, lay the assumptions of a generation. The Vietnam war also exposed and exacerbated differences between generations with those on the younger side of the divide exhibiting greater readiness to take the dove side of the debate.

The Vietnam war overshadowed American relations with both Japan and China. During the 1960s Japan did not yet possess the economic might that pushed it to the forefront of international affairs two decades later. Yet, as Michael Schaller shows, the problems which later bedeviled Washington's relations with Tokyo had their roots in the 1960s. By contrast Arthur Waldron's account of American relations with the People's Republic of China illustrates the limits of American diplomacy: the static nature of this relationship had little to do with American ideas and much to do with internal Chinese politics.

Developments in the Middle East, by contrast, proved susceptible to outside pressures, but the independence of the region's client states remained surprisingly hardy. Douglas Little details the paradox that superpower ties with regional surrogates intensified at the same time as the ability of the Soviet Union and the United States to control the actions of Egypt and Syria and Israel, respectively, declined. Yet despite Washington's heightened relationship with Israel and with the "moderate" states of Iran and Saudi Arabia, to American diplomats Latin America remained the most important area of the developing world. One hundred forty years of the Monroe Doctrine had created an American mind set that found difficulty accepting the autonomy of Latin American nations. The presence of Cuba, ninety-one miles from the Florida coast but controlled by a Communist leader who cooperated closely with the Soviet Union, exacerbated the American obsession. This reality had good and bad consequences. On the one hand, the fear of Communism in large measure spawned the Alliance for Progress, which produced $20 billion in aid to the region during the 1960s. On the other hand, the Cold War engendered various attempts to depose Cuban leader Fidel Castro, the Dominican invasion as well as the perpetually stalwart American support for authoritarian leaders of all descriptions so long as they towed the anti-Communist line.

American policy toward Africa is highlighted by Gerald Thomas. Only in 1960 did the major European colonial powers realize that the sun had indeed set upon their empires. In the next ten years a score of countries achieved their independence. To Washington this sea change offered promise and peril. Seeing the United States as the first liberated colony, administration officials reached out to newly emergent nations. Africa became the site of major Peace Corps programs which stationed college graduates for two years in developing nations. American assistance both under the AID rubric and otherwise flowed as well. More than generosity prompted this response: American officials feared that without assistance, these new countries would turn to the Soviet Union for inspiration and leadership. As in Latin America, the American record is not without stain.

The reputations of both Kennedy and Johnson have suffered in recent years. The historians represented in this volume have all had access to government documents which form the raw material of their craft. On some significant issues, their opinions converge while on others the contributors' arguments differ markedly. Given the proximity of the 1960s to our own time and the passionate nature of the foreign policy debates during that decade, this duality is to be expected. These chapters also illustrate the way in which the United States, at the zenith of its power and influence, often found itself at the mercy of decisions made by other nations and other leaders. Diplomacy is by definition never a one way process but never before were there so many players who had an impact on the superpowers and their foreign relations' decisions. The ability of small countries to withstand the will of the United States is especially startling: in Latin America, in the Middle East, in Southeast Asia, countries which clearly fell within the underdeveloped rubric defied Washington's will.

The portraits that emerge confirm some stereotypes, confound others. What they do not affect is the perception on which this book is based, that the 1960s was the crucial decade of the Cold War. During this decade the two superpowers, as Secretary of State Dean Rusk put it, went eyeball to eyeball against each other and the other side blinked. For its part the Soviet Union apparently drew the lesson from the Cuban Missile crisis that it needed to so build up its arsenal that it could never be forced into a second climbdown. This decision then led

to the overweening Soviet military industrial complex whose domination over resources greatly contributed to the destruction of the Soviet
Union's economy and ultimately, of the Soviet Union itself. While the
Cuban missile crisis may have encouraged Kennedy's growing consciousness, most notably expressed in his June 1963 American University speech, of the perils of the Cold War and the arms race that it had
spawned, the fact remains that the United States continued to build up
its arsenal as well. Faced with unmistakable evidence of a changing
world economy we chose to share the burden rather than to ask if it
needed be borne at all. Taken together, these decisions created the conditions that nurtured the Cold War for two more decades but, paradoxically, then caused it to dissolve in 1991. The Cold War, for so long
the sun around which all American foreign policy rotated, has now
gone from current event to historical fact. To understand the course of
American diplomacy during the 1960s is to comprehend better the reasons for this transformation.

Diane B. Kunz
New Haven, September 1993

NOTES

1. George Kennan, "The Sources of Soviet Conduct," *Foreign Affairs*, 25 (July
1947): 566–582.

1

Men and Policies: 1961–69

•

DAVID KAISER

Despite the change in presidents in November 1963, the continuity of senior foreign policy advisers from 1961 through 1969 is unique in the history of the twentieth century. Presidents Kennedy and Johnson had only one Secretary of State, Dean Rusk; a Secretary of Defense, Robert McNamara, who served for seven years before yielding to Clark Clifford; and just two National Security advisers, McGeorge Bundy and Walt Rostow. Various second-level officials, including George Ball, William Bundy, U. Alexis Johnson, Averell Harriman, Cyrus Vance, and Roswell Gilpatric, played important roles in both administrations as well. This was hardly accidental, since Lyndon Johnson consciously protected himself against charges of deviating from John Kennedy's path by retaining, and relying upon, much of Kennedy's foreign policy team. This course also came naturally to him because of his own lack of personal experience and self-confidence in foreign affairs.

Both the senior foreign policy leadership and the national security bureaucracies they headed generally regarded the containment of Communism as the essence of their policy. The consensus on America's proper world role was probably more clearly defined in 1961 than at any other time in the twentieth century, especially among the East Coast press, the foreign policy establishment, and the diplomatic corps, from which dissenters like George Kennan and the China hands had been purged in the 1950s. Both the Truman and Eisenhower administrations had undergone violent criticism for having allowed the Communists to advance in Europe, Asia, Africa, and Latin America, and Kennedy himself had made the Soviet-American competition the key issue of the 1960 campaign. At the Pentagon, McNamara supervised the expansion of both strategic nuclear and conventional forces, trying both to manage the military more cost-effectively and to find ways to use military power without plunging the world into nuclear war. At State, Rusk, the Assistant Secretary for Asian Affairs during the Korean War, wanted to hold the line against further Communist expansion by any means necessary. The CIA, which had developed extensive covert action capabilities under the Eisenhower administration, had plenty of suggestions for dealing with new crises as well. And in the wake of the collapse of the 1960 Paris summit, with crises breaking out in Laos, the Congo, Cuba, and Berlin, dramatic reductions in tension with the Soviet Union hardly seemed likely. In retrospect, John Lewis Gaddis has identified the 1960s as the era of general, peripheral, and symmetrical containment, a policy whose costs were very likely to exceed its benefits, and which found its logical expression in the catastrophe of the Vietnam War.[1] And because John Kennedy's inaugural address stated this policy so dramatically, and because he brought the team that dominated foreign policy during the 1960s to Washington, many still regard him as an exceptionally aggressive Cold War president.

This view is quite misleading. The emerging record of the Kennedy and Johnson administrations shows some profound differences in the foreign policies of the two presidents, their relationships with their senior advisers, and the ways in which they used the instruments at their disposal. Despite the climate of the times and the cautious views of his Secretary of State, John Kennedy clearly sought some new departures in foreign policy, and looked for men who could help make them, while putting a premium upon consensus within his team. He also proved increasingly reluctant to plunge American military forces into war, even at the most critical point in his presidency, the Cuban missile crisis. In Berlin, in Southeast Asia, and in relations with the Soviet Union, he deviated in one way or another from the most obvious course of action and sought a more innovative approach. By late 1963, détente had become the most important element of his foreign policy, and he clearly intended to continue it.

Policy changed under Lyndon Johnson, partly because he played a very different role. While fully capable of independent judgment, Johnson had much less of a foreign policy agenda of his own, and wanted above all to avoid any disastrous mistakes. He therefore put the highest priority upon following the consensus of his senior advisers and never chose an alternative that they would have rejected. This tactic helped lead him into a full-scale war in Vietnam, and also helped make the years 1965–69 generally unproductive ones in East-West relations, in comparison to either the preceding or succeeding periods. The policies Johnson followed reflected the consensus of the foreign policy establishment and the national security bureaucracies, but they led him and the nation into a divisive disaster.

With the help of the first official presidential transition staff, John F. Kennedy in late 1960 chose a carefully balanced foreign policy team. On the one hand, Kennedy clearly wanted a relatively young and innovative group; on the other, he wanted to build a broad political base. His most important appointments therefore included a junior officer of the Eastern Establishment (Dean Rusk), three prominent Adlai Stevenson Democrats (Chester Bowles, George Ball, and the two-time unsuccessful presidential candidate himself), and two Republicans (Robert McNamara and McGeorge Bundy). Significantly, Kennedy chose Rusk over Arkansas Senator J. William Fulbright, with whom he felt far more comfortable, both because Rusk was the choice of the establishment leaders former Secretary of Defense Robert Lovett and former Secretary of State Dean Acheson, and because Fulbright's appointment might disturb black and Jewish Americans, who resented his public opposition to civil rights. His ambassadorial appointments were probably the most creative in American history. Bowles and Robert Kennedy looked for prominent figures whose experience, rather than their pocketbooks, qualified them to represent the United States in regions as diverse as France (James Gavin), India (economist John Kenneth Galbraith), and the newly independent African nations. He also courageously brought George Kennan back into the government as Ambassador to Yugoslavia.

Within a few months Kennedy discovered, first, that he could not rely on the recommendations of the established national security bureaucracy—which had developed the Bay of Pigs invasion—and, more generally, that his team was having trouble coming up with innovative solutions to diplomatic problems. Confronted with the CIA's plan for a Cuban-exile invasion of Castro's Cuba, Kennedy initially sought to change it so as to reduce the scale of American involvement, increase deniability, and make it possible for the invaders to melt into the Cuban mountains should an uprising fail to take place. He eventually approved it on that basis, consulting a relatively narrow circle of senior advisers. But after the invasion began with air strikes on April 15, its cover story rapidly collapsed, and the impossibility of making it a success within the guidelines Kennedy had established rapidly emerged. The president refused to sacrifice deniability in order to increase the operation's chances and rejected American military intervention. The invasion became a debacle. Administration officials subsequently agreed that the president henceforth treated all the proposals that reached him with far greater skepticism.[2]

Kennedy experienced further problems with his senior advisers during the two other major crises of his first year in office, those in Berlin and Laos. When Kennedy met Khrushchev in Vienna in June, Khrushchev threatened bluntly to sign a separate peace treaty with East Germany and turn control over the access routes to Berlin over to the East Germans. Should the Western powers try to maintain their old rights by force, Khrushchev warned, war would result. Dean Acheson, whom Kennedy had asked in February to review the situation, simply recommended in July that the United States undertake a substantial conventional and military build-up, refuse to negotiate, and prepare to challenge any East German restrictions on Berlin access militarily should the Soviet leader carry out his threat. Kennedy eventually adopted some of the military recommendations, but continued to look for political alternatives, and complained when the State Department failed to provide any. Meanwhile, Secretary of Defense McNamara found to his horror that any American military attempt to reopen access to Berlin would involve the immediate use of tactical nuclear weapons. Kennedy, National Security Adviser McGeorge Bundy, and McNamara began trying to move NATO military strategy away from the Eisenhower administration's reliance upon nuclear weapons, and to build up an effective conventional capability.[3]

Newly available documentation shows that Kennedy himself wanted to move toward some new, more stable settlement of the German problem, but that Dean Rusk and the State Department failed to come up with any new options. Khrushchev's statements at Vienna often indicated that his real interest was some sort of all-German peace treaty, involving recognition of the German Democratic Republic and of the Oder-Neisse frontier.[4] Had Washington been willing to address these questions, the problem would rapidly have become diplomatic rather than military, but such willingness would have also created enormous strains in relations with the West German government, which flatly refused any concessions on either of these points. A planning paper approved by Kennedy in February 1961 raised these questions, but Acheson's famous memorandum of June 29 seems almost completely to have ignored them.[5] American and Western policy focused simply on the maintenance of Western rights in, and access to, West Berlin—a position which, as some Germans complained at the time, virtually invited the East Germans to shut down access between the two halves of the city. After they did so, on August 13, the crisis cooled relatively quickly, but without any larger movement on the German question.

We now know that Kennedy immediately asked the State Department to develop a new negotiating position on Berlin and larger German questions, including even possible separate peace treaties with East and West Germany, but that Rusk and the State Department—apparently still committed to the West German position—dragged their feet. This apparently led to the estrangement between the Kennedy White House and the State Department which Theodore Sorensen, Arthur M. Schlesinger, Jr., and Robert Kennedy all discussed in memoirs.[6] Several months later, in a November 25 interview with Soviet journalist (and son-in-law of Khrushchev) Alexei Adzhubei, Kennedy looked forward to a new agreement on "the problem of Germany and Berlin," but for reasons that are not yet clear, nothing came of it.[7] We shall find, however, that the idea of a new German policy emerged once again in 1963.

Meanwhile, the president had a blunt confrontation with his senior diplomatic and military advisers over Southeast Asia. Crises in Laos and South Vietnam led to several proposals for American military intervention—most of which he rejected—and to the development of an alternative, diplomatic strategy, which few of his senior advisers really favored.

Under Eisenhower, the United States had rejected a neutral government for Laos in favor of a pro-American regime led by Phoumi Nosavan. By early 1961, Phoumi was fighting a losing battle against both neutralist and Communist forces, and in April the administration conducted several top-level discussions of American or SEATO military action. The Bay of Pigs apparently cooled both Kennedy's and several of the Joint Chiefs' enthusiasm for intervention, and the military option gave way to proposals for a conference to discuss the neutralization of the country. "If it hadn't been for Cuba, we might be about to intervene in Laos," Kennedy told Schlesinger on May 3.[8] Averell Harriman, Kennedy's Ambassador-at-large, took charge of the negotiations, and Khrushchev gave them a boost at Vienna in June by agreeing in principle to the neutralization of Laos. Talks began in May, but progressed very slowly. Meanwhile, the decision for a cease-fire and neutralization in Laos unsettled several other Asian allies, especially the South Vietnamese, whose difficulties in coping with their own Communist insurgency had already been recognized. Vice President Johnson made a trip to Southeast Asia to reassure our other allies, but in succeeding months, the combined problems in the Laos negotiations and in South Vietnam—where President Ngo Dinh Diem began looking for new evidence of a firm American commitment—led to new proposals for American military action should the Laos talks fail.

From July through October 1961, Kennedy repeatedly rejected proposals for a larger American military and political commitment in Laos and South Vietnam.[9] On July 28, at the White House, a State Department official presented plans either for American forces in Southern Laos or American military action against North Vietnam—a contingency plan already favored by Walt Rostow, the deputy National Security Adviser, whose responsibilities included Southeast Asia. Kennedy replied that previous military estimates had been over-optimistic, that he wanted new plans examined more carefully, and "remarked that General De Gaulle, out of painful French experience, had spoken with feeling of the difficulty of fighting in this part of the world." Deputy Under Secretary of State U. Alexis Johnson in reply asked specifically for a declaration "that the President would at some future time have a willingness to decide to intervene if the situation seemed to him to require it," and Kennedy replied that he was "at present very reluctant to go into Laos. He believed that the negotiations in Geneva should be pressed forward, that we should not get ourselves badly separated from the British, that the American people were not eager to get into Laos, that nothing would be worse than an unsuccessful intervention in this area, and that he did not yet have confidence in the military practicability of the proposal which had been put before him."[10]

The Joint Chiefs developed further military recommendations for South Vietnam in August, and in mid-September Rostow passed on new recommendations for the implementation of SEATO Plan 5 for intervention in Laos.[11] A few weeks earlier, on August 29, Kennedy had telephoned Averell Harriman after a meeting at the White House to ensure that the ambassador at large would make every effort to reach an agreement with neutralist leader Souvanna Phouma, "since the alternative to an understanding with Souvanna was not one that he would like to contemplate."[12] In Saigon, Ambassador Frederick Nolting on September 18 recommended armed intervention to secure southern Laos for pro-Western forces.[13]

Kennedy agreed in early October to send his special military representative, General Maxwell Taylor, and Walt Rostow on a fact-finding mission to Saigon, a move Rostow had advocated for months. But when Taylor wrote draft instructions asking him to "evaluate what could be accomplished by the introduction of SEATO or United States forces into South Vietnam, determining the role, composition, and probable disposition of such forces," Kennedy rewrote them, eliminating any specific reference to United States or SEATO forces, and stressing "that the initial responsibility for the effective maintenance of the independence of South Vietnam rests with the people and government of that country."[14] When Taylor and Rostow returned with their report in late October, calling for an initial force of 8,000 Americans, Kennedy rejected it again.

While rejecting American ground combat troops, Kennedy in November finally approved an increased advisory effort and an active American air combat role. Before taking these decisions, however, he had another very revealing exchange with his senior foreign policy advisers. On November 15, National Security Adviser McGeorge Bundy wrote Kennedy a rare memorandum on Vietnam, advocating that the United States should express its willingness, *if necessary*, to commit American combat forces to save South Vietnam. If the United States made such a commitment, he felt, it would probably not have to be carried out, but if we refused, "the whole program will be half-hearted." "This conclusion is, I believe," he continued, "the inner conviction of your Vice President, your Secretaries of State and Defense, and the two heads of your special mission [Taylor and Rostow], and that is why I am troubled by your most natural desire to act on other items now, without taking the troop decision. Whatever the reason, this has now become a sort of touchstone of our will."[15]

In a meeting on the same day, Kennedy showed that he was not convinced. The president argued against a major commitment in South Vietnam on the grounds that it did not represent a clear case of aggression, adding that the United States needed, even more than in Berlin, the support of its allies for domestic reasons. "The President said that he could even make a rather strong case against intervening in an area 10,000 miles away against 16,000 guerrillas with a native army of 200,000, where millions have been spent for years with no success. . . . The President compared the obscurity of the issues in Viet Nam to the clarity of the positions in Berlin, the contrast of which could even make leading Democrats wary of proposed activities in the Far East." He continued along these lines despite some opposition from Rusk, from McNamara, and from General Lyman Lemnitzer, the Chairman of the Joint Chiefs of Staff.[16]

That afternoon, Bundy met with Rusk, apparently to draw the Secretary out and convey some of the president's concerns. He wrote up a remarkable record of the talk for Kennedy. Regarding Vietnam, Bundy

> told the Secretary frankly that you [Kennedy] feel the need to have someone on this job that is wholly responsive to your policy, and that you really do not get that sense from most of us. I suggested Averell [Harriman]. He said Averell was needed in Geneva and that Alexis [Johnson] would loyally carry out any policy you directed. I don't think this is the same as having your own man—Alexis isn't that dispassionate—or that much of

an executive. Averell is your man, as Assistant Secretary [for Far Eastern Affairs].

Later, Rusk elaborated his own position:

Secretary [Rusk] thinks the good of our actions depends on belief we mean to hold in Southeast Asia. He knows we may lose, and he knows we want no Korea, but he thinks we *must* try to hold and must show determination to all concerned. He suggests you should let this be a Rusk-McNamara Plan and fire all concerned if it doesn't work. He thinks we *must* meet Khrushchev in Vietnam or suffer a terrible defeat. I attach cables showing what Mr. Rusk told [French Ambassador] Alphand and [British Ambassador] Ormsby Gore. This shows the tone he thinks we must take, and it is obviously important that you either approve or disapprove.

In his talk with Alphand, Rusk had indicated his lack of faith in a negotiated Laotian settlement, flatly rejected such a solution for South Vietnam, and argued that the United States had more of a stake in Southeast Asia than France or Britain, and might have to go it alone.

Bundy concluded by suggesting that Harriman's appointment as Assistant Secretary be accompanied by a more general reshuffle, including the replacement of Chester Bowles as Under Secretary of State and Walt Rostow's move from the White House to the head of State's Policy Planning Council (the job Rostow had originally wanted). Most of the changes he recommended took place about two weeks later.[17]

The aftermath of this episode sheds more light on how Kennedy handled his team. As Assistant Secretary for the Far East, Harriman during the first half of 1962 brought the Laotian talks to a successful conclusion, although he had to put enormous pressure on the American client, Phoumi Nosavan, to do so.[18] Kennedy, as we have seen, approved a substantially increased American advisory presence in South Vietnam, and McNamara and Rusk apparently agreed that the State Department would handle the Laotian negotiations while Defense took responsibility for Vietnam. Kennedy apparently never laid down the law with Rusk and McNamara over the ultimate importance of Southeast Asia, as Bundy had suggested he do, but he repeatedly refused to declare the independence of South Vietnam a vital interest of the United States. Moreover, nearly all talk of a major SEATO or American military intervention in Laos, South Vietnam, or North Vietnam, such as had filled the corridors of State and Defense in the fall of 1961, came to a halt, not to be heard again until December 1963. Instead, McNamara in July 1962 told the Defense Department and the Military Assistance Command, Vietnam, to prepare plans to end the American advisory role within three years.[19] In later years, Rusk frequently proclaimed that Kennedy had committed the United States to the defense of South Vietnam, but this was exactly what he had repeatedly refused to do.

Kennedy's response to the Southeast Asian crisis of 1961 clearly shows that he understood the dilemma of containment that had bedeviled Truman and Eisenhower, and would continue to plague every president through Reagan. On the one hand, the press and public opinion accepted the notion that Communism had to be stopped, with little regard for the strategic importance of the specific territories it threatened, and the national security bureaucracy was always ready with options for intervention. But at the same time, as the Korean War had already shown—and as Lyndon Johnson would once again discover—the American people would not support prolonged, indecisive wars in relatively remote areas, whatever their initial reaction. Only Kennedy among his senior foreign policy team raised these issues during the debates over intervention in Laos and Vietnam, but he obviously regarded them as critical. While he had asked the American people to bear any burden and pay any price to ensure the survival of liberty, he knew that their willingness to respond to his call was inevitably limited.

Kennedy had shown himself far less willing to resort to force in Southeast Asia than his senior advisers. In Laos, he had given Harriman, who shared his view, full authority to resolve the situation, while in South Vietnam he had placed important limits upon what might be done. He obviously understood that his views differed from some of his senior advisers, but as long as he could define the main lines of his policies and find men to execute them, this did not trouble him. Because he increasingly relied upon particular individuals for particular tasks, he increasingly preferred small, "off-the-record" meetings on various foreign policy topics to full-scale National Security Council (NSC) sessions. He wanted, in short, to maintain consensus while allowing certain controversial initiatives to go ahead, and the system he evolved allowed him, usually, to do both.

We now know, indeed, that Kennedy used this technique most dramatically at the most dangerous moment of his presidency, the Cuban missile crisis of October 1962. The famous meetings of the Executive Committee of the National Security Council (the ExCom) allowed the president to hear the varied advice of his subordinates, and to understand who would favor—or even put up with—what. Kennedy hardly emerged as the most "dovish" of the group (to use the metaphor coined shortly after the crisis by journalists Stewart Alsop and Charles Bartlett). Robert McNamara himself initially argued against military action to remove the missiles on the grounds that they did not really alter the strategic balance, but Kennedy clearly realized that the American people would not accept this position. He accepted the naval quarantine proposal partly because the Air Force did not want, and could not guarantee the success of, a limited air strike. But during the week after his announcement of the quarantine, as work on the missile sites continued at a feverish pace, he came under increasing pressure to authorize a full-scale air strike and invasion. Two events made the situation critical on Saturday, October 27: first, an American U-2 plane was shot down over Cuba and the pilot killed, and second, Khrushchev, who the day before had seemed to offer to withdraw the missiles if the United States promised not to invade Cuba, now demanded instead that the United States withdraw its Jupiter missiles from Turkey—an idea put forward earlier in the week by columnist Walter Lippman.

The published transcript of the Saturday meetings shows that Kennedy did not want to invade Cuba and risk war when the whole world knew that the missile trade would have avoided it. NATO and the American public might initially support the war, but they would immediately have second thoughts when things went badly, especially if—as most of them expected—the Russians either struck NATO missile bases in Turkey, or took West Berlin.[20] In the general meeting of the fifteen members of the ExCom, however, his position found relatively little explicit support. Bundy argued that a trade would undermine the confidence of our NATO allies, and Rusk, while expressing contradictory views, seemed at times to agree. The ExCom eventually agreed simply to tell Khrushchev, first, that work on the missile sites had to stop immediately, and, second, that the United States government accepted his private offer of Friday night to remove the offensive Soviet weapons from Cuba if the United States agreed not to invade.[21]

McGeorge Bundy waited until 1988 to reveal that another meeting had convened in the oval office late that afternoon, including only nine men: the president, Bundy, Rusk, McNamara, Robert Kennedy, George Ball, Theodore Sorensen, Roswell Gilpatric, and Llewellyn Thompson. At that meeting, he reported, Dean Rusk suggested that Robert Kennedy, while delivering the agreed-upon message personally to Soviet Ambassador Dobrynin, also make clear that while the administration could make no public deal, the Jupiter missiles in Turkey would shortly be removed, as the president had already directed. (This was, in fact, an exaggeration; while Kennedy had wanted to remove them, he had never issued orders to do so.) The participants agreed to the suggestion, and promised to keep it secret for all time. Robert Kennedy's posthumous memoir, *Thirteen Days* (1969), revealed what he had told Dobrynin, but did not discuss this meeting.[22] And that evening, Rusk told Bundy in 1987, Kennedy told Rusk to prepare a supposedly spontaneous initiative from U Thant, the Secretary General of the United Nations, suggesting a trade of Cuban for Turkish missiles to resolve the crisis, if need be—an initiative Kennedy planned to accept. Because Khrushchev on Sunday did not insist upon a public trade, this step never had to be taken.

Kennedy, in short, had decided by Saturday, October 27, to try to avoid war. The Joint Chiefs, who regarded the moment for war as a favorable one, were largely excluded from the ExCom discussions (only their new chairman, Maxwell Taylor, attended them) and completely excluded from the small-group meeting in the Oval Office. Kennedy wanted to consult all his advisers and keep them all on board, but he had also determined upon a course that most of them would not favor—and which was very politically risky—in order to avoid war. To carry out his plan he had to conceal it from all but his most trusted advisers. This was the system he had evolved.

Returning early in 1963 to his goal of some new accommodation with the Soviets, Kennedy once again went beyond normal procedures to accomplish it. During 1962, Rusk had won a difficult and lengthy debate over the new Ambassador to Moscow, choosing Foy Kohler, a fairly colorless career diplomat, over the objections of Moscow veteran Harriman and of Robert Kennedy.[23] Now, in April 1963, Harriman himself moved from the Far East bureau to Under Secretary for Political Affairs, the third position in the department, behind Rusk and George Ball. Kennedy immediately sent him to Moscow to discuss pending issues in Soviet-American relations: the continuing Soviet presence in Cuba, the North Vietnamese failure to observe the Laos accords, and a possible nuclear test ban. He made some progress, although Khrushchev also wanted to discuss Germany.[24]

To encourage the talks, Kennedy asked Theodore Sorensen to draft a new "peace speech" to deliver at the American University commencement on June 10. Special Counsel Sorensen and Bundy purposely kept the State and Defense Departments out of the drafting process. "The President was determined to put forward a fundamentally new emphasis on the peaceful and the positive in our relations with the Soviets," Sorensen wrote less than two years later. "He did not want that new policy diluted by the usual threats of destruction, boasts of nuclear stockpiles and lectures on Soviet treachery."[25] In the wake of the speech, Harriman returned to Moscow and successfully negotiated the Test Ban Treaty. The Joint Chiefs, after considerable discussion, agreed to support the treaty under the mandate that Kennedy had given them a year earlier: to advise him not merely according to purely military considerations, but also in light of broader political questions.[26]

Kennedy's managerial techniques failed him later in that summer, during the extended crisis over the future of the Diem regime in South Vietnam. On Saturday, August 24, after President Ngo Dinh Diem and his brother Ngo Dinh Nhu had suddenly cracked down on the Buddhist opposition, Harriman and his successor as Assistant Secretary for the Far East, Roger Hilsman, managed to dispatch a cable endorsing a South Vietnamese military move against Nhu, or Diem and Nhu, without full clearance from the Joint Chiefs. General Taylor and Secretary McNamara, who regarded South Vietnam as their main responsibility, reacted very angrily. In a lengthy series of meetings the following week, a very guarded president helped Taylor and McNamara raise doubts about the wisdom of a coup, without actually reversing the policy. The coup collapsed on August 30, but weeks of new discussions failed to agree on the future of the Diem regime. The president on Labor Day called for "changes in policy and perhaps in personnel" in Saigon to enable the government to win the war, but would go no further. On September 16, Michael Forrestal of the NSC bluntly asked McGeorge Bundy to secure a decision for or against a coup and end the private and public bickering among State, CIA, and Defense, but the president never did.[27] Instead, he sent McNamara and Taylor on a new mission to Vietnam, while showing unusual frustration over press leaks.

The crisis was far too complex for any thorough analysis here, but one may fairly say that Washington never developed a coherent policy. McNamara and Taylor reported that the war was making great progress, but agreed that the South Vietnamese government had to change certain policies—as the president had already stated. They also recommended a partial suspension of aid to bring these changes about, and stated that while the United States should take "no initiative . . . to encourage actively a change in government," it should "identify and build contacts with an alternative leadership if and when it appears"— a contradiction born of the need to reconcile the irreconcilable. Lastly, their recommendations, which Kennedy adopted, took care *not* to specify exactly what changes Diem must make.[28]

Washington lost control of policy partly because of the failure to reach a clear decision, and because of another unforeseen factor in the situation, the independence and persistence of the new Ambassador. Kennedy had chosen to fill another difficult and potentially controversial position with a Republican, the 1960 GOP vice-presidential candidate Henry Cabot Lodge, but he had not anticipated how committed Lodge would become to one particular policy—the overthrow of Diem—and how difficult it would be to give him instructions. During the last few days in October, when Lodge was scheduled to return to Washington for consultations—and, at least some administration figures hoped, where he would be replaced—coup rumors began again, and the ambassador delayed his departure and overrode some cautionary instructions from Washington.[29] When the coup took place on November 1, Kennedy was shocked by the assassination of Diem and Nhu. Although the president knew that the Diem government's policies posed enormous problems both in South Vietnam and in the United States, he never seems to have decided definitely that a coup would help. Unable to make up its mind, Washington lost control of policy to Lodge, who encouraged the coup, and the Vietnamese generals who carried it out.

While Vietnam and Laos posed serious problems during 1963, evidence suggests that Kennedy did not intend to make them the major focus of his foreign policy in 1964 and during his second term. The success of the Limited Test Ban treaty had vindicated his years of often frustrating efforts to improve Soviet-American relations, and he clearly hoped to move ahead in that area. Harriman, now the leader in the field, had written a memorandum on the subject for him on July 30, 1963. The obvious possibility, he suggested, was a Nonaggression Pact between NATO and the Warsaw Pact, but he also proposed that Washington finally abandon the policy of nonrecognition of East Germany, the stumbling block to any serious discussions about Germany and Berlin. To recognize East Germany and the Oder-Neisse line, established at the end of World War II as the border between East Germany and Poland, would be popular throughout nearly all of Europe: "We will certainly gain with Poland and Czechoslovakia and help loosen the bonds between them and Moscow if they no longer fear attack by force on the Oder-Neisse line." The policy of nonrecognition that Bonn had insisted upon, he argued, might have served West German interests, but did not serve American ones—and he noted that West German opposition leader Willy Brandt was abandoning it, as well.[30] Kennedy apparently did not reply in writing, but in one of his last press conferences he expressed his hopes that "the chances of war [would] have been reduced over Berlin and perhaps in other areas" by the election next fall.[31] Whether a German initiative could have succeeded remains a very open question. As it turned out, no real progress occurred until 1969, after Willy Brandt had become Chancellor and definitely discarded the legacy of Konrad Adenauer. Still, Adenauer had already stepped down by 1963, and Harriman's proposals echoed suggestions made by Kennedy himself in the late summer of 1961.

Détente with the Communist world, in any event, would have remained a high priority. At the time of his death Kennedy was also using an ad hoc diplomatic channel to discuss normalization of relations with Castro, and he had referred repeatedly to a possible change in China policy during his second term.[32] Such policies certainly could have been carried out without any major changes in personnel. Rumors circulated that Kennedy would replace Dean Rusk—and Rusk himself had insisted in 1960 that he could remain for only one term—but Rusk had a strong constituency on Capitol Hill and a very easy working relationship with McNamara, both of which the president clearly valued. Harriman would have trod on many more toes as Secretary of State, and could just as easily pursue new talks with the Russians in his current position. Kennedy also mentioned the possibility of making McNamara Secretary of State, a step whose consequences can only be guessed at. We have no reason to suspect that Kennedy would have altered the ideological balance of his team, but he was clearly relying more and more on certain members of it to move toward the détente he favored. Changes after his death were subtle, but critical.

The foreign policy catastrophe and the domestic political turmoil that eventually overtook the Johnson administration make it much too easy to forget how Americans viewed Johnson during his first two years in office. By early 1965 the press and the nation generally believed that Johnson not only stood for the same principles as Kennedy, both at home and abroad, but also that he had managed to implement them considerably more effectively. As a legislating president, Johnson by mid-1965 clearly had no equal since Franklin Roosevelt, and he had won reelection over Arizona Senator Barry Goldwater with 60 percent of the popular vote and 486 electoral votes. Despite Johnson's own inexhaustible insecurity on this score, he had quite definitely supplanted his predecessor in his country's esteem, and even within his administration many frequently questioned whether Kennedy would have been able to accomplish as much. In the general euphoria, many senior officials initially managed to overlook some of Johnson's more unnerving features, such as his obsessions with loyalty, confidentiality, and his own image. Certainly he lacked Kennedy's celebrated detachment and his capacity for humor about himself. Kennedy, to be sure, had sometimes complained bitterly about press leaks, but Johnson before long was asking his National Security Adviser, McGeorge Bundy, to submit weekly reports of all his contacts with the press. Under Bundy's successor, Walt Rostow, the reports sometimes were prepared daily.[33]

In fact, Johnson knew considerably more about the legislative process and the details of domestic policy than Kennedy, although it is less certain that he knew more about national electoral politics. He held mainstream views on foreign policy. As Senate Majority Leader during the Eisenhower administration, he had loyally supported the bipartisan containment policy, increased defense spending, and a strong space program.[34] He had never played a major policy-making role as Vice President, although he had made a well-publicized trip to Southeast Asia in the spring of 1961 and had remained a strong supporter of the Diem regime in South Vietnam. Now, as president, his principal goals were domestic, and he viewed foreign policy mainly as an area in which he might make a disastrous mistake. When a Communist takeover reportedly threatened the Dominican Republic in 1965, or when he feared that bombing the wrong targets in North Vietnam might bring Communist China into the war, or when Martin Luther King, Jr.'s accused assassin was arrested in Britain, Johnson could become obsessively involved with the details of foreign policy. During the Dominican crisis the president received lists of suspected Dominican Communists from FBI Director J. Edgar Hoover, and when James Earl Ray was arrested, Johnson dispatched an Assistant Attorney General, Fred Vinson, Jr., with instructions to inspect the cell in which Ray was confined and confirm that it was, in fact, secure.[35] And the minutes of the Tuesday lunch meetings during the Vietnam War confirm that Johnson, Rusk, McNamara, JCS Chairman General Wheeler, and Walt Rostow did spend hours arguing over specific bombing targets.

Johnson, moreover, immediately identified Vietnam as the problem most likely to cause him trouble, and within less than two weeks after becoming president he began prodding the bureaucracy to do more.[36] His political sensitivity regarding the issue began to be seen a few weeks later.

When Henry Cabot Lodge emerged as a Republican presidential possibility, Johnson apparently asked Bundy to examine the cable traffic from Saigon over the last few months, in order to ensure that the administration had met all of Lodge's requests. Johnson had already made clear that he wanted to do everything he could to try to hold the situation in South Vietnam together, but he also wanted to make sure that Lodge could not return home and announce that the administration had failed to take his advice.[37]

Partly because Johnson lacked his own personal foreign policy agenda, he felt no need to field his own foreign policy team. Instead, he retained nearly all of Kennedy's senior advisers, with mixed results. He certainly established a closer relationship with Dean Rusk than Kennedy had, partly because both of them had incurred the displeasure of Robert Kennedy, and he had always been very impressed by McNamara. He did not however seem to have established a relationship of full confidence with Bundy, who was talking about leaving his post by late 1965, and did so a few months later. Whatever his personal feelings about these men, Johnson saw them as symbols of his predecessor's administration, and as insurance against criticism of himself—from Robert Kennedy, in particular—for deviating from Kennedy's path. As a result, they exerted more influence over him than they had over Kennedy, who had treated each of them simply as one of many sources of information as he tried to reach his own conclusions on issues.

Thus, with the situation in South Vietnam continuing to deteriorate, Johnson in 1964 and 1965—like Kennedy in 1961—received a barrage of suggestions for American military intervention in Southeast Asia, initially in the air. Discussions of action against North Vietnam—which seem to have halted entirely for two years beginning in late 1961— began again immediately after Kennedy's death, and grew during 1964. The political situation in South Vietnam was sinking into chaos, the North Vietnamese and Pathet Lao continued to ignore the Laotian accords, and General Khanh, who had taken power in February 1964, began arguing by the spring that bombing North Vietnam would improve the situation in the South. The Joint Chiefs, who before 1962 had always regarded the North as the source of the problem, and eventually Ambassador Lodge, endorsed these suggestions. More critically, McGeorge Bundy in May 1964, speaking for Rusk and McNamara as well as himself, recommended a diplomatic offensive, stressing Washington's limited objectives in Southeast Asia; "the first deployments toward Southeast Asia of U.S. and, hopefully, allied forces . . . on a very large scale, from the beginning, so as to maximize their deterrent impact and their menace," as well as a Congressional resolution authorizing the use of armed force and an "initial strike against the North," combined with proposed peace talks.[38]

Johnson delayed action on these recommendations for some months, although he submitted the Congressional Resolution in August, after the Tonkin Gulf incident, and won an almost unanimous endorsement, in principle, for future American military action to defend South Vietnam.[39] But while declining as yet to endorse their full recommendations, Johnson allowed these senior advisers to define the nature of the American commitment and the stakes in Vietnam and Southeast Asia—something Kennedy had consistently refused to do. When Senate Majority Leader Mike Mansfield—a Montanan who had worked under Johnson himself as Majority Whip—forwarded to Johnson a series of highly pessimistic memoranda on Vietnam that he had given Kennedy during 1962 and 1963, together with a new one, Johnson turned them over to Rusk, McNamara and Bundy for comment.[40] And after the Tonkin Gulf Resolution, Johnson invited Congressional leaders to join an NSC meeting in progress and hear reports and recommendations from McNamara and Rusk—a procedure he repeated in the following year.[41] In effect, Johnson was using the authority of Kennedy's team to establish a consensus. Meanwhile, in late 1964, Rusk, McNamara, and Bundy failed to give Johnson Under Secretary Ball's first major dissenting memo on American policy in Vietnam.[42]

Even after his reelection, Johnson resisted calls for further air strikes against North Vietnam for several more months, arguing that it made little sense to move against the North while the political situation in the South continued to deteriorate. He initially insisted that the South Vietnamese show progress of their own before the United States moved against the North—a condition which, had he maintained it, would have precluded American intervention. But McGeorge Bundy and McNamara, with Rusk on the sidelines, embarked upon a sustained, concerted effort to convince him that escalation had to begin at once to head off a disaster, culminating in Bundy's trip to Vietnam in February 1965. The United States, they argued, had to begin bombing the North in order to improve morale in the South and prevent a disastrous worldwide loss of worldwide American prestige. Johnson eventually assented.[43]

When the bombing was followed by a series of disastrous South Vietnamese military defeats on the ground, Johnson in late spring faced requests for a substantial American ground force intervention as well. Once again, McNamara, Rusk, Bundy, and the Joint Chiefs persuaded him to go ahead, despite their inability to guarantee successful results and the emergence of some vocal and effective opposition. George Ball and Johnson's unofficial adviser Clark Clifford opposed the ground commitment in the lengthy meetings in July 1965 that preceded the decision, but to no avail. Clifford in particular had a much longer and closer relationship with Johnson than any of his senior foreign policy advisers, but although he could hardly have voiced his objections more strenuously, he made little impression. According to Clifford, Press Secretary Bill Moyers—who shared his skepticism—reported in the midst of the discussions that only a "miraculous effort" would change the administration's course—"requiring not only a change in Johnson's mind, but also Rusk's, McNamara's and Bundy's."[44] No such change occurred.

The decision to intervene seemed broadly to reflect the principles of containment as they had been enunciated in the Truman Doctrine speech of March 1947, repeated in John Kennedy's inaugural address, and supported by Lyndon Johnson throughout his political career. For this reason, the decision initially enjoyed the support of most of official Washington, the press, the veterans of the Cold War known as the "Wise Men" whom Johnson began bringing to the White House for advice, and of public opinion as measured in the polls. Indeed, a small panel of a few "wise men" convened to survey the Vietnam situation in early July 1965 had reported that if South Vietnam fell, "not only would Thailand fall under Chinese sway, but that the effects in Japan, India, and even Europe could be most serious." William Bundy would write later that Johnson was concerned not to "fall short of the standards set by those who had played leading parts in World War II and throughout the period of American successes in the Cold War."[45]

All this does not mean, however, that Johnson had no choice in the matter. Despite some postwar statements by Johnson, no contemporary evidence suggests that he feared a disastrous Congressional reaction if he did not intervene, or indeed that either Kennedy or Johnson ever came under Congressional pressure to put American troops in Southeast Asia. Thus, in the spring of 1961, Kennedy had convened a bipartisan group of Senators to convey to Chief of Naval Operations Arleigh Burke their opposition to intervention in Laos.[46] Senate Majority Leader Mike Mansfield had been perhaps the severest critic of our policy toward Diem, and one of the few to suggest bluntly that Vietnam was not worth a war. Now Foreign Relations Committee Chairman J. William Fulbright had joined Mansfield as a skeptic, and Senator Richard Russell of Georgia, the leader of the "Dixiecrats" and a key figure in Johnson's Senate career, had made it clear that he regarded the war as a dubious venture.[47] The majority of the Congress would support escalation unenthusiastically, while a vocal and effective minority would oppose it. Johnson already had the bulk of the Great Society legislation through the Congress by late July 1965. He knew that his Congressional magic was not likely to last much longer in any case, and he also knew that the war carried enormous potential risks.[48]

George Ball and Clark Clifford, moreover, were not the only leading administration figures or presidential intimates to oppose the war. In February 1965, Johnson's chosen successor as Vice President, Hubert Humphrey, had given him a long and well-argued memorandum arguing against escalating the war, largely on political grounds. Humphrey noted that Johnson had just been elected overwhelmingly over an opponent who had favored escalation, that the war would be very hard to explain to the American people, that many Democrats would oppose it, that it would endanger progress on other foreign policy fronts, and that it might easily become a replay of the politically disastrous conflict in Korea. Johnson repaid Humphrey for this excellent advice by freezing him out of all the critical Vietnam discussions during the rest of 1965.[49] In short, had Johnson decided not to escalate and opt for face-saving negotiations, he could have counted on some important support.

The wise men, furthermore, failed to point out that each of Johnson's three immediate predecessors had seen fit to lay the containment policy aside at moments when its costs seemed to outweigh its benefits. Truman rejected intervention in the Chinese civil war, Eisenhower declined to intervene in Indochina in 1954, and Kennedy, as we have seen, rejected several proposals for military intervention in South Vietnam and Laos in 1961. In this instance, however, Johnson, after considerable hesitation, accepted the advice of his inherited foreign policy advisers, Rusk, McNamara, and Bundy, whose advice Kennedy had refused to accept with respect to South Vietnam during 1961. The parallel apparently occurred to Rusk at the time. "What we have done since 1954 to 1961 has not been good enough," he remarked on July 21, 1965. "We should probably have committed ourselves heavier in 1961."[50]

Whether Kennedy would have rejected their advice again in the spring and summer of 1965 will never be known.[51] He had made it clear in 1961 that he did not favor American military action in Southeast Asia, and he had stated as late as September 1963 that the war must be won or lost by the South Vietnamese themselves. In addition, he had stressed in November 1961 the difficulty of securing and maintaining the support of the American people for a war in Vietnam—an issue which received astonishingly little attention in the meetings of July 1965.[52] But Kennedy's decision in 1965 would to some extent have depended upon his assessment of his overall domestic and international political situation, and we cannot know what it would have been.

As it happened, 1965 differed in many ways from 1961, but the differences did not uniformly militate in favor of intervention. On the one hand, our commitment to Southeast Asia was much larger by 1965, the situation in South Vietnam was worse, and our responsibility for it had grown with the overthrow of the Diem regime, to which Kennedy had assented. But on the other hand, the international climate as a whole was substantially more relaxed, the period of maximum tension in Soviet-American relations was over, and the president found himself in a much stronger political position in the wake of the 1964 election. The utter collapse of the South Vietnamese government by the spring of 1965 left it in even worse shape than the pro-American Laotian government of 1961, and either Johnson or Kennedy might have chosen a face-saving neutralization of South Vietnam as well, provided that he felt that its negative political effects could be balanced by foreign policy successes in other parts of the world.

Johnson's decision to escalate, meanwhile, confronted him with the classic dilemma of containment. While his foreign policy team encouraged him to commit troops to South Vietnam, and while public opinion clearly supported this move in principle, the American people were less likely to support the all-out military effort that the Pentagon favored. McNamara's compromise military strategy for Vietnam sought a relatively cheap way out. The Joint Chiefs favored an all-out effort to destroy North Vietnam's will and capability to fight, and the use of any means necessary to defeat the Communist Chinese should they intervene as a result. But McNamara, who had grown accustomed to modifying the Chiefs' maximum recommendations so as to make them politically acceptable, persuaded himself that a smaller and less risky effort would suffice, and Rusk, who apparently planned to refight the Korean War without provoking Chinese intervention, agreed. A limited American effort to show the Communists that they could not win on the ground in the South and had much to fear from the U.S. in the north, they argued, would persuade Hanoi to seek a negotiated peace on American terms. Meanwhile, Johnson in particular insisted on avoiding any acts that might provoke Chinese or Soviet intervention, and also rejected McNamara's call for a reserve call-up. George Ball would remark years later that Dean Rusk saw the situation as another Korean War, "and Korea, so far as he was concerned, had been a great success," with Chinese intervention, apparently, the one great mistake.[53] The Chiefs, who had expressed serious reservations regarding the administration's strategy a year earlier, now signed on.[54]

The escalation of the war eventually destroyed the unanimity at the top of the national security establishment. Meanwhile, it ensured that the aggressive containment Kennedy had proclaimed in his inaugural, rather than the détente he had called for in his American University speech and begun to implement during 1963, would become the focus of Johnson's foreign policy.

The war, to begin with, soaked up a huge portion of the time and energy of the senior foreign policy establishment. The administration, as Kathleen Turner has said, fought a dual war, both against the North Vietnamese and against domestic critics who doubted American progress. As time passed, the need to show progress, moderation, and a sufficient willingness to take risks for peace consumed at least as much time in Washington as the conflict itself.[55] Johnson himself took a nearly obsessive interest in the details of the war, as the records of the Tuesday lunches confirm. No other foreign policy priority, in short, ever came close to challenging Indochina during the Johnson administration. The war figured in 31 of the 77 full NSC meetings called in the five years of the Johnson administration, compared to just 12 out of 45 full meetings under Kennedy. No other topic under Johnson was discussed as many as ten times.[56]

This, in turn, reflected another aspect of the Johnson administration's approach. The senior foreign policy team focused largely upon crisis points, most of them in the Third World, while paying relatively little attention to relations with Western Europe and the East bloc. The NSC under Johnson discussed Cyprus, various African problems, and other Asian questions six times each—the same number as all Western European items combined. The Soviet Union and strategic arms occupied only eight meetings. Crises in the Dominican Republic and the affair over North Korea's seizure of the *Pueblo* also engaged the administration's attention. But the NSC paid no sustained attention to relations with the Soviet Union, which throughout Kennedy's administration had been a top priority.

The lack of sustained diplomatic initiatives under Johnson—as opposed to crisis management—reflected some personnel changes in the State Department. Dean Rusk, as we have seen, could express a forthright opinion in a crisis, but never pursued any sustained policy initiative of his own. The undersecretaries who under Kennedy had made so much of the running, particularly Harriman and Ball, lost their positions or their influence under Johnson—Harriman because Johnson did not trust him, and Ball because of his opposition to the war in Vietnam. Roger Hilsman, who had hoped to change American China policy, had gone even earlier, in early 1964, although the cultural revolution within China probably doomed any possibility of better relations in any event. After the proposed NATO Multilateral Nuclear Force died early in the Johnson years, no major European initiatives emerged to replace it. No talks took place on Berlin or the German problem, as Harriman had proposed in 1963. And while the administration moved slowly toward talks with the Soviets on antiballistic missile and strategic arms limitations, the impetus for such conversations came mainly from the Department of Defense, where McNamara and his subordinates feared the cost of ABM deployment. State's one significant achievement in the field was the nonproliferation treaty, signed in 1968 but unratified until later because of the Soviet invasion of Czechoslovakia.

As other chapters in this volume make clear, the administration's European policy focused on the related problems of the dollar and the cost of our NATO troops, not on easing the East-West conflict that made their presence necessary.[57] These issues had also become much more serious because of the Vietnam War, which had halted and reversed a very significant improvement in the chronic balance of payments problem during 1965, and led to further pressure on the dollar in 1967. To its credit, the Johnson administration eventually increased income taxes to pay for the war and managed to stabilize the gold outflow in 1968. The Nixon administration hastily repealed the income tax surtax, creating the permanent, structural deficit in the federal budget that has been growing ever since, and leading rapidly to the devaluation of the dollar. Without the Vietnam War, however, Johnson might have coped with these problems at far less cost.[58]

As it was, Johnson met with Alexei Kosygin, the Chairman of the Soviet Council of Ministers, only once, at Glassboro, New Jersey, in June 1967. Brezhnev had not yet emerged as the dominant figure within the new Soviet leadership, and the meeting was hastily arranged when Kosygin attended a session of the United Nations in New York. The two men discussed possible peace talks in the Middle East, where Israel had just defeated the Arab states in the Six Day War, and in Vietnam, where the Americans had no immediate hopes. Johnson pushed for the beginning of ABM talks, but on Germany and European security he merely repeated the standard positions of the last ten years.[60] A year later, Johnson apparently hoped to visit Moscow and announce the start of ABM talks, but the Soviet invasion of Czechoslovakia put an end to these plans. The Nixon administration eventually reaped the harvest of Johnson's arms control initiatives.

As it happened, not only did the Johnson administration's foreign policy focus mainly upon the Vietnam War, but also its direction fell into the hands of men—led by Rusk, McNamara, and Walt Rostow—who believed completely in it. The president also committed himself fully to the conflict, and publicly staked his prestige upon victory again and again. Dissenters left the upper reaches of the State Department and the National Security Council Staff, and second-echelon officials found it harder and harder to become involved in serious policy discussions. Assistant Secretary of State for East Asian and Pacific Affairs William Bundy remarked in 1969 that he had experienced a great deal of trouble even finding out what had been decided at the top-level Tuesday lunches, and he did not dare instruct his staff to review our Vietnam policy because of Johnson's obsessive fear of a damaging leak.[61] The increasing dominance of a few committed hawks ultimately made it impossible truly to reverse the policy either in late 1967, when Robert McNamara declared quite rightly that it had failed to achieve its objectives, or in March 1968, after the Tet Offensive brought the same point home to the American people.

The administration's actual strategy in Vietnam represented a compromise from the beginning—a compromise in which most senior political and military leaders, with the apparent exception of Dean Rusk, eventually lost faith. As early as 1964, a remarkable memo from the Joint Chiefs of Staff stated their preferred military objective, "the destruction of the North Vietnamese will and capabilities as necessary to compel the Democratic Government of Vietnam (DRV) to cease providing support to the insurgencies in South Vietnam and Laos."[62] A year later, during the discussions over the American troop commitment, JCS Chairman General Wheeler accepted the risk of Chinese intervention as well, stating, "From the military view, we can handle, if we are determined to do so, China and North Vietnam."[63] But Johnson, McNamara and Rusk, fearing Chinese or Soviet intervention, insisted upon limiting ground operations to South Vietnamese territory. Unwilling to commit the huge forces necessary totally to defeat North Vietnam, they counted on bombing and attrition to persuade Hanoi that it could not win and force a settlement on American terms.

By early 1967, General William Westmoreland, commander of U.S. forces in Vietnam, had concluded that the strategy was not working, and was pushing for more aggressive action, including attacks upon North Vietnamese sanctuaries and trails in Cambodia, Laos, and perhaps North Vietnam, to regain the initiative. Operations to date, he recognized, had not significantly reduced the enemy's ability to fight, and his new plans would require increasing the American troop presence to approximately 700,000 men. This in turn would require a massive reserve call-up, a step Johnson had always resisted. Although Walt Rostow supported an invasion of North Vietnam to compel Hanoi to make peace, Westmoreland failed to carry the day at the White House in the spring of 1967.[64] While rejecting Westmoreland's strategy, the administration devoted the latter part of 1967 to trying to convince the country that the ground war was *not* stalemated, a campaign in which Westmoreland and Ambassador Ellsworth Bunker, who had replaced Lodge in 1967 joined during a well-orchestrated visit home in November 1967.[65] Meanwhile, Westmoreland prevailed in a lengthy controversy with the CIA, securing a National Intelligence Estimate that showed progress in the war of attrition, a conclusion that both civilian and military analysts had rejected.[66]

As early as May 19, 1967, McNamara had argued in a memorandum for the president that the war was essentially deadlocked, that intensified bombing would not work, and that Westmoreland's additional 200,000 troops would risk widening the war but would not win it. He had bluntly advocated stabilizing our troop commitment, confining bombing south of the 20th parallel, and opening talks between the Saigon government and the non-Communist factions of the NLF. He also recommended abandoning the preservation of a non-Communist South Vietnam as an American objective while seeking mutual withdrawal of North Vietnamese and American forces.[67] He repeated that argument in modified form on November 1, but dropped the proposal for negotiations with the NLF. At Johnson's request, Rostow solicited reactions from Rusk, General Taylor, now an unofficial adviser, Ambassador Bunker, General Westmoreland, and unofficial advisers Abe Fortas and Clark Clifford. All of them rejected McNamara's most important recommendations, generally argued for only small modifications to current policy, and hopefully predicted that progress (although not victory) would soon become apparent both to the American people and Hanoi. On November 27, McNamara resigned.[68]

Two months later, the Tet Offensive, while failing in its objectives, showed the American people that the enemy's ability to mount major operations had increased, not decreased, despite thirty months of American effort and more than 20,000 American dead. While a great deal of revisionist literature has now presented Tet as an American battlefield success, American military leaders did not at the time believe that it had vindicated current strategy. Generals Wheeler and Westmoreland immediately renewed their request for 206,000 more troops, and while Wheeler discreetly failed to mention this in Washington, Westmoreland apparently wanted the reinforcements to undertake his long-planned operations in Laos, Cambodia, and North Vietnam.[69] A clear request to escalate the war geographically as well as numerically would undoubtedly have focused debate in Washington more clearly. As is well known, however, McNamara's successor Clark Clifford— highly influenced by his inherited subordinates Townsend Hoopes,

Cyrus Vance, and Paul Warnke—concluded after Tet that the United States had no real plan to win the war. He pressed Johnson to halt bombing north of the 20th parallel—the same proposal McNamara had put forward ten months earlier—and try to begin negotiations. Johnson was deeply shaken when several of the Wise Men, including McGeorge Bundy, former Secretary of State Dean Acheson, and former Treasury Secretary Douglas Dillon, reversed the position they had taken only a few months earlier and suggested that the United States had to begin to disengage.[70] Rusk eventually agreed, apparently because he felt that only a bombing pause could help recapture public support for the war. Johnson announced the partial halt on March 31, and announced his retirement from office—which he had discussed privately for months—at the same time.

Hanoi's prompt and surprising agreement to meet with American representatives to discuss a total bombing halt led to the opening of the Paris talks, and Harriman's return to a position of influence as chief negotiator. It did not however lead to real progress toward a settlement. As Clifford has recently written in his memoirs, a split continued during most of 1968 between himself, his leading civilian subordinates at the Pentagon, Under Secretary of State Nicholas Katzenbach, and negotiators Harriman and Cyrus Vance on the one hand, and Rusk, Rostow, Ambassador Bunker, Johnson confidant and Supreme Court Justice Abe Fortas, and the American military on the other. While Clifford wanted the talks to end the American role during 1968—largely because he remained convinced that we could not win the war—the others viewed them tactically, and still counted on military pressure to help produce a favorable outcome.[71] The administration continued through October to push for various assurances, including one that the DMZ would be respected—a concession neither Johnson nor Nixon ever secured—before halting the bombing. Finally, on the eve of the election, Washington agreed to the halt and the beginning of talks on the assumption that Hanoi would respond appropriately. The talks failed to begin when Saigon, encouraged by the Nixon campaign and by Ambassador Bunker, refused to sit down with the Viet Cong, and Nixon was elected. Meanwhile, the ground war continued at a very high level through 1968.

Johnson's failure truly to reverse his policy during the latter half of 1968 left Clifford, Harriman, and millions of Americans intensely frustrated. In this respect, however, his successor did no better. When Nixon took office the country expected a relatively early peace (he had, after all, intimated that he could end the war quickly during the 1968 campaign), and he encouraged that expectation by beginning peace talks and announcing a token troop withdrawal in the summer of 1969. In the meantime, the war continued at a high level, and 1969, during which nearly 10,000 American soldiers died, became the second-heaviest year of the war after 1968. Nixon wanted to use a mixture of pressure on the Soviet Union and escalation of the war against the North to end the conflict on favorable terms, but in late October 1969, faced with massive demonstrations, he canceled the renewed bombing of the North and the mining of Haiphong harbor. In April 1970 he authorized one of the military's long-desired options, the invasion of Cambodia, but the enormous criticism that resulted led him seriously to begin disengaging for the first time. He eventually ended American participation in the war, but he neither settled the conflict nor strengthened the South Vietnamese to the point that they could defend themselves.

The evaluation of specific periods in Cold War American foreign policy has become both more interesting and more challenging in the wake of the collapse of Communism and the end of that conflict. What one thinks of the policies of any particular administration depends very largely upon one's view of what exactly led to Western victory in the Cold War.

Viewed as a whole, and disregarding for a moment the differences in the Kennedy and Johnson administrations, the 1960s rank with the 1980s as one of the more active decades in Cold War foreign policy. The performance of these administrations should impress those who believe that vigilant, wide-ranging containment, superiority in strategic arms, and covert action in the Third World brought down Communism. Kennedy and Johnson oversaw one of the largest strategic arms build-ups of the whole Cold War, harassed Cuba, helped to bring down leftist governments in Brazil and Greece and to block them in the Dominican Republic and Indonesia, and went to war to stop Communism in Southeast Asia. In practice, their foreign policy resembles Reagan's more than Nixon's or Eisenhower's, and conservatives might therefore be more likely to give the Kennedy-Johnson team high marks than centrists or liberals. Indeed, the neoconservative movement drew heavily on those who believed in such a foreign policy, and who felt that the Democratic Party had abandoned it after Vietnam. It would be very difficult to argue, however, that these policies moved us dramatically nearer victory in the Cold War during the 1960s.

Others might argue that the ups and downs of the 1960s are simply episodes in the 45-year history of containment, a policy whose eventual success was more a matter of time than of short-term tactics. The specific events of the 1960s seem much less important in the wake of the sudden collapse of Communism. Even the foreign policy consequences of the Vietnam War already seem relatively minor. The war did not secure its objective, but neither did it prevent the opening of relations with China under Nixon, or détente with the Soviet Union, or eventual victory in the Cold War. One can even argue, as Walt Rostow in particular has done, that the war allowed some of the impressive economic development in other parts of Southeast Asia to take place, although it was never clear, and it is not clear now, that the consequences of an earlier Communist victory would have spread beyond Indochina. Eventually the war will seem hardly more important to the course of world history than the French wars in Indochina and Algeria that preceded it.

To those like George Kennan, however, who believe that a bitter Cold War made it easier for the Soviets to maintain the cohesion of their state and their alliances, and that the détente of the 1970s accelerated the decay of Communism, the 1960s loom as an era of lost opportunity.[72] Had Kennedy lived through a second term, he might have managed to maintain or increase the momentum of East-West détente, as he clearly hoped to do at the time he died, and scored some of the successes achieved by Richard Nixon. To be sure, as we have seen, a Democratic president would have found it more difficult to undertake the East-West initiatives that Nixon brought to fruition in the 1970s. The West German government was only beginning to relax its inflexible policy, and Moscow and especially Beijing might not yet have been ready for better relations. Still, Kennedy had clearly begun moving in that direction during 1963. Johnson never paid the same kind of sustained attention to East-West relations, and Vietnam, as we have seen, swallowed up most of his administration's foreign policy.

Meanwhile, if the international consequences of 1960s foreign policy may be debated, the domestic ones are not open to dispute. The Vietnam War now looms as one of the more significant events in American political history. Together with the civil rights movement, it split the Democratic Party and ushered in two decades of Republican dominance. It destroyed the Cold War consensus in American foreign policy and alienated much of a whole generation from its government. And it left the country with the painful legacy of a lost war, one which the American public has never fully faced up to.

Like the Korean War—whose domestic political consequences seem largely to have been forgotten in the 1960s—Vietnam laid bare the essential contradiction that bedeviled the American government from 1947 through 1990. During these four decades, successive presidents told the American people that they had to contest the spread of Communism all over the world, and the opposition party rarely missed a chance to claim that the government had failed in this task. In practice, no administration could ever afford the cost of trying to restrain Communism everywhere, and none did so. Truman declined to intervene in the civil war in China, Eisenhower accepted the French defeat in the Indochina War and had to live with Castro in Cuba, the Kennedy, Johnson, Nixon, and Ford administrations could not save Indochina, Carter could not prevent the Soviet invasion of Afghanistan or the Sandinista victory in Nicaragua, and Reagan, for all his rhetoric, confined his "rollback" operations to Grenada. Unlimited containment—and in particular, the commitment of American forces in areas that, in and of themselves, could not be deemed vital to American interests—was never a workable policy, if only because the means required would frequently be revealed to be so much greater than the worth of the short-term ends in view. In practice, successful foreign policy during the Cold War depended upon convincing the American people that the government was doing enough to fight Communism without actually undertaking military operations whose benefits would not match up to their costs. The Johnson administration spectacularly failed this test, and destroyed its effectiveness at home.

NOTES

1. John Lewis Gaddis, *Strategies of Containment* (New York, 1982), pp. 198–273. I would like to thank my colleagues in the Strategy Department of the Naval War College for their comments on this chapter.

2. For the most recent account of the invasion see Michael R. Beschloss, *The Crisis Years. Kennedy and Khrushchev, 1960–1963* (New York, 1991), pp. 100–25. Beschloss presents some evidence that the original plan also included an assassination attempt upon Castro, and that Kennedy refused to intervene partly because it did not take place.

3. Honore M. Catudal, *Kennedy and the Berlin Wall Crisis. A Study in U.S. Decision Making* (Berlin, 1980), pp. 101–56; see also Marc Trachtenberg, "The Berlin Crisis," *History and Strategy* (Princeton, 1991), pp. 169–234, and Thomas Schwartz, *infra*.

4. See Vladislav Zubok, *infra*.

5. W. W. Rostow, *The Diffusion of Power. An Essay in Recent History* (New York, 1972), p. 224; Catudal, *Kennedy and the Wall Crisis*, pp. 144–46.

6. Trachtenberg, "The Berlin Crisis," pp,. 227.

7. Harold W. Chase and Allen H. Lerman, eds., *Kennedy and the Press* (New York, 1965), p. 134.

8. Arthur M. Schlesinger, Jr., *A Thousand Days: John F. Kennedy in the White House* (Boston, 1965), p. 339.

9. Robert Schulzinger's article, *infra*, addresses itself to the American involvement in Vietnam.

10. *FRUS* (1961–63) 1: 109.

11. Ibid., 131.

12. Library of Congress, Harriman papers, box 519, Vietnam, General, 1961, memo of August 29.

13. *FRUS* (1961–63) 1: 133.

14. Ibid., 157, and Maxwell D. Taylor, *Swords and Plowshares* (New York, 1972), pp. 225–6.

15. *FRUS* (1961–63) 1: 253.

16. Ibid., 254.

17. Ibid, 256.

18. The word "successful" must be qualified. The agreement provided for a new government under Souvanna Phouma, unification of the various Laotian armed factions, and withdrawal of North Vietnamese troops from Laos. Only the first of these three objectives was ever reached, but the agreement still left the United States in a much stronger position, since it now had the neutralist forces on its side.

19. See the record of the Honolulu Conference of July 23, 1962, *FRUS* (1961–63) 2: 248.

20. Certainly this belief differs very significantly from that of President Eisenhower in earlier crises, who, as we know now, simply did not believe that the Soviet Union would risk war over Berlin. Had Kennedy shared Eisenhower's confidence—and had he felt strong enough politically to act on it—he would have saved himself a great deal of trouble, both in 1961 over Berlin and in 1962 over Cuba.

21. McGeorge Bundy originally published the transcript in *International Security* 12, no. 3 (1987), pp. 32–92.

22. See McGeorge Bundy, *Danger and Survival. Choices about the Bomb in the First Fifty Years* (New York, 1988), pp. 432–36; Robert Kennedy,*Thirteen Days* (New York, 1969).

23. *Robert Kennedy in His Own Words*, pp. 338–39. The president certainly took the post seriously, and even spoke to his brother about taking it.

24. Beschloss, *The Crisis Years*, pp. 591–94.

25. Theodore C. Sorensen, *Kennedy* (New York, 1965), pp. 730–31.

26. Taylor, *Swords and Plowshares*, pp. 189, 286–87. Taylor acknowledged that the Chiefs regarded the proposed treaty "with controlled enthusiasm," and that they regarded it as a purely military disadvantage.

27. *FRUS* (1961–63) 4: 116.

28. Ibid., 167.

29. See the most revealing comments in *Robert Kennedy in his Own Words*, pp. 402–403. RFK seems to have viewed this particular crisis largely through the eyes of Taylor and McNamara.

30. Library of Congress, Harriman papers, Box 541, Test Ban, Memorandum of July 30, 1963. As Thomas Schwartz points out, *infra*, this was not a com-

pletely new proposition.

31. Press conference, October 9, 1963, Chase and Lehrman, *Kennedy and the Press*, p. 505.

32. William Attwood, a member of the American U.N. delegation, was discussing normalization of relations with Cuban delegates at the U.N. and reporting directly to McGeorge Bundy in November 1963. See Beschloss, *The Crisis Years*, pp. 638–39, 658–59.

33. These memos can be found in the National Security File, Memos to the President, LBJ Library.

34. Robert Dallek, *Lone Star Rising. Lyndon Johnson and his Times, 1908–1960* (New York, 1991), pp. 382–84, 529–32.

35. For the London episode see Philip M. Kaiser, *Journeying Far and Wide: A Political and Diplomatic Memoir* (New York, 1993), pp. 250–51.

36. *FRUS* (1961–63) 4: 336, 337.

37. *FRUS* (1964–68) 1: 73 and note.

38. George McT. Kahin, *Intervention: How America Became Involved in Vietnam* (New York, 1986), pp. 205–13; *FRUS* (1964–1968) 1: 173.

39. As Kahin noted in 1986, it has been well established that the second reported attack on American ships never took place, but we still do not know whether McNamara, in particular, actually believed that it had. Kahin, *Intervention*, pp. 219–223.

40. *FRUS* (1964–68) 1: 8.

41. *FRUS* (1964–1968) 1: 278, 280.

42. Kahin, *Intervention*, pp. 241–45.

43. Kahin, *Intervention*, pp. 249–85.

44. Clark Clifford, *Counsel to the President: A Memoir* (New York, 1991), p. 416.

45. Kahin, *Intervention*, p. 361. The panel included General Omar Bradley, former Deputy Defense Secretary Roswell Gilpatric, former presidential science adviser George Kistiakowsky, former USIA director Arthur Larson, and former U.S. High Commissioner to Germany John J. McCloy. In a remarkable example of doublethink, many administration officials during this period managed simultaneously to argue that North Vietnam feared China and would not want China to intervene in the conflict, and that a North Vietnamese victory would be, above all, a victory for Communist China.

46. The meeting with Burke took place on April 27 and included conservative Republicans and Southern Democrats; see Edward J. Marolda and Oscar P. Fitzgerald, *The United States Navy and the Vietnam Conflict*, (Washington, 1986), 2: 71.

47. On Russell see Brian VanDeMark, *Into the Quagmire: Lyndon Johnson and the Escalation of the Vietnam War* (New York, 1991), pp. 32–33, 160, 208.

48. Harry C. McPherson, *A Political Education* (New York, 1972), p. 268, quotes the president as saying that with Congress, "One year is all you get," and adding that he was bound to lose a great deal of his majority in late 1966 if the war continued.

49. Hubert H. Humphrey, *The Education of a Public Man* (New York, 1976),

pp. 313–328.

50. Kahin, *Intervention*, p. 372.

51. The literature is already deeply divided on this point. Both William J. Rust, *Kennedy In Vietnam* (New York, 1985), and John M. Newman, *JFK and Vietnam* (New York, 1992), tend to conclude that Kennedy would not have escalated, while Kahin, *Intervention*, implies that he might have followed the same course, as does Stanley Karnow, *Vietnam: A History* (New York, 1983.) The expressed opinions of those men who served both Kennedy and Johnson reflect, almost without exception, their own retrospective assessments of the wisdom of escalation.

52. See Kahin, *Intervention*, pp. 367–97. George Ball was virtually the only participant even to raise this issue.

53. Ball Oral History, LBJ Library, p. 33.

54. For the Joint Chiefs' objections see their memorandum to McNamara, June 2, 1964, in *FRUS* (1964–68) 1: no. 191.

55. Kathleen J. Turner, *Lyndon Johnson's Dual War: Vietnam and the Press* (Chicago, 1985).

56. See LBJ Library, National Security Files, Memos for the President, Box 21, vol. 38.

57. See Diane B. Kunz and Thomas Schwartz, *infra*.

58. See Burton I. Kaufmann, "Foreign Aid and the Balance-of-Payments Problem: Vietnam and Johnson's Foreign Economic Policy," Robert Divine, ed., *The Johnson Years, Volume Two* (Lawrence, Kansas, 1987), pp. 79–109.

59. See Arthur Waldron, *infra*.

60. LBJ Library, National Security Files, Countries, Europe & USSR, Box 229, Hollybush.

61. William Bundy oral history, LBJ Library.

62. *FRUS* (1964–68) 1: 191, memo of 2 June 1964.

63. Kahin, *Intervention*, p. 381. "If we are determined to do so" probably meant, "if we are willing to use nuclear weapons."

64. Charles F. Brower IV, "Strategic Reassessment in Vietnam. The Westmoreland 'Alternate Strategy' of 1967–1968,' " *Naval War College Review* 44 no. 2 (Spring 1991): 20–51.

65. Larry Berman, *Lyndon Johnson's War. The Road to Stalemate in Vietnam* (New York, 1989), pp. 115–17.

66. Ibid., pp. 93–113.

67. McNamara for the President, May 19, 1967, Joint Exhibit 955, Westmoreland-CBS Trial.

68. All these memoranda have been collected in LBJL, NSF, Countries, Vietnam, Box 127, Vietnam, March 19, 1970.

69. Brower, "Strategic Reassessment in Vietnam," pp. 40–41.

70. Clifford, *Counsel to the President*, pp. 516–17.

71. Ibid., pp. 528–96.

72. George F. Kennan, "The G.O.P. won the Cold War? Ridiculous," *New York Times*, October 28, 1992, p. A21.

2

Mixing the Sweet with the Sour: Kennedy, Johnson, and Latin America

•

WILLIAM O. WALKER III

"Have we determined what we are going to do about Cuba?" So wondered members of the National Security Council (NSC) at one of their first meetings in 1961 under President John F. Kennedy.[1] The focus on Cuba specifically and on threats from the left to U.S. interests in the hemisphere, generally, set the tone for inter-American relations in the 1960s. The intellectual paladins of the New Frontier, many of whom were college professors from Harvard and MIT, espoused a liberal vision of justice without precedent in the Americas. Yet had the men of the Charles River been less imbued with a strong world view derived from Cold War assumptions, then both national and regional programs for social change and economic progress might possibly have been pursued for their own sake. The irony, of course, is that reform programs would have been much less elaborate if the imposing shadow of the Cold War were not looming over the shoulder of U.S. officials.

It would be a mistake to underestimate the effect of the Cold War in the Americas. By January 1961 the era of the Good Neighbor policy was long over. Wartime prospects for greater reciprocity in hemispheric economic relations had given way to hegemonic autarky on the part of Washington. Both tradition and strategic demands of the early Cold War period had guaranteed that the Economic Charter of the Americas, agreed to at the 1945 Inter-American Conference on the Problems of War and Peace, would echo larger U.S. foreign policy objectives; there would be no special consideration given to Latin American tariff, loan, trade, or investment needs for more than a decade after the war.[2] Former Assistant Secretary of State for Economic Affairs William L. Clayton would write to the newly inaugurated president in February 1961 denouncing the very discriminatory policies he had helped to fashion. He called upon Kennedy not to follow existing policies "designed to set our country economically above and apart from the rest of the world."[3]

Clayton, who equated U.S. security with boldness in economic foreign policy, was advocating an interdependence similar to that Latin Americans had demanded at the 1945 Chapultepec conference. Yet continuity more than change would mark Latin American policy from Eisenhower to Kennedy, and ultimately to Johnson. In sum, policy originated from a fear of communism's potential appeal to impoverished Latin Americans. How the politics of anticommunism in the 1960s affected inter-American relations can be seen by examining the four basic pillars of U.S. policy: containment of Castro and the revolutionary left; foreign aid and trade policy; military assistance; and the Alliance for Progress.[4] The limited ability of the United States to ensure either individual well-being or democracy throughout the region remains a major legacy of Kennedy-Johnson foreign policy and is the principal theme of this chapter.

Eisenhower and Latin America

Latin America's general economic condition was far from encouraging in the late 1950s. As the Argentine economist Raúl Prebisch, executive secretary of the United Nations Economic Commission for Latin America (ECLA), once wrote: "The prevailing social structure posed a serious obstacle to . . . economic and social development." Lack of social mobility, greatly distorted distribution of wealth, and limited investment capital reinforced a conservative status quo that seemed antithetical to growth and development.[5] With both per capita income and terms of trade plunging in Latin America, Prebisch knew that only comprehensive economic and social planning could improve the human condition.[6] One response from ECLA, an organization whose creation the United States had opposed, was to call for increased financial assistance from Washington, a proposal that Assistant Secretary of State Henry F. Holland in March 1955 termed "socialistic."[7] Although Prebisch and U.S. officials could perhaps agree that "the economic difficulties in Latin America [were] properly attributable in major part to deficiencies in the countries themselves,"[8] they did not place comparable faith in privately funded development projects as a solution to Latin America's structural woes. Nevertheless, the limited role for public resources in U.S. economic foreign policy toward Latin America since 1945 seemed to preclude any drastic alteration of policy. "The objective of United States' inter-American policy," Holland told Secretary of State John Foster Dulles in December 1955, "is to persuade the Latin American Governments and peoples to adhere to our political and economic philosophies."[9]

Holland's predecessor, John Moors Cabot, had decried the conditions that Prebisch and like-minded Latin Americans found so threatening to economic development and political stability. Yet for advocating expanded lending authority for the Export-Import Bank, Cabot was removed from his post by Secretary Dulles whose foreign policy priorities—along with those of President Dwight D. Eisenhower—lay outside the Western Hemisphere. This is not to argue that the administration neglected Latin America; it did not. Rather, as historian Stephen G. Rabe points out, a staunch anticommunism permeated U.S. policy to the extent that Eisenhower and Dulles sought to derive political capital from the dispersal of limited military aid.[10]

Economic assistance to Latin America remained essentially a secondary consideration for the administration almost until the disastrous South American trip of Vice-President Richard M. Nixon in the spring of 1958. Involvement in the June 1954 overthrow of President Jacobo Arbenz in Guatemala and the decision on the eve of the Rio Conference that November not to revamp their economic policy blinded U.S. officials to the growing social and economic crisis in the rest of the hemisphere.[11] A report to the NSC in the wake of Nixon's trip expressed much concern over "continuing political instability and intensified economic problems in most of Latin America."[12] Many Latin Americans believed, in the words of the Operations Coordinating Board (OCB) of the NSC, that a much "too low priority has been placed by the U.S. Government on operations in the area."[13]

The remaining years of the Eisenhower presidency were spent in trying to rectify that oversight. Impetus for change within the Department of State came from Assistant Secretary Roy Richard Rubottom, Jr., who had replaced Holland in September 1956. Like Cabot before him, Rubottom sought to promote U.S. interests by focusing on social and economic issues. In February 1959, the NSC formalized Rubottom's approach in NSC 5902/1, which posited a "key role" for Latin America in safeguarding U.S. security. As such, U.S. policy should take cognizance of: "rising aspirations" in the hemisphere; the intensity of Latin American nationalism; problems posed by neutralism, which the Kennedy administration would have to deal with early on in the case of Brazil; demands for rapid social and economic change; and a revived desire for democratic government and the protection of human rights.

Only in that context, U.S. policymakers realized, could military aid become acceptable to the proponents of change and development.[14]

Ever reluctant to engage in large-scale economic aid, the administration argued before Congress that military and economic assistance were interchangeable. Prodded by President Juscelino Kubitschek of Brazil in June 1958 to address the root causes of underdevelopment, the administration finally put aside its philosophical reservations about public assistance—if only to contain the excesses of "Operation Pan America."[15] Seizing the opportunity afforded by Kubitschek's ambitious plan, which must be regarded as a prototype for the Alliance for Progress, Rubottom and others concerned with the fate of Latin America, including the president's brother Milton Eisenhower, Thomas C. Mann, and C. Douglas Dillon, supported dramatic changes in the U.S. position on commodity agreements and convinced the president to support capitalization of an Inter-American Development Bank (IDB) at $1 billion.

If these changes were narrower than Under Secretary of State Dillon would have liked, they were no less significant for that. However tentatively, a fundamental impasse in economic foreign policy had been overcome. Support for coffee and metal prices and access to development capital might stave off the contagion of Communist revolution.[16] Only a serious, revolutionary threat to U.S. interests could reveal how insubstantial the alteration of policy actually was. Kubitschek had hoped that the initial capitalization of the IDB would be as much as $5 billion; he also supported the idea of a "Marshall Plan" for Latin America in the amount of some $40 billion over two decades.[17]

The rise to power of Fidel Castro in Cuba doubtless had a greater inevitability for Latin Americans than for policymakers in the United States. Myopia in Washington was the result of viewing movements for social change primarily through the lens of free trade and private investment. In Cuba, however, and also throughout much of Latin America, the time had come for agrarian reform that not only provided access to productive land for impoverished masses but also assured peasants that their crops would find more profitable markets than before. Raúl Prebisch captured the essence of the agrarian dilemma: "The intimate link between the socioeconomic structure and the structure of power is well known."[18] Castro emphasized this same theme in his address to the United Nations in September 1960.[19] In short, structural inequities had guaranteed the coming of the Cuban Revolution.[20]

Although extremely cautious in its initial responses to Castro, the administration quickly recognized the revolutionary regime. Following a meeting with North American businessmen at the U.S. embassy in Havana on January 6, 1959, Counselor Daniel M. Braddock reported: "Every man present expressed individually and emphatically the view that it would be in the interest of US and of American business in Cuba for US to recognize provisional government as quickly as possible."[21] U.S. policymakers could not seriously object to the overthrow of the dictator Fulgencio Batista without rejecting one of the central premises of NSC 5902/1—opposition to authoritarian governments.[22]

More a modus vivendi than a honeymoon, relations between the Eisenhower administration and Castro soon deteriorated. Adoption of the Agrarian Reform Law and other related measures by mid-1959 moved Washington to consider cutting the sugar quota.[23] Dillon cabled Ambassador Philip W. Bonsal: "Agrarian reform law [is] causing great consternation in U.S. Government and American sugar circles."[24] By the end of the year, despite Ambassador Bonsal's call for patience, Christian A. Herter, who had replaced the ailing Dulles as secretary of state, was advising Eisenhower that Castro ought to be removed from power.[25] Nationalizing Cuba's economy and moving toward neutralism in foreign policy were unacceptable breeches of trust as well as direct threats to the administration's plans for regional development and keeping Communist influence out of the hemisphere.[26]

Even after the recall of Bonsal to Washington in early 1960, Rubottom and Dillon believed that U.S. policy "should carefully mix the sweet with the sour," but the time for accommodation had passed.[27] On March 16 the 5412 Committee, a covert action review group created after the ouster of Arbenz in Guatemala, proposed replacing Castro's regime "with one more devoted to the true interests of the Cuban people and more acceptable to the U.S. in such a manner as to avoid any appearance of U.S. intervention." Presidential authorization came the next day.[28] Covert plans to overthrow Castro continued apace throughout the final year of the Eisenhower administration, highlighted by efforts to destabilize Cuba's economy and to create a political alternative to Castro.[29] During 1960 the administration also began a covert process that resulted in the May 1961 killing of Raphael Leonidas Trujillo Molina, the military dictator of the Dominican Republic.[30]

The Kennedy Transition

The Kennedy administration clearly understood the dichotomy between reform and revolution. And as under Eisenhower, the best antidote for revolution would be economic development and social justice. The difference, as Albert O. Hirschman has noted, was that Castro "made the United States favor a more intensive use of public funds as a principal instrument of foreign policy."[31] Younger, more flamboyant, and more intoxicated by power than their predecessors, the individuals in Kennedy's inner circle generally adhered to the conservatism they inherited in foreign economic policy. Public economic assistance would be used as a necessary pump-priming device—as Eisenhower had begun to do in mid-1960 with the creation of a Social Progress Trust Fund of $500 million to be administered by the IDB—to accelerate the stages of economic growth. The Organization of American States (OAS), with only Cuba in dissent, had ratified the idea of a trust fund at a September 1960 meeting in Bogotá. And yet, it remained axiomatic that expansion of foreign aid for development purposes should in no way threaten to undermine U.S. monetary stability. That is, foreign economic assistance would not be so extensive as to stall the engine of growth of the U.S. economy.[32]

However much Kennedy wanted to fashion a "new deal" for Latin America—the words were Lincoln Gordon's of the Harvard Business School[33]—the political and economic realities in Latin America paradoxically counseled both a sense of urgency and a note of caution. A review of NSC 5902/1, undertaken in April 1960, found turmoil in the Caribbean and part of South America; unstable prices in the coffee, cocoa, and sugar markets; reduced flows of private investment; and intensified penetration of the region by Communist influences.[34]

The preinaugural task force on Latin American affairs, led by Adolf A. Berle, believed that Venezuela and Colombia were the keys to avoiding "a major Cold War in the Caribbean littoral."[35] Berle wrote in his diary that "social revolution is inevitable; it must be dissociated from Communism and its power politics."[36] Subsequently, following a trip to Latin America with the Food for Peace Mission, presidential adviser Arthur M. Schlesinger, Jr., told Kennedy—in words that echoed assessments by Raúl Prebisch— that the chief obstacles to modernization were structural, that ruling oligarchs had made economic growth and social mobility impossible. Without a middle-class revolution, as Rómulo Betancourt was pursuing in Venezuela and Víctor Raúl Haya de la Torre was promising for Peru, radical, and possibly Communist, revolution would be inevitable.[37]

Time for modernization through moderation was running out, Schlesinger warned. Young intellectuals showed signs of doubting whether progressive political parties could ever fulfill their promises. The core of U.S. policy must therefore reflect strong opposition to dictatorship and a clear willingness to support development not only through industrialization but also through extensive land reform, tax reform, and social progress. Alone private enterprise and the customary monetarist solutions of the International Monetary Fund (IMF) would fail. Schlesinger also recommended that the United States reassess traditional relations with military forces because in a number of countries "civilian governments exist on the Army's sufferance."[38]

The evaluation of the transitional task force on economic foreign policy was scarcely less bleak. Headed by George W. Ball, who would serve as under secretary of state for economic affairs, the task force expressed concern over a wide range of economic and financial issues, notably the current balance of payments problem facing the United States, and argued forcefully for greater openness and competition in the world economy. At the same time, the task force called for increased cooperation among the industrial powers of the West in providing economic aid to the underdeveloped areas of the world.

Third World nationalism, unless properly directed, would greatly impede growth and development, task force members feared. Hence, something more than financial and technical assistance was necessary; underdeveloped countries had to have access to markets they could depend on in order to reduce the destabilizing effects of price fluctuations. Moreover, foreign economic aid needed to be restructured from its prior focus on forestalling the spread of communism to funding economic and social reform programs. In that regard, appropriations for the Social Progress Trust Fund under Eisenhower were a step in the right direction, particularly because multilateral institutions including the IDB, the Export- Import Bank, and the International Bank for Reconstruction and Development were engaged as never before in long-term planning. To be sure, anticipatory planning was crucial for the systematic mobilization of local capital resources and introduction of such institutional changes as land reform.[39]

Significantly, the task force report was of two minds about military aid, noting that programs implemented under the Mutual Security Act largely emphasized the dangers of communism and only secondarily contributed, through the use of contingency funds, to sustained economic growth. The contributors to the report argued that military aid and economic assistance were interrelated. As such, some of the military support given to local armed forces might better be expended on innovative nation-building programs than on superfluous defense requirements.[40]

Brazil's Kubitschek had done as much as any leader in Latin America to link economic development and the effective control of subversive activities. Failure to achieve development in fairly short order would substantially retard the realization of Western objectives in the Cold War.[41] From the inception of Kennedy's presidency, U.S. policymakers endeavored to find an appropriate mix for economic and military assistance. Not until March 1962, though, would NSC officials try to resolve this vexing dilemma by adopting more systematic planning procedures.[42]

Given the threat to U.S. interests posed by Castro and a stagnant Latin American economy, the administration's outward optimism in its early months was hardly justified. Progressives including Haya de la Torre, Betancourt, Arturo Frondizi of Argentina, Víctor Paz Estenssoro of Bolivia, and Jânio Quadros of Brazil underlined for Kennedy's advisers the gravity of conditions there.[43] To a considerable extent, Kennedy had compounded the situation by making Castro such a major issue during the campaign. Doing so left little room to reassess the covert operation initiated by Eisenhower and implemented under the auspices of the Central Intelligence Agency (CIA). If the Republicans had "lost" Cuba, then the logic of campaign rhetoric mandated that the Democrats had to recover the island.[44] The military and policymaking disaster of Operation Zapata at the Bay of Pigs in April not only demonstrated the limits of U.S. power but also enhanced Castro's reputation in the hemisphere, as the president himself later admitted.[45]

The Alliance for Progress

Kennedy's oft-quoted inaugural address spoke with a clear voice to "our sister republics south of the border," pledging both a "new alliance for progress" and opposition to "aggression or subversion anywhere in the Americas."[46] Discerning listeners might have wondered how the president's ringing words squared with the Declaration of San José, Costa Rica, at the conclusion of the Seventh Meeting of Consultation of Ministers of Foreign Affairs in late August 1960, at which time the OAS reaffirmed the principle of nonintervention by any American state in the affairs of its sister republics.[47] Yet the tense atmosphere at San José did not prevent the United States from moving ahead with plans to overthrow Castro, an action that would be undertaken for its own sake and as a warning to leftists throughout the hemisphere.[48]

Like its predecessor, the Kennedy administration worried about the effect of non-alignment and the strength of the left in Latin America, especially in such states as Brazil,[49] Colombia, and Venezuela.[50] Walt W. Rostow, assistant to national security adviser McGeorge Bundy

observed that Latin America "was in a new state of torment" and that
Fidel Castro "was actively engaged in subversive action." And Roger
Hilsman, director of intelligence and research in the State Department,
wrote that underdeveloped nations "offered exciting prospects" for
communism.[51] Searching for a means to counter the feared spread of
communism, the OCB— soon to be abolished—enumerated how
administration policies and programs in the Americas could be coordinated. Basic to this effort would be the creation of country teams, internal security programs, and a special group concerned with gaining
multilateral support for U.S. policy toward Cuba.[52]

In the wake of the Bay of Pigs fiasco in mid-April, as the administration endeavored to control the damage done by such a "serious setback" to its foreign policy, several options eased policymakers through
the difficult months. First, the perceived betrayal of Cuban exile forces
had to be overcome, if only for domestic political reasons.[53] Second,
other governments needed to be persuaded of the wisdom of continued pressure against the Castro regime. The goal would not be soon
accomplished, as Latin Americans had expended considerable diplomatic energy in the twentieth century to obtain from Washington formal pledges not to intervene in their internal affairs. Uncertainty about
Washington's Cuban policy was rife throughout Latin America and
would not easily be overcome.[54]

Rostow felt that indications of progress in South Vietnam, "where
success against Communist techniques is conceivable," would bring
most of the OAS into line on Cuba. By the end of 1961, though, the
White House was once again resorting to covert activities in its effort
to eliminate the problems posed by Castro.[55] As we shall see, pressure
against Cuba would soon be accompanied by intensified counterinsurgency training programs for Latin American military and police
forces.

Third, less dramatic but no less important, Kennedy's proposed
Alliance for Progress soon became the centerpiece of Latin American
policy. Administration officials feared that Cuba presented an impressive showcase for Communist revolution, yet they also believed that
the Alliance could serve as an effective counterweight. Outside of Cuba
only Venezuela in early 1961 was engaged in a concerted agrarian
reform program.[56] Significantly, an address to the Pan American Society in New York by Venezuelan Ambassador to the United States José
Antonio Mayobre, who was an economist by training, set the stage for
Kennedy's speech of March 13 formally proposing the Alliance.[57]

In the spirit of Kennedy's Alliance address, Lincoln Gordon defined
the Alliance for Progress as "a sustained and cooperative effort to

accelerate economic growth and social progress throughout Latin America, working through democratic institutions based on respect for the individual." Knowing that the Alliance needed active involvement by governments throughout Latin America in order to succeed, Gordon acknowledged that the program placed the region's democratic institutions under great strain. Even with infusion of considerable public and private capital from the United States, available resources might not be up to the task. Kennedy aide Richard N. Goodwin recalled that U.S. intentions, in retrospect, may seem "naïve, grandiose, even arrogant." And the Commission on United States-Latin American Relations noted in 1974: "The Alliance for Progress was in some measure an attempt to accommodate security considerations with concern for domestic welfare of Latin American nations. The Alliance was a reflection of both generous intention and Cold War considerations."[58]

The struggle to chart the course of social revolution had been joined. If the president actually thought that the fate of Latin America was the most critical issue he had to handle next to Berlin, then giving primary responsibility for the birth of the Alliance to Goodwin—a man who had only once been south of the United States—did not symbolize an auspicious start for the new program.[59] It reflected instead both the arrogance and the idealism endemic to Kennedy's inner circle. In other words, it failed to take into account either the political and economic complexity or the uniqueness of each society in Latin America, not to mention the great difficulty of bringing about long-term development and social justice within existing state structures.

The American republics met at Punta del Este, Uruguay, in August to establish the Alliance. Heading the U.S. delegation was Secretary of the Treasury C. Douglas Dillon; Ernesto "Che" Guevara led Cuba's team of observers. Given the memory of the Bay of Pigs failure and the humiliation suffered by Kennedy at the hands of Soviet premier Nikita S. Khrushchev at their Vienna meeting in June, the White House needed the conference to be a resounding success. Dillon, without presidential authorization, pledged $20 billion in public and private money to the Alliance over a ten-year period; the U.S. government would make $1 billion in public funds available in the first year. The U.S. delegation also discussed commodity price stability, a Latin American common market, and a reciprocal commitment to social reform. The latter controversial proposal, which thrust the United States into the vortex of longstanding domestic debates in much of Latin America, portended social justice through land redistribution, progressive taxation, and resource reallocation for health care, education, and housing.

Negotiation ultimately brought agreement and the Charter of Punta del Este was adopted.[60]

Guevara, who used the occasion of the signing of the charter to denounce the new organization as a tool of U.S. imperialism, subsequently asked Goodwin how Cuba and the United States might reach a modus vivendi. Trade remained essential to the success of the Revolution. In exchange for trade on a pragmatic basis, Cuba, Goodwin recalled, was willing to limit its activities in other Latin American states. Guevara's overture fell on deaf ears in Washington, or so it seems. Without access to more complete documentation, a final assessment of the incident is impossible. For a brief moment, though, Cuba may have considered issuing a self-denying pledge that would have altered the course not only of its revolution but of the Alliance as well. By the end of the year, however, U.S. policymakers, including Goodwin, Brig. Gen. Edward Lansdale, and Robert Kennedy, were hard at work planning Castro's removal from power, even if that meant assassinating the Cuban leader—in what became known as Operation Mongoose.[61]

A fourth option available to U.S. officials after the Bay of Pigs was to concentrate upon trade, aid, and investment policy in the general context of Alliance goals. Walt Rostow believed that Latin American economies required fundamental change; only a few nations had reached the "take-off" stage.[62] In the early days of the administration foreign aid became a policy matter within the purview of the NSC.[63] As much as any other action, linking aid, trade, and investment to security demonstrated the relationship of development to anti-Communist priorities.

Kennedy and Foreign Assistance

Less than two weeks after announcing the Alliance, the president issued a special message on the vital importance of foreign assistance. In the tradition of Harry Truman's Point Four program and the Marshall Plan, Kennedy found the nexus of aid and development in the 1960s essential to the preservation of national security and prosperity. He further observed that "the single most important tool will be long-term development loans at low or no rates of interest." Other than liberal terms would impair the involvement of the Export-Import Bank and private investors in the development loan program. As innovative as Kennedy believed the proposal to be, it was not altogether at odds conceptually with loan policies advocated by Herbert Hoover in his days as secretary of commerce in the Harding and Coolidge administrations.[64]

In dollar terms alone, Kennedy's foreign aid program merited considerable praise. Through 1962 the Social Progress Trust Fund, Food for Peace, the Export-Import Bank, and the Agency for International Development (AID) had channeled more than $2 billion to Latin America.[65] Yet a closer look at the structural conditions in a number recipient countries suggests that the take-off phase for development was still some distance away. Commodity export earnings did not rise appreciably and balance-of-payment loans did little to build currency reserves. What actually occurred has been termed a "financial salvage operation." Trade imbalance remained a grave problem; debt service devoured export earnings; and inflation in such ostensible money markets as Brazil, Chile, Colombia, and Argentina limited prospects for investment. Even net public capital assistance for the decade was less than $5 billion.[66] The presence of the many impediments to development meant that the social justice goals of the Alliance went largely unfulfilled, even where the will to pursue them existed.

The administration did attempt to assess the prospects for economic development, social justice, and democracy throughout Latin America. In the process, it created the means to promote an aid agenda for "liberal America." The Foreign Assistance Act of 1961 would provide the legislative basis for U.S. economic and military aid; AID, in the State Department, would oversee a maze of grant, loan, and technical assistance programs.[67]

A country overview, based upon a document prepared by the State Department's Bureau of Intelligence and Research,[68] must have chastened those U.S. officials who hoped that substantial progress could be achieved with little delay. Unequal taxation, social privilege, glaring inequities in land ownership, and crushing poverty stood in the way of effective dispersal of aid. On the one hand, a fundamental break with the past would be a difficult task even in relatively advanced countries like Chile, Venezuela, Colombia, Brazil, and Argentina where expectations for change were great.

In poor nations, on the other hand, with generally high rates of illiteracy where access to political power was limited— as was the case in Nicaragua, Guatemala, Ecuador, and Paraguay, for example—hopes for social justice remained a luxury for the committed few. Elsewhere poverty and hope stood side-by-side, as in the Dominican Republic thanks to U.S. support for the ouster of the Trujillo regime.[69] A roughly comparable socioeconomic situation existed in Peru as the national elections of June 1962 drew near. Yet Haya de la Torre had moderated the earlier social programs of Peru's APRA party in his quest for political office. Even so, a military *golpe*, or coup, led by U.S.-trained forces in possession of U.S.-supplied equipment dashed the ambitions of Haya's followers, the *Apristas*, to usher in a new era of hope for the many impoverished Peruvians.[70]

The Limits of Counterinsurgency

Peru's experience reveals in microcosm the extent to which Kennedy relied on the actual or potential use of force to achieve his goals in Latin America. In that respect, the foremost means to an end was the elimination of Castro by whatever it took to get the job done. (McGeorge Bundy has termed Operation Zapata "a bad mistake," albeit in a managerial sense.)[71] A proposed plan of action picked October 1962 as the month in which Castro would be replaced, despite acknowledging that "we still know too little about the real situation inside Cuba."[72] Some recently published declassified documents concerning Operation Mongoose indicate the preparation of a contingency plan for U.S. military forces to invade Cuba had a determination been made to do so.[73]

Washington's focus on Castro did not blind policymakers to the need for regional support in containing the Cuban Revolution. Although a few governments did perceive Cuba as a threat to their stability, others believed less in the severity of the threat and only followed the U.S. lead after receiving inducements to do so, largely in the form of increased military assistance. Nicaragua fell within the former category. By the spring of 1962, fifteen Latin American states had severed relations with Cuba. Mexico, Argentina, Brazil, Chile, Ecuador, and Bolivia did not share the administration's extreme concern with Castro, however. And only a bare two-thirds majority voted with the United States to exclude Cuba from the OAS in a meeting at Punta del Este in January 1962.[74]

Brazil's independent policy vis-à-vis Cuba was especially frustrating for Washington. Since the late 1940s the two nations had developed a good relationship, with Brazil the recipient of substantial military and economic largess. Yet Quadros, who had taken office only eleven days after Kennedy, appeared less than grateful in failing to condemn Castro, as the president informed Minister of Finance Clemente Mariani in May 1961. The subsequent replacement of Quadros by João Goulart in August 1961—welcomed at first by new Ambassador Lincoln Gordon—soon alarmed both the Brazilian armed forces and U.S.

officials. Kennedy assistant Schlesinger termed Goulart "a weak and erratic demagogue."[75]

Inevitable delays in getting the Alliance for Progress and foreign aid programs underway made vigilance against communism seem all the more imperative. The administration's determination to revise the structure of military assistance, like other aspects of its Latin American policy, had antecedents in Eisenhower's last year. "Civic-action" programs and military nation building did not begin with Kennedy. The theory linking the military and development held that the armed forces would become supporters of social progress and democracy. Further, it was no small matter that the military in Latin America had for some time identified itself with U.S. security objectives.[76]

These considerations came together in the internal security, or counterinsurgency (CI), programs adopted by the White House. Wars of national liberation and guerrilla warfare, as personified by the exploits of Mao Zedong and Che Guevara, fascinated Rostow, who along with Bundy convinced Kennedy that Latin American armed forces should receive special training in the United States, on site or at the School of the Americas in the Panama Canal Zone.[77] By early 1962 Chairman of the Joint Chiefs of Staff (JCS) Gen. Lyman L. Lemnitzer was associating nascent counterinsurgency programs with the activities of the Alliance for Progress. Civic action efforts, Lemnitzer informed Secretary of Defense Robert S. McNamara, would help by removing "some of the causes of national discontent which generate instability and by encouraging closer relationship between the civilian and military communities."[78] Kennedy thus established a Special Group (CI) by signing National Security Action Memorandum No. 124 on January 18. The president told the graduating class of West Point in 1962 that "a wholly different kind of military training" was required.[79]

Virtually every Latin American government was scheduled to receive training and material assistance in Fiscal Year (FY) 1962; the proposed amount totaled $73.8 million. The operational emphasis was expected to be on internal security and paramilitary operations. A JCS background report delineated the strength of Communist parties in Latin America and warned about their efforts to influence student, agrarian, and labor groups. In commenting on the role of the military in civic action and nation building, the JCS coupled CI with Cold War objectives and observed: "When the military and people become close to each other there is no place for the enemy to hide."[80] By January 1962, the United States was concerned about internal security in the following South American countries: Argentina, Bolivia, Brazil, Chile, Colombia, Ecuador, Paraguay, Peru, Uruguay, and Venezuela. A State

Department assessment report declared that law and order was "vitally important to hemisphere defense."[81]

Consensus among officials in the White House, at AID in the State Department, and in the Defense Department on the primacy of paramilitary operations in Latin American policy emphasized how the Cold War and the Cuban Revolution affected inter-American relations. Anti-Communist regimes, such as the military-imposed government of José María Guido that replaced Arturo Frondizi in Argentina in March 1962, experienced little interruption in U.S. aid. One of Kennedy's assistant secretaries of state for inter- American affairs, Edwin M. Martin, acknowledged that the United States could not always dictate who held political office in the Americas.[82]

The rupture of relations with Peru in the aftermath of a military overthrow of President Manuel Prado in July 1962 does not contradict this general approach to the sensitive issue of recognition. The military seized power, in order to prevent Haya de la Torre from becoming president, as Peru's political factions battled over which one offered the best road to structural reform and, hence, development. The problem for Washington was that the U.S.-trained military responsible for the *golpe* lacked adequate anti-Communist credentials. This oversight was corrected during January 1963 with forays into the provinces to round up suspected rebel agitators. By the time Fernando Belaúnde Terry took over the presidency in July 1963 after being duly elected, U.S. aid to Peru had been resumed.[83]

Critics of counterinsurgency policy have contended that CI doctrine posited the interdependence of security and development but in practice favored the former.[84] Order and stability, the critique asserts, were preconditions for growth and development, and for the fostering of democracy as well.[85] The Latin American political landscape in 1961–62 suggested that CI strategy, as the administration hoped it would be implemented, was often unrelated to existing conditions.

Given such a situation, nation building and civic action programs were not necessarily conducive to either social order or democratic political stability, as the 1964 Mann Doctrine would acknowledge. After visiting Colombia, a U.S. Special Warfare Team reported in March 1962 on the lack of preparation within the Colombian armed forces for CI operations; fortunately, the team reported, that nation's 8,000 Communists "were inept bumblers and posed no real threat to the government."[86] That assessment would be less accurate after 1965 with the rise of organized guerrilla groups. Yet even in 1962 the Special Group (CI) appeared to be much less sanguine about subversion in Colombia than the Special Warfare Team.[87]

Furthermore, existing structural weakness in the region's economy had made it all but impossible for the pump-priming goals of the Alliance for Progress to be met. Accordingly, instead of celebrating how the influx of investment capital was helping to achieve predicted growth rates of 2.5 percent per year, Alliance officials were worrying that tax changes in the Revenue Act of 1962 would serve to retard the allocation of private funds. The clear message was that without the certainty of stability, the movement of capital would be inadequate for development projects. For some months, the administration was reduced to a policy of boosterism; Secretary of Commerce Luther Hodges headed a special pro-investment committee, the Commerce Committee for the Alliance for Progress.[88] What was actually occurring, though, was a turn to the right by an already moderate administration. By October 1963 David Rockefeller, president of Chase Manhattan Bank whose family had longstanding personal and business interests in Latin America, would take charge of the new Business Group for Latin America (BGLA). Kennedy welcomed the formation of the BGLA and promised a close working relationship with the administration.[89]

In Brazil, where private capital had much at stake, the power of the left, manifested—high State Department and White House officials believed—in the weakness of the Goulart regime and its overly close ties to Communists, limited the prospects for private investment and helped to curtail Alliance activities. Nevertheless, even several non-Communist labor leaders doubted that the United States either knew how or actually wanted to help Brazil's working classes. Stressing the gravity of the situation were the bleak findings of an Alliance staff report in August 1962: "U.S. policies and programs are in a state of considerable disarray." AID's efforts in Northeast Brazil did nothing to change that evaluation.[90]

Conditions throughout the hemisphere in autumn 1962 clearly revealed the limited effectiveness of Kennedy's Latin American policy. Structural poverty in El Salvador rendered that country vulnerable to leftist activities and its oligarchy stood in the way of reform; rumors of Communist renewal and a possible *golpe* swirled through Venezuela; instability continued to plague the Dominican Republic. U.S. diplomats in Chile feared that lack of collaboration with the Alliance would open the door to power for the left in the 1964 elections. Colombia seemed to be one nation where the Alliance for Progress was working, yet Kennedy admitted that any decline in coffee prices would harm economic and social programs and possibly lead to a debilitating fiscal crisis.[91]

The Cuban Missile Crisis and After

And then came the Cuban Missile Crisis. Recently released CIA documents suggest that the crisis did not entirely catch the White House off
guard. In any event, policymakers on all sides had fallen victim to mis-
perception and misinformation, and were further hampered by poor
judgment. It has been suggested, too, that Castro argued for a Soviet
nuclear strike against the United States.[92]

A wealth of scholarship attests to our extensive knowledge and
understanding of the missile crisis and how nuclear war was avoided.[93] For present purposes, its instructional purposes are rather different. Available evidence indicates that Castro may have sought a
démarche with the United States after the crisis. Not only were his overtures rebuffed, but Operation Mongoose was also revived, albeit in an
altered form. The target of sabotage became more the daily functioning
of the Cuban state itself than Castro personally.[94] This change reflected
the realization that the Cuban leader had not been easy to depose. A
Standing Group on Cuba was created within the NSC to coordinate
future policy.[95] Furthermore, Washington resumed its effort to align
the American republics against Cuba, building on the broad support
generated during the crisis.[96] This task was simplified after Cuba tried
in November 1963 to assist Venezuelan terrorists. Ultimately, all Latin
American governments except Mexico severed diplomatic relations
and cut off trade with Cuba.[97]

It is also possible to discern an enhanced importance for CI programs in lieu of customary military assistance in White House planning. The administration created the Office of Public Safety (OPS) within AID to equip police forces in developing nations. At the same time,
Special Group (CI) focused its attention on Guatemala, Colombia,
Venezuela, Bolivia, and Ecuador. During the mid-1960s OPS and more
traditional security assistance flowed in substantial amounts to Hon-
duras and Nicaragua as well. Nearly $35 million was authorized for the
Military Assistance Program in Latin America for FY 1963.[98]

Cuba continued to preoccupy the administration in 1963. The Standing Group and the State Department's Cuba Task Force sought to bring
order to Cuban policy, even to the extent of curtailing unauthorized
raids against the island.[99] CIA-sponsored sabotage by exile forces was
a different matter altogether;[100] vigilance in response to perceived Sovi-
et-Cuban threats to the Americas became the defining quality of inter-
American relations. To that end, Goulart's warm overtures to the
Brazilian left deeply troubled CIA analysts.[101] In Guatemala, U.S. wor-

ries that President Miguel Ydígoras Fuentes would permit former president Juan José Arévalo to stand for election were realized, but the military overthrew Ydígoras and put into power Gen. Enrique Peralta apparently with Washington's blessing.[102]

The great fear, as Secretary of State Dean Rusk warned, was that, even without Soviet support, the Cuban example—if not Fidel Castro himself—would encourage "in all countries of Latin America communist parties . . . to establish totalitarian regimes." Consequently, Kennedy's security policy for the Americas had as its fundamental objective the rollback of Cuban influence and the deterrence of further aggression.[103] U.S. officials had to agree by early 1963, however reluctantly, that Alliance programs were not strong enough to serve as the first line of defense against subversion.

Internal reviews of Alliance activities expressed concern over low growth rates, particularly in agriculture. Progress in land reform was also disappointing. In addition, not only was there inadequate private investment, but capital flight brought into question the actual commitment in wealthy sectors of Latin America to Alliance goals.[104] The Peronist *Confederación General de Trabajo* in Argentina added to these criticisms by asking why the Alliance extended assistance to authoritarian regimes that were adamantly opposed to the structural reforms envisioned in the Charter of Punta del Este.[105]

To some critics the very soul of the Alliance for Progress was at risk. It did not help that in the first five years of the Alliance there were nine military coups against constitutional, civilian governments. Furthermore, one of the most revered goals of the Alliance, achieving widespread literacy, seemed to be close at hand not among the putative beneficiaries of Alliance programs but among the masses in Communist Cuba.[106] By November 1963 the Alliance for Progress with its vision of social justice, economic development, and democracy did not possess the urgency that it had in its early days. Kennedy was preoccupied with foreign policy matters in Southeast Asia and nothing Goodwin or Schlesinger might do would recapture his attention.

Johnson's Conservative Course

Lyndon Baines Johnson pledged to follow the lead of his slain predecessor in the Americas. "The most important foreign policy problem I faced," he wrote in his memoirs, "was that of signaling to the world what kind of man I was and what sort of policies I intended to carry out."[107] In the Western Hemisphere, there was much to be done. President Kennedy's legacy, then as now, seemed to be a confused, if not contradictory, one. Under Secretary of State Chester Bowles felt that the administration had, in effect, forsaken the principles of the Alliance—an organization, one scholar argues, that by late 1963 was already in a state of decay. The disarray was the result of bureaucratic disagreement over the direction of policy beyond containing the spread of communism.[108]

Johnson began by making his friend Thomas C. Mann, former ambassador to Mexico, Special Assistant to the President on Latin America, Assistant Secretary of State for Inter-American Affairs, and Coordinator of the Alliance for Progress. This concentration of power in one individual scarcely lasted fifteen months and, as under Kennedy, the position of assistant secretary seemed to be trapped in a revolving door. Yet Mann, unlike his predecessors, left a clear mark on Latin American policy, as we shall see.[109]

Security assessments in the first few months of the Johnson administration followed policy assumptions that Kennedy inherited from Eisenhower and that the "Charles River" group had expanded upon. Castro and the threat of Communist subversion dominated policy deliberations. Not only was the NSC concerned about how the Cuban threat might be countered in the hemisphere, but also about how to induce European allies not to trade with Cuba.[110] The CIA did not believe that "economic difficulties or internal political opposition will cause the collapse of the regime."[111]

Accordingly, local vigilance backed by U.S. aid was deemed as the most effective anti-Castro strategy. Self-help therefore became the hallmark of Johnson's Latin American policy. To be sure, U.S. assistance, whether in the form of CI training or public and private financial initiatives, remained the last line of defense against Communist aggression. A policy of limited autonomy was deemed possible because of the implicit pledge of self-denial the Soviet Union took after the missile crisis.[112] External support for subversion or wars of national liberation thus posed significantly less of a threat after 1962.

In early 1964, the CIA nevertheless expressed marked concern about political stability in the Dominican Republic, Guatemala, Nicaragua, Panama, Colombia, Ecuador, Bolivia, and Venezuela and Brazil where threats from Cuba and the left seemed most ominous. Johnson's coming to power terminated the informal contacts with Cuba that had persisted under Kennedy. Despite hints from Castro that a modus vivendi would benefit both nations, White House officials spurned his appeals.[113]

The early months of the Johnson administration also left the distinct impression that the Alliance for Progress had lost some of its luster.

The creation of the Inter-American Committee on the Alliance for Progress (CIAP) just prior to Kennedy's death signaled that some of the tasks of the Alliance would assume a multilateral form. CIAP would review development plans, chart the availability of resources, identify the sources of funds for projects, and recommend appropriate courses of action. CIAP did not, however, have the authority to enforce its recommendations and, in any event, avoided controversy. The principal weakness of CIAP was that none of the major involved parties, large Latin American states, international lending institutions—especially the IDB, and the U.S. government, submitted to its authority.[114]

In effect, turning the decision-making functions of the Alliance into a multilateral exercise—which its most liberal proponents in Latin America espoused—encouraged the extremist, reactionary elements in Latin America that opposed the movement for social justice. It also gave comfort to the growing number of U.S. policymakers who believed that order must come before progress. The Alliance had therefore become a vehicle for the adoption of positivism, twentieth-century style. This turn of events may have been recognizable in a historical sense, but it called into question the Charter of Punta del Este and limited future policy options for the United States.

The crisis in Panama and OAS reaction to Castro's meddling in Venezuela underlined this neoconservatism. Walt Rostow had seen it coming: "[T]here were no miracles that Washington could perform to bring about accelerated economic and social progress." In Panama, well-paid Zonians, the ruling oligarchy, and horribly poor Panamanian masses co-existed uneasily. Riots broke out over the tearing of a Panamanian flag but did not lead the White House to examine the underlying cause, Panamanian anger over the terms of the 1903 Canal treaty. Instead, Johnson sent Thomas Mann and Secretary of the Army Cyrus Vance to meet with President Roberto Chiari and restore order. U.S. representatives in Panama saw the work of Communists in the demonstrations, whereas progressive Latin Americans feared the riots would have a negative effect on Alliance programs.[115]

Likewise, the United States responded to Cuban adventurism in Venezuela as though Venezuela were one of the last bastions of freedom in a fierce struggle with international communism. Or so Rostow argued, despite previously mentioned indications to the contrary.[116] On 26 July Castro appeared to apologize for sending arms to Venezuelan guerrillas and once again left the door open to a possible accommodation with Washington. Meanwhile, the administration had positioned the OAS behind an unyielding stand, even exaggerating the severity of the rebel threat in order to guarantee OAS acceptance of the economic and diplomatic isolation of the Cuban government. At length, only Mexico declined to follow the U.S. lead.[117]

While plans were underway to condemn Cuba for subversive activities, Secretary Mann announced the doctrine that bears his name. The United States would not inquire into the nature of regimes that were to receive military and economic assistance, an evaluation that several officials in the Kennedy administration had advocated. Support for social reforms thus ceased to be a *sine qua non* for gaining Washington's favor.[118] Policymakers had learned a lesson between 1961 and 1963: To insist upon democratic government as a prerequisite for, or as a complement to, U.S. aid might actually vitiate existing campaigns against subversion. As a result, during its tenure in office, the Johnson administration would evince much greater interest in promoting state stability, however achieved, than in bolstering democratic state structure.

Johnson's and Mann's security-cum-development approach met its first test in Brazil. Johnson knew about and encouraged, if he did not covertly support, Goulart's overthrow in April.[119] The ultranationalism Goulart espoused was a dangerous enough game in hemispheric relations; in Brazilian domestic politics it proved to be suicidal. During what Brazilian economist Celso Furtado defined as a prerevolutionary situation, the rate of inflation nearly tripled; and foreign investment dropped off sharply, as did the overall rate of growth. Goulart refused to adopt tough monetary stabilization policies, and the alternative of nationalizing foreign enterprises was just not feasible. With economic paralysis inevitable, the military responded by putting into place a market-authoritarian regime.[120]

The United States recognized the regime of Humberto Castello Branco with unseemly haste and moved quickly toward renegotiating outstanding loans. Brazilians had "taken their country back from the edge of communism," a highly relieved U.S. official declared. Castello Branco later asserted that one of his major tasks was "to recover the minimum necessary order for the functioning of the national economy." Within six weeks of taking power, the new regime broke relations with Cuba and adopted a foreign policy that the White House could support. The next year Brazil was a steadfast ally during the Dominican crisis.[121] In short, the Brazilian military had become the guardian, as Alfred Stepan concludes, of internal security and national development, which was precisely what the Kennedy and Johnson administrations had intended.[122] That democracy suffered markedly in the process was regrettable, but professionalism and political savvy portended order if not progress.

The Johnson administration responded in an analogous fashion later in 1964 to the ouster from power of Víctor Paz Estensorro in Bolivia. The Kennedy administration had endeavored to promote economic growth and political stability through President Paz, but the vicissitudes of Bolivian politics proved impossible to finesse. Berle found Paz "unable to keep the peace." Gen. René Barrientos Ortuño proved to be rather more adept and, soon after distancing himself from labor and the left, returned his country to relative prosperity under the protective wing of the United States.[123]

The logical culmination of Washington's search for security in Latin America under Kennedy and Johnson came in the Dominican Republic in April 1965 where self-help required a helping hand. U.S. intervention did not constitute an exception to Johnson's style, which Rostow termed "minimum intervention."[124] Rather, it was the apotheosis of the U.S. obsession since January 1961 with subversion. Even so, intervention in Santo Domingo was broadly welcomed then and later in the Americas.[125]

The progressive Juan Bosch had turned out, in Schlesinger's view, to be a far "better short story writer than . . . statesman." Although the White House rued his fall from power in 1963, it is doubtful that U.S. intervention on April 28, 1965 was on the side of Bosch and democracy. Officials simplified the complexities of Dominican politics. Secretary of State Dean Rusk cites the loss of public order and the need to protect U.S. citizens as primary reasons for intervening. Fear of the left, with Bosch as its agent, led Rusk and Mann to oppose his return to power. An OAS force kept the peace until an interim government took over. In 1966 the moderate Joaquín Balaguer was elected president in fair elections.[126]

This intervention occurred, it seems clear in retrospect, because U.S. officials did not believe that they could trust the Dominican military, despite many years of training, to prevent a Communist takeover. At all costs, Cuba could not be allowed to establish another Caribbean base for sabotage and subversion. Accordingly, the nonintervention pledges of the Good Neighbor policy were swept away in maneuvers reminiscent of occupations earlier in the century. Vietnam dove George Ball accepted "the wisdom of our initial landing" but grew concerned as Johnson "became, in effect, the Dominican desk officer"—a leading role that the president would reprise in the Indochina conflict.[127]

Competing Visions of Development

Theoretically as basic to the future of economic growth in Latin America were the efforts of the BGLA. Promoting private investment headed the agenda of the group, which operated under the assumption that receptive capital markets existed throughout Latin America. The BGLA merged with other private organizations to form the 175-member Council for Latin America. As valuable as any other contribution the Council made was supporting before Congress administration requests for foreign aid and Alliance for Progress funding. Also noteworthy was the work of the Council in assisting U.S. efforts to give Latin American labor a stake in the programs of the Alliance through the American Institute for Free Labor Development (AIFLD), which was founded in August 1961. AIFLD was to inculcate a pro-business orientation within labor's putative quest for democratic development. AIFLD-trained labor leaders in Brazil may have played a role in Goulart's ouster.[128]

Reliance on private enterprise to the extent envisioned by the White House led to the perception that officials were playing down the importance of aid and the Alliance. Indeed, Johnson's preoccupation with Vietnam led his advisers to conclude that the U.S. "ideological image" was suffering in Latin America.[129] At the same time, problems attendant to the foreign aid program did not augur well for an improved situation. Slight increases in private investment by mid-1964 from previous years soon were overwhelmed by reports of continuing economic instability, lack of food for a rapidly growing population, and weak institutional structures for putting reform programs into place. Per capita incomes fell considerably short of what was needed to alleviate human misery. And, as the Policy Planning Council of the State Department concluded in a memo calling for a hemispheric summit on development, "actual achievements [in land reform] have been negligible." Buying out the landlords through compensation with an IDB fund, the memo averred, "may well be the critical factor in a number of countries in diffusing a potentially politically explosive situation."[130]

National Security Adviser Walt Rostow proposed a study of how the "frontiers of Latin America" should be systematically developed not only to meet economic needs but also to prevent "the possibilities of Communist insurgency." Lincoln Gordon, serving as assistant secretary of state in September 1966, feared that enumerating the proposed tasks would be seen as a commitment by Washington to carry them out at a time when both institutional feasibility and requisite financing, public and private, were in doubt.[131] Growing U.S. balance of payments deficits may not have resulted from an unfavorable balance of trade with other American republics, but these deficits raised serious doubts about large- scale funding of development projects by the United States.[132]

The efficacy of the self-help approach to development came further into question with the move toward nationalization of foreign-owned enterprises in several Latin American states. In the view of the United States, private enterprise provided the surest road to economic development; statist enterprises offered an opening wedge to socialism, if not communism. Yet diagnoses of Latin America's economy by ECLA and others emphasized, first, structural limitations and, later, dependency upon multinationals as the basic causes of underdevelopment. Even as nationalization became more acceptable as a means of economic control in Latin America, North American businesses turned to the U.S. Congress for statutory help. Some businessmen held that the Hickenlooper Amendment to the 1962 Foreign Assistance Act, sponsored by Sen. Bourke B. Hickenlooper (R-Iowa), would lead to greater private investment in Latin America. The amendment required the president to suspend economic aid automatically to any country that either expropriated the property of or repudiated a contract with a U.S. company. Compensation for expropriation had to begin within six months; otherwise the amendment would take effect.[133]

Leftist intellectuals saw the financial neoconservatism of the Alliance under Johnson as a well-conceived plan to maintain U.S. hegemony. Despite the burdensome U.S. financial obligations elsewhere, particularly in Europe and Indochina, and the rather cautious role of multinational corporations in Latin America, where investments would not be guaranteed until the creation of the Overseas Private Investment Corporation in 1969, reality paled before perceptions of U.S. public and private hegemony. Only in Chile, where AID was extremely active in the mid-1960s, was limited risk insurance available to U.S. companies.[134]

Copper was the object of nationalization efforts in Chile in the 1960s—a country, ironically, to which the BGLA pointed as a showcase of what private enterprise could achieve, a view shared by the Kennedy administration. In part to forestall the rise of the left under Salvador Allende, the Christian Democratic Party of President Eduardo Frei Montalva initiated the Chileanization, or partial purchase, of foreign-owned copper companies. In the last months before the presidential election of September 1964, U.S. officials had worried that "if Allende wins and stays in power, we are in trouble." The left would therefore become a potent political force and nationalization could force Johnson to invoke the Hickenlooper Amendment resulting in the termination of aid. In that event, an alternative to the Alliance might be given credibility.[135]

Both the Chilean left and U.S. officials criticized Frei's move, the one because Chileanization did not go far enough and the other because of the dangerous precedent it set. Allende did, in fact, move toward nationalization of copper in 1970. By that time, foreign private investment had declined markedly and diminished the growth rates Chile experienced in 1965 and 1966. The United States secretly tried in both 1964 and 1970 to prevent Allende's coming to power. When he finally did take office, the Chilean economy was in a noticeably weaker condition than it had been just several years earlier. Ironically, the conservative nature of foreign assistance in response to Chileanization had played into Allende's hands.[136]

As with Chile, foreign investors had long dominated Peru's economy. Two-thirds of U.S. investment, nearly $600 million in all, was in petroleum and mining; land and income distribution were as inequitable as anywhere in the hemisphere. Upon seizing power in October 1968, Gen. Juan Velasco Alvarado endeavored to revitalize Peru's stagnant economy and to terminate dependence on the International Petroleum Company (IPC) and the International Telephone and Telegraph (ITT)-owned telephone company. One year earlier as the value of the sol plummeted, the White House had described Peru's difficulties as "primarily fiscal." At the same time, officials feared that either further currency devaluation or balance of payments problems would provoke a military seizure of power. One formidable obstacle to a *golpe*, they believed, was the active record of private investment in Peru.[137]

Velasco's actions proved them wrong. On several occasions in the 1960s, U.S. officials had tried to force Lima to adopt a conciliatory policy toward IPC, but these efforts were largely unavailing. Ambassador John Wesley Jones rightly worried about expropriation and the subsequent application of the Hickenlooper Amendment. Neither the Johnson nor the Nixon administrations ever invoked it, but after nationalization AID, IDB, the IMF, and the World Bank extended few new credits to Peru. Peru's "third way" to development—a model that favored neither capitalism nor communism—therefore faced destabilizing threats from Washington. President Richard M. Nixon's national security adviser, Henry Kissinger, termed the ultimate settlement of the IPC dispute a consequence of "patient and sustained efforts."

Neutralism in foreign policy, which Dulles and Eisenhower had abhorred, clearly remained anathema to their successors. In sum, Velasco's model of state-sponsored economic development was possible only in theory. The program ended in failure as a result of external financial pressures and because the Velasco regime, like others in Lima before it, was essentially unprepared to deal with the root causes of rural poverty.[138]

Johnson and Military Assistance

Throughout the decade of the Alliance, the United States looked upon military assistance as the final guarantor of order, democracy, and progress. That a new positivism would vanquish the promotion of democracy became evident, however, even before the Mann Doctrine extended to caudillo nationalism Washington's blessing. Stability, Kennedy and Argentine Gen. Pedro Eugenio Aramburu agreed in November 1962, would reduce the threat posed by communism, thus making orderly progress possible.[139]

Military assistance under Johnson accepted this operating assumption, even though the CIA concluded in March 1966 that Communist parties in the hemisphere were in a state of disarray and that neither Cuba nor the Soviet Union were likely to sponsor subversion on a grand scale.[140] Further, the sensitive politics of anticommunism made it difficult to understand how military expenditures could promote liberal economic and social goals.[141] Accordingly, the state and defense departments undertook a review of military assistance policy. Mann believed that "predominant emphasis will continue to be placed on improvements in counter- insurgency and internal security capability."[142] And so it was.

The question was how best to achieve internal security. The Department of Defense under Robert S. McNamara sought cuts in the military grant aid program beyond FY 1965, despite arguments from the State Department that a "problem of latent insurgency" could not adequately be controlled. McNamara, overseeing the build-up of U.S. forces in Indochina, had little interest in grant aid to Latin America. Gordon, who raised the specter of insurgency in Peru and Brazil and widespread urban violence in several other societies, could not persuade Defense to outfit Latin American armed forces as fully as some in State desired. Even though the sale of arms to Latin America between FY 1966 and FY 1969 fell by nearly 50 percent, U.S. officials could not entirely disabuse the Latin American military of the idea that their prestige depended upon acquiring sophisticated, conventional weaponry.[143]

Military-sale policy did not, however, leave armed forces unable to combat insurgencies. U.S. military missions continued to train Latin American military forces, and AID's Public Safety Program provided aid to thousands of police personnel in country or, in select cases, in the United States. Between FY 1961 and FY 1973, OSP grants to Latin America exceeded $56 million.[144] A history of Western Hemisphere security compiled by the Johnson administration gives high marks to the CI program. Victory came for CI in Venezuela in 1963, in Colombia and Guatemala from 1963 to 1968, in Peru in 1965, in Nicaragua in 1967, and in Bolivia in 1967 where guerrillas commanded by Che Guevara were isolated and killed. The CI record nevertheless could not conceal a few major blemishes: Colombian rebels survived; the U.S. ambassador to Guatemala was killed in August 1968; and Che Guevara in death symbolized resistance to U.S. hegemony.[145] Rostow's comment to Johnson that "we and the Latinos have our ups and downs in the counterinsurgency business" seems fatuous in the extreme.[146]

Conclusion

Johnson never gave Latin America the attention that policy and program required. A belated attempt to bring some cohesion to inter-American relations came at a summit meeting, called by the OAS for Punta del Este on April 12–14, 1967. U.S. planners acknowledged the need for renewed economic integration, better educational programs, real agrarian reform, and enhanced trade and investment. Just the same, Johnson refused to commit funds to new Alliance activities until he could review all proposals. The president ultimately adopted economic integration, perhaps through the mechanism of a regional common market or a free trade association, as a way of revitalizing the inter-American system. Johnson's conventional scheme earned the support of Rockefeller's Council for Latin America.[147]

Domestic critics of the administration's proposal objected to their lack of specificity. If Latin American leaders accepted in general the premise of integration, they still wondered about its economic and political costs individually to their nations. The most important unanswered question, raised by Alberto Lleras Camargo of Colombia, concerned trade preferences and access to commodity markets in the United States and Europe. Without such access, integration would largely benefit U.S. businesses while growth in Latin America remained dependent upon the confidence of foreign investors in the frequently volatile economies there.[148]

Lyndon Johnson believed that there existed few problems in the Americas that money and resources could not fix.[149] In an ideal world he may have been right, but Johnson's Latin American policy never saw the light of a clear day. Indochina and fears of Communist subversion shadowed his efforts to pursue policies favorable to development and democracy. The Mann Doctrine, for all intents and purposes, codified the implicit rejection of the original hopes vested in the Alliance. If rhetoric called for the liberation of the human spirit through a multilateral program of development, then the reality of avid monetary conservatism and reliance upon authoritarian governments to preserve order in the face of potential Communist threats proved to be a cruel hoax to progressives who championed the cause of the Alliance.[150]

It cannot be said that the Alliance for Progress effectively brought security to the poor masses of the Americas. Neither in conception nor in execution did Democrat programs confront the intractability of ruling elites in Latin America. However unwittingly, Kennedy and Johnson left a legacy that paved the way for further difficulty in the realization of Alliance goals. The 1960s reified the logic of U.S. hegemony in the hemisphere: The United States had to save Latin Americans from themselves by any available means. (U.S. policies toward Central America in the 1980s and drug control efforts under the Nixon, Reagan, and Bush administrations stand out as two of the foremost examples of this imperative.)

The pursuit of liberal hegemony during the 1960s had an additional, inevitable consequence. Responding to subversion with counterinsurgency warfare contributed to the autonomy of authoritarian regimes. U.S. hegemony, in other words, involved the suborning of undemocratic forces that held onto power for two decades or more in some instances. State structures, as Julio Cotler observes, embody a history that is closely related in Latin America to class structure.[151] Democracy consequently exists in such circumstances more in form than in content. It remains the tragedy of U.S. policy in the 1960s to have supported the many Latin American regimes that considered economic and social progress, and democracy itself, as obstacles to order and stability. Far more toward the rest of the hemisphere than toward Cuba did Washington's policies in the Alliance years mix the sweet with the sour.

NOTES

Abbreviations

AH: Administrative History
AID: Agency for International Development
AMS Jr.: Arthur M. Schlesinger, Jr.
AP Series: Alliance for Progress Series
CI: Counterinsurgency

CIA: Central Intelligence Agency
CK: Carl Kaysen
CO Series: Country Series
CP: Cabinet Papers
D & A Series: Departments and Agencies Series
DS: Department of State
DSB: Department of State Bulletin
FO: Foreign Affairs Files
FRUS: Foreign Relations of the United States
JFK: John F. Kennedy
JFKL: John F. Kennedy Library
Gen.: General
LBJ: Lyndon B. Johnson
LBJL: Lyndon B. Johnson Library
M & M Series: Meetings and Memoranda Series
MBF: McGeorge Bundy Files
MNF: Meeting Notes File
NIEs: National Intelligence Estimates
NSAM: National Security Action Memorandum
NSC: National Security Council
NSF: National Security File
OAS: Organization of American States
OH: Oral History
PAU: Pan American Union
PP: Private Papers
PPP: Public Papers of the President
RS Series: Regional Security Series
S Series: Subjects Series
TM Papers: Teodoro Moscoso Papers
WH: White House
WHB Series: William H. Brubeck Series
WHF: White House Files

1. NSF: M & M Series, NSAM 10, February 6, 1961, Box 328, JFKL.
2. David Green, *The Containment of Latin America: A History of the Myths and Realities of the Good Neighbor Policy* (Chicago, 1971), pp. 172–208; Samuel L. Baily, *The United States and the Development of South America, 1945–1975* (New York, 1976), pp. 40–48; Stephen G. Rabe, "The Elusive Conference," *Diplomatic History* 2 (Summer 1978): 279–94; Roger R. Trask, "The Impact of the Cold War on United States-Latin American Relations," *Diplomatic History* 1 (Summer 1977): 271–84; Chester J. Pach, Jr., "The Containment of U.S. Military Aid to Latin America, 1944–49," *Diplomatic History* 6 (Summer 1982): 225–43. Brazil may have been an exception to this general rule; see Elizabeth A. Cobbs, *The*

Rich Neighbor Policy: Rockefeller and Kaiser in Brazil (New Haven 1992), Gerald K. Haines, *The Americanization of Brazil: A Study of U.S. Cold War Diplomacy in the Third World, 1945–1954* (Wilmington, 1989), and W. Michael Weis, *Cold Warriors and Coups d'Etat: Brazilian-American Relations, 1945–1964.*

3. NSF: RS Series, W. L. Clayton to JFK, February 20, 1961, Box 215, JFKL.

4. See relevant sections of Thomas E. Skidmore and Peter H. Smith, *Modern Latin America*, 3d ed. (New York, 1992) for a fuller accounting of the events of the period.

5. Raúl Prebisch, *Hacia una dinámica del desarrollo latinoamericano* (México y Buenos Aires, 1963), 4. ECLA was created in 1948 as a regional commission of the United Nations, with headquarters in Santiago, Chile, in order to articulate development needs in Latin America; see Albert O. Hirschman, *A Bias for Hope: Essays on Development and Latin America* (New Haven, 1971), pp. 279–311.

6. Prebisch in John Scott, "How Much Progress? A Report to the Publisher of *Time*," November 1963, TM Papers, Alliance for Progress Series, Box 3, JFKL.

7. *FRUS* (1955–57), 6: 314.

8. Ibid., p. 319.

9. Ibid., p. 354.

10. Stephen G. Rabe, *Eisenhower and Latin America: The Foreign Policy of Anti-communism* (Chapel Hill, 1988), pp. 67–70; idem, "Dulles, Latin America, and Cold War Anticommunism," in Richard H. Immerman, ed., *John Foster Dulles and the Diplomacy of the Cold War* (Princeton, 1990), pp. 160–66.

11. Piero Gleijeses, *Shattered Hope: The Guatemalan Revolution and the United States, 1944–1954* (Princeton, 1991); Richard H. Immerman, *The CIA in Guatemala: The Foreign Policy of Intervention* (Austin, 1982); Rabe, *Eisenhower and Latin America*, pp. 70–77, 84.

12. *FRUS* (1958–60), 5: 2.

13. Ibid., p. 23.

14. Ibid., pp. 91–116; NSF: CO Series, Brazil, John M. Cabot to DS, July 12, 1961, Box 12, JFKL; Rabe, *Eisenhower and Latin America*, pp. 100–106.

15. *FRUS* (1958–60), 5: 39–40, 275–76, 676–89, 696–706, 777–81; Burton I. Kaufman, *Trade and Aid: Eisenhower's Foreign Economic Policy, 1953–1961* (Baltimore, 1982), pp. 161–66, 207–11.

16. Rabe, *Eisenhower and Latin America*, pp. 109–16.

17. Ibid., pp. 110, 113.

18. Morris H. Morley, *Imperial State and Revolution: The United States and Cuba, 1952–1986* (New York, 1987), pp. 76–78; Prebisch, *Hacia una dinámica del desarrollo latinoamerica*, 43–52; Prebisch, *Tranformación y desarrollo: La gran tarea de América Latina* (México, 1970), pp. 41, 47 for the quotation.

19. Fidel Castro, "The Problem of Cuba," in James Nelson Goodsell, ed., *Fidel Castro's Personal Revolution in Cuba: 1959–1973* (New York, 1975), pp. 30–32.

20. Hirschman, *A Bias for Hope*, p. 177.

21. Richard E. Welch, Jr., *Response to Revolution: The United States and the Cuban Revolution, 1959–1961* (Chapel Hill, 1985), pp. 32–37; *FRUS* (1958–60), 6: 345 for the quotation.

22. *FRUS* (1958–60), 6: 401–6.

23. Louis A. Pérez, Jr., *Cuba and the United States: Ties of Singular Intimacy* (Athens, GA, 1990), pp. 238–40; Morley, *Imperial State and Revolution*, pp. 81–88.

24. *FRUS* (1958–60), 6: 510.

25. Philip W. Bonsal, *Cuba, Castro, and the United States* (Pittsburgh, 1971), 110–36; Rabe, *Eisenhower and Latin America*, pp. 126–28.

26. *FRUS* (1958–60), 6: 656–58.

27. Ibid., p. 849.

28. Ibid., 850 for the quotation, pp. 861–63.

29. Morley, *Imperial State and Revolution*, pp. 114–30.

30. Rabe, *Eisenhower and Latin America*, pp. 153–62; *FRUS* (1958–60), 5: 806–08.

31. Hirschman, *A Bias for Hope*, p. 177.

32. *FRUS* (1958–60), 5: 221; Arthur M. Schlesinger, Jr., *A Thousand Days: John F. Kennedy in the White House* (Boston, 1965), pp. 177, 190–91; Walt W. Rostow, "The Strategy of Foreign Aid, 1961," NSF: S Series, Foreign Aid, Box 297, JFKL.

33. Lincoln Gordon, *A New Deal for Latin America: The Alliance for Progress* (Cambridge, 1963), 7; Beatrice Bishop Berle and Travis Beal Jacobs, ed., *Navigating the Rapids, 1918–1971: From the Papers of Adolf A. Berle* (New York, 1973), p. 719.

34. *FRUS* (1958–60), 6: 134–40.

35. Berle, *Navigating the Rapids*, 720 for the quotation, pp. 721–25.

36. Ibid., p. 725.

37. WHF: PP AMS Jr., Latin America Report, March 10, 1961, Box WH 14, JFKL.

38. Ibid.

39. George W. Ball, *The Past Has Another Pattern: Memoirs* (New York, 1982), 160–62; NSF: S Series, Foreign Economic Policy Task Force Report, Box 297, JFKL.

40. Ibid., 65, Appendix 2.

41. *FRUS* (1958–60), 5: 679–83, 685.

42. NSF: CK Papers, Foreign Aid, Box 373, JFKL.

43. NSF: RS Series, Latin America, Box 215, JFKL.

44. Richard N. Goodwin, *Remembering America: A Voice from the Sixties* (Boston, 1988), pp. 124–26.

45. Trumbull Higgins, *The Perfect Failure: Kennedy, Eisenhower, and the CIA at the Bay of Pigs* (New York, 1987), p. 174.

46. *PPP: JFK, 1961*, p. 1.

47. PAU, OAS, *Seventh Meeting of Consultation of Ministers of Foreign Affairs*, "Final Act," San José, Costa Rica, August 22–29, 1960.

48. *FRUS* (1958–60), 6: 1064.

49. NSF: CO Series, Brazil, Cabot to DS, July 12, 1961, Box 12, JFKL.

50. NSF: M & M Series, Special Group (CI), Memorandum by U. Alexis Johnson, August 13, 1962, Box 319, JFKL; NSF: CO Series, Venezuela, Teodoro Moscoso to DS, September 1, 1961, Box 192, JFKL; Cole Blasier, *The Hovering Giant: U. S. Responses to Revolutionary Change in Latin America* (Pittsburgh, 1976), pp. 244–45.

51. W. W. Rostow, *The Diffusion of Power: An Essay in Recent History* (New

York, 1972), pp. 164, 208; Roger Hilsman, *To Move a Nation: The Politics of Foreign Policy in the Administration of John F. Kennedy* (Garden City, NY, 1967), p. 161.

52. NSF: RS Series, Latin America, Memorandum for McGeorge Bundy, February 1, 1961, and Memorandum for Bundy, February 3, 1961, Box 215, JFKL.

53. NSF: M & M Series, NSAM 31, March 11, 1961, and NSAM 38, April 13, 1961, Box 329, JFKL; NSF: S Series, Policy Planning, W. W. Rostow memorandum to JFK, April 21, 1961, Box 303, JFKL for the quotation.

54. NSF: CO Series, Mexico, Thomas C. Mann to Ralph A. Dungan, April 1, 1961, Box 141, JFKL; NSF: CO Series, Venezuela, Moscoso to DS, May 18, 1961, Box 192, JFKL; NSF: CO Series, Brazil, L. D. Battle to Dungan, March 16, 1961, Box 12, JFKL; NSF: CO Series, Argentina, Roy R. Rubottom to DS, August 22, 1961, Box 6, JFKL.

55. Laurence Chang and Peter Kornbluh, eds., *The Cuban Missile Crisis, 1962: A National Security Archive Documents Reader* (New York, 1992), pp. 16–21.

56. WHF: PP AMS Jr., "Venezuela: Status of Agrarian Reform Program," February 9, 1961, and "Cuba as a Showcase in Latin America," July 20, 1961, Box WH 14, JFKL.

57. *PPP: JFK, 1961*, pp. 170–75; Schlesinger, *A Thousand Days*, pp. 191–205.

58. Gordon, *A New Deal for Latin America*, pp. 8–11; Goodwin, *Remembering America*, 150; *The Americas in a Changing World: A Report of the Commission on United States-Latin American Relations* (New York, 1975), p. 19.

59. Goodwin, *Remembering America*, pp. 147, 162.

60. Jerome Levinson and Juan de Onís, *The Alliance That Lost Its Way: A Critical Report on the Alliance for Progress* (Chicago, 1970), pp. 59–69; Goodwin, *Remembering America*, 190–95.

61. Goodwin, *Remembering America*, 195–205; Morley, *Imperial State and Revolution*, pp. 148–49; *Alleged Assassination Plots Involving Foreign Leaders: An Interim Report of the Select Committee to Study Governmental Operations* (New York, 1976), pp. 136–39.

62. W. W. Rostow, *The Stages of Economic Growth: A Non- Communist Manifesto*, 2d ed. (New York, 1971), pp. 18, 126–27.

63. NSF: M & M Series, NSAM 6, February 3, 1961, Box 328, JFKL.

64. *PPP: JFK, 1961*, 203–12; NSF: M & M Series, NSAM 130, March 2, 1962, Box 334, JFKL; Joan Hoff Wilson, *American Business and Foreign Policy, 1920–1933* (Lexington, 1970), pp. 101–23; Barbara Stallings, *Banker to the Third World: U. S. Portfolio Investment in Latin America, 1900–1986* (Berkeley and Los Angeles, 1987), pp. 67–75.

65. Stephen G. Rabe, "Controlling Revolutions: Latin America, the Alliance for Progress, and Cold War Anti-Communism," in Thomas G. Paterson, ed., *Kennedy's Quest for Victory: American Foreign Policy, 1961–1963* (New York, 1989), p. 107.

66. Levinson and de Onís, *The Alliance That Lost Its Way*, pp. 133–40.

67. Robert A. Packenham, *Liberal America and the Third World: Political Development Ideas in Foreign Aid and Social Science* (Princeton, 1973), pp. 60–61.

68. WHF: PP AMS Jr., "Latin America—Current Stages of Progress in Key

Socio-Economic Reforms, by Country," September 28, 1961, Box WH 14, JFKL.

69. Rabe, *Eisenhower and Latin America*, 153–62; Piero Gleijeses, *The Dominican Crisis: The 1965 Constitutionalist Revolt and American Intervention*, trans. by Lawrence Lipson (Baltimore, 1978), 25–64; *Alleged Assassination Plots*, pp. 191–215.

70. Fredrick B. Pike, *The United States and the Andean Republics: Peru, Bolivia, and Ecuador* (Cambridge, 1977), pp. 318–19; Schlesinger, *A Thousand Days*, p. 786.

71. NSF: D & A Series, Memorandum to the President, May 16, 1961, Box 290, JFKL.

72. NSF: M & M Series, Special Group (Augmented), "The Cuba Project," February 20, 1962, Box 319, JFKL.

73. Chang and Kornbluh, ed., *Cuban Missile Crisis, 1962*, pp. 40–51; Thomas G. Paterson, "Fixation with Cuba: The Bay of Pigs, Missile Crisis, and Covert War Against Castro," in Paterson, ed., *Kennedy's Quest for Victory*, pp. 137, 148.

74. Paterson, "Fixation with Cuba," 139; John C. Dreier, *The Organization of American States and the Hemisphere Crisis* (New York, 1962), pp. 90–94.

75. Jan Knippers Black, *United States Penetration of Brazil* (Philadelphia, 1977), pp. 162–66, 186; NSF: CO Series, Brazil, Memorandum of Conversation, May 16, 1961, Box 12, JFKL; Ruth Leacock, *Requiem for Revolution: The United States and Brazil, 1961–1969* (Kent, OH, 1990), p. 84; Schlesinger, *A Thousand Days*, p. 790.

76. Rabe, *Eisenhower and Latin America*, 147; *FRUS* (1958–60), 5: 47, 71, 123.

77. NSF: M & M Series, Staff Memoranda, Memorandum for JFK, January 27, 1961, Box 325, JFKL; NSF: M & M Series, NSAM 48, April 23, 1961, Box 329, JFKL; NSF: M & M Series, NSAM 88, September 5, 1961, and September 30, 1961, Box 331, JFKL.

78. NFS: M & M Series, NSAM 118, January 13, 1962, Box 333, JFKL.

79. NSF: M & M Series, NSAM 124, Box 333, JFKL; Hilsman, *To Move a Nation*, p. 415.

80. NSF: M & M Series, NSAM 118, "Appendix B: Military Actions for Latin America, Part II," 45, Box 333, JFKL.

81. NSF: M & M Series, NSAM 134, February 20, 1962, Box 335, JFKL.

82. Joseph S. Tulchin, *Argentina and the United States: A Conflicted Relationship* (Boston, 1990), pp. 119–22; Gary W. Wynia, *Argentina in the Postwar Era: Politics and Economic Policy Making in a Divided Society* (Albuquerque, 1978), pp. 83–111; *DSB* 49 (November 4, 1963): 698–700.

83. Rabe, "Controlling Revolutions," p. 114; Gavin A. Smith and Pedro Cano H., "Some Factors Contributing to Peasant Land Occupations in Peru: The Example of Huasicancha, 1963–1968," in Norman Long and Bryan R. Roberts, ed., *Peasant Cooperation and Capitalist Expansion in Central Peru* (Austin, 1978), p. 171; Julio Cotler, "State and Regime: Comparative Notes on the Southern Cone and the 'Enclave' Societies," in David Collier, ed., *The New Authoritarianism in Latin America* (Princeton, 1979), pp. 276–77. As of August 1, 1992, no NSF documents concerning Peru were open to scholars at the JFKL. The resumption of modified military aid is mentioned in NSF: S Series, Alliance for Progress, October 14, 1962, Box 291, JFKL.

84. NSF: M & M Series, NSAM 182, August 24, 1962, Box 338, JFKL provides a comprehensive look at CI doctrine.

85. D. Michael Shafer, *Deadly Paradigms: The Failure of U. S. Counterinsurgency Policy* (Princeton, 1988), pp. 79–132; Douglas S. Blaufarb, *The Counterinsurgency Era: U. S. Doctrine and Performance* (New York, 1977), pp. 52–88.

86. NSF: M & M Series, Special Group (CI), Report of a Visit to Colombia, March 12, 1962, Box 319, JFKL; Michael McClintock, *Instruments of Statecraft: U. S. Guerrilla Warfare, Counterinsurgency, and Counterterrorism, 1940–1990* (New York, 1992), pp. 222–24.

87. NSF: M & M Series, Special Group (CI) Meetings, April 12, 1962, Box 319, JFKL.

88. NSF: S Series, Alliance for Progress, Moscoso to Carl Kaysen, April 9, 1962, and DS Circular to American Republics, April 4, 1962, Box 290, JFKL.

89. Leacock, *Requiem for Revolution*, pp. 94–95.

90. NSF: CO Series, Brazil, Dean Rusk to JFK, September 15, 1961, Box 12, JFKL; NSF: S Series, Alliance for Progress, Daniel M. Braddock to DS, April 23, 1962, Box 290, JFKL; NSF: S Series, Alliance for Progress, Moscoso to JFK, July 6, 1962, Box 291, JFKL: NSF: S Series, Alliance for Progress, Staff Report, June 16–July 12, 1962, Box 290, JFKL; Riordan Roett, *The Politics of Foreign Aid in Northeast Brazil* (Nashville, 1972).

91. NSF, CO Series, El Salvador, Memorandum for McGeorge Bundy, December 16, 1962, Box 69, JFKL; NSF: CO Series, Venezuela, C. Allan Stewart to DS, August 30, 1962, Box 192, JFKL; NSF: M & M Series, NSAM 153, "Policy Statement on the Dominican Republic," March 15, 1962, Box 336, JFKL; NSF: CO Series, Colombia, JFK to President Alberto Lleras Camargo, May 4, 1962, and Report on Colombia, June 8, 1962, Box 26, JFKL; NSF: WHB Series, Charles W. Cole to DS, October 17, 1962, Box 384, JFKL.

92. *New York Times*, October, 14, 1992, p. A19; *Washington Post*, October 19, 1992, p. A10; *New York Times*, October 20, 1992, p. A4; *New York Times*, October 23, 1992, p. A17; and Chang and Kornbluh, *The Cuban Missile Crisis, 1962*.

93. See, for example, Paterson, "Fixation with Cuba," pp. 140–52; James G. Blight and David A. Welch, *On the Brink: Americans and Soviets Reexamine the Cuban Missile Crisis* (New York, 1989); James A. Nathan, ed., *The Cuban Missile Crisis Revisited* (New York, 1992); Raymond L. Gartoff, *Reflections on the Cuban Missile Crisis*, rev. ed. (Washington, D. C., 1989).

94. Wayne S. Smith, *The Closest of Enemies: A Personal and Diplomatic History of the Castro Years* (New York, 1987), pp. 84–85; Paterson, "Fixation with Cuba," pp. 152–53; *PPP: JFK, 1963*, 243.

95. NSF: M & M Series, NSAM 213, January 8, 1963, Box 339, JFKL.

96. Michael C. Desch, " 'That Deep Mud in Cuba:' The Strategic Threat and U. S. Planning for a Conventional Response during the Missile Crisis," *Security Studies* 1 (Winter 1991): 317–51; NSF: M & M Series, Standing Group Meetings, October 24, 1962, Box 315, JFKL.

97. Stephen G. Rabe, *The Road to OPEC: United States Relations with Venezuela, 1919–1976* (Austin, 1982), pp. 152–53.

98. NSF: M & M Series, Special Group (CI), August 13, 1962, Box 319, JFKL; NSF: M & M Series, NSAM 177, November 1, 1962, Box 338, JFKL; NSAM 206, December 4, 1962, Box 339, JFKL; Walter LaFeber, *Inevitable Revolutions: The United States in Central America* (New York, 1983), p. 151.

99. NSF: M & M Series, Standing Group Meetings, April 23, 1963, Part A, Box 315, JFKL.

100. Ibid., April 30, 1963.

101. Ibid., October 1, 1963.

102. NSF: CO Series, Guatemala, W. H. Brubeck to Bundy, January 21, 1963, Box 101, JFKL; LaFeber, *Inevitable Revolutions*, pp. 164–65.

103. NSF: RS Series, Latin America Vol. 2, Rusk memorandum, August 31, 1963, Box 216, JFKL; NSF: S Series, Basic National Security Policy, section 8, March 25, 1963, Box 294, JFKL.

104. Organization of American States, Inter-American Economic and Social Council, *Report on the First Year of the Alliance for Progress* (Washington, D. C., 1962); TM Papers, AP Series, *Informe Preparado por el Gobierno de los Estados Unidos de América para las Segundas Reuniones Anuales del Consejo Interamericano Economico y Social*, Septiembre de 1963, Box 3, JFKL.

105. *Boletín Informativo Semanal de las Actividades de la Confederación General del Trabajo* 1 (28 de Octubre al 3 de Noviembre de 1963): 4–11.

106. Levinson and de Onís, *The Alliance That Lost Its Way*, pp. 279–81.

107. Lyndon Baines Johnson, *The Vantage Point: Perspectives of the Presidency 1963–1969* (New York, 1971), p. 22.

108. Joseph S. Tulchin, "The United States and Latin America in the 1960s," *Journal of Interamerican Studies and World Affairs* 30 (Spring 1988): 26–27; Chester Bowles OH, JFKL; Christopher Mitchell, "Dominance and Fragmentation in U. S. Latin American Policy," in Julio Cotler and Richard R. Fagen, ed., *Latin America and the United States: The Changing Political Realities* (Stanford, 1974), p. 190; Abraham F. Lowenthal, " 'Liberal,' 'Radical,' and 'Bureaucratic' Perspectives on U. S. Latin American Policy: The Alliance for Progress in Retrospect," in Cotler and Fagen, ed., *Latin America and the United States*, p. 232.

109. AH: AID, Vol. 1, Part 2, 236–237, LBJL.

110. NSF: NSAMs, NSAM 274, December 20, 1963, Box 2, LBJL; NSF: MBF, December 27, 1963, Box 18–19, LBJL.

111. NSF: NIEs, "Situation and Prospects in Cuba," June 14, 1963, Box 8–9, LBJL.

112. Ibid.

113. NSF: CO File, "Latin American Situation Report," January 8, 1964, Box 1, LBJL; Smith, *The Closest of Enemies*, pp. 86–87.

114. AH: DS, Vol. 1, Chap. 6., LBJL; Levinson and de Onís, *The Alliance That Lost Its Way*, pp. 128–31.

115. Rostow, *The Diffusion of Power*, p. 424; Walter LaFeber, *The Panama Canal: The Crisis in Historical Perspective*, expanded ed. (New York, 1979), pp. 132–45; NSF: NSC History, Panama Crisis, 1964, Memorandum of a Conversation, January 10, 1964, and Charles Yost to DS, January 14, 1964, Box 1, LBJL.

116. Rabe, *The Road to OPEC*, p. 154.

117. NSF: NSC Meetings, Meeting No. 523, March 5, 1964, Box 1, LBJL; Smith, *The Closest of Enemies*, 86–90.

118. *New York Times*, March 19, 1964, pp. 1, 2.

119. Phyllis R. Parker, *Brazil and the Quiet Intervention, 1964* (Austin, 1979), pp. 72–83; Vernon A. Walters, *Silent Missions* (New York, 1978), 378–90.

120. Leacock, *Requiem for Revolution*, 201–18; John Sheahan, *Patterns of Development in Latin America: Poverty, Repression, and Economic Strategy* (Princeton, 1987), pp. 186–88.

121. NSF: NSC Meetings, Meeting No. 526, April 3, 1964, Box 1, LBJL; NSF: CO File, Latin America, Mann to Rusk, May 13, 1964, Box 1, LBJL; WHCF: FO 3–2, Richard W. Reuter to LBJ, May 26, 1964, Box 26, LBJL; "Speech by Humberto Castello Branco, 1967," in Brian Loveman and Thomas M. Davies, ed., *The Politics of Antipolitics: The Military in Latin America* (Lincoln, 1978), 193; Johnson, *The Vantage Point*, p. 202.

122. Alfred Stepan, "The New Professionalism of Internal Warfare and Military Role Expansion," in Alfred Stepan, ed., *Authoritarian Brazil: Origins, Policies, and Future* (New Haven, 1973), pp. 47–53.

123. Berle, *Navigating the Rapids*, 799; Herbert S. Klein, *Bolivia: The Evolution of a Multi-Ethnic Society*, 2d ed. (New York, 1992), 242–49; NSF: CO File, Latin America, CIA Memorandum, May 18, 1965, Box 2, LBJL.

124. Rostow, *The Diffusion of Power*, p. 411.

125. Jerome Slater, *Intervention and Negotiation: The United States and the Dominican Revolution* (New York, 1970); Gen. Bruce Palmer, Jr., *Intervention in the Caribbean: The Dominican Crisis of 1965* (Lexington, 1989).

126. Schlesinger, *A Thousand Days*, 773; Dean Rusk, As Told to Richard Rusk, ed. by Daniel S. Papp, *As I Saw It* (New York, 1990), pp. 354–76.

127. Gleijeses, *The Dominican Crisis*, pp. 75–77; Abraham F. Lowenthal, *The Dominican Intervention* (Cambridge, 1972), pp. 151–57; Ball, *The Past Has Another Pattern*, 328–29.

128. NSF: CO File, Latin America, Mann to LBJ, March 15, 1965, Box 2, LBJL; Paul G. Buchanan, "The Impact of U. S. Labor," in Abraham F. Lowenthal, ed., *Exporting Democracy: The United States and Latin America: Themes and Issues* (Baltimore, 1991), 174–75; René Armand Dreifuss, *1964: A Conquista Do Estado: Ação Política, Poder e Golpe de Classe*, 5th ed. (Petrópolis, 1987), pp. 315–19.

129. NSF: Name File, Gordon Chase to Bundy, July 26, 1965, Box 1, LBJL.

130. NSF: CO File, Latin America, Benjamin H. Read to Bundy, June 17, 1964, Box 2, LBJL; NSF: Name File, Bowdler Memos, William P. Bowdler to Bundy, June 24, 1966, Box 1, LBJL; NSF: CO File, Latin America, Policy Planning Council Memo, July 8, 1966, Box 4–5, LBJL.

131. NSF: NSAMs, NSAM 349, Rostow to LBJ, May 27, 1966, and Lincoln Gordon to Rostow, September 8, 1966, Box 8, LBJL.

132. NSF: CO File, Latin America, Gordon to Rostow, May 3, 1967, Box 3, LBJL.

133. Levinson and de Onís, *The Alliance That Lost Its Way*, pp. 12, 144.

134. Paul E. Sigmund, *Multinationals in Latin America: The Politics of Nationalization* (Madison, 1980), pp. 33–42; James Petras and Morris Morley, *The United States and Chile: Imperialism and the Overthrow of the Allende Government* (New York, 1975), p. 24.

135. NSF: CO File, Latin America, Chase to Bundy, March 19, 1964, Box 1, LBJL; NSF: WHB Series, Thomas L. Hughes to Edwin Martin, June 27, 1962, Box 384, JFKL.

136. Petras and Morley, *The United States and Chile*, pp. 131–42; Theodore H. Moran, *Multinational Corporations and the Politics of Dependence: Copper in Chile* (Princeton, 1974), pp. 119–44; Sheahan, *Patterns of Development in Latin America*, pp. 203–15; Paul E. Sigmund, *The Overthrow of Allende and the Politics of Chile, 1964–76* (Pittsburgh, 1977), pp. 57–60, 80–83, 92–118.

137. Sigmund, *Multinationals in Latin America*, 180–82; MNF: "Meeting on Peru," November 8, 1987, Box 2, LBJL.

138. Charles T. Goosdell, "Diplomatic Protection of U. S. Business in Peru," in Daniel A. Sharp, ed., *U. S. Foreign Policy and Peru* (Austin, 1972), pp. 246–52; Sigmund, *Multinationals in Latin America*, pp. 184–96 which includes a discussion of the settlement of the ITT dispute; Sheahan, *Patterns of Development in Latin America*, pp. 257–65; Henry Kissinger, *White House Years* (Boston, 1979), p. 657.

139. NSF: CO Series, Argentina, Memorandum of a Conversation, November 6, 1962, Box 7, JFKL.

140. NSF: CO File, Latin America, CIA Intelligence Memorandum, March 15, 1966, Box 3, LBJL.

141. NSF: NSAMs, NSAM 297, Dungan to LBJ, April 16, 1964, Box 4, LBJL; NSF: CO File, Latin America, NSAM No. 297, April 22, 1964, Box 2, LBJL.

142. NSF: CO File, Latin America, Mann to Martin, January 2, 1965, Box 2, LBJL.

143. NSF: CO File, Latin America, Rusk to Secretary of Defense Robert S. McNamara, November 15, 1966, and Memorandum by Gordon, November 16, 1966, Box 3, LBJL; Michael T. Klare, *American Arms Supermarket* (Austin, 1984), pp. 79, 86–89.

144. Michael T. Klare, *Supplying Repression: U. S. Support for Authoritarian Regimes Abroad* (Washington, 1977), p. 20.

145. AH: DS, Vol. 1, Chap. 6, section C, LBJL.

146. NSF: CO File, Latin America, Rostow to LBJ, September 7, 1967, Box 3, LBJL.

147. AH: DS, Vol. 1, Chap. 6, section B, LBJL; NSF: NSC History, OAS Summit Meeting, April 1967, Memorandum by the Council for Latin America, 16 March 16, 1967, Box 12, LBJL; Johnson, *The Vantage Point*, pp. 347–51; Rostow, *The Diffusion of Power*, pp. 429–30.

148. NSF: CO File, Latin America, Rusk to LBJ, October 14, 1967, Box 3, LBJL; NSF: CO File, Latin America, "Official Latin American Reaction to Summit," April 1967, Box 3, LBJL; Eduardo Frei Montalvo, "The Alliance That Lost Its Way," *Foreign Affairs* 45 (April 1967): 437–48; Walter LaFeber, "Latin American Policy," in Robert A. Divine, ed., *Exploring the Johnson Years* (Austin, 1981), pp. 83–85.

149. CP: Cabinet Meeting, July 10, 1968, Box 14, LBJL.
150. Cole Blasier, "The United States and Democracy in Latin America," in James M. Malloy and Mitchell A. Seligson, ed., *Authoritarians and Democrats: Regime Transition in Latin America* (Pittsburgh, 1987), 219–27; Abraham F. Lowenthal, "Alliance Rhetoric Versus Latin American Reality," *Foreign Affairs* 48 (April 1970): 494–508.
151. Julio Cotler, "A Structural-Historical Approach to the Breakdown of Democratic Institutions: Peru," in Juan J. Linz and Alfred Stepan, ed., *The Breakdown of Democratic Regimes: Latin America* (Baltimore, 1978), pp. 178–79.

BIBLIOGRAPHY

Blasier, Cole. *The Hovering Giant: U.S. Responses to Revolutionary Change in Latin America*. Pittsburgh, 1976.
Blight, James G. and David A. Welch. *On the Brink: Americans and Soviets Reexamine the Cuban Missile Crisis*. New York, 1989.
Divine, Robert A., ed. *Exploring the Johnson Years*. Austin, 1981.
Gleijeses, Piero. *The Dominican Crisis: The 1965 Constitutionalist Revolt and American Intervention*, trans. by Lawrence Lipson. Baltimore, 1978.
Higgins, Trumbull. *The Perfect Failure: Kennedy, Eisenhower, and the CIA at the Bay of Pigs*. New York, 1987.
Klare, Michael T. *American Arms Supermarket*. Austin, 1984.
Leacock, Ruth. *Requiem for Revolution: The United States and Brazil, 1961–1969*. Kent, OH, 1990.
Levinson, Jerome and Juan de Onís, *The Alliance That Lost Its Way: A Critical Report on the Alliance for Progress*. Chicago, 1970.
Morley, Morris H. *Imperial State and Revolution: The United States and Cuba, 1952–1986*. New York, 1987.
Packenham, Robert. *Liberal America and the Third World: Political Development Ideas in Foreign Aid and Social Science*. Princeton, 1973.
Parker, Phyllis R. *Brazil and the Quiet Intervention, 1964*. Austin, 1979.
Petras, James and Morris Morley. *The United States and Chile: Imperialism and the Overthrow of the Allende Government*. New York, 1975.
Rabe, Stephen G. *Eisenhower and Latin America: The Foreign Policy of Anticommunism*. Chapel Hill, 1988.
Shafer, D. Michael. *Deadly Paradigms: The Failure of U.S. Counterinsurgency Policy*. Princeton, 1988.
Sharp, Daniel A., ed. *U.S. Foreign Policy and Peru*. Austin, 1972.
Sigmund, Paul E. *Multinationals in Latin America: The Politics of Nationalization*. Madison, 1980.
Slater, Jerome. *Intervention and Negotiation: The United States and the Dominican Revolution*. New York, 1970.
Weis, W. Michael. *Cold Warriors and Coups d'Etat: Brazilian- American Relations, 1945-1964* (Albuquerque, 1993).
Welch, Richard E., Jr. *Response to Revolution: The United States and the Cuban Revolution, 1959–1961*. Chapel Hill, 1985.

3

Cold War Dollar Diplomacy:
The Other Side of Containment

•

DIANE B. KUNZ

During the 1960s interwoven security questions and monetary issues dominated American policy toward Western Europe. The administrations of John F. Kennedy and Lyndon Johnson increased spending for both guns and butter simultaneously while still retaining the Bretton Woods system. Indeed Johnson particularly wanted to have it all: domestic prosperity, international financial stability, and protection from the Communist threat. That the United States almost pulled off this trick owes much to the extraordinary power of the American economy and the complicated relationship between military matters and money. Cold War tensions rose to their height during this decade with crises in Laos, Berlin, Cuba and Vietnam. Mounting a military response to the perceived Soviet-inspired confrontations affected all major Western economies, the American one most of all. At the same time Western European countries enjoyed record prosperity under the American-led Bretton Woods financial system. As a result, Britain, France, and the Federal Republic of Germany (West Germany) each felt compelled to follow the American lead in both the security and economic spheres. American financial power in the form of loans to prop up the pound contributed to London's decision to retain British troops in West Germany and delayed the British evacuation East of Suez. In a mirror image of the Anglo-American relationship, the German Federal Republic propped up the dollar in exchange for a massive American troop commitment in Europe. After 1963 France increasingly became the free rider, able to carve out its own path, knowing full well that it still derived the benefits of the NATO alliance. As the Kennedy and Johnson administrations struggled to meet the financial and military challenges of their time, they shaped the nature of both their era and our own.

The 1960 Crisis

The Bretton Woods negotiations of 1944 molded the configuration of the postwar monetary world. The resulting agreements created the International Monetary Fund (the IMF), the International Bank for Reconstruction and Development (the IBRD or World Bank) and, more importantly, set up an international financial standard based on the dollar. Each country agreed to maintain a fixed gold value for its currency and the United States additionally promised to sell gold at the price of $35/ounce. This unequivocal commitment made the dollar as good as gold, thereby allowing foreign governments to hold dollars as well as gold as reserves for their currencies. It also made the United States the "free world's" banker with the benefits and burdens that such a position entails. (The Soviet Union and its satellites dwelt in their own closed economic world.)

During the period 1950–1958, while the United States reigned supreme economically, it ran yearly balance of payments deficits.[1] In other words, the amount of money spent abroad by Americans individually, together with U.S. government expenditures, exceeded the equivalent expenditures made by foreigners in the United States. These deficits were in large part due to the combined cost of American foreign aid and defense allocations. As long as American gold stocks remained stable the deficit remained a low-level concern, particularly since the American balance of trade (the difference between the amount of goods a country imports and the amount it exports) remained in surplus.

A new era began in 1958. Western Europe countries, now fully recovered from the devastation spawned by World War II, agreed to make their currencies virtually convertible, i.e., exchangeable into other currencies at the holder's will. Simultaneously, for the first time in the postwar era, American gold stocks significantly declined. Washington officials hoped that this occurrence would prove to be a fluke but it happened again in 1959. Simultaneously the American balance of payments deficit trebled.[2] Not only was this development worrisome for its own sake but also the resulting outflow of American dollars into foreign hands correspondingly increased claims against American gold stocks.

Increasing concerns over the validity of the American commitment to sell gold at $35/ounce burst into view in October 1960 when the price of gold on the London market suddenly jumped over $40/ounce.[3] In response, presidential candidate John F. Kennedy pledged unequivocally that "If elected President I shall not devalue the dollar from the present rate. Rather I shall defend the present value and its soundness."[4] This promise reflected both outer realities and the candidate's inner convictions. Keeping it would define much of his administration's economic policies, both domestic and foreign.

Designing a Foreign Economic Policy

Once elected, Kennedy moved quickly to address foreign economic policy by including this issue as one of several to be tackled by a specific pre-presidential task force. The resulting report, delivered on December 27, 1960, benefitted from the wisdom of leading diplomats and economists, many of whom would soon join the administration. The committee, chaired by George Ball, the designated Under Secretary of State, explicitly rejected reducing military and economic foreign aid or restrictions on capital investment. Neither did the idea of devaluing the dollar find favor. Instead the report advocated what it called an "expansionist solution": increasing American exports abroad and foreign investments in the United States.[5]

Kennedy adopted these views in his February message to Congress on the balance of payments. Again he pledged that the dollar price of gold would remain at $35/ounce. He outlined a variety of measures: increasing international cooperation, special interest rates for dollar holdings of foreign governments and monetary institutions, export promotion, a move toward lower tariffs and a push to convince foreign governments that they should share the cost of foreign aid and defense.[6] In the view of one of Kennedy's domestic economic advisers, James Tobin, the message was "a poor one."[7] Tobin and his colleagues were right to object. Kennedy had been elected during a recession and men like Tobin, Walter Heller, Chairman of the Council of Economic Advisers and Kermit Gordon, Director of the Bureau of the Budget, wanted to follow a Keynsian approach, cutting taxes and interest rates in order to stimulate demand. Unfortunately Kennedy in his balance of payments message had promised to stabilize or, where possible, to lower prices. Furthermore, Kennedy's aim of attracting foreign capital necessitated high short-term interest rates. It would be virtually impossible to meet both the domestic and foreign economic agenda. If it came to a choice Kennedy had now signalled that his allegiance lay with preserving the external value of the dollar.

Kennedy's appointments to the Treasury Department further signalled his conservative approach to international finance. His choice of C. Douglas Dillon as Secretary of the Treasury made political sense; as a Republican who had served as President Dwight Eisenhower's Under Secretary of State, Dillon's presence reassured Wall Street, which had vigorously opposed the Kennedy candidacy. The selection of Robert Roosa, whose views mirrored Dillon's, to be the Under Secretary of the Treasury for Monetary Affairs emphasized Kennedy's embrace of traditional views of international finance. Kennedy's predilection combined with the prejudices held by both Dillon and Roosa produced an international economic policy dominated by a Treasury committed to the maintenance of the Bretton Woods system and "in no mood for radical experiments."[8] Additionally, in each major nation domestic economic and political needs as well as international diplomatic and strategic concerns militated against attempting a major readjustment of the international monetary system. Therefore, during this decade American and most Western European officials always sought the smallest possible changes.

By 1961 the financial order at the least needed realignment. Roosa bore the brunt of the burden of creating devices to prop up the dollar so that it could continue to serve as the world's reserve currency. Using mechanisms such as the London gold pool, swaps, "Roosa Bonds," and the General Agreements to Borrow[9], by 1963 the Treasury had created in Roosa's words "rings of outer and inner defenses for the dollar and financial system"[10]. The military metaphor was an apt choice. Not only was the Treasury mounting a campaign to save the status quo but also many American officials believed that a strong dollar was necessary both for its own sake and in order for the United States to continue to wage the Cold War.

Rather than considering the option of cutting back defense expenditures President Kennedy, for his part, had in his inaugural address proclaimed that the United States would pay any price and bear any burden to meet the challenge posed by the Soviet Union and its allies. Not surprisingly, this attitude contributed to the administration's acknowledgement in October 1963 that the American military presence in Europe would continue indefinitely.[11] Kennedy's foreign policy had a double-barrelled effect on the balance of payments as well as the position of the dollar. Increased military expenditures abroad directly and negatively affected the balance of payments—every dollar spent abroad represented another claim on American reserves. Spending more money for defense also left the government with less for other projects and increased the difficulties inherent in achieving the administration's cherished goal of a tax cut.[12]

The Kennedy administration took steps to ameliorate this situation. Under the aegis of the Cabinet Committee on the Balance of Payments, headed by Dillon, increasingly large amounts of American foreign aid were "tied" to purchases made in the United States. The Defense Department sought to buy as many military supplies as possible in the United States and cut the duty-free allowance for returning servicemen. It also increased the pressure on our allies to aid the American bottom line. As the French and West Germans had large balance of payments surpluses, American officials particularly thought they should contribute to the bolstering of the international financial system and to the cost both of foreign aid and of keeping American servicemen in Europe.[13]

European nations took more eagerly to the first of the notions. The willingness of foreign central banks to subscribe to borrowing agreements, to agree to swaps, and to buy Roosa bonds resulted in the substitution, to a large extent, of interlocking loan agreements for gold settlements.[14] This accommodating attitude did not primarily derive from charity. Europeans, enjoying growth rates far higher that the United States, feared the possibility of a rapid end to American balance of payments deficits because of the shock waves it would send through their own economies. They also remained shy of giving their currencies reserve status. The burden sharing issue, by contrast, would bedevil American relations with European allies throughout the decade and beyond.

That the balance of payments accounts had improved impressively during 1962 provided the administration with a temporary respite. Encouragingly, Congress had passed the Trade Expansion Act of 1962 which granted the President authority to reduce tariffs up to 50 percent on most goods and up to 100 percent on certain selected items under the aegis of GATT (the General Agreement on Tariffs and Trade).[15] The ideological roots of this measure, labeled by one historian "one of the greatest legislative accomplishments of Kennedy's presidency," lay in the long held Democratic belief that tariff barriers were bad for both economic and foreign policy reasons.[16] Previously political concerns outweighed economic incentives for such legislations but now the recovery of Western Europe, the growth of the Common Market, and the problematic American balance of payments position combined to elevate economic considerations.

Because administration officials remained apprehensive about the state of the international payments system, they debated taking preventive measures during this calm period in order to stave off another crisis in the future. Joseph Coppock, Director of the State Department's Foreign Economic Advisory Staff, urged such an approach in order that "the U.S. Government should be able to engage in expansionary policies without having to be concerned with the outflow of gold, with all of its psychological ramifications."

Coppock's plan called for a unilateral Treasury announcement, without prior notification to America's allies, that the Treasury would no longer exchange gold for dollars to foreign governments on demand. Another suggestion called for foreign governments to agree to a "standstill" which would make a very large percentage of their dollars no longer convertible. The advantages of either plan were obvious. Coppock, for one, also thought the administration could sell his plan to American allies by explaining that an ailing American domestic economy would both "weaken our political and psychological position vis-à-vis the Communists [and] lessen our economic capacity to support our military establishment." But the price of such freedom came too high: jettisoning the American commitment to sell gold at $35/ounce to foreign governments on demand would violate an ongoing American pledge to the IMF as well as Kennedy's repeated public promises.[17]

Making matters worse, by mid-1963 indications pointed to an increase in the balance of payments deficit. As the *New York Times* pointed out, with an election around the corner Kennedy feared the political repercussions from failing to live up to his repeated pledges to cure the balance of payments problem.[18] Kennedy responded by delivering to Congress a second balance of payments message while simultaneously urging Congress to pass a tax cut measure which administration economists suggested would stimulate the economy, thereby attracting foreign investments. Simultaneously, the Federal Reserve Board raised American interest rates in order to attract foreign capital immediately. Indications exist that during the final months of his life, Kennedy had begun to question his adherence to traditionalist foreign economic views.[19] Whether his reexamination of long-held assumptions would have led to a different economic policy is a question which will never be answered. What is clear is that the boundaries of American financial policy during the 1960s were in part set by the decisions and dilemmas of our major European allies, Britain, France, and West Germany, each of which faced the first half of the 1960s in very different states of health.

Great Britain: Searching for a Role

The "special relationship" between the United States and Great Britain, our comrade in arms in all twentieth-century wars, hot and cold (excepting Vietnam), was never as close as some writers have maintained. Still, the two countries, particularly their leadership classes, shared many strong bonds and similar perceptions. During the Kennedy era ties of affinity as well as relations with adversaries cemented these connections: Conservative Party Prime Minister Harold Macmillan was related by marriage to the Kennedy clan.[20] While Macmillan had at first been skeptical of Kennedy's qualifications for high office, fearing him too young and inexperienced, the first meetings of the two leaders, held in the spring of 1961, launched an excellent working and growing personal relationship.[21]

The financial dilemma newly facing the United States in 1961 was old hat to British leaders who had been wrestling with strategic and imperial commitments that exceeded Britain's grasp for decades.

Without sufficient reserves Cabinets, both Labour and Conservative, had been determined to retain a strong pound which, among other things, would help cement London's position as an international financial center. Moreover, British officials increasingly viewed the position of the pound and the continuance of the sterling area as glue for the Empire and ballast for the ephemeral Commonwealth which together could substitute for Britain's diminishing tangible power.[22] Britain's foreign financial policy goals in 1961 were exceedingly ambitious: to retain the sterling parity of £1 = $2.80 as well as to continue the sterling area and, by British standards, high social spending and a defense commitment second only to that of the United States. To meet these targets would require both constant British vigilance and continual infusions of foreign cash, primarily from the United States but also from international sources.[23]

In 1961 Britain faced yet another in a series of financial crises. As British officials patched together a multi-billion dollar support package, Macmillan, in a major policy shift, announced that Britain would apply to join the European Economic Community or Common Market.[24] Britain had previously spurned the opportunity to join this organization which in 1961 incorporated a six-nation European free-trading zone that some hoped would become the United States of Europe.[25] Washington had long supported European integration in general and British participation in particular: as Under Secretary of State George Ball informed Prime Minister Macmillan, "the United States believes that the Common Market has played an indispensable role in knitting together the countries of Western Europe. We will continue to support the Common Market as the central element of a moving process toward closer political and economic integration."[26] However, as Ball wrote to the president in August: while the United States wanted to push European integration, the government needed simultaneously to protect

American economic interests. Ball saw no inconsistency between these two goals as he believed that American interests were "consistent with those of the Free World as a whole."[27]

Yet the newly found American awareness of the Common Market's potential price tag did not fundamentally alter the previous American commitment to European integration. Officials took comfort from an optimistic State Department assessment that the net effect of European economic integration would be to expand American exports.[28] More important, the United States had long subscribed to the view that an economically united Europe would be better able to shoulder its share of Cold War generated defense costs.

At the highest level, Anglo-American relations grew increasingly more intimate through the foreign policy vicissitudes of the next two years. During the Cuban missile crisis Kennedy consulted both Macmillan and the president's good friend of twenty-five years standing, British Ambassador to the United States David Ormsby-Gore (Lord Harlech).[29] Soon after this climactic event of the Cold War, Kennedy and Macmillan met in Nassau on December 19, 1962. Prominent among the topics for discussion loomed the question of Skybolt, an American made missile that the United States had promised to Britain in order for it to upgrade its independent nuclear deterrent. Having been convinced by his advisers that the Skybolt program should be canceled, Kennedy now found himself persuaded by Macmillan over the objections of George Ball and others that Britain should receive Polaris missiles. While Macmillan walked away from the summit victorious, French President Charles de Gaulle seized on the Anglo-American agreement as another reason for blocking Britain's inclusion in the Common Market.[30]

De Gaulle's pronouncement, delivered on January 14, 1963, did not come as a total surprise to American officials. Nevertheless, de Gaulle's veto left Britain's European policy in shambles. British and American diplomats agreed that Britain needed to keep the option of joining the Common Market open and that together the two countries should make all attempts to pry the rest of Europe away from de Gaulle's domination.[31] Staying on this track would prove a difficult task for both governments.

The French Connection

In 1945 Charles de Gaulle, then leader of the Free French forces, told President Franklin Roosevelt's personal envoy Harry Hopkins that he "could not understand how they [the United States] can undertake to settle the fate of Europe in the absence of France. . . . The questions of the Rhine would not be settled by America any more than by Russia or by Great Britain. The solution could only be found one day by France or by Germany. Both had long sought it one against the other. Tomorrow they would discover it perhaps by joining together."[32]

This statement summed up de Gaulle's philosophy when he returned to office as the President of France in May 1958. De Gaulle's first three years at the helm of the newly constituted Fifth Republic showed a rare combination of skill and luck. Not only did de Gaulle move quickly toward terminating the bloody and divisive Algerian War but his government also put French national finances on a sound and ever more prosperous basis while simultaneously ending the structural instability that had bedeviled the French Fourth Republic from its creation in 1944 until its collapse fourteen years later.

While Franco-American ties of friendship dated back to the American revolution, de Gaulle's personal experience with American leaders had often been far less than cordial. Indeed Roosevelt consistently had tried to deny de Gaulle the leadership of the Free French forces. Of equal importance, de Gaulle resented the way in which the Eisenhower administration had turned down his September 1958 request to supersede the NATO structure, which he conceived of as American dominated and therefore outdated, with "a three power directorate to determine world-wide strategy."[33]

Nuclear weapons lay at the heart of de Gaulle's demands. He believed that the Soviet nuclear capability had devastating potential consequences for Europe. That the Soviet Union possessed the ability to strike American cities placed the American commitment to defend Europe at jeopardy: would the United States risk its safety to defend Europe? As a result de Gaulle concluded that it was imperative for France, like Britain, to create its own nuclear capability which de Gaulle also thought was the *sine qua non* of sovereign independence in the nuclear age.[34]

The Kennedy administration opposed either the creation of an independent French nuclear capability or the inclusion of France in a three-part power sharing arrangement.[35] Some American officials, notably Ball and Secretary of State Dean Rusk, advocated a two-pronged approach: "eliminate the privileged British situation" regarding nuclear weapons while concurrently creating a vehicle which would "assure our European allies of effective participation in control" over American nuclear forces committed to NATO.[36] Kennedy's action at

Nassau scuttled the first target but plans for the Multilateral Force or MLF, the device for meeting the second goal, became a key part of American policy toward Western Europe well into the Johnson administration. While the British and West German governments went along with the scheme, albeit without enthusiasm, de Gaulle, realizing that "effective participation in control" was tantamount to no control at all, refused to be bought off by the MLF.[37]

The only meeting between the two presidents took place in April 1961. The moment resonated with East-West tensions centering around the future of Berlin, then a city divided between the Western, democratic sector and an Eastern, Communist area. For the previous three years Moscow had demanded the eviction of the Western powers from this city located deep within Communist East Germany. Kennedy's meeting with de Gaulle in Paris, also remembered for Jacqueline Kennedy's rapturous reception (Kennedy quipped that he was "the guy who accompanies Jacqueline Kennedy"[38]), proved amiable on a personal level but unproductive on substantive matters: the gap between the two leaders was too large to be bridged.[39]

The issue of British entry into the Common Market occupied many hours of discussion between French and American diplomats. American officials received troubling signals during 1963. Britain's negotiations with "the Six" had not gone smoothly. Questions of Britain's ties with non-EEC European trading partners as well as to the Commonwealth and Empire, particularly in the realm of agriculture, proved nettlesome. More important, as American Ambassador to the European Communities John Tuthill observed, Britain had been unable to demonstrate to skeptical Europeans that Britain's presence in the Common Market was worth the many concessions it had sought.[40] Adding to the uncertainty, French Foreign Minister Maurice Couve de Murville predicted that the Nassau Agreement reached by Macmillan and Kennedy rendered Britain's entry into the Common Market more difficult.[41]

Bolstered by a huge victory in the National Assembly elections of November 18 and 25, de Gaulle delivered a vintage disquisition on Britain's place in the world at his press conference of January 14, 1963. After reviewing Britain's "insular," "maritime," and "singular" characteristics, he proclaimed Britain not yet ready to join the Common Market.[42] American officials could do little but sputter. George Ball sent McGeorge Bundy, Kennedy's national security adviser, a memorandum comparing the French President's description of Britain to the reply of Manchu Emperor King Chien Lung to George III's Ambassador.[43]

Financial factors placed additional strains on American relations with France. By mid-1962 the French government was running the largest continuing balance of payments surplus in the world. Indeed during the one week period from August 9 to August 16, 1962, French gold and foreign exchange holdings jumped $46.4 million.[44]

The French government had exercised its growing monetary hegemony gingerly at the beginning of the decade. Although officials were upset by the 1960 dollar crisis, Paris had shown "considerable discretion" in converting dollars to gold. This policy of restraint continued through 1961 and into the next year—the Bank of France not only gave solid support to the gold pool but first suggested the idea of swaps.[45]

Increasingly, French officials felt that other countries were not playing the monetary game with the same scruples. This growing belief, combined with the current French balance of payments surpluses and the historic French preference for gold instead of foreign exchange reserves, led the Bank of France to begin consistently converting dollars to gold in 1962. That the French government concurrently repaid all its outstanding Marshall Plan loans as well as a large chunk of other French debts to the United States did not totally assuage American discomfort.[46] Continued friction over American investments in France further inflamed feelings.

Yet this very real tension should not be allowed to obscure the other side of the coin. As a Central Intelligence Agency report pointed out, "France's record of cooperation in assisting the United States in its balance of payments difficulties during recent years is as good as that of any other European nation and better than most."[47] Unfortunately during the autumn of 1963 American officials began to report that de Gaulle's attitude toward the United States had hardened. Ambassador Charles Bohlen informed the State Department that while de Gaulle continued to support the Atlantic Alliance, he was against the idea of the American controlled NATO structure.[48] Events would soon vindicate Bohlen's views.

Reassessing Germany

The question of Germany occupied the central position in the bipolar global confrontation. Divided "temporarily" in 1945, by 1960 large armies from the United States and the Soviet Union faced each other across German territory. The two nation-states, West Germany (the Federal Republic of Germany) and East (the German Democratic Republic) mirrored their protectors' characteristics. Under Walter Ulbricht, East

Germany boasted a Stalinist society with all the accoutrements. West Germany, by contrast, displayed its pro-American nature as proudly as any Kiwanis Club member. Its *Wirtschaftswunder* (economic miracle) had transformed a nation totally wrecked by World War II into a nascent economic powerhouse. Indeed, the decline in American gold reserves during the late 1950s had been matched by a corresponding increase in West German reserves. Fueled by spectacular growth, West Germany's trade surplus in 1960 largely accounted for that year's official gold and foreign exchange increase of $2.4 billion.[49] As the difference between annual American expenditures in West Germany ($650 million) and West Germany's military expenditures in the United States ($230 million) accounted for more than 25 percent of the hard core United States balance of payments deficit in 1960, the Kennedy administration saw in West Germany an obvious solution to its balance of payments problem.[50] Support for taking a firm line on this issue with West Germany ran through the administration. As Secretary of State Dean Rusk wrote to Kennedy, the problem called "for sustained action by the Germans as the major surplus country of the West."[51]

The April 1961 visit of Konrad Adenauer, Chancellor of West Germany, gave the Kennedy administration ample opportunity to air these concerns. At that point Adenauer had been West Germany's only Chancellor, having led the nation since the founding of the divided state in 1949. "Der Alte," as the eighty year old leader was called, had accepted the reality of German division for the foreseeable future and had moved to establish close ties not only with the United States, but also with France, the nation that Germany had invaded three times in seventy years. His visit to Washington had a complicated agenda. Most important, Adenauer wanted to discuss the continuing crisis of Berlin. That city, Germany's former and future capital, located deep in East Germany, had also been divided in the aftermath of World War II. In 1948 the Soviet Union had blockaded the Western zones of the city; ten years later the Soviet government made a similar threat which in 1961 ominously hung over all questions of Western defense.

While the Kennedy administration's first priority remained the Communist danger, after Adenauer arrived American officials also emphasized two aspects of the balance of payments issue: the need for West Germany to contribute to the cost of American troops in Germany and the importance of Germany increasing its foreign aid to less developed nations. Underlying the American urgency regarding financial questions was the administration's belief, expressed in an *aide-memoire* prepared in connection with the West German Chancellor's visit, that under the Bretton Woods system, "a sustained accumulation of gold and other international reserves by any one country is disruptive to the international community."[52] Of course, when the United States possessed the lion's share of such reserves, the imbalance had not seemed as problematic.

Kennedy and Adenauer had two days of discussion. Unlike Macmillan, who had quickly lost his initial skepticism, Adenauer viewed the president "with ill-disguised disdain."[53] The meetings did produce German promises to increase foreign aid and to pay "continuing attention" to the balance of payments problem.[54] During the spring and summer events in Berlin assumed center stage. As discussed more fully in chapters 4 and 5, on August 13, 1961, the East German government constructed a wall across the city of Berlin. Designed as a radical defensive measure to stop the departure of young, talented East Germans tempted by the freer and richer life in the Western zones, the action spawned a major war scare in all Western capitals. Only gradually did it become clear that this step meant the end of Communist claims to the Western parts of Berlin and Germany.

As the Kennedy administration dealt with the Berlin crisis, concurrently officials worked on the MLF scheme. German levels of offset payments rose as a result of an agreement concluded in October 1961 and extended after discussions in September 1962. Indeed, the later discussions "comitt[ed] the Germans to place *orders* fully offsetting the foreign-exchange costs of U.S. forces in Germany during 1963" although the level of payments was "subject to the availability of funds."[55] The increasing closeness between France and West Germany, marked by the signing of a treaty of friendship in January 1963, alarmed some American officials particularly as it occurred concurrently with the French veto of British membership in the Common Market.

Kennedy's trip to Berlin in June 1963 with his moving statement, *"Ich bin ein Berliner,"* captured the hearts of West Germans. Secretary of State Rusk's public promise in October that the United States would maintain its divisions in Germany "as long as there was need for them" won their minds.[56] It would be left to Kennedy's successor to discover the means to pay for this commitment.

Having it All: Johnson's Foreign Economic Policy

Lyndon Johnson came to the White House on November 22, 1963 determined to carry out Kennedy's policies, both actual and anticipated. However, while he adopted Kennedy's domestic economic policy and obtained the enactment of various foreign economic palliatives, Johnson presided over the emasculation, albeit much disguised, of the Bretton Woods system.

As a result of Kennedy's July 1963 measures the American balance of payments deficit on regular transactions decreased in 1963.[57] However, American financial advisers, worried that this respite could well be a fluke, pressed for further action. In response Johnson appointed a Foreign Economic Task Force in July 1964 and Secretary of the Treasury C. Douglas Dillon and other American officials presided over a series of international conferences designed to ameliorate problems in the international financial system. Although the various Kennedy administration initiatives had kept the system functioning, they had not altered the basic problem: Europe's love/hate relationship with American balance of payments deficits. As the United States had pledged to end its deficits within the next five years, another mode of liquidity needed to be created.[58]

To the disappointment of Dillon and Walter Heller, Chairman of the Council of Economic Advisers, the various meetings of the G-10 countries[59] produced "more mouse than elephant."[60] The United States had pushed for a 50 percent increase in IMF member quotas but French representatives adamantly resisted such a large increase.[61] The resulting 25 percent increase was a big disappointment. But for the time being French and American differences remained under wraps. They would not be for long.

With the 1964 landslide election victory safely in his pocket, Johnson had no trouble getting a new package of balance of payments palliatives through Congress. But compared with the previous administration, foreign economic policy became less important. Johnson did not share Kennedy's assumption of the importance of gold reserves and the position of the dollar. Furthermore, Johnson received advice from trusted colleagues that led him to take a sanguine position in 1965. Gardner Ackley, the new Chairman of the Council of Economic Advisers wrote Johnson on December 10, 1964 that the best way to sustain prosperity was to enact tax cuts and a "Great Society" budget, since "If jobs, income and profits keep moving up—and your well-established frugality image is maintained—such a deficit would *not* impair confidence [in the dollar both here and abroad].[62]

Others concurred. Donald Cook, a possible successor to Dillon, and Robert Anderson, Eisenhower's Secretary of the Treasury, both praised the balance of payments program.[63] The gold picture sparkled brighter as well. Since 1962, the White House had utilized a "gold budget" designed to make sure that government officials minimized where ever possible the federal government's drain on the balance of payments. In February Johnson, reviewing the situation, told the Cabinet that "I believe we can assure the people that no savings have been overlooked by the Federal Government."[64] With the administration equally determined to push forward on the so-called Kennedy Round of tariff reduction negotiations, the international economic skies seemed bright.

The British Dilemma

In early 1964 the British economy had entered the end of one of its many postwar "stop-go" cycles: an economic boom had caused a huge increase of imports which began to threaten sterling. During the late summer, as the British election campaign began, the position of the pound took a drastic turn for the worse. Albeit with a tiny margin of four seats, the Labour Party emerged victorious on October 18, for the first time in thirteen years. Immediately the sterling crisis worsened. Faced with looming disaster, the new Prime Minister, Harold Wilson, and his two closest economic advisers, Chancellor of the Exchequer James Callaghan and George Brown, designated head of the new Department of Economic Affairs, met and vetoed any thought of devaluation. Instead, during the next month, the new government took such steps as a 15 percent surcharge on imports of manufactured and semi-manufactured goods, an increase in gasoline and income taxes and the introduction of capital gains and corporation taxes. Equally important, the British government, with American help, put together a $3 billion international short term sterling support package. Although perturbed at the effect of the import surcharge on the American push to lower tariffs and increase exports, the United States publicly took an optimistic view of these steps.

One month later Harold Wilson arrived in Washington for his first visit as Prime Minister. Wilson today is a politician in need of a revisionist rescue. Viewed in 1964 as the British John Kennedy, he has been derided in recent years as the ultimate pragmatist, interested only in power for power's sake. Aware of Wilson's reputation as "too clever by half," Johnson administration officials wished to gain his allegiance for their most pressing European priority: finding a place for the ever more powerful West Germany within the Atlantic Alliance. The administration's only vehicle for accomplishing this goal remained the Multilateral Force. The task ahead was to convince the British that they should accept parity in the MLF with the Germans rather than with the Americans. It would not be easy, especially as the scheme would represent a demotion for the British whose governments since the war had viewed their nation, together with the United States, in a class apart from the rest of the "free world." However, Wilson's deeply felt desire to establish a close relationship with Johnson played into American plans.[65] Other topics for discussion included a British presence in Vietnam, the British military commitment East of Suez (which included bases in Malaya, Singapore, Bahrain and Aden) and help for the pound.[66]

The British defense White Paper of February 1965 proclaimed the success of the Johnson administration's efforts, strongly reiterating the British commitment to the area East of Suez, although the document also decried the high level of expenditures for the BAOR (British Army on the Rhine). However, this report was an interim one; the government would make public its final recommendations in the summer.[67] But while the defense front seemed to be withstanding attack, rumors of a sterling devaluation continued to run rampant in New York. Dillon and Walter Heller, former Chairman of the Council of Economic Advisers, feared such a result both for its own sake and because of the effect it might have on the dollar. A financial crisis might also trigger a British military withdrawal from Europe. As a result the prime minister came to the United States in April to discuss his economic problems with the president as well as the Vietnam situation in light of the escalating bombing campaign.[68]

The deteriorating British financial situation placed economic concerns at the forefront of Anglo-American discussions throughout the next four months.[69] White House officials, trembling at the thought of the double-barrelled effect of a devaluation, debated whether and in what fashion they should aid Britain. If the United States decided to fund a loan, should it be a unilateral or multilateral measure? Officials also discussed whether the United States should attempt to condition any loan on domestic or foreign policy commitments. McGeorge Bundy, National Security adviser, felt that "the British are constantly trying to make narrow bargains on money while they cut back on their wider political and military responsibilities." He suggested that a "British Brigade in Viet Nam would be worth a billion dollars at the moment of truth for Sterling." White House aide Francis Bator put the same point a different way: the British should be told that "anything which could be regarded as even a partial British withdrawal from overseas responsibilities is bound to lead to an agonizing reappraisal here." But Bator simultaneously pointed out that the United States could not assume that current defense expenditures and the pound's present parity would remain absolute British priorities. After all, he opined, "the proposition that devaluation would be a total and *certain* disaster for Wilson is wrong." But Wilson, at this point, did believe that devaluation was unthinkable, thereby granting the administration significant leverage.[70]

The British crisis came to a head at the end of July as the Cabinet agreed to yet another deflationary package. When this remedy proved insufficient, Wilson and Callaghan realized the absolute necessity for further international help. In response, during August and September both Under Secretary of State George Ball and newly appointed Treasury Secretary Henry Fowler visited Britain. They made it clear that American help came with strings: Britain must take stern measures to dampen the domestic economy. Moreover, Ball also "put it to the British on Singapore and our support of the pound." The under secretary reported that it took two talks for Wilson to accept the linkage between the defense of the pound and British overseas commitments. But after the Cabinet agreed to a legal ceiling on wage increases on September 1, an enormously difficult step for a Labour government, Fowler took the lead in organizing international credits totalling $925 million, of which the American government contributed $400 million. The administration donated this significant sum because officials believed that a sterling devaluation would set in train so many lamentable consequences that the United States had no choice but to aid Britain.[71] However, Johnson had decided that a British ground commitment in Vietnam would not be part of the package.[72]

The French Thrust

Concurrently American relations with France grew increasingly strained. President Charles de Gaulle had long subscribed to the gold bloc philosophy expounded by French economist Jacques Rueff since the nineteen twenties. Although during the early sixties the French government had minimized its difficulties with American financial decisions, in February 1965, de Gaulle, again utilizing a news conference, proclaimed war on current international financial practices. His chief objection was to the use of the dollar as a reserve currency. As he correctly pointed out, "the fact that many States in principle accept dollars on the same basis as gold so as to offset, if need be, the deficits in their favor in the American balance of payments, leads the United States to indebt itself abroad at no cost."[73]

Both economic and political factors motivated de Gaulle's attack. Not only was he offended by the U.S. ability to print more dollars to offset balance of payments deficits, but he also firmly believed in gold as a reserve currency.He wanted 80 percent of French reserves in gold and those in the Bank of France, not at the Federal Reserve Bank of New York, as was customary.[74] Of equal importance, de Gaulle resented American domination of the Western alliance and bitterly dissented from American policy in Vietnam. His lack of any rapport with Johnson further exacerbated the situation as did the American President's inattention to European questions.[75]

De Gaulle's monetary thrust, the first of two strikes he would launch against the United States, threatened the financial structure of the postwar world. The second, the French government's announcement of its withdrawal from NATO in March 1966 and the eviction of NATO forces from their French headquarters, seemed to imperil the "free world's" security structure. The estimated price tag of $175–275 million for the evacuation of NATO facilities and personnel from France would also damage the American balance of payments position.[76]

French officials now began to accelerate their gold purchases, intending to convert all new holdings of dollars. Rumors that France was also undermining the pound swept financial markets. Furthermore, French Finance Minister Valery Giscard d'Estaing suggested that all countries should settle accounts only in gold.[77] French officials recognized that the withdrawal of dollars from the reserves of central banks would necessitate the creation of a new reserve unit. They suggested the CRU (variously the Composite or Collective Reserve Unit) which would be backed by a pool of money supplied by G-10 members. Less developed countries also suggested this device in the hope that more money for foreign aid would thereby be available.[78]

In response, the American government did an about-face and agreed to participate in an international conference on reserve unit creation.[79] A number of reasons explain this major change in policy, the most important of which were the departures of Dillon and Roosa, who had been replaced by Treasury Secretary Fowler and presidential adviser Francis Bator.Convinced of the intellectual basis and practical reality of the liquidity crisis, they did not share their predecessors' addiction to the status quo. Fowler immediately showed his seriousness by following up his attendance at the first international conference, held in July 1965, by barnstorming through European capitals. In September, the G-10 Deputies began formally studying the subject. While the United States now enthusiastically backed the idea, the French government almost completely retreated from the notion. Not suprisingly then, the gestation period for the special drawing rights, the name of the new asset, exceeded that of an elephant: the final agreement was not signed until 1969.[80]

Paying the Price

By that time the nature of the balance of payments problem had changed greatly. Vietnam, the monster that overwhelmed Johnson's foreign policy, eventually destroyed the integrity of America's foreign balance sheet as well. An increase in defense expenditures of 30 percent between 1965 and 1966 boded ill for the balance of payments.[81] In November 1965 both Fowler and Bator warned Johnson that "it would be necessary for the government to dramatize the balance of payments programs *as part of the total effort connected with the Viet Nam war*.[82] As Roosa wrote: "These drains accounted in directly measurable form, for two-thirds of the rate of deficit by the autumn of 1966, and indirectly could account for all the remainder."[83] The converse was also true: Fowler concluded that the balance of payments position would not improve until the Vietnam war had, at the very least, been substantially wound down.[84]

In line with Fowler's prediction, the balance of payments deficit for 1966 was very close to the 1965 deficit of $1.3 billion. This amount was half the 1963 and 1964 totals but disappointed officials because the Foreign Policy Task Force had earlier predicted that by 1966 the United States would be in surplus. The American balance sheet for the last quarter of 1966 was not encouraging and treasury department officials predicted that the president must expect significant problems during 1967.[85] On January 1, the president sent yet another balance of payments message to Congress. It advocated extending and strengthening the interest equalization tax (a tax on foreign loans raised in the United States first enacted in 1964), setting up yet another task force, and stimulating exports and foreign capital investment in the United States.[86]

Unfortunately these steps were not enough—they were simply elaborations of the measures previously put into place. Absent the Vietnam complication, they might have done the trick, at least temporarily. But the Southeast Asian conflict had three effects on the balance of payments. First, the war caused the expenditure of billions of additional dollars outside the United States, thereby directly damaging the balance of payments. Secondly, Vietnam-related expenditures, paid for by deficits, not taxes, led to a domestic boom which drove up American inflation, making American products more expensive, thereby hurting the balance of trade. The rapidly dwindling balance of trade surplus (soon to disappear altogether) removed another cushion for the balance of payments. The results of the Kennedy round negotiations under GATT, concluded on June 30, 1967, although in many ways favorable to the United States, could not begin to change this dismaying pattern.[87] Finally, American individuals and corporations, flush with cash, began their addiction to imports and to overseas purchases and investments.[88]

Yet Johnson shirked the task of asking Congress to increase taxes to pay for the war and indeed did not even mention the balance of payments in his 1967 State of the Union address.[89] With dissent over the war growing each month, he wanted nothing less than an opportunity for critics to debate the war. Johnson also feared that Congressional conservatives would use such an opportunity to emasculate the Great Society social programs which were Johnson's pride and joy. That the American people from the president on down were increasingly uneasy at the cost of safeguarding the integrity of the Bretton Woods system played a role too.[90]

This change in attitude is at the center of the difference between Kennedy and Johnson foreign financial policy. Kennedy, raised by a father who did not trust "funny money," viscerally believed that the United States was bound to play by the traditional rules of the monetary game.[91] Johnson apparently did not share this outlook. Faced with a perceived need to defend the dollar, he willingly embraced short-term solutions. Simultaneously, the growing cost of maintaining the Bretton Woods system in its then current state eroded any constituency in favor of a conservative approach. Fortunately for the president, for their own reasons, the Federal Republic of Germany in particular and our other allies in general, were willing to cooperate in two decisions that preserved the shell of Bretton Woods while rendering the reality increasingly specious.

The British Tightrope

The August–September 1965 rescue mission marked the high point of British financial stability. When Harold Wilson arrived at the White House in December for his semi-annual meeting with the president the agenda was full. McGeorge Bundy informed Johnson the same day that Wilson intended to discuss defense policy with the president. The White House knew that Wilson's goal, a cap on Berlin defense expenditures above £2 billion, would necessitate major cuts in existing commitments. No wonder the administration was uneasy: an issue that seemed settled in August had come alive four months later. At the same time the administration found itself forced to defend its Vietnam position to Wilson. The prime minister was in an unenviable position. He wanted to be a loyal ally but found himself increasingly under attack from his party's left wing. A British attempt to reconvene the Geneva conference on Indo-China succeeded only in alienating Washington. But on defense issues Wilson remained sound: the 1966 British defense review balanced "significant savings of money and foreign exchange against comparatively small reduction [of] military capacity," most notably the decision to evacuate the Aden base.[92]

Unfortunately by July 1966, Wilson was, in the words of the State Department's Intelligence Department, "beset by problems."[93] The economy had not improved and Labour party backbenchers were attacking not only the government's East of Suez defense policy but Wilson's leadership as well. In fact on July 19, for the first and only time, Wilson discussed the question of devaluation with his Cabinet. Six ministers favored this step but seventeen, including the Prime Minister and Chancellor of the Exchequer, opposed it. As a result, the Cabinet adopted its latest and most austere economic program. It called for a six-month freeze on wages and prices, cuts in domestic spending, new taxes, and pledged savings of at least £100 million ($280 million) in overseas defense and other government expenditures.[94]

Notwithstanding American knowledge of the prime minister's predicament, officials prepared ambitious agendas for Wilson's visit. George Ball, as usual, offered the most far-reaching one. He suggested that the president could use this moment to talk with Wilson "about the longer-range relations between our two nations" which would entail a redefinition of the special relationship. As Britain could no longer hope to play a world role alone, the administration must encourage the prime minister to lead his country into the Common Market. Such a step would allow Britain to find a new place for itself while serving as a counterweight to France and a palliative for German alienation. The administration also sought to persuade Britain to give up its independent nuclear deterrent, which would improve the chances for nuclear nonproliferation and placate German sensibilities. Although Ball recognized that his ambitious program could not be accomplished overnight, he urged that a start be made, lest the West be once more "confronted with the conditions of a new and dangerous instability."[95]

Wilson arrived on schedule, having survived the announcement of the rigorous U.K. economic program. His American hosts applauded Wilson's tough measures but worried that they might force the United States into greater expenditures. Bator advised that if Wilson asked for American aid for the pound, the president should use Fowler's ambiguous formulation: "no unilateral American aid."[96] As with previous summits all seemed well during Wilson's visit to Washington. But once the prime minister returned home the administration began hearing disturbing noises, particularly regarding the British commitment to Europe. Of all the British suggestions, removing combat troops from Germany remained the most alarming. If Britain weakened its NATO commitment, would Germany not lean toward neutrality? Moreover, the Senate Majority Policy Committee had just approved the so-called Mansfield Resolution, which advocated substantial cuts in American forces in Western Europe (then hovering between 400,000 and 450,000 troops). The Atlantic Alliance seemed fragile indeed.[97]

Watch on the Rhine

The German rescue came as part of the tripartite negotiations among the British, American, and West German governments, designed to increased the amount of offsetting payments made by Bonn in exchange for a continued Anglo-American military presence in the Federal Republic. Political and economic factors put them center stage in 1966. The French pull-out from NATO meant, as Johnson wrote to Wilson, that "our best hope of security in the future is for our two countries to work with the Germans in a meaningful way."[98] While the administration recognized, in George Ball's words, that "this is not the time for major cuts in European defenses, given German sensitivities on this point," at the same time both the United States and the United Kingdom intended to convince the German government to pay for a greater share of the cost of British and American troops stationed in Germany.[99]

The goal was to settle definitively the "offset" issue; that is to say the amount the German government would spend on military equipment in the United States and Britain to offset the balance of payments effect of allied troops stationed in Germany.[100] The United States occupied the pivotal position, torn between wanting to propitiate Bonn and having to prop up London. When West German Chancellor Ludwig Erhard arrived in September 1966, the administration had two aims: to increase German purchases in the United States and Britain to a satisfactory level while persuading the British to make only the most minimal cuts, and to delay these until the offset negotiations had concluded.[101] Erhard, the architect of the German economic miracle, was a man in deep political trouble. He had replaced Adenauer as Chancellor in October 1963 determined to improve relations with the United

States.[102] With the German budget deficit increasing rapidly, he asked Johnson for an extension of time to make the offset payments already due. The American refusal contributed to the fall of the Erhard government the following month.[103]

The offset issue and the related question of possible Anglo-American force reductions now grew increasingly problematic. Shortly after the formation of a new German government led by Kurt-Georg Kiesinger (the so-called "Grand Coalition"), Johnson appointed John J. McCloy, former American High Commissioner of Germany, friend to German leaders and certified "Wise Man," as his representative for a tripartite review of the Alliance in general, and the "equitable sharing of defense and related burdens," in particular.[104] McCloy's appointment indicated how seriously the administration viewed this problem. Simultaneously, officials attempted to find money for the British government; National Security Advisor Walt Rostow had informed Johnson that it would take $35 million in military orders "to permit Wilson to hold his Cabinet together and to unhook from his deadline for the announcement of troop withdrawal from Germany."[105]

During the spring McCloy and his fellow negotiators concentrated on the stickiest point—closing a multi-million dollar gap between the British and German positions on the offset issue. Discussions on this issue reached a satisfactory conclusion in May. Not only did the Federal Republic agree to continue significant offset purchases in the United States but the *Bundesbank* (the German Central Bank) promised to invest $500 million in special medium-term U.S. government securities during the period July 1967-July 1968 and also assented to Anglo-American redeployment of army and air force personnel.[106]

Of more significance, as part of the *quid pro quo* for the continued American military presence in Germany, the *Bundesbank* agreed in writing not to convert any dollars it received as part of Germany's foreign exchange surplus into gold from the United States Treasury.[107] This so-called "Blessing letter" (named for the head of the bank), symbolized two vital facts about the financial world that existed from 1967 until the Nixon shock in August 1971. By promising not to convert any dollars into gold West Germany in effect gave the United States a blank check. The price was clear: in exchange for this guarantee, the United States would continue to bear the brunt of the burden of defending West Germany from the threat posed by the hundreds of thousand of Soviet troops stationed across the border, thereby sparing our ally the financial and political burden of paying for its own defense. The costs of military overextension are clear. But, as the Blessing letter indicates, military hegemony has its benefits. The security connection largely explains the West German subsidy of American balance of payments deficits. Absent that, the dollar's path would have been much rockier.

Blessing's letter marked a major revision of the Bretton Woods system. Dollar convertibility was the foundation of the "free world's" monetary system. Now the *Bundesbank* had renounced its right to demand gold for its dollars from the U.S. Treasury in perpetuity. The image of Bretton Woods remained untarnished but much of the reality had now vanished.

Britain Slides Toward Reality

The events of September 1966 to November 1967 in retrospect have an air of inevitability about them. Increasingly committed to Vietnam, with the American balance of payments position worsening, the Johnson administration worked feverishly to keep an acceptable British military presence in Europe. Measured against this goal, the importance of the British commitment East of Suez and the sterling parity paled. More important, American officials sensed that they were fighting a losing battle.

Some relief came from the settlement of the tripartite negotiations: the West German government agreed to make offsetting purchases in Britain of almost $150 million while the United States pledged to make an additional $19.6 million dollars of such purchases in Britain. Yet it became apparent that the British Cabinet still intended to draw up a timetable for a British withdrawal East of Suez. American officials at one point suggested a twenty-five year multi-billion dollar loan to Britain designed to quash definitively any speculation about the pound. While Chancellor of the Exchequer James Callaghan initially expressed great interest, the plan died after it became obvious that the price would be a British public commitment to retaining the East of Suez defense presence.[108] Now, rather than lobbying directly, Washington encouraged emissaries from former British colonies to pressure London to change its mind. Furthermore, Johnson did a bit of personal politicking with various British newspaper editors.[109]

Wilson intended to arrive in Washington on June 2. In anticipation State Department Under Secretary Foy Kohler prepared a list of talking points for Johnson. Designed to change Wilson's mind, the memorandum enumerated the many adverse consequences of a British decision to pull out from positions East of Suez. Among them, "a hue and cry will immediately go up in this country that the British are abandoning us at the most crucial point since World War II." A British withdrawal would also provide fuel for antiwar critics, give ammunition to Americans urging a withdrawal from Europe, and cause a split in the special relationship. Yet as Ambassador David Bruce warned the administration, the chances of affecting Wilson's plans were slim, particularly since the prime minister, having staked his popularity on his Common Market bid approved by the Cabinet in early May now had to watch de Gaulle scotch his plans again.[110]

In the event the run-up to the Six Day War took center stage during this particular conference. The Middle East was important for its own sake and also because Wilson knew that either the closing of the Suez Canal or an interruption in British oil supplies could grievously harm the position of sterling. Moreover, a weak currency always suffers during a political crisis, especially since in the pre-1973 world of fixed rates any move to sell sterling was virtually a no-lose proposition.

As with every encounter, Wilson made no unpleasant announcements while in Washington. But in July the penny dropped—London announced that Britain would cut its forces in Singapore and Malaysia in half by 1970–71 and withdraw altogether within a few years.[111] Yet Walter Heller reassured the administration in September that both Wilson and Callaghan were "as firmly committed as ever to holding the value of the pound."[112]

Events proved otherwise. The British dock strike, which began on September 18, provided the final blow. Lasting more than eight weeks, this unfortunate confrontation convinced foreign investors that wage restraints, the centerpiece of Wilson's economic nostrums, would soon be jettisoned. As a result the pound faced renewed pressure. By early November the British government had decided that the question was not whether but when it should devalue sterling. Administration officials spent the second week of the month attempting to cobble together an international rescue package only to find that the kind of package that might have persuaded the Wilson government earlier in the year no longer had any effect.[113] Henceforward the administration pursued two goals: to bolster the British position by minimizing or eliminating other European devaluations and to limit the damage to the dollar, obviously the next target.[114] On November 18 the British government announced that it had devalued the pound to £1 = $2.40 (14%).[115] So ended the Anglo-American campaign which had consumed so much energy during the preceding three years.

The events of 1964–67 reveal the strengths and limitations of positive economic diplomacy. Much has been made of the Johnson administration's linkage of a sterling support package with a British commitment East of Suez during the summer of 1965. It should first be noted that there was nothing disreputable about this link; borrowers always learn that acquiring a lender means gaining a partner. More important, this coupling worked only because the Wilson government had independently rejected devaluation and itself wanted to retain its presence East of Suez. For the preceding twenty years British governments, both Conservative and Labour, for political, diplomatic, financial, and psychological reasons, had viewed the position of the pound as sacrosanct. With the nation still committed to an imperial role, no British prime minister had wanted to announce a withdrawal East of Suez, an action that would truly signal the end of empire. As Francis Bator wrote in July 1965: "if [Wilson] makes an absolute objective of $2.80—then of course we are in the saddle and can impose whatever terms we wish."[116] However, once the British government itself decided that neither the sterling parity nor a British presence East of Suez were worth the candle, American sticks and American carrots proved equally useless. Economic power can be a necessary condition for change; it is never a sufficient one. This lesson is one we would learn again in later years.

The Final Engagement

What substance remained in the Bretton Woods system soon became imperiled. The British devaluation of sterling placed enormous strains on the dollar. Speculators surged into the London gold market buying gold in the hopes of reaping a large gain if the United States decided to sever the link of $35/ounce gold. Increasing industrial and ornamental requirements for gold added to the pressure as new production failed to keep up with demand. Johnson aides had long pondered the risk of another run on gold. Now that the fear had become reality, Washington decided to take on the speculators.[117] The gold pool arrangement, which the United States had vigorously supported for seven years, provided the first line of defense, losing hundreds of millions of dollars worth of gold in the process.[118]

Between November and January the administration tried to stem this tide. On the domestic front, the president conferred with Congressional leaders seeking to apprise them of the international situation and simultaneously to ascertain the political and economic price they would exact for a tax increase. Concurrently, Treasury Under Secretary Frederick Deming toured European capitals drumming up support for the dollar and the gold pool.[119] By mid-December the balance of pay-

ments deficit "threaten[ed] to turn the year into a disaster."[120] Furthermore, gold losses had brought the American reserves almost to the
point at which penalties would accrue for violating the legal require-
ment that the Treasury hold a "gold cover" equal to 25 percent of the
dollars circulating in the United States. On New Year's Day Johnson
released another balance of payment program combining voluntary
action and mandatory controls on American direct investment abroad.
He also urged Congress to raise taxes and, in mid-January, requested
the end of the gold cover restriction.[121]

Contingency planning continued. Discussions shifted from the academic to the actual during the second week of March "as world financial markets had a bad case of the shakes." The gold pool came under
heavy pressure, recording the loss on Friday, March 8 of $179 million,
the second largest on record. With a weakened Johnson unable either
to prosecute the war abroad or to obtain the tax increase he sought at
home, speculators increased their bets against the United States Treasury. Sterling again came under siege as well.[122] As the foreign policy
wise men met with Johnson to discuss Vietnam policy in the wake of
the Tet offensive, Fowler convened his own "wise men," including former administration members Dillon, Roosa, and Heller and financial
titans such as David Rockefeller. They recommended pushing Congress to enact the tax increase bill and ending the gold pool agreement
but "unanimously opposed an increase in the price of gold as a way of
dealing with the present crisis."[123]

Financial advisers met in constant session, agreeing, as National
Security adviser Walt Rostow informed the president on March 14, "we
can't go on as is, hoping that something will turn up." On the same day,
the gold cover legislation passed Congress. With the news that gold
pool losses on that day exceeded $400 million, Johnson requested that
British authorities immediately close the gold market.[124]

Over the weekend finance ministers gathered in Washington. The
allies proved cooperative and the ideas mooted by American officials
received almost universal acceptance. Only France failed to support
the American suggestions.[125] Other nations had no desire to call the
entire Bretton Woods system into question, much preferring the benefits and willing to bear the burdens of the status quo. The key change
was the bifurcation of the gold market into two tiers: an official market
where monetary authorities would buy and sell gold at $35/ounce and
a commodity market where the price of gold would fluctuate freely
according to supply and demand.[126]

When the free world's central bankers released their final communique on March 17, another part of the Bretton Woods system had

become history. Now the American commitment to sell gold at $35/ounce ran only to foreign governments and central banks, the most important of which had promised in the Blessing letter not to exercise this right. Economist Arthur Okun wrote Johnson that the new gold policy was only a temporary expedient to help the international system until more fundamental changes were made but added that it provided the American government with a breathing space to correct its balance of payments.[127] The Nixon administration decided instead to dispense openly with the American commitment to sell gold at $35/ounce on August 15, 1971.

Conclusion

The jury will long debate the costs and benefits of American monetary and security policy toward Western Europe during the 1960s. Clearly the Cold War drained enormous amounts of American money throughout this decade. On the other hand, our allies increasingly could and did share the burden, both military and financial. Paradoxically, while American military commitments strained the balance of payments, they also increasingly bought the United States freedom from the pressure of worrying about the issue. No matter the cost to West Germany and other countries of absorbing dollars, the reality of the American defense umbrella together with freedom from controversial domestic decisions more than made up for it. Now that the Cold War has become history, we may find that being the only superpower is a far more expensive proposition than living in a bipolar world.

NOTES

1. The exception was 1957—that year's surplus was an anomalous one deriving from the British financial travail during the Suez crisis of the previous year.

2. John F. Kennedy Presidential Library, Boston, Massachusetts, Pre-Presidential Papers, Box 1073, Nitze, "Memorandum on U.S. Balance of Payments," November 24, 1959.

3. Paul Volcker and Toyoo Gyohten, *Changing Fortunes: The World's Money and the Threat to American Leadership* (New York, 1992), p. 21.

4. Robert V. Roosa, *The Dollar and World Liquidity* (New York, 1967), Appendix II, "A Statement by Senator John F. Kennedy on the Balance of Payments," October 31, 1960, p. 268.

5. JFKL, Pre-Presidential Box 1073, "Report to the Honorable John F. Kennedy by the Task Force on the Balance of Payments," December 27, 1960.

6. Roosa, Appendix, III, "The United States Balance of Payments and the Gold Outflow from the United States," February 6, 1961.

7. JFKL, Kermit Gordon Papers, Box 24, Tobin to Heller and Gordon, February 7, 1961.

8. Volcker/Gyohten, p. 25.

9. The London gold pool was an arrangement under which major Western economic nations promised to supply enough gold to the London market to keep the price at $35/ounce. "Swap Agreements" allowed governments almost instantly to borrow other currencies in times of crisis. Roosa Bonds permitted the American government to issue bonds in foreign currencies. The General Agreements to Borrow is the label for a mechanism under which the governments of nations with the ten largest Western economies agreed to provide a $6 billion line of credit to the IMF to be made available to member nations.

10. Volcker/Gyohten, p. 32.

11. JFKL, NSF Box 342, "National Security Action Memorandum No. 270, October 29, 1963.

12. American defense spending rose more than 15% from 1960 to 1962. See Paul Kennedy, *The Rise and Fall of the Great Powers* (New York, 1987, 1989), p. 384.

13. See, e.g., JFKL, National Security Files Box 325, Bator, "Draft Sketch of a U.S. Negotiating Position at DAG," March 14, 1961; Box 297A, Komer Memorandum for the President, March 2, 1963.

14. Charles A. Coombs, *The Arena of International Finance* (New York, 1976), p. 174–75.

15. GATT, the General Agreement of Trade and Tariffs, is a specialized agency of the United Nations which provides a mechanism for international tariff negotiations.

16. William S. Borden, "Defending Hegemony: American Foreign Economic Policy," in Thomas S. Paterson, ed., *Kennedy's Quest for Victory: American Foreign Policy, 1961–1963* (Oxford, 1989), p. 69. See also, Thomas W. Zeiler, *American Trade and Power in the 1960s* (New York, 1992).

17. Harry S. Truman Library, Dean Acheson Papers, State Department and White House, Memorandum on Gold Agreement Proposal, July 24, 1962; Turpin to Ball with enclosures, August 17, 1962; JFKL, Gordon Papers, Box 32, Coppock to Gordon with enclosures, August 10, 1962. (Courtesy of Marc Trachtenberg.)

18. *New York Times*, September 30, 1963.

19. Author's interview with James Tobin, January 21, 1993.

20. Mrs. Macmillan's nephew, the Marquess of Hartington, had married John F. Kennedy's sister Kathleen. Both husband and wife had died during the 1940s.

21. Alistair Horne, *Macmillan 1957–1986: Volume 2* (London, 1989), pp. 280–281.

22. The sterling area consisted of countries that kept their reserves in London, used the Bank of England as their central banker and generally followed London's lead in financial and trading matters.

23. For example, according to a 1966 Defense Department report, the United Kingdom "now" spent 6.8% of her Gross National Product for defense while the United States spent 8.8% and West Germany 5%. Lyndon Baines Johnson Library, Austin, Texas, National Security Files, Memos to President Box 10, McNamara to President, September 19, 1966.

24. On the support credits see, JFKL, NSF Box 170, Memorandum for the President: U.K. Request for Assistance from the International Monetary Fund, July 28, 1961.

25. The nations consisted of West Germany, France, Belgium, Luxembourg, Italy and the Netherlands.

26. JFKL, NSF Box 170, "Great Britain and the Common Market: Summary of Mr. Ball's Memorandum of May 10, 1961 replying to Prime Minister Mac Millan [sic]."

27. JFKL, NSF Box 170, Memorandum for the President: Certain Implications for American Policy of Prime Minister Macmillan's Statement on the EEC, August 7, 1961.

28. JFKL, NSF Box 170, Ball Memorandum to the President, August 23, 1961.

29. Horne, *Macmillan*, pp. 367–375; Michael R. Beschloss, *The Crisis Years: Kennedy and Khrushchev 1960–1963* (New York, 1991), pp. 475–477, 494, 499–500.

30. See, e.g., Horne, *Macmillan*, pp. 432–444; Arthur M. Schlesinger, *A Thousand Days: John F. Kennedy in the White House* (New York, 1965, 1971), pp. 783–788; JFKL, Henry Brandon Oral History interview with David Nunnerly.

31. JFKL, NSF, Box 171, Memorandum of Conversation: "Where Do We Go From Here?," January 18, 1963.

32. JFKL, NSF Box 72, "President de Gaulle in Discussion with H. Hopkins and Ambassador Caffery on January 27, 1945."

33. JFKL, NSF Box 70, Memorandum: "A New Approach to France," April 21, 1961.

34. Jean Lacouture, *De Gaulle: The Ruler 1945–1970* (New York, 1991), pp. 368–369.

35. See, e.g., JFKL, NSF Box 70, Memorandum of Conversation concerning Tripartite Consultation, March 10, 1961; Paris to SD, No. 4522, April 20, 1961.

36. JFKL, NSF Box 70, Memorandum: "A New Approach to France," April 21, 1961.

37. See chapter 4 below.

38. Lacouture, *De Gaulle*, p. 372.

39. JFKL, NSF Box 170, Memorandum of Conversation with the President and the Congressional Leadership, June 7, 1961.

40. JFKL, NSF, Box 170a, Brussels to State Department, No. ECBUS 594, December 17, 1962.

41. JFKL, NSF Box 71A, Paris to SD, No. 2595, December 24, 1962.

42. JFKL, NSF Box 72, General De Gaulle's Press Conference of January 14, 1963.

43. JFKL, NSF Box 72, Ball to Bundy, January 23, 1963.

44. JFKL, NSF Box 71A, Memorandum for the President, July 18, 1962; Paris

to SD, No. 938, August 23, 1962.

45. Coombs, *Arena of International Finance*, pp. 174–175.

46. Ibid.; JFKL, NSF Box 71A, Paris to SD, No. 45, July 3, 1962; SD to Paris, No. 71, July 6, 1962, SD to Paris, No. Deptel 143, July 9, 1962.

47. JFKL, NSF Box 72, CIA Office of Current Intelligence, "The Impact of French Economic Policy on US Interests," March 20, 1963.

48. JFKL, NSF Box 72, Bohlen, "Continuing Elements of De Gaulle's Foreign Policy;, August 7, 1963; "Report from Paris," September 26, 1963.

49. JFKL, Personal Office Files Box 117a, "Chancellor Adenauer's Visit—Washington, April 12–13, 1961—Summary Review of German Economy"; POF Box 116a, "Memorandum for the President: Germany's Payments Position with the United States and the Rest of the World," March 1961.

50. JFKL, POF Box 116a, Dillon Memorandum for the President concerning Balance of Payments, April 7, 1992.

51. JFKL, POF Box 116a, Rusk Memorandum for the President, February 15, 1961.

52. JFKL, POF Box 117a, "Chancellor Adenauer's Visit, Washington, April 12–13, 1961: United States Aide Memoire on the Balance-of-Payments Situation."

53. Henry Ashby Turner, Jr., *The Two Germanies Since 1945* (Yale, 1987), p. 89.

54. JFKL, POF Box 116a, Joint Communique, April 1961.

55. HSTL, Dean Acheson Papers, State Department and White House, "Report to the President on Balance of Payments" February 25, 1963. (Courtesy of Marc Trachtenberg.)

56. JFKL, NSF Box 342, "Excerpt from Proposed Speech by Secretary Rusk at Frankfurt, Germany, on Sunday, October 27, 1963."

57. LBJL, White House Central Files FO Box 32, Memorandum, "The Balance of Payments," April 22, 1964.

58. JFKL, Chayes Box 2, Roosa, "Agenda for Money and the Balance of Payments," September 23, 1964.

59. This grouping of the ten (later eleven) largest economies in the Western world took as its chief responsibility the structure of the international monetary system. The countries were: the United States, Canada, Britain, France, the German Federal Republic, Italy, Belgium, the Netherlands, Sweden and Japan. Switzerland joined later.

60. LBJL, Francis M. Bator Papers, Chronological Files Box 1, Memorandum for the President, August 10, 1964.

61. Each member of the International Monetary Fund contributed to the organization its quota 25% in gold and the balance in the member's own currency. The IMF then made these amounts available to member nations facing financial problems. With the United States after 1964 among the borrowing nations, Washington had a real interest in increasing these assessments.

62. LBJL, WHCFFO Box 32, Ackley to President, December 10, 1964.

63. LBJL, NSF Memoranda for the President (MP), Box 2, McGeorge Bundy Memorandum to the President, January 25, 1965.

64. LBJL, WHCF Fi Box 51, Memorandum for George Reedy, February 13, 1965.

65. Author's interview with Roy Jenkins, June 28, 1990; LBJ, NSF, MP Box 3, Bundy to Johnson, April 14, 1965.

66. LBJL, NSF-Country Files Box 214, Acheson to President, December 3, 1964; Box 213, Ball to President, December 5, 1964.

67. LBJL, NSF-CF Box 207, State Department Research Memorandum, March 5, 1965.

68. LBJL, NSF-CF Box 207, Heller to President, March 30, 1965; NSF; MP Box 3, Rusk to President, April 14, 1965.

69. The British government had a balance of payments deficit of $2,090 million in 1964 while at the same time its reserves only equaled $2,519 million. Source, LBJ, NSF-CF Box 215, Summers to Hinton, June 21, 1965.

70. LBJL, WHCF Co Box 12, Heller to President, June 17, 1965; NSF-CF Box 215, Memorandum to Bundy, June 1, 1965, "The Issue of Further Financial Assistance to the UK," Bator, Agenda: Preparation for Trend, July 28, 1965, Bator to Bundy, July 29, 1965; NSF-CF Box 207, Eckstein to Ackley, June 11, 1965; NSF, MP Box 4, Bundy to President, July 28, 1965.

71. LBJL, NSF-CF Box 215, Ball, "British Sterling Crisis," August 6, 1965. See also, James Callaghan, *Time and Chance* (London, 1987, 1988), pp. 181–89; Clive Ponting, *Breach of Promise: Labour in Power 1964–1970* (London, 1989), pp. 42–54.

72. LBJL, NSF MP Box 4, Bundy to President, August 2 and September 10, 1965.

73. Library of Congress, W. Averill Harriman Papers, Box 454, Text of President de Gaulle's Eleventh Press Conference, February 4, 1965.

74. Lacouture, *De Gaulle*, p. 381.

75. Ibid., p. 379.

76. LBJL, NSF-NSC Meetings Box 2, Summary Notes of 566th NSC Meeting, December 13, 1966.

77. LBJL,WHCF Co Box 175, Visit of Foreign Minister Couve de Murville, Background Papers, February 16, 1965.

78. Roosa, pp. 228–9; Coombs, p. 189.

79. Volcker/Gyohten, p. 44.

80. Special Drawing Rights are reserve assets allocated to each country on the basis of their IMF quota. The SDRs were originally linked to the dollar at $35/ounce gold. SDRs floated when the dollar did; they are now linked to a "basket" of various currencies.

81. Kennedy, *Rise and Fall*, p. 384.

82. LBJL, NSF, MP Box 5, Bator Memorandum for the President, November 16, 1965.

83. Roosa, *Dollar*, p. 215.

84. LBJL, WHCF FO Box 33, Remarks by the Honorable Henry H. Fowler at a News Conference on the Balance of Payments, February 14, 1966.

85. LBJL, WHCF Co Box 34, "Balance of Payments," December 1, 1966.

86. LBJL, Administrative Histories: Treasury Department, Chapter IX, Bal-

ance of Payments, pp. 26–27.

87. Zeiler., *American Trade and Power*, pp. 236–9 and 243–5.

88. See, e.g., LBJL, WHCF CO Box 34, Morton to Valenti, February 28, 1966.

89. Federal Reserve Bank of New York, New York, New York, IMF 798.3, Coombs Memorandum to Files, January 26, 1967.

90. See Roosa, *Dollar*, p. 219.

91. John Morton Blum, *Years of Discord: American Politics and Society, 1961–1974* (New York, 1991), p. 56. See also, JFKL, Theodore Sorenson Oral History where Sorenson states, "he gave to [the balance of payment problems] an urgency of crisis proportions which I often wondered whether they deserved."

92. LBJL, NSF-CF Box 209, London to SD, No. 3936, February 22, 1966.

93. LBJL, NSF, MP Box 8, President to Prime Minister, May 27, 1966, Bruce to Acting Secretary, No. 5768, June 2, 1966, President to Prime Minister, June 14, 1966, Rostow to Palliser, June 16, 1966.

94. LBJL, NSF-CF Box 209, Intelligence Note, July 27, 1966; Tony Benn, *Out of the Wilderness: Diaries 1963–1967* (London, 1987, 1988), pp. 457–458; Callaghan, *Time and Chance*, pp. 198–200.

95. LBJL, NSF-CF Box 209, Ball to President, July 22, 1966.

96. LBJL, Council of Economic Advisers Papers, Box 2, Ackley to President, July 19, 1966; NSF-CF Box 209, Intelligence Note, July 21, 1966; MP, Box 7, Bator to President, July 28, 1966.

97. LBJL, NSF-NSC Histories Box 50, President to Prime Minister, August 26, 1966, Mansfield to President, August 31, 1966; NSF-CF Box 172, SD to Paris, No. 36429, August 26, 1966; NSF-CF Box 210-2, Memorandum of Conversation, August 17, 1966.

98. LBJL, NSF-CF Box 58, Bator to President, March 18, 1965, President to De Gaulle, March 22, 1966, President to Wilson, March 23, 1966; Author's interview with Walt Rostow, January 23–25, 1991; Maurice Couve de Murville, *Le monde en face* (Paris, 1989), pp. 39-40; Lyndon Baines Johnson, *The Vantage Point: Perspectives of the Presidency 1963–1969* (New York, 1971), p. 305.

99. LBJL, NSF, MP Box 7, Ball to President, May 19, 1966.

100. The then current German commitment was to place $1.35 billion of military orders in the United States in calendar years 1965–1966 and to make payments of that amount in U.S. fiscal years 1966–1967. LBJ, NSF, MP Box 10, McNamara to President, September 19, 1966.

101. LBJL, NSF-NSC Histories Box 50, Bator Memos to President, September 21, 1966; Memos to the President Box 10, Rostow Memos to President, September 29, 1966.

102. Turner, *Two Germanies*, p. 89.

103. See e.g., JFKL, George McGhee Oral History; LBJL, Bator Papers, Chronological Box 3, Memorandum for the President, September 25, 1966.

104. LBJL, NSC-NSF Histories Box 50, President to McCloy, October 6, 1966.

105. LBJL, WHCF CO Box 49, Draft message from Rostow to President, autumn 1966; NSC-NSF Histories Box 50, Bator to President, November 18,

1966.

106. LBJ, NSF-NSC Histories Box 50, Bator to President, March 17, 1967, McCloy to President, March 22, 1967; Box 51, State Department Press Release No. 104, May 2, 1967.

107. LBJL, NSC-NSF Histories Box 50, Blessing to Martin, March 30, 1967; Kiesinger to Blessing, March 30, 1967.

108. Callaghan, *Time and Chance*, p. 211.

109. LBJL, NSF-CF Box 210–12, London to SD, No. 8404, April 14, 1967, London to SD, No. 8493, April 18, 1967; Box 202, SD to London et al., No. 193089, May 12, 1967; NSF-Name File Box 1, Bator to President, May 19, 1967.

110. LBJL, NSF-CF Box 216, Kohler to Rostow, May 26, 1967; Bruce to SD, No. 9929, May 30, 1967.

111. Denis Healey, *The Time of My Life* (London, 1989), p. 293.

112. LBJL, NSF Name File Box 7, Bruce to SD, No. 1487, August 30, 1967; WHCF, Co Box 8, Heller to President, September 9, 1967.

113. Callaghan, *Time and Chance*, pp. 213–224; Austen Morgan, *Harold Wilson* (London, 1992), pp. 312–13.

114. Fowler had warned the President that a sterling devaluation would trigger widespread monetary unrest. LBJL, NSF-NSC Histories Box 53, Fowler to President, November 13, 1967.

115. LBJL, WHCF, Co. Box 49, Fowler to President, October 19, 1967, Statement by Chancellor of the Exchequer, November 18, 1967; NSF-NSC Histories Box 53, Rostow Memos to President, November 13, 1967.

116. LBJL, NSF-CF, Box 215, Bator to Bundy, July 29, 1965.

117. LBJL, NSF-NSC Histories Box 53, Fowler Memorandum to President, November 13, 1967.

118. In the first three business days after the British devaluation alone, the pool lost $177 million. The United States supplied 60% of the gold, the major European nations (excluding France) the balance. LBJL, NSF-NSC History, Box 53, Rostow to President, November 22, 1967.

119. LBJL, Meetings Notes, Box 2, Notes on the President's Meeting with the Leadership, November 19, 1967; Notes on the President's Meeting with the Bipartisan Leadership, November 20, 1967; Council of Economic Advisers Box 2, Ackley to President, November 27, 1967.

120. LBJL, WHCF Fi Box 50, Ackley Memorandum to President, December 21, 1967.

121. LBJL, NSC/NSF Box 54, Statement by the President on the Balance of Payments, January 1, 1968.

122. LBJL, WHCF Co Box 50, Arthur Okun Memorandum to President, March 9, 1968.

123. LBJL, NSF-NSC Histories Box 53, Rostow Memorandum to the President, March 9, 1968.

124. LBJL, NSF-NSC Histories Box 53, "The Gold Crisis," p. 12.

125. See LBJL, NSF-CF Box 173/4, Central Intelligence Agency, "French Actions in the Recent Gold Crisis."

126. See, e.g., LBJL, NSC-NSF Box 53, Position Paper for Gold Pool Negotiations, March 16–17, 1968; "Communique Concerning Discussions held by the Governors of the Central Banks."
127. LBJL, CEA Box 2, Okun Memorandum to President, March 28, 1968.

BIBLIOGRAPHY

Calleo, David P. *The Imperious Economy*. Cambridge, 1982.
Johnson, Lyndon Baines. *The Vantage Point: Perspectives on the Presidency 1963-1969*. New York, 1971.
Lacouture, Jean, *De Gaulle: The Ruler 1945-1970*. New York, 1991.
Odell, John S. *U. S. International Monetary Policy: Markets, Power and Ideas as Sources of Change*. Princeton, 1982.
Pimlott, Ben. *Harold Wilson*. London, 1992.
Roosa, Robert V. *The Dollar and World Liquidity*. New York, 1967.
Tobin, James. *The New Economics One Decade Older*. Princeton, 1974.
Treverton, Gregory F. *The Dollar Drain and American Forces in Germany: Managing the Political Economies of Alliance*. Athens, 1978.
Volcker, Paul A., and Gyohten, Toyoo. *Changing Fortunes: The World's Money and the Threat to American Leadership*. New York, 1992.

4

Victories and Defeats in the Long Twilight Struggle: The United States and Western Europe in the 1960s

•

THOMAS ALAN SCHWARTZ

In his inaugural address, President John F. Kennedy called upon Americans to "bear the burden of the long twilight struggle" against Communism, a struggle that might not come to an end in their lifetimes or their children's. The new president had no doubt that the central arena of that struggle remained Western Europe, where the United States had fought two wars, and feared that a third, potentially nuclear, conflict, might break out.

Historians have not been kind to the Kennedy-Johnson policies toward Western Europe. Frank Costigliola, in an analysis of Kennedy's approach, condemned the president for talking about a "New Atlantic Community," while seeking American hegemony over the countries of Western Europe. Worse than that, his policies were an abject failure. [Kennedy's] "Grand Design lay in shambles by 1963. Kennedy had failed to build the Atlantic Alliance into an Atlantic community. His successors failed to try."[1] Michael Beschloss, in a recent treatment of Kennedy's diplomacy, criticizes Kennedy for "rarely showing the magnanimity that should have been expected of a superior power," and provoking the Soviets to flex their muscles in Berlin and Cuba, and then, after humiliation in the missile crisis, to engage in an expensive arms race with the West.[2] For his part, Lyndon Johnson's foreign policy is rarely treated sympathetically. It is usually summarized by one word—Vietnam.[3] Johnson's neglect of Europe has been reciprocated by historians, who usually skip from Kennedy's crises to Nixon's formalization of détente in the early 1970s.[4]

This chapter is not as critical because it assesses the Kennedy-Johnson policies less in terms of idealistic outcomes and more in relation to what actually happened. The decade began with American power preeminent, and with the focus of foreign policy on Europe. Dwight Eisenhower's administration had accustomed Americans to the Cold War, but it left his successor with unresolved and potentially dangerous issues.

Unfinished Business: The Eisenhower Legacy

No American president has been more identified with Western Europe than Dwight Eisenhower. Having been the Supreme Commander of Allied Forces in World War II and the first general to lead NATO after the war, Eisenhower always kept Western Europe and the Atlantic Alliance in the forefront of his concerns. A strong believer in European unity, Eisenhower never wavered in his conviction that strong ties between the United States and Europe were central to peace and stability. Eisenhower was a genuine hero to most Europeans, respected by British Prime Minister Harold Macmillan and even by French President Charles de Gaulle. For the Germans, whom Eisenhower had so thoroughly defeated, his policies allowed a return to international respectability and importance. Secretary of State John Foster Dulles and German Chancellor Konrad Adenauer even developed a close personal relationship based on their strong anti-Communism and religious convictions. Yet it was in relation to Germany that the Eisenhower administration left a number of unresolved questions to its successor.

First and foremost among these was the Berlin question. In November 1958, Soviet Premier Nikita Khrushchev announced that the time had come to "renounce the remnants of the occupation regime in Berlin." In a note delivered to the Western powers, Khrushchev described Berlin, the city deep within the heart of East Germany, as "a dangerous center of contradiction between the Great Powers . . . a smoldering fuse that has been connected to a powder keg." The Soviets declared that if a suitable four-power accord was not reached within the next six months, the USSR would sign a separate peace treaty with East Germany, and hand over control of traffic to it. This would force the West to deal with a regime that they did not recognize as legitimate if they wanted to preserve their access to West Berlin. The Soviets further proposed that West Berlin be transformed into a "demilitarized free city," which would be free of foreign troops and required to make its own arrangements with the East German regime.[5]

So began a three year war of nerves, with Khrushchev periodically issuing new threats and ultimatums, and then allowing them to expire quietly. Why Berlin? At the time many argued the Khrushchev's challenge was simply Soviet expansionism, a test of the West similar to those that Hitler had made in the 1930s. But many also recognized the problem that West Berlin posed to the Soviet empire's most western outpost. East Germany (formally, the German Democratic Republic) was losing its most skilled and talented people to the lure of the West, an escape that could be made on a subway ride from East to West Berlin. The country's population shrank during the 1950s from 18 million to 16 million, and the refugee flow threatened to destroy the Communist state. At the same time Berlin was also a place of unique Western vulnerability at a time of Soviet strategic inferiority. It was the most exposed outpost in America's worldwide imperium, and Khrushchev knew that he could always get the attention of the West by threatening the city. He compared Berlin to a "corn on the toe of the West—he could always get a holler by stepping on it." In his competition with the Chinese for leadership of the Communist movement, pressure on Berlin was an important asset.

Khrushchev's repeated threats over Berlin also reflected a genuine concern over Germany's growing power within the Western alliance, its demand for reunification and the return of its lost territories in the East, and the possibility that it might acquire nuclear weapons. As Germany rearmed and grew in strength in the 1950s, Khrushchev believed that it was only a matter of time before it acquired nuclear weapons. The Soviets were particularly concerned about the young German Defense Minister Franz-Josef Strauss, whose nationalist rhetoric and demands that Germans not be "the footsoldiers for American atomic knights," seemed to indicate the risks a nuclear-armed Germany might pose.[6] Khrushchev may have sought to use the Berlin issue to force the United States to recognize both the legitimacy of the division of Germany *and* the need to prevent Germany from acquiring nuclear weapons.[7]

Even if Soviet objectives in the crisis were essentially "defensive," they still struck at one of the foundations of the "dual containment" strategy that Eisenhower and Dulles had pursued toward the Soviet Union and Germany. Part of the price for keeping West Germany solidly within the Western camp was strong support for the goal of reunification and the treatment of Germany as an equal within the alliance. Neither Eisenhower nor Dulles could imagine that a country with a history like Germany's could be kept divided, and they feared that any Western hesitation on this issue could encourage a nationalist reaction.

The Berlin ultimatums seemed to force a choice between support for eventual German reunification and the possibility of conflict in Europe. Eisenhower remained calm and agreed to negotiate Berlin's status, but not at the expense of the Western presence.[8] He acknowledged that the city's position was "abnormal," but the U-2 crisis of May 1960 ended whatever chance Eisenhower may have had of negotiating some arrangement with the Soviets.

The second unresolved issue was that of nuclear sharing, a question that related to Soviet fears of a nuclear Germany. Eisenhower's administration was known for its strategy of "massive retaliation," a policy of relying on the use of nuclear weapons in the event of war. As the Soviet Union developed its own arsenal, and with its demonstration of its missile capability with the space satellite Sputnik, doubts grew over whether the United States would use its nuclear weapons to defend Western Europe, especially if it were placing its own cities at risk. One of the principal doubters was French President de Gaulle, who returned to power in 1958 determined to reassert France's role as a great power. Rebuffed by Eisenhower for his proposal to establish a Franco-American-British directorate of NATO, de Gaulle was determined to separate France from the NATO alliance and acquire an independent nuclear capability. His ambitions concerned Americans who feared that his example would encourage the West Germans to demand their own nuclear program in the interests of "equality."[9] This "nuclear nationalism" increased the possibility of the fragmentation of the alliance and the potential for war. At the same time, Eisenhower recognized that the European desire for control over nuclear weapons reflected the need to have some control over their own security and their own fate.

For this reason Eisenhower enthusiastically backed the idea of a "Multilateral Force," a seaborne nuclear missile force directly under NATO command. The submarines or ships would be manned by different nationalities, thus putting a European finger on the nuclear trigger. Proposed by Robert Bowie, one of the designers of ill-fated "European Defense Community" in the early 1950s, the MLF was designed to encourage a more unified Europe to play an active role in its own defense, and to provide an outlet for German nuclear ambitions.[10] The MLF would be accompanied by a conventional force build-up as well to raise the threshold at which nuclear war might begin.[11] Eisenhower never stopped arguing that the United States should decrease its responsibilities in Europe, and his support for the MLF flowed from that conviction as well.

Eisenhower's concern about America's responsibilities grew even stronger in the wake of problems with the balance of payments. The return to European currency convertibility in 1958 led to a growing American balance of payments deficit and a decline of more than $4 billion in America's gold reserves.[12] In late 1960, Eisenhower sent his Treasury Secretary, Robert Anderson, and Under Secretary of State, Douglas Dillon, to see Adenauer to ask for a payment of $650 million. The Germans rejected the demand for direct support costs, as these smacked of "occupation costs" and were politically impossible. They made a tentative offer to increase their foreign aid program, speed up the payment of their postwar debt, and make more military purchases in the United States. Anderson warned the Germans that this might mean a cutback in the number of American troops, but that decision awaited the Kennedy administration.[13]

The Transition

John Kennedy entered the White House after a presidential campaign focused on getting the country "moving again" after the supposed languor of the Eisenhower years. Questions about Western Europe, particularly Berlin, had not played a major role in the campaign, and Kennedy was relatively free of commitments, especially compared with his militant stance on Cuba. Still, there were indications that his presidency would bring new thinking on America's relationship with Europe. As a senator one of his major foreign policy addresses had been an attack on French policy in Algeria, a speech that earned him the suspicion of Atlanticists like the former Secretary of State, Dean Acheson. In a 1957 article in *Foreign Affairs*, Kennedy argued that, "American policy [in Germany] has let itself be lashed too tightly to a single German government and party," and concluded, somewhat prematurely, that the "age of Adenauer is over."[14] Kennedy had also written a note to George Kennan after the latter called for American disengagement from Central Europe, praising Kennan's willingness to challenge the "rigid" policies of Dulles and Eisenhower. But during the campaign itself Kennedy had largely followed the advice of his political aides who urged him to steer clear of the European situation. As Fred Holborn warned Kennedy before a Wisconsin speech, likely to include not only Germans but also Poles, even if the "Adenauer policy has come to a dead end," this was "no excuse for us openly to embarrass the Germans or to proclaim the perpetual division of Germany."[15]

On other European questions, Kennedy's election signalled both change and continuity with the Eisenhower era. Kennedy shared

Eisenhower's concern about moving away from "massive retaliation" and updating NATO's strategy for the 1960s, but his campaign was more influenced by General Maxwell Taylor's proposal to increase the size of America's conventional forces. In the event of a Soviet attack, Kennedy told his advisers, he wanted more choices than "surrender or annihilation." Kennedy was also far more interested than his predecessor in the problem of nuclear proliferation and control over nuclear weapons.[16] His campaign rhetoric about a "missile gap" and the decline in America's strength augured an increase in defense spending as an early priority, even though he shared with Eisenhower a concern about America's increasingly unfavorable balance of payments problem.

The Berlin Crisis

The election results were not even official when Kennedy received word that the Russians would welcome an early summit meeting. Khrushchev made it clear that he wanted an opportunity to meet with Kennedy to deal with the "cancer" of Berlin. For his part Kennedy tried to avoid dealing immediately with an issue that he perceived correctly, as Henry Owen put it to be "the most pregnant with disaster," and the most likely *"casus belli"* on the horizon.[17] On February 17, 1961, the Soviet leader sent a note to Adenauer demanding a peace treaty and the resolution of Berlin's status by the end of the year, or "the Soviet Union . . . will sign a peace treaty with the GDR. That will also mean ending the occupation regime in West Berlin with all the attendant consequences."[18] In March Kennedy still instructed his ambassador to Moscow, Llewellyn Thompson, to avoid the subject of Berlin in a planned conversation with the Soviet leader.[19] Wanting a clean slate from which to begin negotiations, the administration renounced the concessions Eisenhower had made on Berlin and Kennedy asked Acheson to prepare a report on NATO and Germany.[20]

The Acheson report set off a wide ranging debate within the administration, dividing hardliners from those who wanted to find some formula to negotiate with the Russians. During the first visit by British Prime Minister Harold Macmillan, Acheson laid out what Schlesinger later called a "bloodcurdling" recital."[21] "All courses of action are dangerous and unpromising, but inaction is even worse." The former Secretary of State believed that "a willingness to fight for Berlin" was necessary. Among the military countermeasures that Acheson favored was sending a division down the *Autobahn*, thus making it clear to the

Russians that the United States would not allow access to Berlin to be cut off. If the Russians reacted, the West could rally its forces and rearm as it had in the Korean War.[22] Although he did not agree entirely with Acheson's proposal, Bundy called it "first-rate" and argued that "Berlin is no place for compromise and our general friendliness and eagerness for improvement on many other points really requires strength here in order to be rightly understood."[23]

Behind Acheson's tough stance was his assumption that the Berlin crisis was much more than an assault on a capitalist enclave in Communist territory. To Acheson and others who urged a hard line, Berlin was the preeminent symbol of Western determination, the Atlantic alliance, and America's ties with West Germany. In Acheson's view, Khrushchev was challenging America's will and seeking America's humiliation. While Acheson did not oppose any negotiations, he believed that "a rush to negotiate" would be interpreted as weakness. Khrushchev's provocation was a sign to Acheson that increasing Soviet strength had reduced his fear of war with the West. Acheson, echoing his own experience as Secretary of State, wanted to negotiate from a position of strength, and believed that the United States would have to risk a conflict in order to re-establish that position.[24]

For others in the Kennedy administration, among them Averell Harriman and Adlai Stevenson, the Acheson position symbolized all that had been wrong with the Eisenhower and Dulles "rigid" foreign policies. Gearing their appeal to a president whose inaugural address included a pledge to never "fear to negotiate," the softliners urged Kennedy to take a less militant stance. Referring specifically to Stevenson and Harriman, Arthur Schlesinger told Kennedy that the Acheson presentation had "deeply dismayed" many of the Americans and the British as well. He argued that Acheson was "committing the United States to dangerous positions" before there had been any chance to test the possibility of negotiations. He conceded that Acheson's position might prove "valid," but felt it was a "grave error to start out with it as a major premise of our policy."[25] Behind these arguments was the conviction, as Henry Kissinger put it, that "firmness should be related to the substance of our negotiation position," and that refusing to talk should not become a test of American resolve. Kissinger proposed developing an alternative "Kennedy Plan" for Central Europe to seize the diplomatic advantage from the Soviets.[26] Among the points that Acheson's opponents were willing to consider in negotiations were an all-Berlin Free City, Germany's eastern border, and "alternatives to our traditional position on reunification and the recognition of East Germany."[27] They disputed Acheson's contention that the pressure on

Berlin was a "test of will," arguing that the Soviet leader's primary aim was a "solution to his liking of the Berlin problem and the two Germanies issue."[28]

Although the·softliners primarily stressed their desire for negotiations, their viewpoints also represented a significant break from Acheson's orthodoxy about Germany and Berlin. They had far more sympathy with Russian concerns about Germany's growing power, and far less willingness to allow Adenauer's political position to be the central concern of American policymakers. Repeating the Western mantra about German reunification had no appeal to them, as Bundy would comment, in referring to a State Department White Paper on Berlin, "it repeatedly refers to German unity in a tone which suggests that we really believe such unity is possible in the reasonable future. We do not believe that, and other nations know we don't."[29] Acheson's critics saw themselves as willing to face the reality that postwar Germany would remain divided, and that this reality was far more preferable from the American point of view than efforts aimed at reunification that might lead to instability and even war.

Kennedy postponed a final decision on America's Berlin policy until after the Vienna summit meeting with Khrushchev. The failure of the American-supported Cuban exiles at the Bay of Pigs may have encouraged the Soviet leader to press Kennedy even harder on the Berlin question at Vienna. Khrushchev again insisted that Berlin was "the most dangerous spot in the world," a "thorn" and an "ulcer" that must be eliminated. He attacked the "dominant position" of Germany in NATO, and stressed that "two German states exist," and "a united Germany is not practical because the Germans themselves do not want it." Kennedy tried to defend the American position in Berlin, noting its importance as a symbol of American commitment to Western Europe and adding, "If we were to leave West Berlin, Europe would be abandoned as well." Kennedy may have weakened his own position by acknowledging, as Eisenhower had, that the Berlin situation was not satisfactory, but that "it is not the right time now to change the situation in Berlin and the balance in general." (As Beschloss aptly notes, coming just a few weeks after the Americans had sought to change the balance in Cuba, this argument was not likely to sway Khrushchev.[30])

Grim and angry after the summit, Kennedy told one of his aides that "It seems silly for us to be facing an atomic war over a treaty preserving Berlin as the future capital of a reunited Germany when all of us know that Germany will probably never be reunited."[31] However silly it was, Kennedy knew that Berlin had become a critical test of his foreign policy. In July 1961 Kennedy and his advisers debated policy on

Berlin. Acheson and his allies, including Vice President Johnson, insisted that Kennedy "support a full program of decisive action," including a declaration of national emergency.[32] Opponents argued that would provoke further escalation of the crisis, alienate world opinion, and "leave the propaganda and diplomatic initiative to Khrushchev."[33] From outside the administration came calls from prominent Senators such as Mike Mansfield to guarantee Berlin as a "free city" as a first step toward German reunification.[34] Senator J. William Fulbright taking a slightly different view, argued that there were now "two German states which cannot be united under any conditions now conceivable," and proposed that Berlin become the new headquarters for the United Nations.[35] But what is more striking than these suggestions is the strong public support that Americans displayed for the status quo in Berlin. One Gallup Poll in late July showed support for keeping American forces in Berlin "even at the risk of war" was at 82 percent.[36] To that extent, Berlin was a good place to take a stand, at least in terms of rallying public support for a military buildup that could be useful not only in Berlin, but also in other trouble spots around the world.

With domestic support assured, Kennedy approved a military buildup similar to what Acheson had recommended, hoping both to demonstrate to Khrushchev the American determination to stay in Berlin, and convince the Soviet leader *and* the American people that the United States would be undertaking negotiations from a position of strength. Kennedy would not follow Acheson the entire distance, trimming his request by $800 million and refusing his suggestion of immediate mobilization and a declaration of national emergency. Still, Kennedy's increases in military spending since January amounted to almost $6 billion, a substantial increase in America's nuclear and conventional strength. The president made his announcement in a nationally televised speech on July 25, 1961, in which he reiterated to the American people that "We cannot and will not permit the Communists to drive us out of Berlin."[37] The $3.25 billion he requested for defense would allow an expansion of the army from 875,000 to 1 million, and an increase from 11 to 16 combat-ready divisions. Kennedy also called up 51,000 reservists and encouraged the building and stocking of more fallout shelters. To indicate a willingness to negotiate, Kennedy acknowledged the Soviet Union's "historical concern" for security against "ravaging invasions" from Central Europe. The United States was willing to "remove any irritants" in West Berlin but not at the expense of the city's freedom.[38]

Kennedy's speech intensified the crisis atmosphere surrounding the city, and East Germans streamed into the city in ever-increasing numbers, totaling 30,000 in July, and reaching 4,000 on August 12, 1961, the day before the Berlin Wall was established. The administration's reaction to the Soviet move might be best summarized in Kennedy's remark that "a wall is a hell of a lot better than a war." Although the administration may not have known the full specifics or the exact timing of the East German/Soviet move, Kennedy and his advisers were not totally surprised by the move, having expected some action to prevent the GDR's hemorrhaging. In Kennedy's July 25 speech he referred only to the defense of *West* Berlin, and remarked that the "endangered frontier of freedom runs through divided Berlin." Fulbright had told a national television audience on July 30 that "I don't understand why the East Germans don't close their border because I think they have a right to close it."[39] Walter Heller warned Kennedy that there was the possibility of an "uprising [in East Germany] in response to either a separate peace treaty or a blockade . . . "[40] Kennedy's silence after the Wall was built may have been designed to avoid inflaming the situation further, as some had accused the United States of doing during the Hungarian rebellion in 1956. Although he sent Vice President Johnson to West Berlin to show American support, and appointed the hero of the Berlin Blockade, General Lucius Clay, as his special envoy, Kennedy acted cautiously. While the Wall was an affront to human rights and a violation of Allied agreements, Kennedy judged that it was not an issue over which Americans would fight. Indeed, by confirming the status quo, there was hope that the Wall might signal an end to the crisis.

Most American leaders expected that the Wall was the opening shot in the Soviet escalation of the crisis. Kennedy quickly asked Defense Secretary Robert McNamara to accelerate military preparations and move ahead on civil defense. But he also wanted to move ahead quickly on negotiations, making it "plain to our three allies that this is what we mean to do and that they must come along or stay behind." The Wall spurred Kennedy to move away faster from the traditional American position on Berlin, and he insisted that "our proposals . . . should *not* look like warmed-over stuff from 1959." The U.S. should "protect our support for the *idea* of self-determination, the *idea* of all-Germany, and the *fact* of viable, protected freedom in West Berlin." He was willing to move away from occupation rights if "other strong guarantees can be designed."[41] Kennedy's push for a new American position is also reflected in the proposals of Carl Kaysen, one of Bundy's assistants on the National Security Council. Kaysen argued for a defensive interpretation of the Soviet policy toward Berlin, and expressed sympathy for Soviet desires to "place some limitation on the military power of

West Germany." In return for guaranteeing the freedom of West Berlin, Kaysen argued that the West should offer to recognize the Oder-Neisse line as Germany's eastern frontier, some form of recognition of the GDR as the government of East Germany, and some type of "nuclear free zone in Germany."[42] Averell Harriman echoed this view, arguing that since Khrushchev "means what he says when he told me as well as others that 'We would never agree to a united Germany under social-ism . . . and I will never agree to a united Germany under your sys-tem,' " the United States should move to a "de facto recognition or acceptance of the East German regime," and some type of "denu-clearized control of West Germany and East Germany."[43]

This drift in American thinking led to a sharp deterioration in rela-tions with the Adenauer government. The chancellor had openly regretted the loss of his once close partnership with Dulles and feared Kennedy's election might bring advisers like Stevenson and Harriman to prominence, both of whom he considered soft on the question of rec-ognizing East Germany. Briefly reassured by Acheson in April, the chancellor had little rapport with the young president, who felt Ade-nauer was "talking not only to a different generation but to a different era, a different world."[44] The American reaction to the Wall further confirmed the chancellor's skepticism, though his own slow response to Berlin's plight did little to endear him to that city's population. In the midst of an electoral campaign, the chancellor worried about the Amer-ican position on negotiations, especially some type of nuclear-free zone in Germany. He warned Kennedy that "a special military status for any country of Western Europe, particularly the Federal Republic, will mean an open invitation to the Soviet Union to push further into West-ern Europe."[45] This was the same thing he had been saying for years, and the Kennedy people were tired of the message. The Germans also believed they were being told "almost categorically that it was a waste of time even for negotiating purposes to talk about the reunification of Germany," and that the United States "was moving toward something which was indistinguishable from *de facto* recognition of East Ger-many."[46]

If these were the changes, the Americans were careful not to put them explicitly to Adenauer on his November visit to Washington. Before Adenauer arrived, Bundy told Kennedy that "everyone agrees the Chancellor needs a shot in the arm—maybe you've tried already, but another try might help."[47] The chancellor agreed that the Ameri-cans should continue talks with the Soviets on Berlin and to provide more German soldiers for defense, in return for which Kennedy agreed not to negotiate Germany's eastern boundary, the recognition of the

GDR, or any neutralization of Central Europe. Kennedy rejected Adenauer's demand for German participation in any nuclear decision making in the event that a conventional war was about to escalate to a nuclear conflict.[48]

The negotiations on Berlin began late in 1961, despite the heightening of tensions that had come with the Soviet resumption of nuclear testing in late August, and a tense standoff between American and Soviet forces in Berlin. On Friday October 27, 1961, American and Soviet tanks faced each other near Checkpoint Charlie, which divided the U.S. and USSR zones. To head off a confrontation, the president sent a secret message to Khrushchev that indicated that if the American and Soviet tanks would both depart without incident, the president was prepared to demonstrate a "certain flexibility" on the Berlin issue."[49] Kennedy may also have reinforced his message by indicating to the Soviets how overwhelming America's nuclear superiority was. In a speech on October 21, 1961, by Roswell Gilpatric, McNamara's deputy at the Defense Department, the "missile gap" was publicly laid to rest. Gilpatric announced that "the total number of our nuclear delivery vehicles . . . is in the tens of thousands, and of course we have more than one warhead for each vehicle." The United States had "a second strike capability which is at least as extensive as what the Soviets can deliver by striking first."[50] Combined with the buildup in conventional strength, this public pronouncement of American nuclear superiority may explain why Kennedy believed he could now show some "flexibility" on Berlin.

The administration proposed an "International Access Authority for Berlin," with a membership including neutral countries, which would govern air and road access between West Germany and West Berlin."[51] Adenauer attacked the idea, arguing that the plan could not be implemented and that he did not have "the slightest hope that these [United States-Soviet] soundings will lead to a result."[52] He disliked the measure of recognition that such an authority would give to East Germany, and doubted that neutral countries could play any effective role. Washington retaliated with the extraordinary step of asking for the recall of the German Ambassador to Washington, Wilhelm Grewe, who was considered "just a bit too pushy with his advocacy of Bonn's unpopular policies." Grewe may also have been the source of destructive leaks in Washington on the Berlin negotiations.[53] To some extent the administration believed that the Germans had nowhere else to go, and that it held the all the cards. As Roger Hilsman told Secretary of State Dean Rusk, "The West Germans realize that the viability of the West German state and the integrity of its territory are dependent directly as well as ultimately upon the US security guarantee, irrespective of the medium through which it is applied."[54]

Some recent accounts have argued that the administration was preparing to go quite far in its search for a diplomatic settlement of the Berlin crisis, what Acheson called "a humiliating defeat over Berlin."[55] While this may be an exaggeration, there is also reason to doubt Arthur Schlesinger's description that the crisis "faded away."[56] Soviet interference with air traffic in the city, the continued killing of escapees, and Soviet protests over the harassment of its personnel kept Berlin in the forefront of American concerns until the missile crisis in Cuba. Indeed many of the administration's reactions during the crisis betrayed the fear that the missiles in Cuba might be designed to gain concessions in Berlin. To that extent, the Cuban Missile crisis may well have been, in Marc Trachtenberg's phrase, "the final phase of the Berlin Crisis."[57]

Despite—or because of—Kennedy's successful handling of the Cuban crisis, Khrushchev continued to plead with him "to solve the German question because the next crisis, possibly of no lesser danger, can be caused by the German question."[58] Khrushchev may have known of Kennedy's irritation with Adenauer when he asked, "Should really you and we—two great states—submit willingly or unwillingly, our policy, the interests of our states to the old-aged man who both morally and physically is with one foot in grave?"[59] Whatever irritations the chancellor had caused him, Kennedy would not take the bait and criticize Adenauer. He told Khrushchev that his assertion that Adenauer controlled his policy missed "entirely the true nature of the problem that confronts us in Central Europe. For her the vital interests of many states are involved—on your side as well as ours."[60] A more confident Kennedy—confident in both his own leadership and America's military superiority—was still interested in a settlement, but could also rest more comfortably with the status quo in Berlin.

The Nuclear Question and de Gaulle

The stabilization of the status quo in Berlin was the most significant achievement of Kennedy's "Grand Design" for Europe, a policy that proved neither grand nor much of a design. Borrowed from the title of a book by the journalist Joseph Kraft, the Grand Design was a "vision of North America and Western Europe happily joined by policies and institutions in common pursuit of economic expansion and military defense."[61] Kennedy used a July 4 speech in Philadelphia to call for a new "Declaration of Interdependence" between the United States and

Western Europe. The administration contained many high officials, among them George Ball, Livingston Merchant, Thomas Finletter, Henry Owen, and Walt Rostow, who shared the conviction that the United States could best nurture the Atlantic relationship by playing a key role in the process of European unification. The "theologians," as they came to be called, shared the conviction that the key to future peace and stability was the peaceful integration of West Germany on terms of equality with other European nations. But the objectives of the group ran counter to the administration's new military strategy of "flexible response" and met powerful resistance in Western Europe.

"Flexible response" was Kennedy's attempt to deal with what he called the "absurdity" of resorting to all-out nuclear war in the event that one Russian soldier crossed into West Germany. In adopting this new doctrine, the administration assumed that the Soviet threat to Europe was real, but that it could also take the form of local, non-nuclear aggression. To provide the president with a range of choices, NATO needed to strengthen its conventional forces across the board.[62] Flexible response also extended to the nuclear realm, with the argument that America had to have a variety of nuclear war-fighting strategies, and not simply an all-out assault on Soviet military targets and cities. This would give the president more bargaining power and flexibility, and perhaps reduce casualties. In Acheson's report on Berlin, he also emphasized the need to obtain centralized control over nuclear forces, and emphasized the need to control any independent nuclear forces that the British or French might possess.[63] The report did allow that the Europeans could satisfy their nuclear desires through a "Multilateral Force" (MLF), provided that it operated under American control.[64]

Kennedy announced the new policy in a speech to the Canadian Parliament in Ottawa, stating that the United States would commit five Polaris submarines to the NATO command. He added that he looked "to the possibility of eventually establishing a NATO seaborne force, which would be truly multilateral in ownership and control, if this should be desired and found feasible by our allies, once NATO's non-nuclear goals have been achieved."[65] The last phrase, "once NATO's non-nuclear goals have been achieved," departed from Eisenhower's less demanding policy, and did not elicit much European enthusiasm.[66] Europeans were concerned that a buildup of conventional forces might tempt the United States to accept a limited war in Europe and be unwilling to use its nuclear deterrent against the Soviet Union. The Berlin crisis temporarily sidetracked the issue, but in November 1961, after Adenauer stated that NATO should have the authority to use nuclear weapons without prior authorization from the United States, Secretary of State Dean Rusk publicly reaffirmed the MLF offer. He told the NATO Ministerial Meeting the next month that the United States "considers that a multilateral force is the means of deploying MRBMs [medium range ballistic missiles] most consistent with NATO cohesion."[67] Only a few months later at another NATO meeting, Secretary of Defense Robert McNamara strongly condemned the British and French nuclear forces: "In short, limited nuclear capacities operating independently are dangerous, expensive, prone to obsolescence, and lacking credibility as a deterrent."[68] McNamara reaffirmed the Kennedy administration's support for the MLF, but his disparaging comments made it clear that the MLF was a political tactic rather than a military necessity.

Political concerns were always central to the MLF. On the one hand was the fear that with the British and the French developing national nuclear deterrents, could the Germans be kept from wanting to follow the same path? As they did with the European Defense Community, Americans officials devised a scheme that would keep the Germans from the sense of discrimination.[69] To forestall the "resentment that might develop from Germany's continued exclusion from the nuclear club," the United States proposed the MLF, thus giving Germany the appearance of equality.[70] Along with this purpose came the hope that the MLF, sponsored and partially financed by the United States, might prove more attractive to the British and the French than their expensive national nuclear deterrents. Finally, the "theologians" hoped that the MLF would spur the drive toward European unity. They hoped to use the offer to share control of nuclear weapons as a way to encourage the Europeans to create a single unified political executive that could share authority with an American President. With such an executive, the United States might someday hand over its veto over control of nuclear weapons. (Schlesinger notes that Kennedy never really contemplated giving up the American veto, but the theologians hoped that he or some future president might be so convinced.)[71]

The MLF that Kennedy offered Europe underwent considerable change from the time of the Bowie report and Eisenhower's proposals. Kennedy sharply curtailed the number of nuclear warheads for the MLF—the Europeans would control only 4 percent of the deterrent stationed in the NATO area—and Admiral Hyman Rickover's opposition had prevented the MLF from consisting of the more militarily useful submarines. What was left was a proposed fleet of 25 surface ships each carrying nuclear armed Polaris missiles. The ships' crews were to come from at least three different NATO countries, with no single nation supplying enough men to control the ship itself. However, even though the Navy concluded that the proposal was technically feasible, skepticism about its workability and opposition in Western Europe remained.

This American scheme for Europe met its primary opponent in the legendary French leader, General Charles de Gaulle. When Kennedy reaffirmed his opposition to de Gaulle's proposed tripartite directorate of NATO, de Gaulle's determination "to disengage France, not from the Atlantic alliance, which I intended to maintain by way of ultimate precaution, but from the integration realized by NATO under American command."[72] Critical to this independence was de Gaulle's drive to develop the *force de frappe*, an independent nuclear deterrent.[73] But De Gaulle's assertion of independence from the United States involved not only nuclear weapons, but also expanded ties to the Soviet Union, China, and Eastern Europe, and an aggressive courting of Adenauer's Germany. During the Berlin crisis the general took a public stand that was tougher than Kennedy's, arguing that no concessions should be made to the Russians. De Gaulle encouraged Adenauer's growing doubts about America's reliability, hoping to use the Franco-German relationship to assert France's leadership in Europe. Adenauer, whose goal of reconciliation with France was a lifelong dream, accepted "the slightly unequal aspect of the contract" in return for France's support for Germany's defense and its eventual reunification.[74]

The British were also unwilling to play the role that advocates of the MLF had set for them. In the face of McNamara's harsh criticism, Harold Macmillan was determined to maintain Britain's independent nuclear deterrent, something that represented "a major part of his political platform."[75] To modernize this deterrent, the British had counted on the Skybolt missile, an early version of what would later be called cruise missiles. Repeated failures in the testing program led McNamara to cancel development, precipitating the worst crisis in U.S.-British relations since the Suez crisis of 1956. The theologians hoped that this would lead to the British scrapping their nuclear deterrent and joining the MLF. When George Ball tried to make the case for Britain's joining the MLF, Macmillan replied disdainfully, "You don't expect our chaps to share their grog with Turks, do you?"[76] At the Nassau conference in December 1962 Kennedy decided against the theologians, opting to help the politically embarrassed Macmillan by offering him the Polaris submarine instead. Knowing that such a demonstration of the Anglo-American special relationship would infuriate de Gaulle, Kennedy made a similar offer of Polaris to the French.[77] De Gaulle, who had supported Kennedy during the Cuban Missile crisis but saw the event as confirmation of his view that America would act irrespective of Europe's interests, was not about to be persuaded. The French leader viewed the offer as too little too late, and would use the Anglo-American deal as a pretext to veto British entry into the Common Market.

Kennedy was disappointed over the general's action, as he had hoped that Britain's entry would produce "an outward-looking Europe with a strong American connection."[78] However, only a week later, in an action that would shock Washington, the French and Germans signed a Friendship Treaty, which committed the two nations to close coordination in all matters of foreign policy and seemed to augur a new political configuration in Europe. "Wild rumors" circulated that the treaty would lead Bonn to "negotiate with Moscow for a whole new European arrangement."[79] Some speculated that a Paris-Bonn deal with Moscow might lead to a neutral and reunited Germany, and the end of NATO. To head off such an arrangement, Kennedy pushed the MLF concept, telling the NSC that "even though de Gaulle is opposed, . . . a multilateral force will increase our influence in Europe and provide a way to guide NATO and keep it strong."[80] Kennedy told a conservative critic that with "the political instability of so many European nations, I am even less willing to leave the decision of nuclear peace or war in the hands of myriad individual nations and leaders . . . "and that what the United States sought was a *"new arrangement which maintains the indivisibility of the nuclear deterrent while giving the Europeans real participation in its maintenance and management."*[81] The president sent a mission to Europe headed by Livingston Merchant to give "new impetus to the multilateral force project."[82] The president remained concerned that America be seen as responding to European concerns, especially German concerns about equal treatment. Walt Rostow acknowledged that, "It may seem odd to create such an elaborate structure merely to solve the problem of Germany's nuclear role," but then listed the Marshall Plan, NATO, the Schuman Plan and the Common Market, and concluded "the truth is that most of our creative innovations in European policy since 1945 have been more or less directly the result of efforts to solve aspects of the German problem."[83]

Still, doubts remained about the MLF. The German situation seemed less pressing, especially after more Atlanticist-oriented German leaders inserted a clause in the Franco-German treaty that made it clear Germany would not go back on any of its multilateral commitments.[84] Kennedy himself expressed doubts when he told a news conference, "It may be that when the proposal is examined in detail they [the Europeans] may not feel it provides sufficient additional security to warrant additional expenditures of money, and may decide that the present arrangement is satisfactory. That, we, of course, would accept."[85] McGeorge Bundy warned Kennedy before his June 1963 trip to Europe that the MLF had "only grudging support among the very people in whose interest the force has been designed." Bundy played on one of Kennedy's chief concerns when he expressed the fear that the U.S. might appear as the "nuclear rearmers of Germany," and this might affect the prospects for success of negotiations for a nuclear test ban treaty with the Soviets. Surveying the situation in Europe, Bundy took issue with the optimism of the theologians and concluded that although it was "essential that we not back away too sharply from the MLF," the U.S. should "take off any sense of deadline," widening the proposal to consider other goals such as "consultation, control, alternative weapons systems, coordination of existing nuclear forces in the West and non-proliferation."[86] Bundy clearly hoped that the MLF would fail, but that the onus would fall on the Europeans and not the American government.

Kennedy's triumphal European trip of June 1963, with its famous "Ich bin ein Berliner," speech and the extraordinary demonstration of his popularity in Europe, yielded only the most modest of European commitments to pursue the MLF. Though the president did not kill the proposal before November 1963, he did hope that it would fade away.[87] Kennedy's own efforts were directed at fulfilling the promise of his American University speech, and its call to "reexamine our attitude toward the Cold War," recognizing the Russian people "for their many achievements," and recognizing as well that "no nation had ever suffered more than the Soviet Union during the war." The most basic link between the two countries was "that we all inhabit this small planet. We all breathe the same air. We all cherish our children's future. And we are all mortal."[88]

The signing of the test-ban treaty with Britain and the Soviet Union in August 1963 was the first achievement of these small steps toward détente, and it unsettled some European governments. De Gaulle denounced the treaty and refused to sign, while the Adenauer government, in its last months in office, expressed concern that East German agreement to the treaty might imply recognition. The Germans continued to fear "their interests would be overridden in deals between the two superpowers."[89] When those concerns were satisfied, they called the accord "a partial success," hoping that it might lead to further negotiations on such issues as reunification. (The Bundestag would approve the treaty in June 1964.)[90]

Kennedy's assassination on November 22, 1963, stunned Europeans, eliciting an extraordinary outpouring of grief and emotion. Kennedy's popularity in Europe had been at its highest point shortly before the assassination, with some 83 percent in Germany, and similar figures elsewhere, expressing approval of his leadership. Surveys later demonstrated that most Europeans felt like they had lost their own leader, "their Super Chancellor." Kennedy's youth, charm, and style appealed to a Europe led by octogenarian leaders from the war years. Europeans realized that the United States held Western Europe's fate in its hands, and this created a powerful bond, a sense of shared fate. The American Ambassador to London, David Bruce, noted that "recognition of [Kennedy's] position as leader of the free world was, at last, ungrudgingly accorded him."[91]

Lyndon Johnson, the MLF, and Détente

With such a traumatic transition of power, Lyndon Johnson sought to preserve a continuity of policy with his slain predecessor. As vice president he had played a restrained and uncomfortable role in the world of Camelot. Sent to Berlin in August 1961 to affirm the U.S. commitment to Berlin, Johnson pledged American "lives, fortunes, and sacred honor," to its defense.[92] Johnson had been deeply moved by the outpouring of public support in the divided city and, like many Americans in this period, struck by the gratitude of Germans who had only recently been America's enemies.[93] When he was vice president, he had brought Adenauer down to his ranch, leading to the rather incongruous sight of the aged Rhinelander in an oversized cowboy hat. As one of the most successful Senate leaders of his generation and an acknowledged master in the art of politics and power, Johnson believed that "the global political elite constituted a club like the Senate, not even as big."[94]

One of the first leaders Johnson met was Ludwig Erhard, Konrad Adenauer's successor and the man given credit for Germany's "Economic Miracle." Erhard's accession to the chancellorship was a triumph for the "Atlanticists" in the conservative Christian Democratic party over the Gaullist faction. That group was led by Adenauer and the dynamic Franz Josef Strauss, the former Defense Minister whose outspoken insistence on obtaining nuclear weapons for the German army had worried foreign observers.[95] Erhard was firmly pro-American and determined to court Johnson, and was pleased when an early meeting in Texas was arranged. Johnson, for his part, knew that Erhard was "anxious to build up his own image in Germany as a world statesman and international political leader," and that he attached "the highest political importance to his visit."[96]

At the meeting the two leaders seemed very much in sync, both personally and politically. Johnson told Erhard that the United States was "going down the road to peace, with or without others, and asked the chancellor to be more flexible toward the Soviet Union. With the first opening of the Berlin Wall for Christmas visits, the possibilities for a relaxation of tensions seemed auspicious. For his part Erhard was eager to distinguish himself from Adenauer's hardline policies, and to "search for new paths toward East-West agreements."[97] Johnson's early life had been spent in a part of southwest Texas which had drawn many German settlers, and he believed he had a special understanding of Germans. He took Erhard out deer hunting, and then to a number of German-American communities near the ranch. At the end of the visit Erhard exulted to a German reporter, "I love President Johnson, and he loves me."[98]

The MLF did not play a significant role in these talks, though Johnson did raise it with Macmillan's successor, Prime Minister Sir Alec Douglas-Home. In LBJ's briefing papers for the visit, Rusk urged him to tell Douglas-Home that "we intend to move forward with the MLF and hope Britain will join," adding in a handwritten note, "Important— if you don't say it, they'll claim the U.S. doesn't care."[99] Rusk's comment indicates that in the vacuum after Kennedy's death, State Department supporters stepped forward to urge Johnson to renew Kennedy's commitment to the nuclear sharing project. At a critical meeting on April 10, 1964, they presented the case for the MLF to the new president. George Ball argued that the MLF would "give Germans a legitimate role in the defense of the alliance, but on a leash." Thomas Finletter, the U.S. Ambassador to NATO, reported that the Europeans had the impression Johnson wasn't interested in the project. He argued that the "U.S. had to stop being diffident about the MLF."[100] The only major reservations about the MLF came from William Foster, head of the Arms Control and Disarmament Agency, who worried that the MLF would damage chance for a nuclear nonproliferation treaty.[101]

Johnson took up the challenge that Finletter presented. The president was most interested in the argument that Germany would have to be treated as an equal with regard to nuclear weapons. In characteristic language, Johnson told his advisers, "the Germans have gone off the reservation twice in our lifetimes, and we've got to make sure that doesn't happen again, that they don't go berserk."[102] Rostow reinforced Johnson's fears when he told him, "if the multilateral solution is shot down now, as it was in 1932, the swing to the Right is all too likely to repeat itself."[103] Johnson drew his historical analogies from an even more distant past, fearing that failure to give Germany a respectable role in nuclear defense might lead them "to break out again like Kaiser Bill and get us into World War III."[104] Johnson was even willing to set a year-end deadline for signing a treaty, and in a speech to newspaper editors later that month announced, "We support the establishment of a multilateral nuclear force composed of those nations that wish to participate."[105]

Johnson's deadline brought the MLF to the center of American diplomacy toward Europe, with ambassadors urged to press their host countries for approval, and the USIA seeking the dispel the impression that the MLF was a bilateral U.S.-German arrangement.[106] But while the U.S. pressure elicited more support for the proposal, it also served to motivate the opposition. As early as June 1964 David Klein, an aide to Bundy, argued that the administration should "take time to assess MLF developments since April," as "the political facts of European life were not candidly and frankly stated."[107] As the deadline approached, French attacks on the "two horned and apparently powerless body" of MLF increased.[108] The Russians also stepped up their criticism, repeating their attack on giving the German "revanchists" nuclear weapons and contending that the MLF would doom a nuclear nonproliferation treaty.[109]

After President Johnson's landslide victory, a conference was arranged with the new British Prime Minister Harold Wilson, whose Labour Party held a four-seat margin in the House of Commons. Labour had opposed an independent British nuclear deterrent while in opposition, but once in power began to reverse itself. The MLF remained unpopular, and in the weeks before Wilson's visit, Bundy established a special committee, composed of himself, Ball, Rusk, and McNamara, to work out a negotiating position. Bundy was particularly interested in evaluating the European prospects for MLF, and suspected, as Klein had warned months earlier, that the picture being presented by MLF advocates was seriously flawed. As new information came in, Johnson's doubts about the project grew. The president was struck by the assessment that German support for the MLF was lukewarm and that one of the reasons Germany supported it was "it also believes that we want it very badly."[110] Henry Kissinger told Bundy that "it is simply wrong to allege that the future orientation of the Federal Republic depends on pushing through the MLF."[111] More important, Johnson began to canvas the Senate, where he found little support for the proposal. Conservatives disliked any sharing of the nuclear trigger, while liberals believed the MLF "would further imperil the prospects for arms control and divide the NATO alliance, all without adding to the security of the United States."[112] Wilson arrived in the

United States with a compromise proposal—an Atlantic Nuclear Force (ANF), which replaced the mixed-manned ships with various national components, thereby preserving British ownership of its V-Bomber and Polaris fleets. The Prime Minister might have been prepared to deal on the MLF, but Johnson decided that there was no good reason to continue to push the idea. "If Europe isn't for it," the president told a small group of his advisers, "then the hell with it." [113] American pressure for the MLF would end, and although the Europeans were welcome to devise their own solution, the MLF would no longer be the centerpiece of America's NATO policy. To make sure that everyone got the message, Johnson deliberately leaked his directive ending the American efforts to James Reston of the *New York Times*.

The demise of the MLF signalled two important changes toward Western Europe, both initiated during the Kennedy administration and confirmed under Johnson. The first was a disengagement from the post-1945 intensive preoccupation with European issues, and a reluctance to propose solutions to such problems as European unity and the German question. Kennedy had come to this attitude when he and the Belgian leader Henri Spaak in May 1963 that "the whole debate about an atomic force in Europe . . . is really useless, because Berlin is secure, and Europe as a whole is well protected. What really matters at this point is the rest of the world."[114]

For Johnson, the "rest of the world" would include the Dominican Republic, where the United States landed forces in early 1965, and more important, Southeast Asia, with the beginning of bombing raids on North Vietnam in February 1965 and the increase in American troop strength. The escalation of the war in Vietnam served to complete America's alienation from de Gaulle's France, as the general continued his independent course, recognizing the People's Republic of China and condemning American policy. The final step came in 1966 when the general officially pulled France out of NATO's military organization. Johnson, whose relationship with de Gaulle never recovered from a misunderstanding they had at Kennedy's funeral, was stung by the attacks on his Vietnam policy but avoided personal criticism.[115] When the demand for withdrawal of American forces from France came, Johnson stifled the urge of his advisers to hit back sharply, fearing this would only confirm de Gaulle's claim of American domination. The president told his aides, "When a man asks you to leave his house, you don't argue; you get your hat and go."[116]

The second change came in confirming the greater emphasis toward détente with Soviet Union over solving internal alliance disputes. Fears about the effects of the MLF on nuclear proliferation and arms control negotiations were important to the opposition in the United States. The Johnson administration was determined to pursue these negotiations, as well as encourage the West Germans in what German Foreign Minister Gerhard Schroeder called their pursuit of a "relationship of confidence" with Eastern Europe and a more realistic view of East Germany.[117] Johnson told Erhard that he believed that a policy of détente was the best approach to German reunification and progress with the Soviets.[118] However, Johnson's argument was, at best, a partial truth. The State Department's Policy Planning Council undertook a reexamination of American policy toward Germany, and concluded that although negotiations served Western interests in other ways, "a settlement based on the reunification of Germany in freedom cannot in the foreseeable future be obtained." The Soviet and Polish opposition to reunification rested on "more than ideology; they believe that the status quo is essential to their national interests." Unless there were "profound internal political change," even an end to the Cold War, they were likely to continue to hold these views. While urging a strengthening of American cooperation with Germany, the report called for "a sound and candid relationship" which urged Bonn to develop a "more active Eastern policy." It concluded that such a policy would enable the West "to live with a divided Germany indefinitely if necessary."[119]

It would be wrong to believe that the change in American policy caused German leaders to pursue an *Ostpolitik*, though Willy Brandt, the Socialist mayor of Berlin, argued that the American acceptance of the status quo in Berlin pushed him in that direction. To some extent, McGhee argued, the United States and West Germany were thinking along parallel lines about improving relations with the East. The Germans continued to fear that their interests might be sacrificed by the United States in its pursuit of such items as a nonproliferation treaty. Bonn hoped that an official renunciation of the MLF would be a bargaining chip for reunification.[120] (The major concession the Germans gained in the nuclear field was McNamara's Nuclear Planning Group within NATO, which gave the allies, especially the Germans, a greater insight and input into allied discussions of military strategy and nuclear weapons.) Despite German misgivings, the Johnson administration pushed ahead toward détente. On October 7, 1966, Johnson told a conference of editorial writers that "we must improve the East-West environment in order to achieve the unification of Germany in the context of a larger, peaceful, and prosperous Europe."[121] The author of the speech, Zbigniew Brzezinski, modestly believed that it "fundamentally reversed the priorities of the United States in Western Europe."[122]

This exaggeration aside, the speech was an important signal, and expressed "a doctrine congenial in Europe, different from de Gaulle's, without quarreling."[123] Johnson also affirmed that the United States respected "the integrity of a nation's boundary lines," and encouraged the removal of territorial and border disputes, a none-too-subtle reference to Germany's refusal to recognize the Oder-Neisse line and the loss of its eastern territories. McGhee had sought a last minute change that would have softened the reference, but the State Department insisted it remain, to provide "gentle support to those people in Germany who want slowly to back away from a self-defeating position."[124] The administration's priorities were the Nonproliferation Treaty, which was signed in 1968, and a strategic arms control agreement with the Soviets, which Johnson discussed with Soviet Premier Kosygin in June 1967 in Glassboro, New Jersey. By December 1967 NATO adopted the Harmel Report on the future of the alliance and affirmed that "military security and a policy of détente are not contradictory but complementary."[125]

Johnson and the Trilateral Negotiations[126]

The pressures encouraging détente were not solely political in nature.[127] Back in 1961 Kennedy had told advisers that the two things that worried him most were "nuclear war and the payments deficit,"[128] and in his first meeting with Adenauer, the president appealed to him to "find some way to ease the balance-of-payments burden."[129] In November 1961, they reached an agreement whereby Germany, over a two-year period, would buy American military equipment and services worth $1.35 billion. The "offset" agreements were renewed for successive two year periods through to 1966, and the payments "approximate[d] American military expenditures in the Federal Republic."[130] Attempts to negotiate a similar agreement with France failed, though the British were able to get the Germans to agree to help offset partially the cost of their own British Army on the Rhine (BAOR).

By 1966 the escalation of the war in Vietnam had increased the payments deficit dramatically and brought a crisis over NATO's future. In mid-July, Senator Mike Mansfield warned Johnson that unless American forces in Europe were reduced, he and other Democrats would pressure him to do so by Senate resolution. Problems in the British economy kept the pound sterling under severe pressure, culminating in a run on the pound in July 1966. In early 1966, the German economy faced its first severe recession of the postwar period, and the Erhard government faced a large budget deficit. Under pressure to curb government spending, especially the expensive—and questionable—purchases of American military equipment,[131] Germany was badly lagging in fulfilling its offset orders.[132] Erhard told Washington that he needed significant relief from the offset payments, but with the French withdrawal, both Washington and London feared that cutbacks would weaken the alliance. They wanted more, not fewer, payments.[133]

In late August 1966 the United States suggested a form of "Trilateral Negotiations" between the U.S., Britain, and Germany to resolve the offset problem. Erhard preferred coming to Washington, as McGhee warned Johnson, to "throw himself on your mercy, citing Germany's past performance as a loyal ally."[134] Johnson liked Erhard, but the pressures of Vietnam had already affected their relationship. At their December 1965 meeting, Johnson had pressed Erhard for more German nonmilitary assistance in Vietnam. McGhee later recalled how "the tall rangy figure of Johnson towered over the comparatively small figure of the chancellor," threatening that, "Now we are going to find out who are friends are, . . . now was the time for Germany to pay us back." Erhard appeared uncomfortable, "verging on fright," with the change in the man "who had taken him touring the ranch only two years previously."[135]

Johnson was more restrained at their September 1966 meeting, aware that Erhard was in trouble, and hoping to avoid any responsibility for his demise.[136] Press reports made it clear that Erhard "badly needs a success at the White House,"[137] but Johnson, facing strong resistance from Secretary of Defense McNamara and the Treasury Department, could not allow a "stretching out" of the offset payments.[138] Although Erhard implied that his successor might "take a different view of loyalty to the United States," he put up little resistance.[139] When he returned to Germany and proposed a tax increase to meet the offset payment, Erhard's government collapsed. The chancellor's resignation set off a vehement "wave of criticism of the U.S. . . . so excessive as to hint at a basic instability in the German political psyche."[140] The new government consisted of a "Grand Coalition" between the Christian Democrats and the Social Democratic Party. Kurt Kiesinger from the Gaullist faction of the CDU became chancellor, with SPD leader Willy Brandt taking over as foreign minister.

To handle the Trilateral negotiations, Johnson appointed John J. McCloy, the former American High Commissioner in Germany.[141] McCloy strongly opposed significant troop reductions, and argued against the idea that the level of forces should depend on the offset payments. Supported by the State Department, McCloy convinced Johnson to detach American force levels from the offset costs, and to accept a solution that would allow any balance of payments gains and losses to be neutralized by financial transactions. In a meeting on March 1, 1967, Johnson emphasized to McCloy his political problems at home: "The Congressional position is three to one for substantial cuts; the only one who will slug it out and hold out is [Senate Republican leader Everett] Dirksen; he has German grandparents as I have; the rest of them will run just like turkeys," Johnson told McCloy, "I know my Germans. You know I lived in Fredericksburg; they are great people; but by God they are as stingy as Hell." Johnson emphasized how critically important it was for the Germans "to put something in the family pot." They would have to help the British as well, as a British withdrawal would encourage demands for a similar American action. To McCloy's warning that "you are on the verge of the collapse of the Alliance," Johnson replied, "I can't do it alone."[142]

Johnson didn't have to. The Germans agreed to purchase and hold some $500 million in U.S. Government medium-term securities and, even more importantly, agreed to make public their intention to refrain from buying gold.[143] The U.S withdrew one division and 96 aircraft, although for appearance's sake, these forces remained committed to NATO. The British proved more difficult, and the Americans had to increase their own spending in Britain to help the Germans reach a 90 percent offset of the foreign exchange costs of the BAOR. McCloy wrote Johnson that "although from time to time the trading instincts of your Fredericksburg Germans cropped out in the F.R.G. representatives, I am not certain that the subtler but still acquisitive instincts of the British are any less formidable."[144]

The Trilateral Agreements of May 1967 served as stopgap measure, temporarily holding the alliance together through a serious crisis and the adjustment to France's withdrawal. They gave Johnson the weapon he needed to fend off Congressional challenges. When Senator Stuart Symington a Missouri Democrat and an ally of Mansfield, proposed cutting U.S. forces in Europe by 50,000 in June 1968, Johnson rallied his forces, arguing that "we do not want to cut out any of our muscle, . . . [and] open another front by drawing down [our] forces in Europe."[145] The Soviet suppression of the Prague Spring in August 1968 gave Europe a "severe case of angst."[146] It also gave NATO a much needed "shot in the arm," and slowed the demand for further troop withdrawals.[147]

The Trilateral Agreements also underlined the deterioration in America's power that had been caused by the war in Vietnam. More important, the intensely unpopular war did incalculable damage to

America's image in Western Europe. The conflict occasioned student demonstrations in all the European capitals and attacks on symbols of the United States. The prestige of the United States in Europe, at its height in the early 1960s, reached its nadir during the Vietnam era, with one survey in May 1967 finding some 80 percent of the Europeans opposing American policy.[148] By 1968 Lyndon Johnson, who had once postponed a European tour because of a fear his reception would not match Kennedy's, could not travel in the United States without violent protests, let alone venture abroad.

Conclusions

From the perspective of American prestige in Europe, a contemporary observer in 1969 could be forgiven for seeing the 1960s as an unmitigated disaster for the United States. However, the actual outcome of the Kennedy and Johnson policies was more positive than it appeared at the time. The two presidents recognized the legitimate security concerns of the Soviet Union and Eastern European countries, something which Eisenhower and Dulles were reluctant to acknowledge, at least publicly. The Cold War was successfully "stabilized" in Western Europe without bloodshed, and only through such stabilization could the conflict "evolve" into a more peaceful competition, and one in which the West's advantages became more apparent. Of critical importance, West Germany was both pushed and encouraged to begin a course of reconciliation with its Eastern neighbors and the Soviet Union. Certainly there were those in Germany who wanted to move in that direction, but because of the enormous role played by the United States in the Federal Republic, these groups might have found it far more difficult without American support. The Atlantic Alliance also survived both de Gaulle's challenge and the often misguided enthusiasms of its own advocates. American power declined, but this was inevitable, even if hastened by the Vietnam war. And from the perspective of the 1990s, it is worth recognizing that the harsh political atmosphere of the United States in the early 1960s, with rigid anti-Communism joined with powerful right-wing political forces, might have brought a far worse outcome than Kennedy and Johnson achieved. Kennedy and Johnson sought "victory" in the Cold War, but they defined that victory in very different terms than many of their contemporaries. Despite all the recent political rhetoric about "who won the Cold War," it is worth recognizing that the Kennedy-Johnson years helped set the nation on the road to a strategy that balanced the

American people's strong desire for stability and peace with its nuclear-armed rival, and their underlying sense of outrage about the division of the continent, and hope that it would succumb eventually to the tide of freedom. We have far too many examples in history of leaders who did not achieve such a balance to dismiss this achievement too quickly.

NOTES

1. Frank Costigliola, "The Pursuit of Atlantic Community: Nuclear Arms, Dollars, and Berlin," in Thomas Paterson, ed., *Kennedy's Quest for Victory* (New York, 1989), pp. 24 and 56.

2. Michael R. Beschloss, *The Crisis Years* (New York, 1991), p. 702.

3. For the best treatment see Larry Berman, *Lyndon Johnson's War* (New York, 1990).

4. For example, Beschloss, *The Crisis Years*, p. 702.

5. United States Department of State, *Documents on Germany, 1944–1985* (Washington, 1986), pp. 552–559.

6. *Time*, April 4, 1960, p. 52.

7. Beschloss, *The Crisis Years*, p. 173. Research in the recently opened East German archives indicates that the East German communist leader, Walter Ulbricht, played a very significant role in the Berlin crisis, even inititating a number of the confrontations with the Western Allies. Letters indicate that Khrushchev felt the need to caution Ulbricht from acting too provocatively. Hope M. Harrison, "Inside the SED Archives: A Researcher's Diary," *Cold War International History Project Bulletin* (Fall 1992), p. 31.

8. Stephen Ambrose, *Eisenhower the President*, Vol. 2, (New York, 1984), p. 503.

9. The best discussion of this remains Catherine Kelleher, *Germany and the Politics of Nuclear Weapons* (New York, 1975), esp. pp. 21–29, and 92–94.

10. Dwight D. Eisenhower Presidential Library, Abilene, Kansas, Box 9, White House Office, Robert Bowie, "The North Atlantic Nations: Tasks for the 1960s," August 1960.

11. For a discussion of the Bowie Report and its implications, see John Steinbruner, *The Cybernetic Theory of Decision* (Princeton, N.J., 1974), pp. 188–198.

12. The balance of payments question is treated fully in Chapter 3 above

13. Gregory Treverton, *The Dollar Drain and American Forces in Germany* (Athens, Ohio, 1978), p. 33.

14. John F. Kennedy, "A Democrat Looks at Foreign Affairs," *Foreign Affairs*, October 1957, p. 6.

15. John F. Kennedy Presidential Library, Boston, Massachusetts, Pre-Presidential Senate Files, Box 559, Memo, Holborn to JFK, April 8, 1959.

16. McGeorge Bundy, *Danger and Survival* (New York, 1988), p. 489.

17. JFKL, National Security File, Box 75, Memo, Owen to Bundy, May 17, 1961.

18. *Documents on Germany*, pp. 723–727.

19. Beschloss, *The Crisis Years*, p. 175.

20. Arthur Schlesinger, *A Thousand Days* (New York, 1965), p. 353.

21. Ibid., p. 354.

22. Declassified Documents Collection (DDC) 1985/2547, Dean Acheson, Memo for the President, April 3, 1961.

23. JFKL, NSF, Box 75–81, Bundy to JFK, April 4, 1961.

24. Beschloss, p. 243.

25. JFKL, POF, Box 65, Schlesinger, Memo for the President, April 6, 1961.

26. JFKL, NSF, Box 75–81, Kissinger, Memo for Bundy, July 14, 1961.

27. JFKL, POF, Box 116a, Memo, Sorenson to JFK, July 17, 1961.

28. JFKL, NSF, Box 75–81, Roger Hilsman to Kohler, June 30, 1961.

29. JFKL, NSF, Box 82–91, Memo, Bundy to JFK, August 11, 1961.

30. Beschloss, *The Crisis Years*, pp. 215–217.

31. Kenneth O'Donnell and David Powers with Joe McCarthy, *Johnny We Hardly Knew Ye* (Boston, 1972), pp. 292, 298–300.

32. JFKL, NSF, Box 82–91, Memo, Bundy to JFK, "NSC discussion of July 17, 1961," July 24, 1961.

33. JFKL, POF, Box 116a, Memo, Sorenson to JFK, July 17, 1961.

34. Beschloss, *The Crisis Years*, p. 239

35. JFKL, POF, Box 116a, J. W. Fulbright to Kenneth O'Donnell, June 7, 1961.

36. George H. Gallup, *The Gallup Poll*, Vol. 3 (New York, 1972), p. 1729.

37. *Documents on Germany*, pp. 762–765.

38. Ibid., p. 765.

39. Beschloss, *The Crisis Years*, p. 264.

40. JFKL, POF, Box 116a, Memo, Heller to JFK, August 2, 1961.

41. JFKL, NSF, Box 82–91, Kennedy to Rusk, August 21, 1961.

42. JFKL, NSF, Box 82–91, Carl Kaysen, "Thoughts on Germany," August 22, 1961.

43. JFKL, NSF, Box 82–91, Harriman to JFK, September 1, 1961.

44. Beschloss, *The Crisis Years*, p. 241.

45. JFKL, POF, Box 116a, Adenauer to JFK, October 4, 1961.

46. Harry S. Truman Presidential Library, Independence, Missouri, Papers of Dean Acheson, Box 85, Memo of conversation with Grewe, October 11, 1961.

47. JFKL, POF, Box 116a, Bundy to JFK, November 21, 1961.

48. Beschloss, *The Crisis Years*, p. 341

49. The best account of this confrontation is Raymond L. Garthoff, "Berlin 1961: The Record Corrected," *Foreign Policy*, 84, Fall 1991, pp. 142–156.

50. Beschloss, *The Crisis Years*, pp. 330–331. Beschloss argues that the Gilpatric speech "provocatively undermined Khrushchev's position in the Kremlin and in the world," and was a key factor in leading to the decision to deploy missiles in Cuba. However, his evidence for the importance of the speech to Khrushchev is very thin.

51. JFKL, NSF, Box 75–81, Kaysen memo, March 3, 1962.

52. *Documents on Germany*, p. 814.

53. *Time*, May 18, 1962, p. 22

54. JFKL, NSF, Box 75–81, Hilsman to Rusk, August 3, 1962.

55. Acheson to Truman, September 21, 1961, quoted in Marc Trachtenberg, *History and Strategy* (Princeton, N.J., 1991), p. 230.

56. Schlesinger, *A Thousand Days*, p. 369.

57. Trachtenberg, *History and Strategy*, p. 231.

58. National Security Archive, Washington, D.C., Cuban Missile Crisis Documents, Khrushchev to JFK, October 30, 1962.

59. NSA, Cuban documents, Khrushchev to JFK, November 22, 1962.

60. NSA, Cuban documents, JFK to Khrushchev, December 14, 1962

61. Schlesinger, *A Thousand Days*, p. 769.

62. John Yoo, "Three Faces of Hegemony," Senior Honors Thesis, Harvard University, 1989, p. 60. This is one of the best treatments of the MLF episode based on the documents now available.

63. Acheson's thinking on this point had been strongly influenced by Albert Wohlstetter, whose work for the RAND Corporation on strategic nuclear policy had identified him as one of the leading civilian analysts. Steinbruner, *Cybernetic Theory of Decision*, pp. 201–203.

64. JFKL, NSF, Box 221, Dean Acheson, "A Review of North Atlantic Problems for the Future," March 1, 1961.

65. Lyndon B. Johnson Presidential Library, Austin, Texas, NSF, Box 23, "Early History of the MLF," undated.

66. Schlesinger, *A Thousand Days*, p. 778.

67. LBJL, NSF, Box 23, "Early History of MLF," undated.

68. *New York Times*, June 7, 1962. This contains a reprint of McNamara's speech at the University of Michigan, the unclassified record of his Athens talk.

69. For the American role in the European Defense Community, see Thomas A. Schwartz, *America's Germany* (Cambridge, Mass., 1991), pp. 210–234.

70. George Ball, *The Past Has Another Pattern* (New York, 1982), p. 260.

71. Schlesinger, *A Thousand Days*, p. 797.

72. Charles de Gaulle, *Memoirs of Hope: Renewal and Endeavor*, translated by Terence Kilmartin (New York, 1971), p. 202.

73. The French nuclear forces in the early 1960s possessed great destructive power but were extremely few in number, and as late as the 1980s, McGeorge Bundy estimated that they, along with the British and Chinese, constituted only a small fraction of the more than 50,000 nuclear warheads in existence. Bundy, p. 584.

74. Jean Lacouture, *De Gaulle: The Ruler, 1945–1970*, trans. Alan Sheridan (New York, 1991), p. 335.

75. Alistair Horne, *Harold Macmillan, 1957–1986: Volume 2* (New York, 1989), p. 433.

76. Ball, *Past Has Another Pattern*, p. 267.

77. Horne, *Macmillan*, p. 444. Horne notes that a "key difference [between

the offer to the British and the one to the French] was, of course, that while Britain was capable of making her own nuclear warheads for Polaris France was not, and was not now being offered the essential know-how by Kennedy."

78. JFKL, POF, Box 116, Bundy to JFK, January 30, 1963.

79. Ball, *Past Has Another Pattern*, p. 271.

80. "Remarks of President Kennedy to the National Security Council Meeting of January 22, 1963," CDDS 1986;2274, quoted in Yoo, "Three Faces of Hegemony," p. 73.

81. JFKL, POF, Box 31, JFK to Clare Booth Luce, February 17, 1963.

82. JFKL, NSF, Box 75–81, Memo of Conversation, MLF, March 21, 1963.

83. JFKL, POF, Box 65, Memo, Rostow to JFK, February 19, 1963. The Schuman Plan, proposed by French Foreign Minister Robert Schuman in May 1950, called for the merging of the German and French coal and steel industries. Two years later, the Euopean Coal and Steel Community accomplished this goal, in a treaty ratified by Germany, France, Italy, the Netherlands, Belgium, and Luxembourg.

84. Frank Ninkovich, *Germany and the United States* (Boston, 1988), p. 144.

85. *Newsweek*, March 25, 1963, p. 48.

86. LBJL, NSF, Box 23, Bundy to JFK, "The MLF and the European Tour," June 15, 1963.

87. Yoo, "Three Faces of Hegemony," p. 74

88. "The Strategy of Peace," June 10, 1963, *"Let the Word Go Forth": The Speeches, Statements and Writings of John F. Kennedy, 1947–1963*, ed. Theodore Sorenson (New York, 1988), pp. 282–290.

89. *Newsweek*, August 5, 1963, p. 19.

90. George McGhee, the U.S. Ambassador to Germany from 1963 to 1968, estimated that such issues of German confidence in the United States arose "on an average of every two to three months and typically involved US force levels in Germany, the reunification issue, American statements that implied any lessening of confidence in Germany, or the importance the US attached to its relations with the Federal Republic." George McGhee, *At the Creation of a New Germany* (New Haven, 1989), p.92.

91. Costigliola, "The Pursuit of Atlantic Community," p. 24.

92. Rostow argues that he deliberately wrote Johnson's strong words in the post-Wall atmosphere to leave no doubt that the United States would stay in Berlin. LBJL, Walt Rostow, Oral History, p. 9.

93. Costigliola, "The Pursuit of Atlantic Community," p. 43.

94. Richard Barnet, *The Alliance* (New York, 1983), p. 237.

95. The Russians thought Strauss, "the most aggressive-minded man in West Germany." Beschloss, p. 222.

96. LBJL, NSF, Box 190, Memo, Rusk to LBJ, December 26, 1963.

97. *Time*, January 10, 1964, p. 23.

98. Barnet, *The Alliance*, p. 240.

99. LBJL, NSF Country File, Box 211, Rusk to LBJ, February 7, 1964.

100. LBJL, NSF Subject File, Box 23, Memo, Discussion of MLF, April 11,

1964.

101. LBJL, Henry Owen, Oral History, p. 11.

102. LBJL, Gerard Smith, Oral History, p. 7.

103. LBJL, NSF-SF, Box 23, Rostow to LBJ, December 5, 1963.

104. Philip Geyelin, *Lyndon B. Johnson and the World* (New York, 1966), p. 159.

105. Barnet, *The Alliance*, p. 240.

106. LBJL, NSF-SF, Box 23, USIA Circular, "MLF Information Activities," June 1, 1964.

107. LBJL, NSF-SF, Box 22, Klein to Bundy, "The MLF and All That," June 20, 1964.

108. Lacouture, *De Gaulle*, p. 359.

109. LBJL, Gerard Smith, Oral History, p. 10.

110. LBJL, NSF-SF, Box 23, Martin Hillenbrand to Klein, November 25, 1964.

111. LBJL, NSF, Files of McGeorge Bundy, Box 15, Kissinger to Bundy, November 27, 1964.

112. LBJL, NSF-SF, Box 23, Letter, Joseph Clark and eight other senators to Rusk, September 7, 1964.

113. Richard Neustadt, Memo of Conversation, "Wilson Visit and the MLF," December 6, 1964. I want to thank Professor Ernest R. May for providing me a copy of this document. In this same memorandum, the President pointed out that he wasn't impressed by the argument that America had committed its "prestige" behind the MLF and had to save "face." In characteristic language, ironic in light of the impending war in Vietnam, Johnson commented while you're trying to save face, "you'll lose your ass."

114. Schlesinger, *A Thousand Days*, p. 797.

115. LBJL, David Bruce, Oral History, p. 7.

116. Lyndon Johnson, *The Vantage Point* (New York, 1971), p. 305.

117. *Newsweek*, May 3, 1965, p. 38.

118. McGhee, *At the Creation of a New Germany*, p. 148.

119. LBJL, NSF-CF, Box 186, "A Reexamination of Premises on the German Problem," December 9, 1965.

120. LBJL, George McGhee, Oral History, p. 14.

121. LBJL, NSF Speech File, Box 5, Speech to Editorial Writers, October 7, 1966.

122. LBJL, Zbigniew Brzezinski, Oral History, p. 10. Brzezinski claimed he got Johnson to give the speech by suggesting to the White House that Robert Kennedy was planning to attack Johnson's European policy.

123. LBJL, NSF Speech File, Box 5, Rostow to LBJ, October 6, 1966.

124. LBJL, NSF Speech File, Box 5, Bator to LBJ, October 13, 1966.

125. Barnet, *The Alliance*, p. 289.

126. The issue is discussed extensively in chapter 3 above.

127. Schlesinger, *A Thousand Days*, p. 601.

128. JFKL, POF, Box 116a, Memo, Dillon to JFK, April 7, 1961.

129. Treverton, *Dollar Drain*, p. 33.

130. By the end of 1966 roughly three-quarters of the military deficit in the

balance of payments was attributable to the Vietnam conflict, and it continued to worsen until the end of Johnson's presidency. David Wightman, "Money and Security," *Rivista di storia economica*, 5 (1988), p. 57. My thanks to the Johnson Library for making this article available to me.

131. Some of these purchases, like the F-104 Starfighter planes, had already had an alarming run of 66 accidents. Treverton, *Dollar Drain*, p. 65.

132. Wightman, "Money and Security," p. 46. By September 1, 1966 Germany had placed less than half the orders due by the end of 1966, and made less than 25 percent of the payments due by the end of the agreement in June 1967.

133. Treverton, *Dollar Drain*, p. 36.

134. McGhee, *At the Creation of a New Germany*, p. 190.

135. Ibid., p. 184.

136. Francis Bator told LBJ that "for us it is important –even more than Erhard's survival–that we not appear the culprit if he falls." Bator feared that this would make the future of U.S.-German relations a central issue in the fight to succeed Erhard. LBJL, NSF, NSC History, Trilateral Negotiations and NATO, 1966–67 (TNN), Box 50, Bator to LBJ, September 25, 1966,

137. *Time*, September 30, 1966, p. 29.

138. To meet an estimated yearly gap of $500 million between what the Germans would pay and what the costs were, McNamara advocated reducing American spending in Europe by $200 million, and considering the withdrawal of a significant number of American combat personnel, which he acknowledged would have a "traumatic" effect on NATO. LBJL, NSF, NSC History, TNN, Box 50, McNamara to LBJ, September 19, 1966.

139. McGhee, *At the Creation of a New Germany*, pp. 192–193.

140. *Newsweek*, November 14, 1966, p. 41.

141. Kai Bird, *The Chairman* (New York, 1992), esp. pp. 590–593.

142. LBJL, NSF, NSC History, TNN, Box 50, LBJ to McCloy, March 1, 1967, and Memorandum for the Record, "President's Conversation with John J. McCloy," March 2, 1967.

143. LBJL, NSF, NSC History, TNN, Box 50, McCloy to LBJ, May 17, 1967. See the extensive discussion of this point in chapter 3, above.

144. LBJL, NSF, NSC History, TNN, Box 50, McCloy to LBJ, March 22, 1967.

145. LBJL, Papers of Thomas Johnson, Box 3, Tom Johnson's Notes on Tuesday Lunch, July 2, 1968.

146. *Time*, October 4, 1968, p. 28.

147. LBJL, Charles Bohlen, Oral History, p. 21.

148. Barnet, *The Alliance*, p. 264.

SELECT BIBLIOGRAPHY

Barnet, Richard. *The Alliance*. New York, 1983.
Beschloss, Michael R., *The Crisis Years*. New York, 1991.
Bundy, McGeorge, *Danger and Survival*. New York, 1988.

Hanrieder, Wolfram. *Germany, America, Europe.* New Haven, 1989.
Ninkovich, Frank. *Germany and the United States.* Boston, 1988.
Slusser, Robert M. *The Berlin Crisis of 1961.* Baltimore, 1973.
Steinbruner, John D. *The Cybernetic Theory of Decision.* Princeton, 1974.
Trachtenberg, Marc. *History and Strategy.* Princeton, 1991.
Treverton, Gregory F. *The Dollar Drain and American Forces in Germany.* Athens, Ohio, 1978.

Mrs. Kennedy and Latin American diplomats applauding Kennedy's Alliance for Progress speech, March 13, 1961.

COURTESY OF THE JOHN F. KENNEDY LIBRARY

Kennedy welcoming Ghana's President Kwame Nkrumah in March 1961.

Kennedy and British Prime Minister Harold Macmillan meeting in December 1961. COURTESY OF THE JOHN F. KENNEDY LIBRARY

President and Mrs. Kennedy entertaining French Minister of Culture André Malraux, May 1962. COURTESY OF THE JOHN F. KENNEDY LIBRARY

President Kennedy and Soviet Premier Nikita Khrushchev meet in Vienna, June 1961. COURTESY OF THE JOHN F. KENNEDY LIBRARY

President Johnson and Soviet Premier Alexi Kosygin, June 23, 1967.
COURTESY OF THE LYNDON BAINES JOHNSON LIBRARY

President and Mrs. Johnson touring the LBJ Ranch with German Chancellor
Ludwig Erhard in December 1963.

The "Wise Men" groups of senior American foreign policy advisers meets with President Johnson and his team three days before the President's March 31, 1968 announcement of a partial bombing halt over North Vietnam and his decision not to seek another term.   COURTESY OF THE LYNDON BAINES JOHNSON LIBRARY

Israeli Foreign Minister Abba Evan meets with President Johnson, Secretary of Defense Robert McNamara, and other advisers before the Six Day War, May 1967.   COURTESY OF THE LYNDON BAINES JOHNSON LIBRARY

South Vietnamese President Nguyen Van Thieu contemplating the world, July 1968. COURTESY OF THE LYNDON BAINES JOHNSON LIBRARY

5

Unwrapping the Enigma: What Was Behind the Soviet Challenge in the 1960s?

•

VLADISLAV M. ZUBOK

Students of contemporary history cannot escape a question after the dismal collapse of the Soviet empire: did American diplomacy in the 1960s blow the Soviet "historic challenge" out of proportion? During this decade the Soviet Union could not solve its fundamental problems. It failed to shake off the strangling political and ideological legacy of Stalin years, to move from the stage of industrialization to subsequent phases of economic development, to restore its agriculture and to develop modern outlets for centripetal forces of nationalism.[1]

Soviet foreign policy in the 1960s suffered a growing discrepancy between its search for stability and its confrontational bipolar vision— a discrepancy all the more acute due to fissures in the Cold War order and to the slowdown of Soviet economy.[2] However, these long-range developments were largely overshadowed and concealed from U.S. policymakers by imminent threats: the Soviet Union was rapidly becoming a military superpower with nuclear capabilities more or less equal to those of the United States while simultaneously, the Soviet (known as "Communist") model of political mobilization and indus-trialization seemed to take root among the newly independent nations of Asia and Africa.

During January 1961, when a change of political generations took place in Washington, the Soviet leadership consisted of those who owed their career to Josef Stalin's purges and whose formative experi-ence had occurred in the 1930s. Foot-soldiers of Stalin's "revolution from above," this generation came of age amid the Soviet defeat and triumph in the Second World War, followed by the nuclear shadow of the Cold War—and arrived under Leonid Brezhnev as the most conservative and visionless cohort in Soviet political history.

Khrushchev was a link that still tied this generation to the period of its *Sturm und Drang*. He had been propelled to the Politburo by Stalin in 1938 and in conducting world affairs never fully liberated himself from Stalin's legacy. For one thing, he was both a ruthless practitioner of the crudest form of realpolitik and a believer in the eventual demise of world capitalism. Contradictory only to outsiders, this combination was not a unique one for "mature Stalinism" and related Khrushchev both to his dead boss and to his defeated rivals Vyacheslav Molotov and Georgi Malenkov.

At the age of sixty-seven in 1961, the First Secretary, still at full power, controlled and influenced many aspects of Soviet domestic and foreign policy. Yet, their outreach was so global, their national security tasks so enormous, and Soviet diplomacy so diverse, that even a workaholic leader could not single-handedly run Soviet foreign policy, especially since, unlike the foreign policy of any other state in the world, Soviet external relations combined three, not two dimensions, each representing different means and/or motives in striving for security and power. In addition to the state diplomacy and the military policy, Soviet foreign policy included a heavy dose of party diplomacy.

The latter was a linear descendant of the Communist International, a huge semi-public, semi-clandestine network in existence from 1919 to 1943 that helped Moscow to control dozens of Communist parties and thousands of "fellow-travelers" around the world. During the early Cold War a special coordinating bureau, the Cominform, ran the network. After Stalin's death the relationship between Moscow and foreign Communists became a two-way street: in order to guarantee an allegiance of foreign "friends" Moscow had to increase its economic aid and military assistance to them. Even more it concerned the nationalist forces in developing countries: the Soviet leadership put them into the category of "progressive forces" and decided to win them over by massive aid. The more the Communist movement became a sham, the costlier was party diplomacy for the Soviet economy, but to abandon it meant to give up in the Cold War and, even worse, to admit that the global Communist crusade had fizzled out. Moreover, in the early 1960s, most Soviet leaders genuinely believed that Soviet military growth and foreign expansion were only a corollary of the historic inevitability of the Soviet system and Communist ideas. "The idea of world revolution," discarded in the official propaganda under Stalin, "continued its subconscious existence, nourished by the hopes for an upcoming crisis of capitalism."[3]

The combination of the three dimensions in Soviet foreign policy was far from constant. After World War II "state" diplomacy played a prominent role, but, as prospects of accommodation with the United States grew dimmer, the party and military considerations increasingly contributed to Stalin's hard line in his relations with the West.[4] During the first eight years after Stalin's death in 1953 party diplomacy lost much of its luster and importance, but still predominated in relations with Eastern Europe and, until the mid-1960s, with China. The party's ideological considerations nested in the central committee and were supported by a huge budget and an impressive propaganda machine.[5] Their presence in foreign policy decision-making were especially considerable, when matters of creed ("proletarian internationalism," solidarity in "anti-imperialist struggle," etc.) were involved.

In the 1960s "state" diplomacy was clearly predominant over party diplomacy in foreign policy outside the socialist bloc of Eastern Europe and in Asia. Diplomats also made some gains in their standing vis-à-vis the military, as the focus of Soviet security doctrine was shifting from immediate war danger to long-term coexistence with Western powers. A virtual taboo on result-oriented negotiations (instead of propaganda productions) with the West gradually was lifted. Test-ban and other arms control efforts forced even the top-brass in Moscow to learn the art of negotiations with the "enemy number one"—the United States. The Ministry of Foreign Affairs and its embassies abroad worked along with the political police (KGB) to cultivate confidential channels with governments, and, in a broader sense, with "establishments" of the United States and other Western countries.[6] Another expanding venue for state diplomacy was in the relations with developing countries of the Arab East, India, Indonesia and new African states.

The military dimension in Soviet foreign policy was at first synonymous with the occupation of Eastern Europe as a means of providing a "territorial buffer" for the Soviet armed forces. In the missile era the Soviet leadership—prodded by fierce arms competition with the United States—continued to consider the military strategic potential to be the only possible foundation for security and the precondition for peaceful coexistence with the West. Missiles and nuclear tests were regarded as essential for negotiations from "a position of strength." Military aid became a major way of expanding Soviet influence in developing countries. Further, Soviet military stratagems were always based on a notion of a *blitzkrieg* response to a "foreign aggression," i.e. through continental offensive operations from Eastern Europe, which guaranteed a virtual veto on any radical departures from the status quo in this region.[7]

Khrushchev, like Stalin before him, let those three dimensions evolve, interact, and sometimes clash among themselves, but reserved a final decision for himself. At the Soviet Chairman's disposal was a personal network of advisers who briefed him on crucial issues and helped shape his decisions. Sometimes they were professionals: from the Foreign Ministry (V. Kuznetsov, A. Dobrynin, L. Ilyichev), the KGB (A. Shelepin), the Ministry of Defense (R. Malinovsky) and military intelligence (GRU) (I. Serov). Often they were talented journalists-turned-emissaries, through whom Khrushchev negotiated with foreign public and state figures. His second group included his son-in-law A. Adzhubei, M. Kharlamov, Zhukov, and Satyukov.[8] This personal network never evolved into a formal structure, like the National Security Council in the United States. But the "Adzhubei gang" often worked as a substitute for the NSC, especially when Khrushchev wanted to surprise the world with new foreign policy "initiatives." Many "spontaneous" decisions of the Chairman can be attributed to the influence of his immediate circle of advisers.[9]

After 1957 Khrushchev's personal interventions into foreign policy became a permanent practice. He ousted his rivals Molotov and Malenkov from the leadership. Erudite strategist Dmitry Shepilov was replaced in the Foreign Ministry with dour and docile Andrei Gromyko. Khrushchev's personal style of policy-making (after his demotion it was branded as "hare-brained") made a particular impact on Soviet support of "liberation movements," particularly in Cuba and in the Congo, on relations with People's Republic of China, on Soviet-American relations and on the Berlin issue.

Yet while it might be attractive for historians to reduce the study of Soviet foreign policy to the fits and moods of the chairman, it would be a mistake to do so.[10] The three dimensions of Soviet external relations took on, to a varying degree, a momentum of their own, restricting any leader's room for maneuver, especially when it concerned vital issues of Soviet security. One such issue was the "German problem," and another was relations with the United States.

The Berlin crisis is often presented as the best example of Khrushchev's strategy of "detente through intimidation." Many Western scholars, from Adam Ulam to John Gaddis, believe that the Soviets were on the offensive and that their grand design consisted of using West Berlin's vulnerability as a lever to force the West, particularly the

United States and West Germany, to agree to a compromise settlement of the German problem, acceptable to the Soviets and their East German allies. What stopped Khrushchev half-way, forcing him to be satisfied with the Berlin Wall, seemed to be U.S. nuclear superiority.[11] But declassified documents from Soviet archives reveal a somewhat different story.

As evidence both old and new indicates, Khrushchev had reason to believe that the Kennedy administration would undo the confrontational anti-Soviet course of its predecessors and move closer to a compromise on the German settlement. He also believed Kennedy would not go to war over West Berlin, and would share the Soviet interest in preventing nuclearization of West Germany.[12]

From his intelligence Khrushchev learned that the new president would be a good negotiating partner and, perhaps, even "another Roosevelt."[13] One memo of Presidential adviser Walt Rostow to Kennedy that reached Khrushchev's desk recommended that the administration "prepare a new position for talks on the German problem, that might include the Berlin-border agreement" (i.e. a guaranteed access to West Berlin in exchange for recognition of the German-Polish border).[14] He also learned that Arthur Schlesinger Jr., another adviser to Kennedy, had mentioned in private that the U.N. custodianship over West Berlin "would be the best solution of the problem."[15]

There is a widespread view that Khrushchev came to the U.S.-Soviet summit in Vienna, on June 3–4, 1961, intending to "frighten" a young Kennedy, and even to take advantage of his predicament after the Bay of Pigs.[16] However, through the winter and spring of 1961 the predominant mood in Moscow was for accommodation, not for a test of wills. Diplomatic concerns clearly prevailed over party propaganda or military approaches. Confidential channels with the White House were quickly established, mostly through a Soviet intelligence officer Georgi Bolshakov.[17] There were many confidential contacts between foreign minister Andrei Gromyko and his first deputy Vasily Kuznetsov on the Soviet side, and ambassador Llewellyn Thompson and the president's adviser on disarmament, John J. McCloy. The outcome, aside from the summit in Vienna, was bilateral negotiations on disarmament from May through July. Gromyko, reflecting the predominant mood in Moscow, urged negotiators to be flexible and "to demonstrate the Soviet willingness for accommodation with the United States."[18]

At that time the party's Secretariat appointed a special panel headed by Boris Ponomarev to look into ways of improving public dimension of U.S.-Soviet relations. Among the recommendations sent to that commission were the following: to create an American Studies Institute at the Council of Ministers, to allow immigration of 500 elderly Soviet citizens to their American relatives, to pay honoraria to translated American authors, to resume the student exchange and to restore the Jewish theater and periodicals, closed by Stalin in 1953.[19] In a word, the Soviets expected that a summit in Vienna would be a stepping stone to Kennedy's visit to Moscow.[20]

Why then a fiasco in Vienna? It has been suggested that the general discussion on world politics started by president Kennedy was a mistake. Certainly the president's discourse on "freezing" the global status quo must have enraged the chairman, who in January had come out to support "wars of national liberation."[21] Another author portrays the summit as a case of cognitive incompatibility, the clash between two political cultures and civilizations.[22]

However, at the core of Vienna's failure were very specific issues: the German problem and the issue of West Berlin, not ideological clashes over the social or geopolitical balance of power. Khrushchev's perceptions were important, but they stemmed from Kennedy's attitudes, not from the Communist doctrine. First, Kennedy seemed to have acknowledged the geopolitical equilibrium between the "Sino-Soviet bloc" and the West, as well as the inevitability of global social changes in favor of "socialism." Second, the U.S. President came to Vienna with nothing to say on the German problem and even took a step back from Eisenhower's acceptance of the situation in West Berlin as "abnormal."[23] Despite the earlier promising signals, Kennedy excluded Germany and Berlin from his agenda. For the Soviet Chairman it was an invitation to more pressure. In exasperation, Khrushchev even passed up two important opportunities—a possible preliminary agreement on the nuclear test ban and a settlement in Laos. As a result Khrushchev concluded the meeting on a grim note demanding a German peace treaty or threatening war.[24] As the records reveal, he was bluffing.

Soviet motives behind the Berlin crisis were strictly defensive: to stabilize the Communist regime of Walter Ulbricht in East Germany and to check the potential political and military might of West Germany. Finally, Khrushchev realized that no détente in Europe or with the United States would be possible until the German problem was somehow settled among the four occupying powers. The issue of West Berlin was the key to all these goals. In Khrushchev's words, West Berlin "became a stumbling block and destroyed relations among former allies as well as between the East and the West."[25]

The rising tide of refugees to West Berlin became an embarrassment for claims of the inevitable victory of socialism over capitalism and made all proclamations about a new "correlation of forces" in the world look like a sham. But reports to the Presidium (Politburo) proved that the bleeding of East Germany (GDR) could be stopped only by closing the border with West Berlin, and that the Soviet leadership preferred to avoid.[26] The building of the Wall would have demonstrated that socialism was losing its economic competition with the West.

What about the separate Soviet-East German peace treaty with which Khrushchev threatened the West? Available records reveal that both the chairman and Ulbricht preferred not to sign this treaty, since that could have triggered a Western economic blockade and the Soviets would have to bail out its hapless satellite. There were, no doubt, fears of military conflict over West Berlin lurking in the back of Khrushchev's mind.

Party and military concerns in Soviet foreign policy threatened to develop an irresistible momentum toward a separate treaty. It was known in the West[27] that Ulbricht skillfully played on Moscow's concerns; the GDR leadership was the tail that wagged the dog in this case. Ulbricht's plan was to cut West Berlin off from West Germany, if necessary by force. He also pursued a utopian goal of surpassing West German living standards. East German leadership expected the Soviets to help on both scores—with their armed shield and their gold reserve. After 1960 the GDR leaders benefited from the growing Sino-Soviet split and the secession of Albania from Moscow's domination: the Soviet ideological hegemony in the Communist bloc could no longer be taken for granted. Also, they exploited Moscow's fears that a conflict might flare up any minute between the two German states that would draw in the Soviet Union and NATO.[28] Resisting East German pressure on West Berlin, Khrushchev proposed at the meeting of Communist leaders in March 1961 in Moscow that if he failed to reach agreement with Kennedy or Adenauer, the Communist bloc would "begin preparations for conclusion" of a separate treaty with the GDR.[29] After Vienna Khrushchev was taken up on his word.

The common concern in Moscow, East Berlin, and elsewhere in Warsaw Pact was not about a war, but about a Western economic blockade and sanctions. Ulbricht and other Communist leaders did not know that the Soviet Union's nuclear forces were inferior to those of the United States. But even Khrushchev, who was fully aware this was the case still believed in the Soviet thermonuclear deterrent. The Soviet embassy in Washington alerted him very early to the fact that the new president was a realist and a responsible person, a "typical pragmatist," who sought "a possibility of mutually satisfactory settlement" of the U.S.-Soviet relations "on the basis of mutual willingness to avoid nuclear war."[30]

After Khrushchev had recklessly provoked the U.S. president into a public "chicken game" (some American historians criticized Kennedy for being provoked), the Soviet leader's assessments changed. He began to stress the danger of inadvertent war with the United States, the threat of losing control over the situation. He went as far as to "defend" Kennedy before the next meeting of Communist leaders on August 5, 1961, when the final decision on a separate treaty had to be made:

"Kennedy seems to be in a bind, for Kennedy represents one party, and Rusk another. . . . [The United States is] a barely governable state . . . So you can never be safe with the United States. War might happen too. . . . Kennedy is a pretty unknown quantity in politics, so in his situation I feel empathy with him, because he is a light-weight both for the Republicans, and for the Democrats, and the state is too big, the state is powerful and it poses certain dangers."

Unlike Dulles, Kennedy might not have enough of a reputation as a "hard-liner" to stop "on the brink" of military conflict with the Soviet Union. "The situation is very grave there," Khrushchev concluded and added, with a touch of apology: "It looks as if I am a propagandist for Kennedy, to make you less stern about him."[31]

Economic concerns also deterred Khrushchev from excessive provocations of the West. Earlier, at the end of 1960, the West German government abrogated trade agreements with the GDR. Ulbricht demanded emergency Soviet aid in pig iron, food products (some of which the Soviets had to import for hard currency), and 68 tons of gold. Alexei Kosygin, expressing the view of Soviet economic planners, balked at these demands.[32] For many Soviet officials Ulbricht began to seem an intolerable burden, and they hardly concealed their resentment from Americans.[33] The fact of East Germany's economic dependence on the FRG dawned upon the Kremlin rulers in the midst of the Berlin crisis and came as an unpleasant shock to Khrushchev. Khrushchev promised to expand economic assistance and even admitted that "we all were guilty" for not having liberated the GDR economically. But this episode alerted him to the weakness of Eastern positions in the Berlin crisis and must have swayed him toward the idea of the Wall.

The Soviet leader allowed Ulbricht to close the borders with West Berlin on August 13, but said "not a millimeter further." Earlier he had been informed, both through confidential channels and the Soviet embassy, that William Fulbright and Charles Bohlen thought that tightening the border controls was an acceptable way to diffuse the crisis. It looks as if he had raised the ante first, and then came up with a solution that could be sold both in the East and in the West.[34] Did

Khrushchev try to extricate himself from the pledge to Ulbricht by deliberately cranking up tension? We will probably never know. Yet, the outcome of the August meeting got Khrushchev off the hook he had designed himself. The gridlock of the "party" and the military interests that threatened to engulf Soviet foreign policy into escalation of the crisis had been averted through the formula of "negotiation from a position of strength." Unlike the days of Eisenhower, this time Khrushchev managed to maintain the confidential channel to the White House; a flurry of diplomatic and informal contacts after August 13 led to Gromyko-Rusk negotiations on the German and Berlin issues. While using these talks to let off the steam (Khrushchev seemed not to expect more), the Soviet leadership searched for another opening in its relationship with Bonn, expecting more cooperation from the aging Chancellor and his opposition.[35]

As to the "strength" side of the formula, Khrushchev suspended his plan of armed forces reductions, introduced in January 1960. He also sanctioned, without advance warning, a break in the two-year moratorium on nuclear testing that the U.S., Great Britain, and the Soviet Union had observed informally since 1958. A 50-megaton bomb was dropped over Novaya Zemlya near the Arctic, and the KGB networks were used to impress the West with the full Soviet readiness to use force in case of a conflict. In this vein also he allowed a test of the American resolve concerning West Berlin: would they tolerate East German control over the sectorial border in clear violation of the occupational rules? A well-known result of this decision was the famous tank standoff at Checkpoint Charlie on October 26–28.[36]

When the Twenty-Second Party Congress opened in Moscow in October 1961, Khrushchev had foreign policy under control, sharply restricting its "party" dimension and winning support from the military. He secretly communicated with Kennedy and both leaders called the tanks back from the brink. The main proponent of aggressive "internationalism," the Maoist leadership in China, was isolated at the August conference and humiliated at the Congress, when Khrushchev orchestrated a vehement anti-Stalin (and, by inference, anti-Mao) campaign. Yuri Andropov and Boris Ponomarev in the Central Committee, as well as officials in the Ministry of Foreign Affairs and the military, unanimously agreed that the Berlin crisis had to be ended. The Red Army, at the Presidium's order, fortified defense lines along sectorial borders in Berlin.[37] When Mikhail Pervukhin, Soviet ambassador in East Berlin, informed Moscow that Ulbricht was perhaps still thinking about altering the status quo in Berlin, the East German leader was summoned to Moscow for a serious talk. On June 6–9, 1962

Khrushchev, Kosygin, Gromyko, and Marshal Ivan Konev spoke to the unruly leader of the satellite nation. Even in the absence of records, it is plausible to suggest that some sort of unwritten agreement on the status quo had been reached.[38]

Despite a very "cold" fall and winter of 1961, the post-Wall events signalled a new development in U.S.-Soviet relations. The confidential channel allowed Khrushchev and Kennedy to coordinate deescalation of the Berlin crisis and to avert "miscalculations."[39] However, in the short run it played a more ambiguous role, since the Soviet leadership took Kennedy's penchant for secret settlements as an encouragement to continue its gambling.

Khrushchev succeeded in portraying his bluffing as a success, but he was not sure that in the next round he would not be left hanging on the ropes. By spring 1962 convincing evidence indicated that his vision of geopolitical balance ("correlation of forces") was under attack both from the Chinese Communists and the West. On October 21, 1961 Deputy Secretary of Defense Roswell Gilpatric revealed that the "missile gap" was not in the Soviets' favor, but strongly favored the U.S., a sign that Kennedy might be under pressure to abandon his support for qualitative equivalence between the two blocs. The promise of improved Soviet-West German relations disappeared by April 1962: all politicians in the FRG, as well as in Washington, insisted on the ousting of Ulbricht as a precondition to any deal.

Another crisis loomed in Cuba. In Vienna Kennedy admitted that the U.S.-supported invasion of the island to overthrow the Castro regime had been a mistake. But the president's words did not seem to be a guarantee against another intervention. The Soviets were alerted by their intelligence that the president had been tricked into that adventure by the CIA. In February 1962 Khrushchev learned that Pentagon had approved a "Cuban project," stipulating that the Castro regime could be overthrown by October, with a possible role for the U.S. military. Naval exercises to fight an imaginary dictator "Ortsac" had been scheduled at that time in the Caribbean. Along with other reports on the Kennedy-ordered CIA operation to kill the Cuban leader (later declassified as "Operation Mongoose"), this intelligence could be interpreted as signalling the preparation for another invasion in Cuba—perhaps even without Kennedy's formal approval.[40]

Khrushchev felt it would be impossible to save Cuba in this case—almost the same way that Kennedy had felt about Berlin. "I was haunted by the knowledge that the Americans could not stomach having Castro's Cuba right next to them," Khrushchev later recalled. "Our aim was to strengthen and to reinforce Cuba. But how were we supposed to do that? With diplomatic notes and TASS statements?"[41]

It was not the strategic disparity, laid bare by the Gilpatric speech, that had been the primary motive behind Khrushchev's decision to send missiles to Cuba.[42] However, the risk of "losing Cuba" would have brought this disparity into the most painful and embarrassing perspective for the Soviet leader, already irked by the adamant refusal of the American government to accept the Soviet Union as a legitimate and equal superpower. "They treat us as if we were schoolboys," ranted Khrushchev. The conclusion came almost naturally: "The Americans had surrounded our country with military bases and threatened us with nuclear weapons, and now they would learn just what it feels like to have enemy missiles pointing at you; we'd be doing nothing more than giving them a little of their own medicine."[43]

The decision fitted well both "party" and military interests. It provided "socialist" Cuba with a powerful deterrent against invasion and joined Cuban and Soviet leadership together by bonds of "internationalist duty" to the cause of anti-imperialist struggle. It also sought to boost the moral of the Soviet military and to help suppress a complex of inferiority toward the United States.

What about "state" diplomacy—i.e. a prospect of negotiations with Kennedy? Early in 1962 the leading Soviet "think-tank' (IMEMO) warned Khrushchev that the domestic situation in the United States was extremely volatile: there was a powerful right-wing opposition to Kennedy that would never recognize "the new correlation of forces." Another crisis like the Berlin crisis might help the opposition to prevail over "forces of realism"—"in that case we would lose many of those opportunities that are available now in the US-Soviet relations."[44] However, Khrushchev, buoyed by the success of the wall, seemed to believe that the U.S. president, when presented with another *fait accompli*, i.e. Soviet missiles in Cuba, would again swallow it and acknowledge the strategic equivalence between the two blocs. The Soviet leader, already experienced in American electoral dynamics, planned to reveal the secret missile deployments after the November mid-term elections.

In pursuit of secrecy, Khrushchev even compromised his confidential channel to the U.S. President. Neither Georgi Bolshakov, nor Anatoly Dobrynin, the new Soviet ambassador in Washington, knew about preparations in Cuba.[45]

In late spring an agreement with Castro had been achieved; it became a draft of a mutual assistance treaty and the First Operational Department of the General Staff worked out the details of the operation "Anadyr"—the secret dispatch of 40,000 troops and 43 medium-range missiles to Cuba.[46] The military implemented it flawlessly, except for one point—deception and camouflage of missile deployment—where a unique mix of incompetence and negligence, so characteristic of the Soviet system in general, proved fatal for the whole operation.

It is almost commonplace to praise both Kennedy and Khrushchev for their management of the crisis. In all fairness, one has to admit that confusion and fear played a larger role than hard-headed calculations. Khrushchev's reactions to Kennedy's actions and the establishment of an American "quarantine" around Cuba betrayed his panicked reaction which combined outrage, belligerence, fear, and a plea for accommodation. Later he gave a self-serving explanation for his retreat, attributing it to several factors: the unpreparedness of a nuclear deterrent ("the warheads were not yet there"); Kennedy's pledge not to attack Cuba ("although not exactly the one we wanted") and Kennedy's warnings that the military and the right-wingers might force Kennedy's hand, if a compromise wasn't reached ("it was somewhere between threat and prayer"). In correspondence with the Cuban leader Khrushchev assured Castro that the highest motive in his actions was the "proletarian internationalist duty."[47]

Yet, as in the Berlin crisis, the simple truth was that Khrushchev dreaded an unintentional nuclear war and sacrificed the "party" considerations in order to avoid it.[48] "It wasn't in the interests of socialism to allow the crisis over Cuba to develop into a thermonuclear war," Khrushchev told the Supreme Soviet in December 1962: "Why should we invite ourselves to go to the Devil? . . . Nobody has yet returned from there to tell us that it is better there than it is on earth."[49] Alone with his colleagues at the Presidium he conceded it was "another peace of Brest," an unmistakable reference to the negotiations in Brest-Litovsk in 1918, when Lenin, faced with a choice between promotion of the world revolution and the survival of the Soviet state, had chosen the latter.[50]

In the foreign ministry and among the military commanders many might have agreed with a crude remark of Deputy Foreign Minister Vasily Kuznetsov, that Khrushchev had "shitted in his pants."[51] Hasty trouble-shooting looked like capitulation in the final phase of the crisis in November, when under Kennedy's unrelenting pressure Khrushchev completely the flouted interests of his Cuban ally and gave away Castro's only bargaining chip, Soviet-made IL-28 fighter-bombers.[52] Through these steps Khrushchev antagonized Castro and almost "lost" Cuba—this time to the People's Republic of China (PRC), since the Chinese Communists shared Cuba's hurt feelings, though they were unable to take ameliorative actions.[53]

When Kuznetsov at the outset of the crisis proposed that Khrushchev respond by bringing further pressure on Berlin, the Soviet Chairman said harshly: "We do not need that kind of advice. We already have one adventure to get through"[54] The Soviet leader clearly treated the Berlin crisis as a closed issue, the revival of which could only aggravate the Soviet predicament. So much for the major bargaining chip in Soviet "state" foreign policy. To a certain extent the military component suffered also: the outcome of operation "Anadyr" humiliated the Soviet military and rubbed their noses in American naval supremacy. But those in the military who appreciated the nuclear danger approved Khrushchev's retreat.[55]

The Cuban Missile Crisis left Khrushchev's synthesis of "negotiations from the position of strength" in a shambles. Trying to get beyond the crisis as soon as possible, the Soviet leader quickly unwrapped a negotiating package: a nonaggression pact between NATO and the Warsaw Pact, measures to prevent a surprise attack (old Soviet proposals of May 10, 1955) and a German peace treaty. He even made Kennedy a party to his predicament, which squeezed the Soviet leader between pressures from the Chinese and Cuban Communists, as well as from dogmatics in Moscow. "Our friends," he wrote, "are trying to convince us . . . that imperialism cannot be trusted, that is that you cannot be trusted."[56] Khrushchev needed harder evidence than the dismantling of obsolete U.S. missiles in Turkey to demonstrate to comrades that his foreign policy worked.

The aftermath of the crisis opened new opportunities for U.S.-Soviet contacts. In 1963 a "sudden flowering of mutual amiability" took place.[57] National security establishments both in Washington and Moscow were eager to prevent any direct clashes between superpowers. Among the results of this climate were the opening of a hot-line to back up the confidential channel[58], a joint United Nations resolution pledging a nuclear-free outer space, the signing of the test-ban treaty (July 25, 1963)[59]; and Kennedy's famous commencement speech at American University in June 1963 in which he played down Cold War antagonisms, implicitly recognized the Soviet regime's legitimacy, and stressed the mutual interest in avoiding nuclear war. There were other agreements, one of them marking the inauspicious start of massive Soviet imports of wheat from the American continent.

The test-ban treaty was a reasonable solution to the diplomatic deadlock caused by U.S.-Soviet haggling over the number of on-site inspections to monitor underground testing. Soviet stubbornness was not, however, caused only by a mania for secrecy and closeness. Early in the Kennedy presidency Soviet officials hinted that a compromise could be found.[60] Yet they strongly suspected that the American insistence on more inspections simply masked a desire to win a propaganda contest and block an agreement on underground nuclear tests.

The treaty meant that the Soviets ceased playing propaganda games with disarmament—something they had been doing since September 1959. Despite the incomplete character of the treaty (underground testing was allowed), its benefits for global environment and human health were immeasurable. For the first time since 1955 Moscow had adopted a serious approach to arms control. The disarmament propaganda was swept aside by more immediate concerns: a need for tangible and impressive results from negotiations with the West and a concern about the nuclearization of the PRC and West Germany. The test-ban treaty, the first between the Soviet Union and the United States since the onset of the Cold War, immediately satisfied the first motive. As to the FRG, in the Soviet leadership's view, its government in 1963–65 was exercising an effective veto on U.S. decisions on Central Europe and longed for nuclear status. Khrushchev believed that the FRG might get access to nuclear weapons through the U.S-sponsored plan of Multilateral Forces (MLF) in Western Europe.[61]

The concern about China's nuclear program had long been known to policymakers in Washington as partly motivating Soviet interest in arms control.[62] Taken in the military and "state" dimension, China, until recently a major strategic asset, quickly turned into the biggest challenge. On the eve of the Moscow negotiations, the Central Committee of the Communist Party of the Soviet Union (CPSU) had exchanged public denunciations with Beijing, for the first time publicly recognizing the Sino-Soviet split. As a Central Committee insider recalled: "From 1962–1964 the Chinese factor weakened the position of the Stalinists in the USSR. As it developed, the conflict with China had positive influences on the policies of Khrushchev. . . . The debate with the Chinese leaders provided the anti-Stalinists with the opportunity, while defending our policies, to speak out on many political and ideological subjects that had lately become taboo."[63]

Polemics with Mao, a strong opponent of the U.S.-Soviet détente, helped remove obstacles on the road to arms control and other forms of cooperation with the West. Why, then, did Khrushchev refuse to discuss the issue during the talks on the test-ban and why didn't he immediately go further along the road toward a nuclear nonproliferation treaty? Events after Khrushchev's fall demonstrated that an inertia of ideological stereotypes, maintained by the party apparat, still delayed a reassessment of Sino-Soviet relations in the Kremlin. Only a handful of experts on China and a few party bureaucrats, including Yuri Andropov, realized that the split had been caused by more serious factors than ideological nuances and the Mao-Khrushchev quarrel.

Many in Soviet political and military circles believed until 1965 that the old "friendship" with Beijing could still be resumed.[64] Khrushchev came to the opposite conclusion much earlier. He stopped looking over his shoulder at Beijing thereby increasing his room for political maneuver in U.S.-Soviet relations. Yet he must have felt that his colleagues held him personally responsible for the split, as well as for the Cuban missile crisis. Certainly he could not openly cooperate with "the imperialists" in order "to deny," as Walt Rostow put it, "the Chicoms a nuclear capability" or to expect a cooperative action with Americans to preclude China's nuclear weapons development.[65] In addition, he was afraid lest the United States play what would be called later "a Chinese card." These fears were without grounds: neither the Kennedy nor the Johnson administrations were ready for new relations with the PRC.[66] Khrushchev passed the split's headache to his successors: China's first atomic mushroom celebrated his forced retirement in October 1964.

The Cuban missile crisis did not cause a reexamination of Soviet international doctrines, particularly the belief in the aggressive nature of Western imperialism and in Moscow's "internationalist duty" to support radical regimes and movements in the Third World which opposed it. Comparison of Soviet motives and behavior in two crises, the Berlin and Cuban, reveal that Khrushchev, even at the peak of his gambling, was torn between two dimensions of Soviet foreign policy, the party and the state, with military interests breaking the tie between the two. Specifically, Khrushchev could not stick to the principle of geopolitical stability that Kennedy proposed in Vienna, even if it would be clearly in Soviet interests, at least as far as Eastern Europe and the GDR were concerned. Even the missile crisis could not transcend the deep dichotomy in Soviet behavior.

One product of the crisis, though a highly perishable one, was personal chemistry between the Soviet Chairman and the U.S. president. Khrushchev trusted Kennedy as he never trusted Eisenhower, the president who had "betrayed" him by sending the U-2 plane into Russia. The Soviet Chairman heartily congratulated the U.S. president in 1962 on the electoral defeat of his rival Richard Nixon in the California gubernatorial election and seemed confident that, with Kennedy in the White House for four more years, both leaders would be able to move toward dismantling of Cold War antagonisms.[67] Kennedy's death reverberated in Khrushchev's mind for years, as he harked back to missed opportunities in the post-crisis negotiating.[68]

The "window of opportunity" closed very fast on the two leaders. The arms race raged on; old confrontations between the two blocs were spilling over into the fierce and bloody fighting on the rim of Asia—in the sands of Sinai and the jungles of Vietnam. Modern attempts to detach the reputations of both leaders from later developments are unconvincing: it would have been as hard for Kennedy to pull out of Vietnam in 1965, as for Khrushchev to pull his punches against the Prague Spring in 1968. The passing "thaw" of 1963, as well as the "détente" in the 1970s did not end the Cold War, but rather underlined a search for predictability in the bipolar competition. Leaders on both sides decided to introduce some stabilizing measures to check each other's awesome and threatening power.

In October 1964, a Plenary Meeting of the Communist Central Committee in Moscow forced Khrushchev into retirement and unleashed another succession crisis (called a period of "collective leadership"), the third in Soviet history. Till the end of the decade there was no single leader of Soviet foreign policy. For "state" diplomacy it was a period of accumulation and waiting. The party and military dimensions, especially the latter, gained considerably from the domestic turmoil, as rivals in the leadership jockeyed for support of the key bureaucratic interests.

Extensive growth of the Soviet economy and limited attempts to raise the system's efficiency (Kosygin's reforms) provided the Kremlin with enough resources for global involvement and massive programs of strategic and conventional rearmament.[69] But even in these relatively "fat" years the Soviet economy was 50 to 75 percent smaller than the U.S. economy and running into the problems that would later mire the whole Soviet society in stagnation and decline. The U.S. economy had already coped, more or less successfully, with the problems of "mass consumption" and automation, and Western Europe and Japan were catching up swiftly. At the same time the Soviet economy remained a captive of the "late, late" industrialization and its leadership was frozen in a Siberian permafrost of the command-administrative system.

The military complex was an exception, but only to a certain extent. Machine-building ministries, gigantic "metal-eaters," provided a basis for a multistoried military-industrial castle with two crowning towers—the aerospace and nuclear industries. The inexorable drive of the arms race forced the Soviet leadership to compete with Americans both in numbers and quality. The result was an exponential growth of Soviet military expenditures in the 1960s from $36.9 to $89.8 billion, from 9 to 12 percent of GNP, if not higher.[70]

Various circumstances made the Soviet race for numerical parity almost inevitable. Deficiencies in the first generation of Soviet ICBMs made aerospace firms delay massive deployment of strategic rocket forces by almost four years while a new generation of missiles was in the making. When Khrushchev finally made a decision to put ICBMs on assembly lines, he acted under severe strain: the Kennedy-Johnson administrations had been implementing the biggest missile buildup in the U.S. history. Even if the Cuban missile crisis opened the eyes of Khrushchev and the handful of his advisers to the danger of nuclear brinkmanship, it also alerted them and many more in the military and party elites to the sharp disparity in strategic and naval forces. During the Cuban missile crisis the Soviets had only 44 operational ICBMs and 6 more on testing grounds—a ratio of 1:17 in American favor.[71] But already in 1965–66 the Soviets, according to Western estimates, had doubled their arsenal of ICBMs; from then on the Soviet ICBM force grew by about 300 new silo launchers a year.[72] For the new leadership the liquidation of disparity became a prerequisite for negotiations with the West. The new cycle of the arms race not only contributed to "some retardation in the progress of détente"[73]; but also in the longer run the race for an elusive goal of parity became a hallmark of the Brezhnev regime and became a sacred cow for the military establishment.[74]

Aside from this dubious pledge, the "collective leadership" took a cautious, even hands-off, approach to foreign policy; it ruled on the platform of tranquility and amelioration of living standards. In addition the new ruling junta had no experience in foreign affairs. Khrushchev had regarded foreign policy and national security as his fiefdom, while the rest of Politburo and party Secretaries had to satisfy their egos in domestic affairs. The removal of Khrushchev automatically exposed the unpreparedness of the top political leadership to deal with risky and complicated matters of world policy. Alexander Shelepin, a former KGB chief, and Mikhail Suslov, a Party Secretary, were perhaps the only members of the new leadership who had experience in international affairs. Shelepin had created powerful networks, but his ambition scared the majority and his political star quickly faded.[75] The new Prime Minister, Alexei Kosygin, educated and a workaholic, first took control of foreign policy, but even he occupied himself primarily with economic reforms. Chairman of the Supreme Soviet Nikolai Podgorny and the rest of the Politburo rarely transcended their background of plant managers and party secretaries.

Leonid Brezhnev, a new First Secretary of the CPSU and the future leader, had his first contact with foreign policy in his ceremonial role of Chairman of the Supreme Soviet's Presidium. In those days Foreign Minister Gromyko never forgot to brief Brezhnev, thereby earning his gratitude and his long tenure when Brezhnev became the undisputed boss. Brezhnev could act as a statesman (later, when he took interest in U.S.-Soviet relations, he spent hours on arms control issues), but he rarely took the leadership on issues, if there was not already a consensus. In 1964–1968, because he still did not have a loyal majority in the Politburo, Brezhnev spent all his time on coalition-building, and often acted as a "fence-sitter," since Kosygin, Shelepin, and their groups took positions on most foreign policy initiatives.[76]

A number of leaders (Kosygin, Suslov, Shelepin) still believed it was possible to restore the Sino-Soviet axis and placed their hopes on Zhou Enlai. In January 1965, when the first substantial discussion on foreign policy took place in the Politburo, this "China Lobby" criticized Andrei Gromyko and Yuri Andropov, who had presented an outline of policy in the spirit of post-1962 pragmatism.[77] The authors were berated for insufficient "class position" and "class consciousness," excessive "leniency toward imperialism," and a disregard for measures to restore unity with "natural" allies and "class brothers" in the PRC. Brezhnev stayed out of the debate. As a result, Kosygin got a mandate to travel to China and clarify misunderstandings. The trip, which ended in failure, incidentally, revealed the Soviet leaders' egregious blindness to geopolitical and domestic concerns that pitted the Asian giant against Moscow. After this incident the Chinese lobby calmed down. The Soviet leadership managed to grasp that it was impossible to mend fences with China without a humiliating surrender on vital points of domestic and foreign policy.[78]

The revival of ideological motives embedded in the party dimension inevitably clashed with the state policy of détente. In January 1965 the "Chinese lobby" sunk Gromyko-Andropov proposals aimed at improving relations with the United States and Western European countries. Soviet–West German bilateral relations, a crucial element of Khrushchev's foreign policy, were also put on ice: many in the Kremlin did not want to let down "friends" in the GDR, and Ulbricht resisted any talks with the Grand Coalition in the FRG.[79]

The mood in the Politburo held that there was no need to hurry with détente: the deployment of Soviet ICBMs made the Soviet "position of strength" more credible every year; meanwhile the "anti-imperialist struggle" in the Far and Middle East bestowed on the Soviets many allies in this region. Finally American military involvement in Vietnam's civil war, especially the bombing raids against North Vietnam, which coincided with Kosygin's visit to Hanoi, did not put the Johnson administration in the Kremlin's good graces.

The course of inertial confrontation taken by the collective leadership added to the enormous burden of the arms race. The Soviet military budget had been growing steadily since 1961. In addition to the missile race, the post-Khrushchev leadership began a ruinous naval race with the United States. Western estimates of Soviet direct expenditures on aid to Vietnam stand at $1.6 billion. In fact it was much more: Soviet military advisers also trained Vietnamese troops and organized the air-defense system.[80] Other major recipients of Soviet aid were Syria and Egypt. In 1966–1967 Egypt owed the Soviets about 15 billion rubles. However, unlike the Vietnamese, the Egyptians disappointed Moscow's General Staff: in the Arab-Israeli Six Day War in June 1967, the Egyptian army was demolished, thereby placing all Soviet investments in the Middle East in jeopardy.

Again the foreign policy of the collective leadership seemed to be in shambles. According to a Soviet historian "dismay and confusion" ruled in the Kremlin. For the first time the Politburo was forced to rely on diplomacy and opened talks with Western "imperialists" about a mutually acceptable settlement in the Middle East. Brezhnev, Kosygin, and Podgorny spent nights without sleep, even using the hot-line for the first time, trying to bring about a possible compromise with the United States and Western Europe. With instructions from the Politburo, later in June Kosygin flew to the Special U.N. Session and met with Lyndon Johnson in Glassboro, New Jersey, half-way between New York and Washington, in the first U.S.- Soviet summit since Vienna. The Soviet leader and the U.S. President found each other on different wavelengths. Johnson was interested primarily in starting negotiations on strategic arms, not in a possible arrangement for the Middle East. The superpowers' interests in that region remained polar: the Kremlin broke diplomatic relations with Israel and started to rearm and retrain the Egyptian army for a war of revenge, at a larger scale and cost than before.[81]

The precarious balance in Moscow between the state diplomacy of détente and the other two dimensions of Soviet foreign policy was maintained despite the Soviet invasion of Czechoslovakia in August 1968. The anatomy of this case characterized the style of the collective leadership as much as the Berlin crisis was emblematic of Khrushchev's style in national security affairs. The government of Alexander Dubcek in Prague never planned to leave the Warsaw Treaty and attempted to control the process of reforms. But the Kremlin believed it was "losing" Czechoslovakia. Several key factors contributed to the decision: the astonishing pace of the Czechoslovak reforms, panicky information from the Soviet embassy in Prague, pressure from the Polish leader Wladislaw Gomulka and the GDR chief Walter Ulbricht to put an end to the subversive influence of the Prague Spring, and bureaucratic momentum in favor of all-cost preservation of the Soviet security buffers acquired after the Second World War.[82]

The decision to intervene was dictated as much by "internationalist duty" as by military concerns. Czechoslovakia, unlike Hungary in 1956, occupied a strategic corridor between NATO and the Soviet Union, and was the jewel in the crown of Soviet military-industrial nexus.[83] In August the fear of losing Czechoslovakia, along with Soviet military strongholds in Eastern Europe, brought all skeptics in the leadership (Andropov, Ponomarev, Gromyko, Kosygin, and Brezhnev himself) over to the side of dedicated interventionists (Podgorny, Ukrainian party chief Shelest, Mazurov, Ulbricht, and Gomulka).[84] Only the narrow circle of professional "Americanists" in the Central Committee apparatus and the mid-level bureaucracies of the Ministry of Foreign Affairs (MFA) and KGB thought the invasion was a mistake.

After the occupation of Czechoslovakia the Kremlin leaders, to their astonishment, discovered that the whole nation was against them, not just pockets of "counterrevolutionaries." For a while the chances of political restoration of a pro-Soviet regime in the country looked very bleak. Brezhnev and Kosygin, in secret meetings in Moscow, vowed to repeat the Hungarian bloodbath, rather than to capitulate and lose the country to the West—but their speeches betrayed despair.[85]

The "normalization" in Czechoslovakia restored political smugness in Moscow. The outcome was the infamous "Brezhnev Doctrine," which expressed a determination not to let the Communist tide turn back, precluded any defections from the Soviet-run alliance and promised to intervene whenever a regime in any of them was in jeopardy. The restoration of this Stalinist message, diluted in previous years, tied the Soviet foreign policy to the crumbling pillars of the Communist temple and severely handicapped the Soviet diplomacy of détente. Rigid commitments to Eastern European regimes and the expanding aid to radical regimes in the Third World led Moscow down the road to imperial overextension.[86] The collective leadership could not, nor did it attempt to stop this dangerous process.

By the late 1960s the gloom in U.S.-Soviet relations began to dissipate. Foreign policy elites on both sides gradually learned to deal with each other. Stodgy Secretary of State Dean Rusk and Gromyko, tagged "Great Stone Face," or "Grim-Grom," developed a mutual respect and understanding. Their talks were the learning process, or, as Rusk put it, they created "a broader basis for understanding each other's societies."[87]

In January 1967 President Johnson proposed to reach an understanding with the Soviets "which would curb the strategic arms race." It was Americans now, not Soviets, who were trying to bring the other side to the negotiating table. The Johnson administration acted under the increasing financial burden of the Vietnam war and domestic spending, and in a quest for rationality in the weird world of military strategy decided to freeze missile buildup unilaterally at the level of "sufficiency." The Americans' interest was to encourage the Soviets to do the same and to prevent them from deploying a defensive anti-ballistic missile system (ABM), which would have catapulted both superpowers into another cycle of the arms race.[88]

In the eyes of some Soviet officials, it must have seemed ironic that Americans worried about the costs of the arms race. Even years later many in Moscow bureaucracies believed that, aside from the doctrine of "flexible response," the Kennedy administration had enforced the so-called "Rowen strategy": a plan to drive the Soviet economy into exhaustion through the nuclear-missile race.[89] From another angle Johnson's initiative looked like a vindication of the old wisdom "build first, then negotiate," that Khrushchev's successors had opted for. And for many novices to the discourse on nuclear strategic stability the very idea of renouncing the defense against strategic missiles seemed to be dangerous nonsense, if not an "imperialist trap." These suspicions, together with raw feelings about the U.S. role in Vietnam, did not make them overeager to respond to the American offer.

But the Soviets were sophisticated enough to begin immediate preparations for talks, even as Kosygin, then a primary Soviet statesman, continued to voice doubts in public. Both Gromyko and Defense Minister Rodion Malinovsky were sufficiently impressed with the Kennedy missile buildup and American technological superiority to lobby in favor of taking this chance to curb further U.S. breakthroughs. They put together a working group of their subordinates, some of whom had participated in disarmament and test-ban negotiations. This was a real beginning for the Soviet professional arms control elite. The Malinovsky-Gromyko efforts resulted in *Pravda*'s clarification in February 1967, that "the Soviet Government was ready to discuss the problem of averting a new arms race, both in offensive and defensive weapons."[90]

Initially, when the United States led by several years in the missile deployment, the Soviet leadership pushed for the cuts in offensive strategic systems. While Soviet ICBMs became operational in ever greater numbers, the Kremlin leadership still vacillated. In part, as in other cases, this stance illustrated the lack of bureaucratic, as well as political momentum: the Soviet arms controllers never had positions in government comparable to McNamara's "whiz-kids" in the Pentagon and to Arms Control and Disarmament Agency (ACDA) professionals at the State Department. With Malinovsky's death late in 1967, Gromyko lost a crucial ally: Andrei Grechko, the new head of the Defense Ministry, was notoriously suspicious about negotiations with "the number one enemy." Nevertheless the bureaucratic momentum steadily grew, some military leaders learned to trust their diplomatic fellows, and the sober vision of the nuclear deadlock percolated up into the top leadership.[91]

The Kremlin hierarchy learned about arms control from two sources: American counterparts and a new group of Soviet "technocrats." The recognition of the futility of Anti-Ballistic Missile defense was the most striking example. When Kosygin met Johnson in Glassboro, he did not have any prepared position on this subject and therefore spoke in favor of reductions of offensive arms. While he expressed doubts that strategic defense could be a primary source of a new arms race, he seemed influenced, perhaps even swayed, by McNamara's vehement advocacy of strategic stability.[92] A more regular instrument of education appeared with the creation, in early 1968, of a Politburo commission, chaired by Dmitry Ustinov, a veteran of military industries. It included Grechko, Gromyko, head of the Military-Industrial Commission L. V. Smirnov and M. Keldysh, the President of the Soviet Academy of Sciences—all of them regular participants in the Politburo's Defense Council. Keldysh, with his enormous scientific reputation, became for Brezhnev and Kosygin what McNamara was for Johnson: a convincing advocate in favor of limits on ABM defense, thereby clearing the way to negotiations. In May 1968, the Soviets indicated their readiness for the Strategic Arms Limitations Talks (SALT). Successful deployment of Soviet ICBMs and strategic submarines with missiles (SLBMs) undoubtedly made this decision easier for the Kremlin. Very quickly an agreement was reached for a Kosygin-Johnson summit in Leningrad at the end of September.[93]

The invasion of Czechoslovakia on August 20–21, 1968 derailed those plans. Arms control diplomacy seemed to have no deterring effect at all on Soviet interventionism. Could the United States achieve anything by linking the summit with support of the Prague spring? According to Jiri Valenta, "The Johnson administration could either have tacitly warned the Soviet leadership through diplomatic channels about the dangerous consequences of an intervention for both superpowers in the field of arms limitation, or have left the Soviet leadership guessing about a U.S. response."[94]

But at this stage both superpowers were preoccupied lest the "Prague Spring" endanger the much-desired stability in Europe. An informal U.S. spokesman, Henry Kissinger, warned the Czech leaders "not to repeat Imre Nagy's mistake" of seceding from the Warsaw Treaty Organization as Hungary had tried in 1956.[95] As a result the interventionists in Moscow could act feeling certain that the Americans would not become involved. As Dobrynin explained later to Rusk, the two subjects, invasion and arms talks, had "doubtless been on different tracks" in the minds of the Kremlin leadership.[96]

After the invasion, Johnson reluctantly suspended a planned summit. However, as soon as he and his advisers became certain that the occupation would not spread into Romania (which after the Cuban missile crisis had begun a secret quest for rapprochement with the United States)[97], they resumed communications with Moscow through Dobrynin, pushing for the last-minute summit before the inauguration of the next president. The Soviets initially agreed. The First Deputy Premier Kirill Mazurov, one of the primary executioners of the Prague Spring, called for "normalization of relations" and resumption of negotiations. But now, as the Soviets were knocking in the door, President-Elect Richard Nixon decided to postpone SALT, in order to use it later for his own geostrategic aims, first of all in Vietnam.[98]

Conclusion

In retrospect, Johnson's rush for a summit with Moscow, much criticized then and later,[99] had been not only a symptom of his beleaguered Presidency, but also a reflection of deeper interests. The origins of SALT, like the Kennedy-Khrushchev "thaw" in 1963, proved that both sides preferred to put an end to the reckless brinkmanship and instability of the early Cold War. This search for security through arms control and, in a larger sense, for a Cold War order, had been first pronounced in Kennedy's stand in Vienna, reappeared in the aftermath of the Cuban Missile Crisis, and by the late 1960s became accepted by the Soviet rulers.[100] Before curbing their own arsenals, the superpowers arranged to sign, on July 1, 1968, the multilateral nonproliferation treaty, a preventive measure viewed, with some sense, by China and other countries as a second (after the test-ban) stone in the construction of geostrategic status quo.

This trend was not so much a product of the Soviet military buildup;

taken apart from other factors, a unilateral thrust in armaments could only trigger a counteraction, as it often did in the history of U.S.- Soviet confrontation. This time, however, the imminent approach of strategic parity coincided with doctrinal rethinking on both sides and with the "Vietnam syndrome" in the United States. The degradation and weakening of the party component in Soviet foreign policy continued during the 1960s, as the structures of the Communist world were ripped apart by centrifugal forces from Prague to Beijing.

Willy-nilly the Kremlin rulers gravitated to common sense. Arms control became a top issue on the agenda of the Kremlin. It facilitated education of the Soviet leadership and somewhat curbed the influence party priorities played in Soviet foreign policy. SALT negotiations became a catalyst of this process.

The basic question remains, how adequate and effective was American diplomacy in dealing with the Soviet challenge in the 1960s? The Kennedy and Johnson administrations, if measured by common wisdom of the time, fared quite well in adapting the strategies of containment to new realities and managing dangerous crises. They also can be praised for shifting the focus from confrontation to negotiation. However, it wouldn't be wholly unreasonable to take a step further back and reassess the common wisdom itself, in light of better knowledge and understanding of the Soviet side's motives. After all, the revolutionary enhancement of technical capabilities and the increase of "human intelligence" during the 1960s made the Soviet actions and intentions more "transparent" to the U.S. leadership than most historians and political scientists had believed, and perhaps can still imagine.[101]

Conservation of the Soviet regime in its immediate post-Stalin stage under Khrushchev and beyond was based on a promise of peace and better life for increasingly unhappy Soviet populace. The confrontations over Berlin and Cuba had revived fears of war and led the Kremlin to renounce the goal of "historic victory" in favor of strategic parity and cooperation with the United States. Professionals, especially younger experts in Soviet national security elites, took an increasingly critical view of Soviet foreign policy from a viewpoint of *realpolitik*, if not more radical ones.[102] However, the Soviet leadership clung to the tenets of national security and drew only narrow lessons from the perils of nuclear standoff and the new "diffusion of power" in the world.[103] A hulk of old strategic thinking was anchored to the enormous role of the military-industrial interests in Soviet economy, interests that united party bureaucracy with economic management.

American policies and changes in the international environment certainly affected Soviet foreign policy, as it moved from "overextension" in the beginning of the 1960s toward more cautious attitudes in the middle of the decade. But the bipolar Cold War vision survived, along with the commitments it entailed, largely due to the failure of domestic reforms, economic and political. One can agree with an American scholar that "Khrushchev's and Brezhnev's misguided attempts to reconcile détente and expansionism" could be largely explained "by the increased cartelization of the political system, owing to the ossification of the institutions and ideas of Stalin's revolution from above."[104] In this sense the sixties planted the seeds of Brezhnev's imperial overextension. Gorbachev's u-turn in foreign policy fifteen years later, motivated initially by the Krushchevian blueprints in the area of unilateral disarmament and propaganda, ended up in renunciation of imperial policies and the empire itself.

The brief assessment in this chapter portrays American diplomacy largely to be as much a captive of the Cold War confrontation as was the Soviet Union's. The Kennedy and Johnson administrations highlighted and promoted the military, geostrategic aspects of U.S.-Soviet relations, in part to educate the Soviet leadership and check its military might but, in even greater measure, to respond to its own domestic pressures. It proved reluctant to take the lead in changes, such as building economic and cultural bridges to Eastern Europe or improving relations with China. In part, U.S. policymakers seemed to be hesitant to upset the strategic stability and, of course, the American imbroglio in Vietnam after 1964 sapped political will for rapprochement with any Communist regimes in Europe and Asia.

In conclusion, an improved understanding of the Soviet side in the history of U.S.-Soviet diplomacy during the 1960s makes one beware of deficiencies of both *realpolitik* and economic approaches to world diplomacy. While balance of power and economic motives were clearly in ascendance in Soviet policy-making, Soviet foreign policy as a whole remained a unique combination of state, military, and party dimensions, inherited from the previous historic period and resistant to outside pressures for change. Largely because of that, any attempts to make the Soviet Union more manageable—by instruments of diplomacy only—during the 1960s and later, in the Nixon-Kissinger period, were bound to fail. Other measures helped to dilute the Soviet challenge of the 1960s: as the Soviet people became increasingly aware of the realities of the world outside, their expectations and interests came into tacit collision with the old mode of resource distribution that the regime had maintained since Stalin's times. Détente and trade with the West helped accelerate this development. But meanwhile the imperial outreach of the Soviet Union continued, propelled by a bureaucratic gridlock of domestic interests, leaving the Soviet Union as the toughest challenge to American diplomacy.

NOTES

1. See, Paul Kennedy, *The Rise and Fall of Great Powers: Economic Change and Military Conflict from 1500 to 2000.* (New York, 1987), pp. 491–494; John L. Gaddis, *The United States and the End of the Cold War. Implications, Reconsiderations, Provocations* (New York, 1992), pp. 160–161; Walt W. Rostow, "Eastern Europe and the Soviet Union Seen as Problems in Economic Development" (manuscript) October 1990; Bohdan Nahaylo and Victor Swoboda, *Soviet Disunion. A History of the Nationalities Problem in the USSR,* (New York: Free Press, 1990), ch. 10, 11.

2. Kennedy, *The Rise and Fall,* pp. 397, 430.

3. S. V. Kuleshov, ed. , *Nashe otechestvo. Opit politicheskoi istorii* (Our country: Essays in Political History), vol. 2 (Moscow: TERRA, 1991), p. 470.

4. Konstanine Pleshakov and Vladislav Zubok, "The Soviets and the Cold War Dynamics," in David Reynolds, ed., *The Origins of the Cold War in Europe* (New Haven, forthcoming).

5. The international Department (*mezhdunarodni otdel*), headed by Boris Ponomarev, inherited the Comintern/Cominform networks in capitalist countries, primarily in France, Italy, to a lesser extent in Great Britain and Northern America. Its twin-brother (called simply "department" - *otdel*), presided by Yuri Andropov , was reponsible for relations with "socialist countries. " Both had excellent relations with the Party Secretariat, where at least two Secretaries, Otto Kuusinen and Mikhail Suslov, shared their perspective and concerns.

6. Military intelligence (GRU) had other priorities, but sometimes formed a troika with these two organizations.

7. Khrushchev's flirting with the idea of only nuclear deterrence had never been popular with the Soviet military. After his ouster the Soviets continued to rely on both nuclear and conventional deterrence, using the monumental presence of Soviet troops in Eastern Europe as the latter. See, David Holloway, *The Soviet Union and the Arms Race,* 2nd ed. (New Haven, 1984), pp. 40–41; also Raymond Garthoff, *Deterrence and the Revolution in Soviet Military Doctrine* (Washington, 1990); Maj-Gen Valentin Larionov, *Tiazhkii put' poznania: iz istorii izdernoi strategii* (The Hard Way of Learning: From the History of Nuclear Strategy), manuscript, pp. 7–8).

8. Adzhubei was editor-in-chief of *Izvestia,* a major official daily, second only to *Pravda,* whose editor was Satyukov. Kharlamov was a head of the State Television and Radio; Zhukov headed the Society of Cultural Relations Abroad (VOKS).

9. This was the predominent opinion among the "professionals." The author's talk with Gen. Sergei Kondrashov, and Ambassador Vladimir Yerofeev, Moscow, January 14, 1993; on Khrushchev's entourage see: Georgi Arba-

tov, *The System: An Insider's Life in Soviet Politics* (New York, 1992), pp. 83–91; Fedor Burlatsky, *Khrushchev and the First Russian Spring: The Era of Khrushchev Through the Eyes of His Advisor.* (New York, 1991), pp. 183–195.

10. See, Michael Beschloss, *The Crisis Years: Kennedy and Khrushchev, 1960–1963* (New York, 1991).

11. Adam Ulam, *The Rivals: America and Russia Since World War II* (New York, 1971), pp. 295, 327; Gaddis, *Russia, the Soviet Union and the United States: An Interpretive History,* 2nd ed. (New York, 1990), p. 246; also Marc Trachtenberg, *History and Strategy* (Princeton, 1991), pp. 169–334.

12. Beschloss, The Crisis Years, p. 225; Vladislav Zubok, *The New Soviet Evidence on the Berlin Crisis, 1958–1962* (archival findings), pp. 16–18—a paper prepared for the conference "The New Evidence on the Cold War," Moscow, January 12–15, 1993.

13. In October–November 1960 a delegation of Soviet "public figures," including Khrushchev's crony, writer Alexander Korneichuk, attended a Dartmouth conference. Korneichuk met with Averell Harriman and Walt Rostow, two of Kennedy's advisers. In December Rostow traveled to Moscow to take part in the Pugwash conference, where he met Kuznetsov and other Soviet foreign policy officials.

14. Pyotr Abrasimov to Khrushchev, February 8, 1961—Tsentr Khraneniia Sovremennoi Dokumentatsii (The Archives of the former Central Committee of the CPSU, Moscow), [hereafter TsKhSD], Collection 5, Opis 30, Box 365, p. 29.

15. TsKhSD, Collection 5, Series 49, Box 365, p. 25.

16. Adam Ulam, *Expansion and Coexistence: Soviet Foreign Policy, 1917–1973,* 2nd ed. (New York, 1974), p. 653; Beschloss, *The Crisis Years,* 150; another view is in Arthur Schlesinger Jr., *A Thousand Days, John F. Kennedy in the White House,* (Boston, 1965), p. 378.

17. Bolshakov, a KGB officer, transmitted information through Robert Kennedy. Sometimes he acted on instructions of the Presidium, but soon he became a "personal agent" of Khrushchev, who contacted him through the KGB or even directly through his emissaries, like Adzhubei, etc.—see, Beschloss, *The Crisis Years,* pp. 153–157; informal talk with Adzhubei at his dacha near Moscow in June, 1990; a draft of instruction to Bolshakov for his talk with RFK, written by Kuznetsov and M. Zakharov (Defense Ministry) between May 10 and 18, 1961 (the document is in the Presidential Archives).

18. Kuznetsov's memos to the Central Committee on March 24 and 28, 1961—Archiv vneshnei politiki Rossiiskloi Federatsii (The Archives of the Ministry of Foreign Affairs of RSFSR—later referred to as AVP RF), Collection 047, Series 7, Box 127, Folder 23, pp. 59, 65; Gromyko's suggestions on the instructions for disarmament talks—Ibid, pp. 76, 89.

19. TsKhSD, Collection 4, Series 16, Box 944, pp. 38–53.

20. A visit of the U. S. president to the Soviet Union had important symbolic and political significance for Khrushchev and the Soviet leadership. It would have meant world recognition of Soviet policies of "peaceful coexistence." The U-2 incident forced Khrushchev to cancel his invitation to Eisenhower, but he

continued to look for an opportune moment to reissue an invitation to the next U.S. president. On April 26, 1961, the eve of the Vienna summit, V. Kuznetsov included in his list of possible discussion topics prepared for Khrushchev a briefing on "a possible invitation of John Kennedy to visit the Soviet Union" (the text is in the Presidential Archives).

21. Beschloss, *The Crisis Years*, pp. 205–206.

22. Fedor Burlatsky, *Khrushchev*, p. 182.

23. Vienna Meeting Between the Bresident and Chairman Khrushchev, June 3–4, 1961—John F. Kennedy Library, POF:CO:USSR, Box 126, folder 12; M. Beschloss, *The Crisis Years*, pp. 215–220; G. M. Kornienko, "Upushchennaia vozmozhnost. Vstrecha N. S. Khrushcheva i J. Kennedi d Vene v 1961" (A missed opportunity, the meeting of Khrushchev and Kennedy in Vienna in 1961"), *Novaia i Noveishaia Istoriia*, No. 2 (Spring 1992), p. 100. Kornyenko was a Councellor at the Soviet embassy in Washington at the time of the summit, and was informed about the background, preparations, and outcome of the conference. He also studied the Soviet transcripts of the meetings in Vienna, along with other archival documents.

24. The Soviet leader even remarked that it is better to have a war now, before even more destructive weapons would emerge. This wild remark was omitted both in the American and Soviet transcripts of the summit, Kornienko, *Upushchennaia Vozmoshnist*, 101.

25. Jerrold Schecter with Vyacheslav Luchkov, ed., *Khrushchev Remembers: The Glasnost Tapes* (Boston, 1990), p. 163.

26. Z. Vodopianova, V. Zubok, *The New Soviet Evidence on the Berlin Crisis 1958–62*, a research paper presented at the Conference on the new evidence on the Cold War, January 13–16, 1993, Moscow, p. 11.

27. See, Hannes Adomeit, *Soviet Risk-Taking and Crisis Behavior: A Theoretical and Empirical Analysis* (London, 1982), p. 273.

28. TsKhSD, Collection 5, Series 50, Box 226, pp. 25, 34, 35; Zubok, *New Soviet Evidence*, 12; p. Honore Catudal, *Kennedy and the Berlin Wall Crisis. A Case Study in U. S. Decision-Making* (Berlin, 1980), pp. 48–54.

29. Soveshchanie pervikh sekretarei TsK kommunisticheskich i rabochikh partii sotsialisticheskikh stran dlya obmena mneniiami po voprosam, sviazannym s podgotovkoi i zakliucheniiem germanskogo mirnogo dogovora (Conference of the first secretaries of Central Committees of communist and working parties to exchange views on the issues related to preparation and conclusion of the German peace treaty), August 3–5, 1961. Transcripts of sessions—TsKhSD, Collection 4, additional materials, p. 2.

30. Collection 5, Series 30, Box 335, pp. 96, 100, 103; G. M. Kornienko, "Novoye o Karibskov Krizise"(The New Evidence on the Cuban Missile Crisis), *Novaia i Noveishaia Istoriia* No. 3 (May-June, 1991), 82.

31. "Soveshchaniie" Transcripts, pp. 157, 158, 159, 183.

32. Memo of meetings between Khrushchev and Ulbricht on November 30, 1969—AVP RF, Collection "referentura GDR," 1961, Series 57, Box 385, folder 030, 2.

33. Henry Kissinger to the Office of the White House on his conversations with Soviet Delegates to the Pugwash Conference at Stowe, Vermont, September 19, 1961—National Security Archive, the Berlin Crisis files.

34. Peter Wyden, *Wall: The Inside Story of Divided Berlin* (New York: 1989),pp. 85–90; Catudal, *Kennedy and the Berlin Wall*, p. 50; Kornienko, *Upushchennaia vozmozhnost*, pp. 104–106.

35. Indeed, the first contacts in November 1961–January 1962 demonstrated first glimmer of what later became known as *Ostpolitik* in the FRG. See, *Sluzhebnii Obzor Otnosheniii mezhdu SSSR i FRG v 1949–1970* (The official outline of USSR-FRG relations in 1949–1970, prepared by the Historico-Diplomatic Department of the Ministry of Foreign Affairs [MFA])—TsKhSD, Collection 5, Series 69, Box 578, pp. 34–36; also Zubok, *New Soviet Evidence*, pp. 29–30.

36. From the viewpoint of many mid-rank Soviet officials, this episode was the moment when both superpowers were closest to a hot war. It seems that Soviet intelligence mistook the military exercises, ordered by American general Lucius Clay in West Berlin, for the decision to storm the Wall. See on that, Raymond Garthoff, "Berlin 1961: The Record Corrected," *Foreign Policy*, No. 84 (Fall 1991): 142–156.

37. Gromyko and Malinovsky, On measures to control the border between West Berlin and the GDR: A draft of the Politburo decision, November 13, 1961 (the document is in the Presidential Archives).

38. TsKhSD, Collection 5, Series 49, Box 488, pp. 1–5.

39. M. Beschloss, *The Crisis Years*, 333–335; Garthoff, "Berlin, 1961," p. 145.

40. Kornienko, "Novoie o Karibskom krizise," 80; J. G. Blight, D. A. Welch, *On the Brink*. (New York, 1990), p. 329. At the Soviet-Cuban-American conference in Moscow in January 1989 many former participants of the Cuban Missile crisis, including U. S. Secretary of Defense Robert McNamara agreed, that, from Moscow's vantage point, it was a very credible proposition.

41. *Khrushchev Remembers*, p. 170.

42. This view was supported in Gaddis, *Russia, the Soviet Union and the United States*, p. 246.

43. *Khrushchev Remembers*, pp. 493, 494.

44. A. A. Arzumanyan's letter to Khrushchev on January 3, 1962—TsKhSD, Collection 5, Series 30, Box 398, ll 69, 73–75, 84–85.

45. James G. Blight, *The Shattered Crystal Ball: Fear and Learning in the Cuban Missile Crisis* (Savage, 1990), p. 17.

46. General Anatoly Gribkov disclosed the details of military planning and implementation of the operation to the participants of the Cuban-Soviet-American conference in Havana, January 1992. By the time U-2 reconnaissance discovered the sites of middle-range ballistic missiles (MRBMs), 42 were almost operational. This deterrent core was protected by a formidable force in all directions, in the air, and in particular from the sea. The Soviet "provisional" troops, headed by General Issa Plyev, numbered 43,000 men. There were batteries of SAMs and wings of fighter-bombers Il-28. Gribkov also revealed that the Soviet commander in Cuba had at his disposal six tactical nuclear launch-

ers with nine warheads he could use without clearance with Moscow. This meant, of course, that any American conventional operation against Cuba could have led to the use of tactical nuclear weapons with a sure "trip-wire" effect, resulting in a general nuclear war. See, Arthur Schlesinger Jr., "Four Days with Fidel: A Havana Diary," *The New York Review of Books*, March 26, 1992, pp. 22–23; Dino A. Brugiouni, ed. by Robert F. McCort, *Eyeball to Eyeball. The Inside Story of the Cuban Missile Crisis* (New York: Random House, 1991); now the Defense Ministry file on "Anadyr" is declassified, see Bruce J. Allyn, James G. Blight, "Closer Than We Knew," *The New York Times*, November 2, 1992, p. A14.

47. *Khrushchev Remembers*, pp. 172, 175–176, 177; the same reasons can be found in Khrushchev's letter to Castro on January 31, 1963, see the U.S.-Russia-Cuba Project. Documents Released January 21, 1992. The National Press Club, Washington D. C., in *Brown University News* (Providence, RI), February 1992.

48. Blight, *The Shattered Crystal Ball*, pp. 163, 170.

49. *Documents on International Affairs, 1962*, p. 260, quoted in Gaddis, *Russia, the Soviet Union and the United States*, p. 254.

50. My interview with Boris Ponomarev, June 1990, Moscow. He was present at the meeting in Novo-Ogarevo, late October 1962.

51. Kornienko, "Novoie of Karibskom krizise," 88; Interview with Kornienko, November 22, 1989, Moscow.

52. Philip Brenner, "Kennedy and Khrushchev on Cuba: Two Stages, Three Parties," *Problems of Communism. Special Edition*, p. 25.

53. Khrushchev's letter to Castro, January 31, 1962.

54. O. Troyanovsky, "Karibski krizis—vzglyad iz Kermlya" (The Cuban Missile Crisis—As It Looked from the Kremlin), *Mezhdunarodnaya Zhizn*, Moscow, No. 3–4 (March-April, 1992): 174; also quoted in Arthur Schlesinger. "Four Days with Fidel," p. 23.

55. The "big scare" came when the U-2 had been shot down above Cuba on Pliyev's order—Interview with Lieutenant-General Boris T. Surikov, who was in the commanding bunker of the Soviet Air Defence during the crisis, January 1990, Moscow.

56. William Taubman, "The Correspondence: Khrushchev's Motives and His Views of Kennedy," *Problems of Communism. Special Issue.*, p. 17; Zubok, "The Missile Crisis and the Problem of Soviet Learning," Ibid., p. 20, 21; Khrushchev's Letter to Kennedy, December 10, 1962, Ibid., p. 112.

57. Gaddis, *Russia, the Soviet Union and the United States*, p. 256.

58. This idea was proposed first by Leo Szilard to Khrushchev in 1960 during his stay in the United Nations. Khrushchev reacted positively, but decided not to make it a Soviet initiative until the White House would express a definite interest.—TsKhSD, Collection 4, Series 16, Box 907, p. 57.

59. The treaty, concluded by the United States, the Soviet Union and Great Britain, banned nuclear tests on the land surface, in the atmosphere and in space. The TBT was a result of four years of negotiations with initial goal of reaching a comprehensive ban on nuclear testing. The treaty reduced grave

environmental issue of nuclear fall-out, but underground tests continued—see, Glenn T. Seaborg, Benjamin S. Loeb, *Kennedy, Khrushchev and the Test Ban* (Berkeley, 1981).

60. Alexander Fomin to Robert H. Eastbrook, 20 March 1961— NSF:CO:USSR, Box. 176, JFKL.

61. From the American perspective, the MLF "would head off nuclear proliferation by giving Germany . . . more participation in the West's deterrent apparatus."—Frank Coṣtigliola, "The Pursuit of Atlantic Community: Nuclear Arms, Dollars, and Berlin," in Thomas G. Paterson, ed., *Kennedy's Quest for Victory. American Foreign Policy, 1961–1963* (Oxford, 1989), p. 51; for the Soviet assessments: *Sluzhebnii obzor otnoshenii SSSR s FRG*, pp. 38–39.

62. In the spring of 1961 Feklisov-Fomin told an American interlocutor that he forsaw Chinese nuclear weapons within a year and a half. In July 1963, when asked by Averell Harriman, Khrushchev responded it would be years before China would have nuclear weapons—Fomin to Eastbrook; Glenn Seaborg, with Benjamin Loeb, *Kennedy, Krushchev, and the Test Ban* (Berkeley, 1981) 238–239; also Robin Edmonds, *Soviet Foreign Policy, 1962–1973: The Paradox of Super Power.* (London, 1975), p. 31.

63. Georgi Arbatov, *The System*, p. 95; Fedor Burlatsky, *Khrushchev*, pp. 185–186.

64. Arbatov, *The System*, pp. 113–118; author's interview with Fedor Mochulsky, July 1992, Moscow. Mochulsky was a councillor of the Soviet embassy in Beijing in 1962–65.

65. O. Troyanovsky, "Karibski krizis," 178–179; Rostow to the President, July 5, 1963, NSF, Box 265 ACDA-Disarmament, Harriman Trip to Moscow, JFKL.

66. See Gordon Chang, "JFK, China, and the Bomb," *Journal of American History*, 72 (March 1988): 1287–1310; also the same author, *Friends and Enemies. The United States, China, and the Soviet Union, 1948–1972* (Stanford: Stanford University Press, 1990), pp. 236–237, 251–252.

67. Khrushchev's Letters to Kennedy, November 11 and 13, 1962, *Problems of Communism*, pp. 84, 91.

68. Beschloss, *The Crisis Years*, pp. 676–677; *Khrushchev Remembers*, p. 505; Sergei Khrushchev, *Khrushchev on Khrushchev: An Inside Account of the Man and His Era* (Boston, 1990), p. 51.

69. On Soviet economic performance and problems in the 1960s see, Roger Munting, *The Economic Development of the USSR* (London, 1982), pp. 149–159; Alec Nove, *Economic History of the USSR* (New York, 1982), pp. 355–377.

70. The figures produced by the "Correlates-of-War" project, quoted in Kennedy, *The Rise and Fall*, p. 118; The methodological basis for this quantification is not certain, for even now official figures of real Soviet defense expenditures cannot be obtained. For other figures see Holloway, *Soviet Union and the Arms Race*, pp. 114, 118; for methodological problems see Aron -Kazenelinboigen, *Sovetskaia politika i eknomika* (Soviet politics and economy), vol 2. (New York, 1988), pp. 88–125; Western estimates of Soviet defense expenditure as a

proportion of GNP in Holloway, *Soviet Union and the Arms Race*, p. 118.

71. Georgi Kornienko, "On the ABM Treaty," A lecture at the Advanced School for Disarmament and International Security, The Institute of the U. S. and Canada Studies, Moscow, November 1989; Holloway, *Soviet Union and the Arms Race*, pp. 85–86.

72. Ibid., pp. 58–59.

73. Robert S. McNamara, *The Essence of Security* (New York, 1968), pp. 57–59; quoted in Gaddis, *Russia, the Soviet Union*, p. 261.

74. Raymond Garthoff, *Detente and Confrontation, American-Soviet Relations from Nixon to Reagan* (Washington, DC, 1985), pp. 37, 753–754.

75. Vladimir Semichastny, the KGB chief, was Shelepin's protege. Chief of Staff Marshal Sergei Biryuzov was also close to Shelepin's group—Georgi Arbatov, *The System*, p. 109.

76. George Breslauer, *Khrushchev and Brezhnev as Leaders: Building Authority in Soviet Politics* (London, 1982), pp. 179–199; S. V. Kuleshov, *Nashe Otechestrvo*, p. 500; Interview with Georgi Kornienko on Brezhnev's "grooming" by Gromyko and on Brezhnev as a détente's statesman, January, 1990, Moscow.

77. For simplicity I use the name "Politburo," even though at that time this crucial decision-making body still was known as the Central Committee Presidium.

78. Arbatov, *The System*, pp. 113–115, 117–118.

79. Michael J. Sodaro, *Moscow, Germany and the West. From Khrushchev to Gorbachev* (Ithaca, 1990), pp. 72–82, 93–100, 103–107.

80. International Institute for Strategic Studies, *Strategic Survey*, 1972 (London, 1973), pp. 49–50; cited in Gaddis, *Russia, the Soviet Union and the United States*, p. 263; on other forms of aid see Roy Medvedev, *Lichnost i epokha. Politicheskii portret L. I. Brezhneva* (Political portrait of Brezhnev), Vol. 1 (Moskva: Novosti, 1991), p. 187.

81. Medvedev, ibid., pp. 188–189; Lyndon Johnson, *The Vantage Point: Perspectives on the Presidency, 1963–1968* (New York: 1971), pp. 297–301, 481–485.

82. Jiri Valenta, *Soviet Intervention in Czechoslovakia, 1968: Anatomy of a Decision*. Revised Edition (Baltimore, 1991), pp. 12, 125–126, 144–145, 175; Roy Medvedev, *Brezhnev*, p. 199.

83. Sakharov recalled that Efim Slavsky, a minister of the Medium Machine Building (analogue to the Department of Energy in the U. S.) was among the hard-liners.

84. Arbatov, *The System*, pp. 140–141 (he mentions that Stepan Chervonenko, then a Soviet ambassador in Czechoslovakia, related to him Brezhnev's concern for his own position: "After all, it will look as if I lost Czechoslovakia"); also in Valenta, *Soviet Intervention*, 144; Medvedev, *Brezhnev*, p. 202.

85. "The Murder Will Come Out," *New Times*, No. 8, 1991, 24–26.

86. Jack Snyder, *Myths of the Empire. Domestic Politics and International Ambition* (Ithaca, 1991).

87. Dean Rusk, *As I Saw It* (New York, 1990), pp. 357, 358–359.

88. Lyndon B. Johnson, *The Vantage Point*, pp. 479–480; for more specifics see

John Newhouse, *Cold Dawn. The Story of SALT.* (New York, 1973), pp. 78–89; Strobe Talbott, *The Master of the Game: Paul Nitze and the Nuclear Peace* (New York, 1988), pp. 99–101.

89. *Kratkii Obzor Vnutrennei i Vneshnei Politiki Soedinennikh Shtatov, Osnovnikh Napravlenii Voenno-Politicheskogo Kursa Americanskogo Pravitelstva v period s 1961 po 1970 godi* (Moscow 1988), p. 20 (an unclassified review of the U. S. domestic, foreign and military policies in 1961–1970, composed in the research division of the Soviet military intelligence (GRU) and based on its original reports. Henry Rowen was McNamara's aide in the Pentagon in the early 1960s. The existence of this strategy is a matter of dispute, but the Soviets really believed it had existed, and, as the author discovered, continued to believe even now, after the collapse of the Soviet Union.

90. Quoted in Newhouse, *The Cold Dawn*, p. 90; on the Soviet internal politics see, author's interviews with Georgi Kornienko, who had been part of the expert group, and also with Major-General Valentin Larionov, a retired professor of the Academy of the Soviet General Staff, December 1989, January 1990, Moscow; also from Kornienko's lecture "*On the ABM Treaty.*"

91. At first the group of arms control experts included Georgi Kornienko, a head of the U. S. Directorate of the Ministry of Foreign Affairs, Kirill Novikov, a head of the Ministry's Department of International Organizations, General Chernyakhovsky, a head of the Operational Directorate (Rocket Forces) of the General Staff. Later the group was expanded with experts from the Directorate of Armaments of the General Staff, the Military-Industrial Commission at the Council of Ministers, the Defense Department of the Central Committee's apparatus—Interview with Kornienko, June 1991, Moscow; Kornienko, "*On the ABM Treaty.*"

92. Ibid. In his lecture Kornienko used quotations from the Soviet transcripts of Glassboro meetings that are still classified); also see, Gordon R. Wihmiller, *U. S. -Soviet Summits: An Account of East-West Diplomacy at the Top, 1955–1985* (New York, 1986), p. 152; Glenn Seaborg, with Benjamin Loeb, *Stemming the Tide: Arms Control in the Johnson Years* (Lexington, MA, 1987), pp. 427–430.

93. Kornienko, "On the ABM Treaty"; Newhouse, *The Cold Dawn*, p. 130.

94. Valenta, *Soviet Intervention*, p. 133.

95. Quoted in Ibid., p. 191.

96. Seaborg, *Stemming the Tide*, p. 438; The transcripts of the WTO meeting in Moscow after the invasion don't even mention the U. S. reaction—"Murder Will Come Out," *New Times*, 1991, No. 8–9.

97. Raymond Garthoff at the Conference on the New Evidence on the Cold War, January 15, 1993, Moscow.

98. Minutes of NSC Meetings, August 23, September 4, 1968, NSF, Meetings, Box 2, LBJL; W. W. Rostow to the President, NSF, Rostow File, Ibid; author's interview with Walt Rostow on February 19, 1991 in Austin, Texas; Johnson, *The Vantage Point*, p. 490; Richard Nixon, *The Memoirs*, Vol. 1 (New York, 1979), pp. 428, 429.

99. John J. McCloy to the President, Dec. 14, 1968, NSF, Rostow files, Box. 11, LBJL.

100. On this "new maturity" in U. S. -Soviet relations see, John Gaddis, *The Long Peace: Inquiries into the History of the Cold War* (New York: Oxford, 1987), pp. 239–243.

101. On the revolution in intelligence, see Gaddis, *The Long Peace*, pp. 199–206; on "humint" see Jerrold Shechter and Peter Deriabin, *The Spy Who Saved the World: How a Soviet Colonel Changed the Course of the Cold War* (New York, 1992); a recent conference on the Cuban Missile Crisis, sponsored by the Central Intelligence Agency, revealed that the Kennedy Administration had been informed from many sources about the missile deployments in Cuba, but had ignored this evidence. *The New York Times*, October 14, 1992.

102. In a sign of growing tension within Soviet elites some KGB, military and diplomatic officials either switched to the Western side in the Cold War or had to live a dual life. On the extreme side of this palitra was a GRU officer and double-agent Oleg Penkovsky. On the moderate side, Sergei N. Khrushchev, at the end of the 1960s managed to send the tapes with his father's memoirs for storage in the United States.

103. On the "lessons" on the American side, see: Walt W. Rostow. *The Diffusion of Power* (New York, 1972).

104. Snyder, *Myths of Empire*, p. 252.

RECOMMENDED READING

Arbatov, Georgi. *The System: An Insider's Life in Soviet Politics*. New York: 1992.

Beschloss, Michael. *The Crisis Years: Kennedy and Khrushchev, 1960–1963*. New York: 1991.

Gaddis, John. *The Long Peace: Inquiries into the History of the Cold War*. New York: 1987.

Schecter, Jerrold with Vyacheslav Luchkov, ed. *Khrushchev Remembers. The Glasnost Tapes* Boston: 1990.

Ulam, Adam. *The Rivals: America and Russia Since World War II*. New York, 1971.

6

"It's Easy to Win a War on Paper": The United States and Vietnam, 1961–1968

•

ROBERT D. SCHULZINGER

From 1961 to 1968 U.S. involvement in the war in Vietnam grew from a marginal issue into an obsession. A war in Southeast Asia, an area policymakers considered significant but distinctly subordinate to U.S. interests in Europe and the competition with the Soviet Union, gradually absorbed nearly all of Washington's attention. What began as an effort to fortify the policy of containment and enhance the credibility of American threats of the use of force against Communism, ended by alarming U.S. allies in Europe and Asia, destroying domestic consensus over foreign policy, and contributing to the collapse of trust in political leaders and institutions. Throughout the administrations of John F. Kennedy and Lyndon B. Johnson, officials waged what they considered a limited war, designed to compel the North Vietnamese to quit the battle and convince the National Liberation Front (NLF) to abandon their guerrilla activities against the Saigon authorities. Yet American participation in the war failed to establish a viable government in the Republic of Vietnam (South Vietnam), capable of defending itself against Communist insurgents or an invasion from the North. Intervention created an unhealthy dependence on the United States. The more the Americans did, the less the Saigon government could or would do in its own behalf.

American policy makers persistently misunderstood fast changing conditions within Vietnam. Some critics of U.S. involvement claimed that what journalist Frances Fitzgerald characterized as the Americans' "invincible ignorance" of Vietnamese history, culture, and society made failure virtually inevitable.[1] It was understandable, however.

What the Americans attempted in Vietnam had little relevance to what happened in that country.

Intervention originated during the Truman and Eisenhower administrations as part of the Cold War. It continued in the 1960s because of the perceptions, memories, hopes for the future, concerns over domestic politics, and the personalities and rivalries of high officials. Officials in both the Kennedy and Johnson administrations tried to build on and surpass the records of their predecessors in Vietnam. Under Kennedy American participation rose gradually, preparing the way for a dramatic escalation under Johnson. Sometime in the period 1964–1965 the U.S. commitment passed a point of no return; by 1968 the war pushed aside all other issues of U.S. foreign relations and domestic politics.

The New Frontier and Vietnam

Kennedy won the presidency in 1960 with promises to lift public policy from the torpor he claimed had characterized the Eisenhower administration's conduct since 1957. He pledged to "get America moving again," and shortly after taking office he asked his staff "how do we get moving" on Vietnam.[2] The question reflected Kennedy's own longstanding interest in Vietnam. While a senator he had belonged to the American Friends of Vietnam. He had been one of the staunchest supporters of Ngo Dinh Diem, the President of the Republic of Vietnam since 1955. Like most advocates of containment in the 1950s, Kennedy believed that an anticommunist Southeast Asia stood as a bulwark against the People's Republic of China. Americans expressed ambivalence toward nationalist movements in the region. They offered some support in the hopes that independence movements could create viable noncommunist nations. At the same time Americans feared that Asian nationalists might align with Communists.

Both the Truman and Eisenhower administrations supported France in its war with a Vietnamese Communist/nationalist alignment, the Vietminh, led by Ho Chi Minh. That war ended in 1954 when the Vietminh defeated the French at Dienbienphu. The United States attended the Geneva conference that followed Dienbienphu but Washington refused to sign the Geneva agreements. The accords called for elections throughout Vietnam within two years and created a temporary ceasefire line at the seventeenth parallel. Soon after Geneva the United States supplanted France as the major sponsor of the anticommunist elements in the southern sector of the country. The Central Intelligence Agency encouraged hundreds of thousands of mostly Catholic Vietnamese to flee from the North to the South. The U.S. embassy backed the political aspirations of Ngo Dinh Diem, a nationalist who had been in the United States during the French-Vietminh war. In 1955 Diem became the president of a separate, independent Republic of Vietnam in the South. With American backing he refused to participate in the country-wide elections promised at Geneva, and Vietnam was divided into two states, one Communist and one noncommunist.

Additional attention to Southeast Asia generally and Vietnam specifically was timely in early 1961. A three way guerrilla war between Communist, anticommunist and neutralist factions gathered intensity in Laos.[3] On December 20, 1960 the remnants of the Vietminh remaining in the South had formed a National Liberation Front and had initiated a guerrilla war against the government of President Diem. The Saigon government rested on the narrow social foundations of wealthy landowners, French educated civil servants, and Catholics, who made up fewer than 20 percent of the population. Walt W. Rostow, formerly an economist at the Massachusetts Institute of Technology, and now on the staff of the National Security Council, responded to Kennedy's plea for action by recommending that South Vietnam be used as a showcase for the ways in which academic theories of economic development could by applied to the competition between the United States and the Soviet Union in the poor areas of the world. Rostow traveled to Vietnam in May 1961 and soon after his return Kennedy approved his suggestion that the United States increase its aid to Vietnam by $42 million above the $220 million it currently spent yearly to aid the South Vietnamese government.

Kennedy also accepted the suggestions for the more assertive use of armed forces made by General Maxwell Taylor, who had grown dissatisfied with the Eisenhower administration's disdain for ground troops. The president sent hundreds of additional U.S. army soldiers to South Vietnam to train the soldiers of the Army of the Republic of Vietnam (ARVN). He ordered 400 Special Forces (nicknamed Green Berets for their distinctive headgear) to lead 9,000 mountain tribesmen in an effort to stop infiltration of forces from North Vietnam. He directed the CIA to conduct commando raids against the North. The United States provided weapons for local militias to use against the Communist insurgents (known colloquially as the Viet Cong). By the end of 1961 3,205 American advisers were in South Vietnam, and the number climbed to 9,000 the next year. These advisers moved hundreds of thousands of Vietnamese peasants from their homes to so-called strategic hamlets, designed to deprive the Viet Cong guerrillas of access to food and support from the local population.

Planners in Washington hailed the strategic hamlets as a "quantum leap" in the war effort, but the creation of these new villages also hastened the ongoing disruption of daily life in South Vietnam.[4] The movement of such large numbers of farmers from their traditional lands strained the resources of the South Vietnamese government and provided the National Liberation Front with propaganda to use against Saigon. The policy only alienated the rural population from the central authorities. Soon the South Vietnamese air force began bombing, napalming, and dropping defoliants on areas evacuated by the peasants removed to the strategic hamlets. Air actions took an enormous toll on the Viet Cong, but they also killed thousands of civilians. The NLF turned the destruction wreaked on the countryside to its own advantage by telling farmers who remained in their homes that the government was attacking its own citizens. American reporters, expressing skepticism that the Saigon government was winning the war, questioned General Paul D. Harkins, commander of the Military Advisory Command, Vietnam (MACV), about the complaints that indiscriminate bombing was alienating the peasantry from the Saigon government. Napalm, he replied "really puts the fear of God into the Viet Cong, and that is what counts."[5]

From the beginning of the Kennedy administration American optimism and eagerness to progress in the war collided with President Diem's resistance to making his government more responsive to the South Vietnamese people. In May 1961 Vice President Johnson visited Saigon. Although he praised Diem as the "Winston Churchill of Southeast Asia," he added that South Vietnam needed to "pursue vigorously appropriate measures . . . to achieve a happy and prosperous society." A British diplomat who witnessed Johnson's speech cabled the Foreign Office that the Americans were full of plans to reform South Vietnam, but these blueprints were as useful as sticking "thickening paper over the cracks after the previous layer has split."[6] By 1962 Americans had grown frustrated with Diem's unwillingness to delegate authority and broaden the base of his support. His insularity affected the war effort, and the ARVN refused to take the initiative against the Viet Cong. Theodore Heavner, deputy director of the State Department's working group on Vietnam, complained that American officials in comfortable offices in Washington or Saigon were brimming with ideas, but "it's easy to win a war on paper." He worried that the Vietnamese "don't change quickly," and the Viet Cong's continued offensive did not provide much time.[7]

American officials grew increasingly apprehensive as conditions in South Vietnam deteriorated in 1963. Their anxiety led them to redouble efforts to persuade or force the government of South Vietnam to change. The war went badly, the NLF fought better than the ARVN, and Diem's support nearly collapsed in the face of an uprising by Buddhists who made up a majority of the population of the South. On January 2, 1963 a Viet Cong battalion, outnumbered four to one, scored a major victory over ARVN forces, supported by armor, artillery, and U.S. army helicopters, at the town of Ap Bac, approximately 35 miles southwest of Saigon. Reports in the *Washington Post* and the *New York Times* of a "major defeat" brought the issue before the public.[8] The staff of the national security council became alarmed after receiving an angry report on the battle from Colonel John Paul Vann, the American adviser to the ARVN forces. Vann berated the Vietnamese for their "damn miserable" performance and accused their officers of cowardice.[9]

The White House reacted to the catastrophe at Ap Bac and the bad publicity it generated by looking for a new ambassador. A staff member of the national security council wrote that a "single strong executive" was needed to "use all the leverage we have to persuade Diem to adopt policies which we espouse."[10] In the summer the administration asked a prominent Republican, Henry Cabot Lodge, to become U.S. ambassador to Vietnam. The Americans wanted a popular government in Saigon, one that could foster nationalist, anticommunist fervor on the part of the largely rural and Buddhist population. Only such a government had a chance to create an armed force that could move effectively against the NLF fighters. Currently the leadership of the ARVN seemed more interested in preserving their own privileges than in fighting the war. For his part Diem worried more about disloyal army officers threatening his regime than he did about fighting the Viet Cong.

American anxiety regarding Diem's unpopularity and his army's reluctance to fight boiled over in the summer of 1963. Religious leaders of the Buddhist majority had long resented the rule of the Ngo family. Diem, a self-contained, ascetic, almost mystical man, relied on the advice of his brother, Ngo Dinh Nhu, and Tran Le Xuan (his brother's wife, better known as Madame Nhu). The Ngos barely concealed their contempt for Buddhism and rejected calls to relax restrictions on Buddhist religious and political activities. In May, the long-simmering dispute erupted into street demonstrations in which the Buddhists' demanded to fly their religious flags. The government, responding with clubs, tear gas, and gunfire, killed several demonstrators. Further demonstrations took place for the next month, climaxing on June 11. On that day a seventy-three-year old Buddhist monk, Thich Quang

Duc, turned the local Buddhist rebellion into an international crisis by pouring gasoline over himself and burning himself to death in the midst of a busy Saigon intersection. He had alerted members of the international press before taking his life and gory pictures of his suicide were captured on film and broadcast around the world.

The shocking images horrified Americans who previously had given little thought to Vietnam. Senator Frank Church, an Idaho Demo-crat, told the Foreign Relations Committee that "such grisly scenes have not been witnessed since the Christian martyrs walked hand-in-hand into the Roman arenas."[11] President Kennedy told ambassador-designate Lodge that "no news picture in history has generated as much emotion around the world as that one had."[12] Soon after the immolation the State Department pressed Diem to reach an agreement with the Buddhists to defuse the crisis. Within the White House, how-ever, staff members of the national security council quickly abandoned what little hope remained of encouraging the Diem government to reform. They decided to move up the date of Lodge's ambassadorship and quietly informed South Vietnam's vice-president that the United States was ready to support him if President Diem were to lose power. Negotiations with the Buddhists did not end the demonstrations, and another burned himself in August. Madame Nhu's outrageous com-ment that the Buddhists had only "barbecued a *bonze* [monk] with imported gasoline" provoked the White House to inform Diem that he had to get his sister-in-law out of the country.[13] Diem responded on August 21 by proclaiming martial law. His brother Nhu's special forces and police units raided Buddhist pagodas throughout the country, arresting monks and killing several who refused custody.

Lodge, who arrived in Saigon the next day,immediately learned of a plot on the part of several of the ARVN's top generals to oust Nhu and possibly Diem. The South Vietnamese president had survived several earlier coup attempts, but now the generals believed they had, for the first time, the unqualified backing of the United States. The ambas-sador supported their efforts, as did Michael Forrestal, the staff mem-ber on the National Security Council in charge of Vietnam, and Assis-tant Secretary of State for Far Eastern Affairs Roger Hilsman. Acting in the absence of the president, who was vacationing on Cape Cod, For-restal prepared a cable to Lodge promising the generals "direct sup-port" should they oust Diem.[14] Despite assurance of U.S. backing, the generals aborted their coup on August 31, fearful that Diem had learned of their plans.

Their reluctance to go forward without certainty of success left American officials more perplexed than ever about what to do about

Vietnam. Most American officials were almost desperate for a government in Vietnam eager to press the war against the Viet Cong. As plans for the coup unraveled in late August, Secretary of Defense McNamara, Chairman of the Joint Chiefs of Staff Maxwell Taylor, and CIA director John McCone expressed support for Diem. But the current government was preoccupied with the Buddhists and a dissatisfied army. By the end of August, Washington had lost all confidence in the Diem government. Moreover, future relations between the Kennedy administration and Diem were likely to get even worse, since Diem suspected that Lodge had joined with his rivals in the ARVN. The plotters' desire for more aggressive action against the Viet Cong made Diem and Nhu wonder if fighting the Communists was in their own personal best interests.

In September, the future of U.S. policy toward Vietnam riveted the public. Kennedy addressed Vietnam in several interviews. He said "we are for those things which help win the war there. What interferes with the war effort, we oppose." He identified Diem and Nhu as interfering with the war. "I don't think the war can be won," he told Walter Cronkite "unless the people [of South Vietnam] support the effort, and in my opinion, in the last two months, the government has gotten out of touch with the people." He thought the Saigon government might regain some of that trust, as he signaled the American desire for Diem to drop his brother: "with changes in policy and perhaps with personnel, I think it can."[15] Some journalists in Vietnam and academic experts went much further and publicly called for an end to support of Diem. Stanley Karnow, reporting in the *Saturday Evening Post* on the battles between the government and the Buddhists, condemned the Ngo family as "the strongest communist allies in the country. . . . They have sown suspicion and chaos."[16] Cornell political science professor George McT. Kahin, later a severe critic of U.S. escalation of the war, encouraged Senator Church to "press the administration to . . . take the calculated risk of opening the way for new leadership, rather than *half* encouraging this while at the same time continuing with the existing policy of backing Nhu and Diem."[17]

Behind the scenes the White House moved fitfully toward a final break with Diem. Rumors flew that Nhu was looking to make a "deal with North Vietnam for a truce in the war, a complete removal of the US presence and a neutralist" South Vietnam.[18] Kennedy sent two fact-finding missions to Vietnam in September. The first, led by Marine General Victor Krulak and Joseph A. Mendenhall, a Foreign Service officer who had served in Vietnam, returned with wildly divergent opinions. Krulak supported Diem and reported that despite the political divisions with the Buddhists the war was going well. Mendenhall, on the other hand, brought back a gloomy assessment of a religious civil war and a government on the verge of collapse. An exasperated president asked "you two did visit the same country, didn't you?" After his advisers debated whether the war was being won or if the Diem government could be salvaged, Kennedy exploded. "This is impossible," he said, "we can't run a policy when there are such divergent views on the same set of facts."[19]

Kennedy thereupon sent another fact-finding mission to Saigon led by Secretary of Defense McNamara and Chairman of the Joint Chiefs of Staff Taylor, both strong supporters of the war. Both men returned optimistic about the military effort. They proposed that the 16,000-man U.S. advisory contingent could be withdrawn in 1965 if things continued to go well. They also proposed that the president remove a 1,000-man construction battalion once it finished its work at the end of 1963. Kennedy agreed to do so but an additional 1,000 men were to be sent as their replacements. McNamara and Taylor presented a much grimmer view of an unpopular and oppressive Diem government. They suggested that the announcement of proposed troop withdrawals would be another mode of pressuring Diem.

By the middle of October communications had broken down between Washington and Diem. Nhu publicly charged that the cuts in U.S. aid to his country had "initiated a process of disintegration" in Vietnam.[20] The generals who had plotted Diem's overthrow in August once more approached the United States to determine its attitude. The White House responded that it "did not wish to stimulate" a coup but would not "thwart" one either. Internally, White House officials wanted to make certain that the coup would succeed and that it could maintain a "plausible denial" of Lodge's involvement.[21] On October 29, Kennedy met with his Vietnam advisers to discuss the prospects for a coup, but once more they reached no consensus. On November 1 the Vietnamese generals moved anyway, convinced that once they succeeded support would flow from the United States. The army installed General Duong Van Minh as president. Lodge, informed in advance of the plot, made only a perfunctory offer to Diem and Nhu of safe conduct out of the country. They refused, and the next morning they were murdered in an armored car after having been captured by their military opponents. When Kennedy heard the news, his face turned white, and he fled from the room. He had been one of Diem's earliest supporters; now he wanted him replaced as president, not slain. Three weeks later he too was murdered.

Kennedy bequeathed a terrible legacy on Vietnam to his successor,

Lyndon Johnson. The United States was committed to participation in a civil war in Vietnam, without guarantees of success. Sixteen thousand U.S. Army, Navy and Marine Corps troops led ARVN soldiers in daily operations against the NLF, who exercised control over large parts of the countryside. In later years, when the war turned into a catastrophe for the United States, some of Kennedy's loyal supporters claimed that he had contemplated withdrawing U.S. forces from Vietnam. Purportedly, Kennedy had told Kenneth O'Donnell, his appointments secretary, and senate majority leader Mike Mansfield that he wanted to wait until the election of 1964 and then withdraw. He may have made such remarks, although there is no contemporary evidence of them. Even if he did, they represent more musings born of the frustrations of dealing with Diem than an acceptance of a Communist triumph.

Johnson's Vain Effort to Stay the Course

While the Kennedy administration had undertaken a reassessment of its tactics in Vietnam in September and October, the basic policy remained victory in the civil war over the NLF. Until the end Kennedy told Diem that he gave "absolute priority to the defeat of the Communists." He maintained the same position publicly. In remarks prepared for delivery in Dallas on the afternoon of November 22 he would have maintained that Americans "dare not weary of the task" of supporting South Vietnam no matter how "risky and costly" that support might be.[22] Yet by November 1963 the White House recognized a trilemma in U.S. policy toward Vietnam: doing more, doing less, or doing the same all entailed enormous risks.

Johnson became president promising continuity with his predecessor's personnel and policies. Keeping the advisers proved easy: Johnson told each White House staff member how vital he was to the success of the new administration. Determining precise policy proved far more difficult in the case of Vietnam. From November 1963 until July 1965 Johnson alternated between activism and passivity in setting Vietnam policy. He took a series of steps, some smaller, some larger, which, taken together, made the war a fully American affair.

The advisers Johnson retained had an interest in the success of the policy of American intervention to determine the government of South Vietnam. They agreed that abandonment of the U.S. commitment to Vietnam would represent a setback in the Cold War competition with Communism. Reversing the course of additional involvement in Vietnam also held domestic political perils. According to national security adviser McGeorge Bundy, "if we should be the first to quit in Saigon" Johnson would face the same sort of damage that President Harry Truman and Secretary of State Dean Acheson encountered when the Korean War went badly.[23] The coup of November 1, 1963 did not foster the political stability or renewed South Vietnamese war effort expected by planners who had recommended American participation in Diem's ouster. Complicity in the coup had breached a significant threshold. Now Americans were willing to say directly who they wanted to take charge in Saigon and what policies they should pursue. Other Vietnamese factions, dissatisfied with the authorities, now justifiably could look to Washington for support. Faced with what Ambassador Lodge characterized as the deep "dry rot and lassitude" within the government of South Vietnam, the new Johnson administration looked for ways to stiffen the nerve of the authorities in Saigon.[24]

In January 1964 Johnson's militant advisers decided that the war had reached the point of a "definitive crisis." Walt Rostow warned of widespread defeatism in South Vietnam that could contribute to "the greatest setback to U.S. interests in the world scene in many years." To reverse the sense that the United States lacked a "viable concept for winning the war" he advocated "a direct political-military showdown with Hanoi" before the end of the year.[25] Johnson would not go so far in an election year, hoping to keep the Vietnam story off the front pages and the evening news before election day. Johnson did not directly discourage his subordinates from pursuing an assertive Vietnam policy, but hoped for a delay in any showdown with the North. He seemed to agree with national security adviser McGeorge Bundy's caution that the worst political damage would come from appearing to "quit Saigon." With the situation so desperate, the time was not ripe to contemplate a peaceful settlement. "*When* we are stronger," Bundy wrote, "*then* we can face negotiations."[26]

In late January 1964 the Pentagon helped engineer another coup in Saigon, replacing General Minh with General Nguyen Khanh. Americans in Saigon and Washington spent the next six months looking for ways to demonstrate United States support for the government of South Vietnam. McNamara and Taylor returned to Vietnam in March and May. They reported that "the situation has unquestionably been growing worse" since September 1963. The Viet Cong controlled 40 percent of the territory and the Saigon government was discouraged about the morale of the ARVN fighters. General Khanh told the Americans that only some "glamorous, dramatic victory," perhaps involving a U.S.-led invasion, would rally the South Vietnamese.[27] Neither General William Westmoreland, the new U.S. commander in the South, nor

President Johnson would contemplate action against the North in the spring. Westmoreland thought that such activities would divert the ARVN from less theatrical, but more productive actions clearing the NLF from the area around Saigon and the Mekong River Delta. Wanting to run in November as a leader of a country at peace supported by a wide popular consensus Johnson resisted too. He remembered how Chinese intervention in the Korean war had nearly ruined the Truman administration, and he would not approve moves that might provoke a similar intervention in Vietnam.

American policymakers still believed that the Saigon government needed assurances from Washington to boost morale. In June the president's principal advisers floated the idea of a congressional resolution supporting American air or ground action against the north. The State Department prepared a draft of such a resolution, but Johnson declined to submit it. Congress was debating a wide-ranging civil rights bill, an important element on Johnson's domestic agenda. Johnson also did not want to draw attention to Vietnam before the Republican convention met in mid July. The Republicans nominated Senator Barry Goldwater, who had accused Johnson of inaction in Vietnam during the spring primary season.

In early August, however, two controversial incidents off the coast of North Vietnam revived the idea of introducing such a congressional resolution and provided excuses for the first air strikes by U.S. forces against the North. Two U.S. destroyers, the *Maddox* and the *C. Turner Joy*, had conducted so-called De Soto patrols in connection with a covert operation, OPLAN 34-A. In De Soto patrols the American vessels supported the activities of the South Vietnamese navy by conducting surveillance, sometimes within the 12 mile coastal limits claimed by North Vietnam, along the North Vietnamese coast bordering the Gulf of Tonkin. The destroyers approached the coast in order to provoke the operators of coastal radar installations to activate their machines. The radars would then emit radio signals that would reveal their location to the sophisticated electronic equipment on the American ships. In response, the *Maddox* and the *C. Turner Joy* would notify the accompanying South Vietnamese patrol boats of the position of the North's radar, allowing the South Vietnamese to attack.

These De Soto patrols provoked the North Vietnamese navy to attack the *Maddox* on the night of August 2. Two nights later the commander of the *C. Turner Joy* believed that his destroyer also was under attack and ordered his gunners to return fire. They did so but hit nothing, probably because there were no North Vietnamese ships in the area and no attack had occurred. Nevertheless, Johnson ordered air strikes against four North Vietnamese bases and submitted to Congress the resolution prepared earlier in the spring. McNamara testified before Congress that both the *Maddox* and the *C. Turner Joy* had been attacked, although at the time he knew that only scanty evidence existed of the second attack. He also clearly did not tell the truth when he assured lawmakers that "the *Maddox* was operating in international waters and was carrying out a routine patrol of the type we carry out all over the world at all times."[28]

McNamara's testimony and the conviction, expressed by Secretary of State Dean Rusk, that "an immediate and direct reaction by us is necessary," carried the day in Congress. On August 7 both houses passed the Gulf of Tonkin Resolution authorizing the president to "take all necessary measures to repel any armed attack against the forces of the United States and to prevent any further aggression." The resolution also authorized the president "upon the request of any nation in Southeast Asia, to take . . . all measures including the use of armed force to assist" in its defense and resistance against aggression or subversion.[29] The vote in the House of Representatives was unanimous, while in the Senate only two Democrats, Ernest Greuning of Alaska and Wayne Morse of Oregon, voted no. The resolution's extraordinarily broad grant of authority had no time limit. Later Johnson would use it to justify the greatly expanded American role in the war.

The Tonkin Gulf Resolution and the limited air strikes against the North did little to fulfill the planners' hopes of bolstering the morale of General Khanh's government. The moody and impatient Khanh wanted the United States to mount a continuing bombing campaign. Assistant Secretary of State for Far Eastern Affairs William P. Bundy thought that Khanh's chances of remaining in power were only 50–50. He told Johnson that "even if the situation in our own view does go a bit better, we have problems in maintaining morale."[30]

Yet the resolution and the air raids of August removed Vietnam from the political debate during the 1964 election in the United States. Johnson followed the advice of his assistant Bill Moyers to "keep the public debate on Vietnam to as low a level as possible."[31] Goldwater dropped his earlier condemnations of Johnson's timidity. The president broadcast an air of moderation toward the war, refusing to recommend either withdrawal or intensification. Most of his listeners believed that he wanted to keep the United States out of a full-scale shooting war while at the same time preventing a Communist victory. Most supported that course. He made one major campaign speech on Vietnam in which he sounded moderate while leaving considerable room for a deeper U.S. commitment at a later date. He said that only

"as a last resort" would he "start dropping bombs around that are likely to involve American boys in a war in Asia with 700 million Chinese."
He could not predict the future, he said, but "we are not going north
and drop bombs at this stage of the game, and we are not going south
and run out and leave it for the Communists to take over."[32]

The Americanization of the War

The point of no return for the United States came in 1965. By June Johnson had taken a series of decisions that transformed the fighting into an
American war. In July the president presided over a celebrated discussion with his key advisers about whether to increase the number of U.S.
ground forces by 100,000 and call up the reserves. These discussions
ratified earlier decisions to increase the American involvement in the
air and ground war. They represented the last chance to reverse course,
but by the time they occurred Johnson had so deeply committed the
United States to the fighting that it seemed far easier to Johnson and his
advisers to go forward than to diminish their involvement.

Throughout this period of gradually increasing American involvement the Johnson administration strived to keep the participation limited. Planners expected to break the will of the North Vietnamese, force
them to stop the NLF fighters, without at the same time provoking
retaliation from the Soviet Union or China. Most officials thought that
limiting the geographical extent of the war would lessen the impact on
the American public, sustaining support for it. Johnson and his advisers did not want the war to get out of hand: to "get the American people too angry" as Dean Rusk put it.[33] An aroused public might demand
greater force and the administration would lose control of management of the war. It became nearly impossible to limit the war and wage
it effectively. Every step up the ladder of escalation alarmed the Soviets and Chinese and soon provoked reactions from a growing antiwar
movement at home.

Political instability had persisted in South Vietnam after the U.S.
presidential election of 1964. In December Senator Mike Mansfield
warned Johnson that "we remain on a course in Vietnam which takes
us further and further out onto the sagging limb."[34] The succession of
military regimes drove Johnson nearly apoplectic. "I don't want to hear
any more of this coup shit," he exploded to aides.[35] A continuous series
of high-level visits went from Washington to Saigon and returned with
the conclusion that the war was nearly lost. The morale of the ARVN
had continued to sink as the initiative in the battle passed to the NLF

fighters. ARVN field commanders and the government in Saigon seemed paralyzed with fear that the United States would not support them. In this atmosphere U.S. military advisers continued their search for morale boosters for the Saigon regime. General Maxwell Taylor, appointed ambassador to Vietnam in the summer of 1964, told Johnson early in 1965 that a program of air raids, lasting longer than the retaliatory strike of the previous August, would "inject some life into the dejected spirits" in Saigon. Johnson was willing to try, but recognized that the air raids had more to do with encouraging the flagging spirits in Saigon than changing the military fortunes of the war. He predicted to Taylor that "this guerrilla war cannot be won from the air." Taylor thought it would buy time and "bring pressure on the will of the chiefs of the Democratic Republic of Vietnam [North Vietnam]. As practical men, they cannot wish to see the fruits of ten years of labor destroyed by slowly escalating air attacks."[36]

The program of sustained bombing of the North, code named Operation Rolling Thunder, began in February. On February 7 NLF fighters fired artillery at the barracks of American marine base at Pleiku in the central highlands of Vietnam, destroying ten planes and killing eight Americans and wounding 126. American officials considered the attack another episode in a series, but they believed that the cumulative impact of assaults on Americans would panic the already demoralized South Vietnamese. After first ordering a single retaliatory strike against the North, Johnson authorized Rolling Thunder on February 13. The bombing was extensive. In April U.S. and South Vietnamese air force and navy planes flew 3,600 monthly sorties against fuel depots, bridges, munitions factories, and power plants in the North.

As had been the case for the previous several years, the results of the offensive did not meet expectations. In early March national security adviser McGeorge Bundy presented Johnson his gloomy assessment that "the chances of a turn around in South Vietnam remain less than even."[37] Morale of the South Vietnamese government did not rebound sharply, because the infiltration of supplies and troops continued virtually unabated from the North to the South. North Vietnam quickly adapted to round-the-clock bombing. There were few industrial targets in the north and the North Vietnamese used darkness and cloud cover to rebuild destroyed highways and railroad bridges. Aware that Rolling Thunder offered little more than a temporary respite from the Viet Cong's ability to strike at will against the ARVN, General Westmoreland called for the American troops to conduct ground operations on their own throughout the South. The time had come, he told the president in March "to put our own finger in the dike."[38]

Johnson still resisted a complete Americanization of the war. Speaking at Johns Hopkins University in April he offered "unconditional negotiations" with North Vietnam to end the war. He promised a development agency modeled on the Tennessee Valley Authority to serve nations along the Mekong River. Hanoi responded by demanding that the United States quit Vietnam and the South accept the program of the NLF to end the war. A few low-ranking officials in Washington, fretful about the direction the war was taking, thought that Hanoi had not flatly turned Johnson down, only provided "a statement of final objectives."[39] Yet Johnson and his top advisers chose to regard the North Vietnamese statement as a rejection of calls to negotiate, setting the stage for the final, decisive escalation of U.S. participation in the war.

In early May, McNamara, Taylor, and Westmoreland met in Honolulu. Reluctantly agreeing that bombing alone would not force the North and the NLF to stop their war against Saigon, they decided that American forces had to fight the war on the ground in the South if the Saigon government were to have a chance to stabilize. Still, concerned about the implications of Americans fighting throughout the South, they called for 40,000 additional U.S. soldiers to fight within fifty miles of American enclaves on the coast of Vietnam.

The enclave strategy lasted barely a month. The NLF operated at will in the remainder of the South and the Saigon government, now led by Air Marshall Nguyen Cao Ky, lost more authority daily. Westmoreland requested an additional 150,000 troops to carry the war throughout the South. McNamara returned to Vietnam and decided that Westmoreland was right. He recommended that Johnson approve sending an additional 100,000 men to Vietnam and ask Congress to authorize the potential call up of an additional 236,000 reservists. He told the president that "The situation in South Vietnam is worse than a year ago (when it was worse than a year before that). After a few months of stalemate, the tempo of the war has quickened."[40]

McNamara framed two starkly unappealing choices: (1) To cut U.S. losses and leave under the best conditions possible—"almost certainly conditions humiliating the United States and damaging to our future effectiveness on the world scene." (2) To continue with present level of U.S. forces, approximately 75,000. That would make the U.S. position progressively weaker and "would confront us later with a choice between withdrawal and an emergency expansion of forces, perhaps too late to do any good." Rejecting both, McNamara concluded that Johnson could do nothing but follow his third option: "Expand promptly and substantially the U.S. military pressure against the Viet

Cong in the South and maintain military pressure against the North Vietnamese in the North." While no guarantee of eventual success "this alternative would stave off defeat in the short run and offer a good chance of producing a favorable settlement in the longer run."[41]

In late July, Johnson consulted with his principal advisers on the future of American involvement in the ground war. In a series of meetings Johnson appeared frustrated with the inability of the South Vietnamese to make progress, bewildered at the unresponsiveness of the North to his proposals for negotiations, and skeptical about the usefulness of the dispatch of additional United States troops. Most of all, however, he agreed with nearly all of the advisers that the costs of an NLF victory were unacceptably high, because it would shake world confidence in American credibility. Secretary of the Navy Paul Nitze, primarily interested in maintaining good relations with Europe and appearing strong to the Soviet Union, remarked that "the shape of the world will change" were the United States to acknowledge that "we couldn't beat the VC." Secretary of the Army Stanley Resor concurred that "we can't go back on our commitment. Our allies are watching carefully."[42]

The only course tolerable to Johnson was continuation of a gradual buildup of U.S. forces—the very policy that had not succeeded in defeating the NLF or bolstering the morale of the South Vietnamese government for the previous year. He hoped to keep the buildup quiet and present it as a continuation of policy, not a dramatically increased American commitment. He expected that by downplaying the significance of the new commitment he would avoid a divisive public debate and prevent the sort of public war weariness that had wrecked the Truman administration during the Korean war. At the height of his authority with Congress, he feared that congressional discussion of Vietnam would interfere with passage of his ambitious program of domestic reform legislation, the Great Society.

The July reappraisals held elements of tragedy—and folly. Jack Valenti, a political adviser, told the president he wanted to "weep because the options are so narrow and the choices are so barren."[43] A sentimental man, Johnson liked this sort of histrionics from subordinates eager to show their empathy for the burdens borne by the chief executive. For his part, the president often expressed greater awareness of the risks than did some of his more militant advisers. Johnson voiced doubts about the usefulness of additional U.S. troops. He once turned to General Earle Wheeler, chairman of the Joint Chiefs of Staff, and asked: "Tell me this. What will happen if we put in 100,000 more men and then two, three years later, you tell me we need 500,000 more?

How would you expect me to respond to that? And what makes you think that Ho Chi Minh won't put in another 100,000 and match us every bit of the way?" To which Wheeler replied: "That makes greater bodies of men from North Vietnam, which will allow us to cream them."[44] Johnson's fears proved prophetic, and Wheeler's reply foretold some of the military's foolish and wasteful tactics of attrition with which they waged the war. Johnson also recognized the fragility of public support for the war. When the Secretary of the Army pointed to public opinion polls showing strong support for a continuation of the American commitment, Johnson, an old political professional, rebuked him: "But if you make a commitment to jump off a building, and you find out how high it is, you may withdraw that commitment."[45]

Only one of Johnson's principal advisers, Under Secretary of State George Ball, openly voiced dissent from the prevailing willingness to go forward with 100,000 more soldiers. He thought that the United States could not win in Vietnam without risk of drawing China, and possibly even the Soviet Union, into the fighting. Ball thought that public opinion would not tolerate a long war. The longer the war went on and casualties mounted there would be demands by an impatient public "to strike at the very jugular of North Vietnam." Ball thought that even greater dangers to U.S. credibility existed should the war go on for more than a year. "If the war is long and protracted, as I believe it will be," he said "then we will suffer because the world's greatest power cannot defeat guerrillas." Ball referred to the long history of Vietnamese fighting outsiders and doubted that "an army of westerners can successfully fight orientals in an Asian jungle." Johnson seemed struck by the image. "This is important," the president told McNamara and Wheeler. "Can Westerners, in the absence of accurate intelligence, successfully fight Asians in jungle rice paddies?"[46]

No other advisers joined with Ball in expressing such pessimism in the public meetings. Sensing that Johnson believed the risk of a Communist victory greater than the challenges of greater commitment, they recommended sending the troops McNamara thought were needed. Long-time presidential adviser Clark Clifford did telephone a dissent. He too doubted that the United States could win: China and the Soviet Union would see to it that the NLF continued to fight. China was likely to send in troops, as they had done in the Korean war. He accurately predicted an unacceptably high number of U.S. fatalities. "If we lose 50,000 men there," he forecast, "it will be a catastrophe for the country. Five years, billions of dollars, hundreds of thousands of men—this is not for us."[47] In the end, however, Clifford supported Johnson's decision to increase the American troop commitment.

Eventually the president and all of his advisers with the exception of Ball, and possibly Clifford, concurred that adding 100,000 Americans to the 90,000 troops already in Vietnam would stave off defeat without provoking a backlash against the war in Congress or with the public. Johnson and most advisers hoped to characterize the doubling of troops as only a continuation of current policy. To that end they rejected McNamara's request to call up reserves. Even so, Johnson's advisers worried about the implications of the Americanization of the war. Horace Busby, one of Johnson's most politically astute advisers, told the president that it was "self-deceptive" to claim that the troop buildup represented only an extension of what the U.S. had done in the past several years.[48] Yet Johnson encouraged such deception, hoping to maintain the wide consensus in support of his policies.

Johnson informed congressional leaders on July 27 of the decision to send another 100,000 soldiers but not to call up reserves. Most Democratic and Republican leaders expressed support. Speaker of the House John McCormack thought there was no alternative. He reflected that the "lesson of Hitler and Mussolini is clear."[49] Republican leader Gerald Ford agreed. The mood among members of Congress not called to the White House was apprehensive. Mike Mansfield, Johnson's successor as majority leader, told the president that many senators supported the president because they sensed "that your objective [is] not to get in deeply." Lawmakers worried about the administration's inability to define success in Vietnam. "Even if you win, totally," Mansfield reported, "you still do not come out well. What have you achieved? It is by no means a 'vital' area of U.S. concern." Senators sensed deep currents of public anxiety. They noted that the French had never used conscripts in their war in Indochina. News of casualties among American draftees could ignite angry revulsion at the war. Mansfield told Johnson that "the country is backing the president on Vietnam primarily because he is president, not necessarily out of any understanding or sympathy with policies on Vietnam; beneath the support there is deep concern . . . which could explode at any time; in addition racial factors at home could become involved."[50]

Johnson could not be deflected by these reservations. He believed that the cost of seeing the NLF win quickly appeared too great. He announced the dispatch of additional troops at a low-key mid-day press conference on July 28, 1965. For the rest of 1965 the White House continued to insist that the additional troops did not change American policy in Vietnam, and Johnson stressed the Great Society as the centerpiece of his administration's accomplishments. When Secretary of the Treasury Henry Fowler complained that the fighting strained the economy and had caused prices to rise, the White House warned him to keep his views quiet. "What the President doesn't want to do," Bill Moyers told Fowler, "is, in essence, say to the business community that we have declared war in Vietnam."[51] Keeping the buildup quiet, however, backfired dramatically. The stealth with which Johnson announced the additional commitment of American troops contributed later to a wide belief that administration officials did not tell the truth, and a wide "credibility gap" opened.

Whether declared or not, the United States was fully at war after July 1965. The decision to send an additional 100,000 troops by the end of 1965 did not stop the buildup. During 1966 and 1967 the number of U.S. soldiers in Vietnam rose from 190,000 to 535,000. Many were conscripts, and perhaps as many as half of those who ostensibly volunteered did so because they faced induction through selective service. Yet this huge expeditionary force could not prevail against the NLF and several hundred thousand regulars from the North Vietnamese People's Liberation Army.

Fighting the War

The NLF and North Vietnamese decided when to engage the Americans and ARVN forces, thereby limiting their own casualties until the time they expected the Americans would weary of the war. General Westmoreland tried unsuccessfully to counter their tactics with an attrition strategy of his own. He sent giant B-52 bombers and smaller fighter-bombers over South Vietnam to terrorize the Viet Cong. After the bombers had prepared the battlefield helicopter-borne American units descended on the countryside on search and destroy missions to root out and kill enemy soldiers. Americans would fly out from their bases in the morning, pursue the Viet Cong or North Vietnamese in firefights, and return to bases in the evening. The tokens of progress in the war became the "body count" of soldiers killed, rather than territory captured or decapitation of the enemy's command and control structure. Westmoreland adopted the procedure because it seemed to provide the quantifiable data that McNamara insisted upon. Washington and MACV headquarters in Saigon hoped to reach an elusive crossover point at which they destroyed troops faster than North Vietnam could replace them. The lightning helicopter raids also reduced American casualties by limiting their exposure to hostile fire. The procedure encouraged serious abuses. Official reliance on the body count induced soldiers to shoot first without asking questions. A marine recalled that "any Vietnamese out at night was the enemy."[52]

The NLF continued political organization in rural South Vietnam in the face of the punishment inflicted by the American bombers. Critics of the tactics of helicopter borne search and destroy operations complained that the United States was leaving the countryside to the Communists. A correspondent berated a general, "How do you expect our forces to win the hearts and minds of the people when all they do is take off from one army base and fly overhead at 1,500 feet while Charlie [a nickname for the NLF] is sitting down there and he's got 'em by the testicles jerking, and every time he jerks their hearts and minds follow?"[53]

Americans expected the ARVN to motivate the local peasantry to cooperate with the government and create popular local authorities. Yet the vast buildup of U.S. troops contributed to the ARVN's dependency. By the fall of 1966, McNamara recognized as much. He reported that the so-called pacification program, designed to encourage the peasantry to rally round the Saigon government, was "thoroughly stalled." Even if the Americans spent more time in the countryside, "it is known that we do not intend to stay; if our efforts worked at all, it would merely postpone the eventual confrontation of the VC and GVN [government of Vietnam] infrastructures. The GVN must do the job; and I am convinced that drastic reform is needed if the GVN is going to be able to do it." He ruefully told the president, "I see no reasonable way to bring the war to an end soon. Enemy morale has not been broken . . . and he has adopted a strategy of attriting our national will."[54]

The national will grew weary and the mood ever bleaker as the war dragged on. Richard Goodwin, a speechwriter coopted from the Kennedy camp, believed that Johnson became clinically paranoid. Goodwin recorded in his diary Johnson's intense reactions to criticism of the U.S. involvement in the war: "I can't trust anybody anymore. . . . I'm going to get rid of anybody who doesn't agree with my policies. I'm not going in the liberal direction. There's no future with them. They're just out to get me, always have been."[55] By the middle of 1966 Goodwin, Under Secretary of State George Ball, and national security adviser McGeorge Bundy had all left. The others had joined Ball in opposing further American involvement in the war and wanted a negotiated settlement. Walt Rostow, the new national security adviser, remained a hawk. He consistently bolstered Johnson's morale by likening his difficulties to those of "Lincoln in 1864" when it appeared certain that he would lose the presidential election.[56] By the end of the year, McNamara, who Johnson continually praised as the "star of the cabinet,"[57] wanted to stop bombing the north and explore negotiations with Hanoi.

Johnson faced unwelcome criticism from fellow Democrats. Arkansas Senator J. William Fulbright, chairman of the Foreign Relations Committee, reversed his support for the war in September 1965. He undertook a crash course in the history of American policy toward Vietnam. Fulbright's chief of staff informed him in early 1966 that "the powerful force of nationalism, which was instrumental in freeing Vietnam from the French, has been captured by the Viet Cong." Fulbright was particularly downcast by reports that "U.S. Vietnamese polices are found to be highly objectionable in Northern Europe: the Labor [*sic*] government in Britain would fall if it were to offer troops for use in Vietnam; the position of France [a persistent critic] is clear; the Japanese government would fall if it were to support the U.S. in Vietnam; Germany provides only medical support—just enough to encourage the United States not to withdraw its troops from Germany and Berlin."[58] In February 1966 Fulbright chaired televised hearings on the U.S. role in Vietnam. Numerous academic, military, and diplomatic experts, many of whom had been architects of American policy in the Cold War, told the committee that the United States risked jeopardizing its most cherished relations with European allies.

In the fall Fulbright planned more hearings in 1967 on the declining role of the Untied States in the world. His staff arranged for prominent witnesses "with strong personalities" to testify to "gain and retain both television and broad press coverage."[59] Johnson reacted peevishly. He alternately invited Fulbright to the White House and ordered aides to investigate him. "It's easier to satisfy Ho Chi Minh than it is Fulbright," he would explode.[60] The president loved derogatory reports on the senator. He was cheered by the news that an Israeli diplomat thought that Fulbright "reminded him of a 'modestly endowed don' at Oxford. He was full of historic parallels which did not bear serious examination."[61] He encouraged the FBI to circulate comparisons of the positions taken by Fulbright at the 1966 hearing and those of the U.S. Communist party.

Such derision could not stem the tide of criticism from within the Democratic party. Nor could gestures toward the North such as temporary halts in the bombing of North Vietnam during the Christmas and New Year holidays in 1965–1966 and the Vietnamese observance of Tet, the lunar New Year, 1967. By 1967 about a dozen prominent senators opposed the war. They persistently called on the president to end the bombing of the North in order to encourage negotiations with Hanoi. Opposition to the president's conduct of the war from Robert F.

Kennedy, elected to the U.S. Senate from New York State in 1964, represented the most serious blow to Johnson from within the Democratic party. Ambassador at Large Averell Harriman warned Kennedy that his dissent would be considered "support for Hanoi against your government," a charge Kennedy resented.[62] Kennedy berated Johnson for not permanently "halting the bombing in exchange for a beginning of negotiations."[63] The White House complained that such dissent only made it more difficult to begin meaningful negotiations with the North. "We must avoid 'negotiating with ourselves,' " Rostow told Johnson. In any event the White House remained as skeptical about the North's intentions in proclaiming their willingness to begin negotiations as it had been at the beginning of the buildup. "The North Vietnamese might merely be seeking alternative methods of achieving the domination of South Vietnam," Rostow warned.[64]

But Senator Kennedy's criticism had a powerful impact on some of the late President Kennedy's lieutenants who had advised Johnson. McNamara had already concluded that additional bombing of the North would not hasten the end of the war. In mid-1967, former national security adviser McGeorge Bundy reversed his earlier doubts about the danger to the position of the United States and the Saigon government in seeking negotiations. He urged Johnson to put a ceiling on the number of U.S. troops to be sent to Vietnam and halt the strategic bombing of the North. Additional escalation would not compel the North to yield and anxiety about the extent of the future U.S. commitment "is now having destructive effects on the national will."[65]

An even greater challenge to Johnson's authority came from a revived citizens' peace movement. Beginning in the spring of 1965, opponents of the war organized teach-ins on college campuses. The first occurred on the night of March 24–25 on the campus of the University of Michigan. Scores of prominent academic critics of the war lectured dozens of large audiences about Vietnam's historic resistance to outsiders, the failure of the French to quell the Communist uprising, the support in the North for the government of Ho Chi Minh, the unpopularity of the Southern authorities, and the destruction wreaked by U.S. bombs and search and destroy operations. The peace movement also sponsored huge demonstrations against administration policies, encouraged young men to question and then resist the draft, and in 1968 spearheaded an effort to replace Johnson as the Democratic presidential nominee with someone who could extricate the United States from the morass of Vietnam.

Public opposition to the war surged in the spring of 1967. Antiwar organizers hoped to undermine the Johnson administration's "claim to legitimacy through the electoral process."[66] On April 15 about 100,000 people gathered in New York City and another 50,000 in San Francisco listened to speakers from the antiwar and civil rights movements call for an end to the war and a rededication to racial equality at home. Martin Luther King, Jr., who previously had expressed quiet misgivings about the war, addressed the crowd in New York. Opponents of the war encouraged speculation that King and the prominent pediatrician Benjamin Spock might run for president and vice president, respectively, in 1968. White House press secretary George Christian responded by providing columnists with copies of FBI reports alleging King's close connection to members of the American Communist party.[67]

The president became frantic as plans developed for a massive march of more than 100,000 on Washington in October 1967 to demand a bombing halt and immediate negotiations to end the war. At a cabinet meeting, he asked his Attorney General, Ramsey Clark, who had usually been solicitous of the civil liberties of antiwar demonstrators, "Who are the sponsoring groups? Pacifists? Communists?"

Clark replied, "There is a heavy representation of extreme left wing groups with long lines of Communist affiliations."

Secretary of State Rusk interjected, "Wouldn't it help to leak that?"

Clark responded that "the fact of Communist involvement and encouragement has been given to some columnists."

"Let's see more," Johnson added.[68]

Public war weariness rose dramatically in the fall of 1967. Antiwar activities, failure to achieve victory, and television coverage of the devastation wrought in Vietnam profoundly depressed many Americans. The public remained deeply divided between those who wanted stronger action to end the war quickly and those who favored negotiations. From the beginning of 1967 until the march on Washington in October the proportion of the public who believed that getting into the war had been a mistake rose from 30 percent to 46 percent. Only 10 percent of the public wanted the U.S. to withdraw from the fighting, but only 28 percent approved of the way Johnson was handling the war. A plurality of the public was neither hawk nor dove but wanted the war to end and bring relief from daily reports of death, destruction, and futility.

By the middle of 1967 the Johnson administration seemed ready for serious negotiations with Hanoi. Earlier that year the White House had summarily rejected efforts by two newspaper editors to act as go-betweens with the North Vietnamese. It paid more attention to overtures from Polish representatives to open communications with

Hanoi. Eventually, however, Washington concluded that the Polish diplomats spoke only for themselves and could not deliver representatives with the authority to make commitments on behalf of Hanoi.

In the late summer and early fall of 1967 the Johnson administration felt such serious pressure to show progress that it sent its own private intermediary, Harvard professor Henry Kissinger, to Paris to seek North Vietnamese negotiating partners. In talks, code named Pennsylvania, Kissinger relayed to the North Vietnamese an administration offer to cease bombing with the understanding that a pause would lead to prompt formal negotiations with the North. The United States would not demand that North Vietnam remove its troops from the South, but would expect the North not to take advantage of a bombing pause to increase its supplies flowing to the South. The United States would remain committed to the government of South Vietnam, now headed by President Nguyen Van Thieu and Vice President Nguyen Cao Ky, both elected in September. The United States might permit NLF participation in a coalition government, but the NLF would have to drop its revolutionary program. North Vietnam expressed some interest in Kissinger's proposals once the United States stopped bombing within a ten mile radius around Hanoi. Yet Hanoi wanted a complete bombing halt before going forward. It rejected the "words of peace" coming from Washington as "only trickery." Johnson suspected trickery on Hanoi's part and believed they "are keeping this channel going just because we are not bombing Hanoi." Finally the president accepted the judgment of two of his more militant advisers, Supreme Court Justice Abe Fortas and Maxwell Taylor, to keep bombing. Taylor believed that the North had made its first genuine response, but he cautioned "by showing weakness we could prejudice any possible negotiations." Fortas, perhaps closest to Johnson's thinking, recommended that Kissinger tell the North Vietnamese "thanks, it's too bad. You know you could have gotten somewhere if you had really wanted to." Pennsylvania then collapsed.[69]

With the disintegration of the Pennsylvania channel, Johnson sank into gloom, skeptical of the value of escalation but unwilling to stop the bombing to move negotiations forward. In November he accepted McNamara's resignation as Secretary of Defense and announced that the following March long-time Democratic party adviser Clark Clifford would replace him. After McNamara's announced departure the president's remaining advisers became more militant. Clifford himself changed his initial position resisting involvement in the war to advocating continued bombing. He expressed doubts about the North's commitment to negotiate through private intermediaries. "I do not think they will use *this type of channel* when they are serious about really doing something." He believed that a bombing halt would invariably fail to yield negotiations, and the United States would increase its troop levels in the aftermath.[70] William Bundy, Dean Rusk, Walt Rostow, and Maxwell Taylor further agreed that Johnson could not satisfy his domestic critics with a bombing halt. Instead, the president hoped that an optimistic assessment of the war from the battlefield commander might reduce public dissatisfaction. In November General Westmoreland returned to Washington and told a joint session of Congress that the North Vietnamese and Viet Cong could not resist much longer and he hoped the American part of the war effort could end within two years.

Nevertheless, worries persisted among Johnson's civilian advisers that the war had so torn apart the country and reduced the position of the United States in the world. At the end of 1967 Johnson assembled a group of so-called Wise Men, senior foreign policy advisers who had served presidents since 1940, to advise him on Vietnam. They supported continuation of bombing but warned that "endless, inconclusive fighting" had become the "most serious cause of domestic disquiet."[71] They urged him to review American participation in the ground war and find ways of reducing American casualties. Johnson agreed about the need to lower public anxiety, but he seemed almost muscle bound with ambivalence. "We'll do all we can to win the war," he told another group of senior advisers as they considered the merits of sending U.S. troops across the border into Cambodia.[72]

1968

All planning for the future changed abruptly on January 30, 1968. At 2:45 that morning, during Tet, the Vietnamese New Year, a squad of nineteen Viet Cong commandos blasted their way through the wall surrounding the U.S. embassy in Saigon. The attack on the embassy came as part of a coordinated Viet Cong–North Vietnamese offensive against the population centers of South Vietnam during the Tet truce. Benefitting from complete surprise, NLF and North Vietnamese units fought the Americans and ARVN for control of forty-four provincial capitals, five of six major cities, and sixty-four district capitals. The most intense fighting lasted about two weeks, and in most areas the Americans and South Vietnam repulsed the attackers. Casualties on the Communist side were enormous, as many as 40,000 dead, while the ARVN and Americans lost about 3,400 men. The Tet offensive took an enormous toll on the civilian population, with as many as one million refugees swelling already teeming camps.

General Westmoreland considered the results of Tet a major defeat for the North and the NLF. A more important loss was suffered, however, at home, where televised scenes of the grisly fighting turned public opinion against continuing the war. After Tet 78 percent of the public told opinion pollsters that they did not think the United States was making progress in the war. A minuscule 26 percent approved of Johnson's handling of it. In New Hampshire pollsters detected signs of life in what had appeared to be a quixotic campaign by Minnesota Senator Eugene McCarthy to challenge Johnson in that state's presidential preference primary.

Johnson asked Clark Clifford to take a hard look at Vietnam policies before officially taking over as Secretary of Defense on March 1. Specifically, he wanted Clifford's advice on Westmoreland's request for an additional 206,000 troops. Clifford, reminded of the discussions of July 1965, concluded that Westmoreland could not guarantee victory with the additional soldiers, but only postpone a Communist triumph. Reverting to his earlier skepticism, Clifford advised the president not to endorse sending more soldiers to Vietnam. Instead, he pressed for negotiations, to be initiated by a bombing halt.

Johnson, remaining torn, convened another series of high-level meetings in March to discuss options. Clifford presented the case for deescalation while Rostow and Rusk counseled militancy. An astonishingly strong showing by Senator McCarthy in the new Hampshire primary and Robert Kennedy's entry into the presidential race a few days later raised the stakes even further. During the last week in March Johnson reconvened the Wise Men. He lamented that "there has been a panic" in the country since the *New York Times* published news of Westmoreland's request for an additional 206,000 troops. He estimated the cost of such an additional deployment at $15 billion. The position of the dollar and the British pound would be affected. Already France demanded payment for its dollars in gold, costing the U.S. about $1 billion of its reserves. Johnson seemed nearly to weep as he told his advisers about Kennedy's plan to convene a commission of notables to decide future Vietnam policy. "I will have overwhelming disapproval in the polls and the election. I will go down the drain. I don't want the whole alliance and the military pulled down with it."[73] The Wise Men reversed their earlier support for a militant course and urged Johnson to seek a negotiated settlement. Dean Acheson, reflecting his own agony during the Korean War, explained that the United States "could no longer do the job we set out to do in the time we have left and we must take steps to disengage."[74] Johnson seemed bereft. "Everybody is recommending surrender," he complained on March 28.[75]

Three days later Johnson capitulated. In a nationally broadcast speech on the evening of March 31, he announced a partial bombing halt that would stop the U.S. attacks everywhere over North Vietnam with the exception of the immediate vicinity of the Demilitarized Zone. He offered to expand the bombing pause to cover all of North Vietnam if Hanoi would not reinforce its troops in the South. He said that he was appointing Averell Harriman as a representative to explore prospects for opening negotiations with the North Vietnamese and NLF. Finally, he promised to devote himself to peace for the remainder of the year. Accordingly, "I shall not seek, nor will I accept the nomination of my party for another term as your president."[76]

U.S. policy toward Vietnam in the remaining nine and one half months of the Johnson administration recapitulated the tragic and farcical elements of the previous four and one half years. Johnson continued to vacillate between hastening negotiations and increasing the military pressure. His principal advisers disagreed more openly than ever before about whether to bomb the North more heavily or move more quickly toward negotiations. Their divisions caused policy to lurch more suddenly after Johnson announced he would not seek reelection. With the sharp diminution in his political power, public attention focused on the competition among Eugene McCarthy, Robert Kennedy, and Vice President Hubert Humphrey on the Democratic side and Richard Nixon and New York Governor Nelson Rockefeller on the Republican side to elect his successor.

The president became a maudlin and forlorn figure shortly after his surprising announcement. He expressed second thoughts almost from the day he proclaimed the partial bombing halt and the appointment of Harriman. He complained that the first calls he received after his speech came from the wife of Senator McCarthy and Senators Edward Kennedy, Ernest Greuning, and George McGovern, all prominent dissenters from his policies in Vietnam. "I knew something was wrong," he told his senior advisers, "when all of them approved."[77] He met Robert Kennedy in the White House on the morning of April 3 to tell him that "the situation confronted by the nation [was] the most serious he had seen in the course of his life." He "would do his very best to get peace," but "he was not optimistic." He assured Kennedy that he did not "hate him or dislike him" and that he would not play a major role in the upcoming presidential campaign.[78]

Johnson then worked on creating the instructions for Harriman to carry with him. Harriman, accompanied by Deputy Defense Secretary

Cyrus Vance, went to Paris to explore whether North Vietnam would join "prompt and serious substantive talks looking for peace in Vietnam."[79] Harriman was told that the United States would stop all air, naval, and air bombardment against the North provided Hanoi would agree to begin talks within 3 to 7 days after bombing stopped. The United States also insisted that the North not take advantage of the total cessation of bombing by improving its military position in the South. While the negotiators were empowered to discuss a bombing halt, American diplomats dealing with Saigon and military officers feared the consequences of such a move. Ellsworth Bunker, the Ambassador to Saigon, warned Johnson about the dangers of a "collapse in morale in South Vietnam during negotiations" should the United States contemplate a total bombing halt over the north.[80] The Joint Chiefs of Staff also noted that "operations against North Vietnam provide major leverage to our negotiators, and the price of cessation of such action should be high."[81]

After a few weeks of discussion about where to hold preliminary conversations, Harriman and Vance went to Paris in May to begin a frustrating six month exercise in opening substantive conversations with the North. Harriman, thinking that arranging peace in Vietnam would cap a distinguished career, and Clifford wanted to go much further than Johnson's other aides. Harriman approached the negotiations with a view toward the forthcoming presidential election. His first priority was "not permitting [the continuation of the war] to elect Nixon as president."[82] Almost immediately the American negotiators ran into suspicions from the North that the United States wanted to increase the bombing and fears from the South that Washington intended to exclude Saigon from the conversations. Harriman and Vance tried energetically tried to overcome Communist objections to recognition of the legitimacy of the government of South Vietnam with plans for negotiations on the basis of "your side [the North and the NLF], our side [the South Vietnamese government and the United States]." The South tentatively accepted this formula in July, "so long as the Government of Vietnam played the major role in 'our' side."[83]

Saigon's reservations all but negated any progress Harriman and Vance made with the North Vietnamese, yet Harriman pressed Johnson to make concessions to the North Vietnamese. In late July Harriman urged Johnson to stop all bombing of the North in response to the Communists' apparent reduction in activity in the South. Vice-President Humphrey, assured of the Democratic nomination after the murder of Robert Kennedy on June 6, concurred. According to Harriman, Johnson "went through the roof" when he learned that Humphrey endorsed a bombing halt.[84] Harriman and Clifford thought that Johnson wanted to see Humphrey defeated in the fall. Ellsworth Bunker, the ambassador to Saigon, Rostow, and Rusk all opposed declaring a total bombing halt for fear of provoking a collapse in Saigon. Johnson instructed Rusk to hold a press conference at which the Secretary of State condemned the Communists for intransigence.

Shocking events in Czechoslovakia and Chicago overshadowed the Paris negotiations in August. Harriman believed that Johnson's refusal to halt the bombing at the end of July represented "a historic tragedy." It made "Johnson look rigid regarding Vietnam," and may have convinced some fence-sitting Kremlin leaders that they had nothing to lose by ordering Soviet tanks into Prague to crush a liberal government.[85] A week later the Democratic Party nominated Hubert Humphrey for the presidency in a tumultuous convention in Chicago. Johnson refused Humphrey's entreaties to compromise with antiwar Democrats over a platform plank on Vietnam. The convention narrowly endorsed the administration's handling of the war. On the same night Humphrey was nominated the Chicago police force went mad, beating and teargassing a crowd of some ten thousand demonstrators who had come to the city to protest administration policy on Vietnam.

Humphrey left Chicago badly trailing Nixon in public opinion surveys. The Republican nominee fed the widespread suspicion that Johnson had mishandled the war. Nixon had advocated escalation in the early days and now condemned the Johnson administration for stalemate. He refused to offer specific recommendations to break the impasse, because he claimed that to do so would interfere with the ongoing negotiations. Yet he did reply affirmatively to a reporter's question asking if he had a plan to end the war. Humphrey remained loyal to Johnson's policy throughout September, while requesting permission to take a more independent position. None was forthcoming. Eventually, relying on the advice of George Ball, who had left his position as U.S. representative to the United Nations, he separated himself from current policy at a speech in Salt Lake City on September 30. He endorsed a total bombing halt "as an acceptable risk for peace, because I believe that it could lead to a success in negotiations and a shorter war."[86]

Humphrey's presidential campaign gained momentum after his Salt Lake City Speech, and the tempo of negotiations in Paris picked up as well. On October 18 Harriman and Vance reached what they considered to be a breakthrough with Xuan Thuy of North Vietnam. The United States would halt all bombing over the North and the Communists satisfied the Americans that they would not take advantage of a bombing halt to reinforce their forces in the South. The "our side, your side" formula seemed a basis for seating the delegates. In this way the North would give tacit recognition to the government of the South while the United States would extend the same sort of acknowledgment of the NLF. The North Vietnamese mocked the Americans for deferring to the South's concerns. "Usually the man leads the horse," complained the north's Le Duc Tho. "This time the horse is leading the man."[87] The U.S. negotiators in Paris would agree to let the North Vietnamese have a few days to send diplomats to Paris and open formal talks three to seven days after the bombing halt. Once more, however, the White House did not want to go as far as Harriman proposed. Johnson would "rather not stop the bombing" until the Communist representatives actually arrived in Paris. "It could badly hurt us," he said if they had a week in which to resupply their forces in the South.[88] The White House ordered Harriman and Vance to insist on negotiations opening no more than twenty-four hours after the bombing halt.

Harriman and Vance dutifully reported Washington's conditions and negotiations continued. In the meantime, rumors that Johnson was on the verge of announcing a bombing halt sent the Nixon campaign into a panic. Anna Chennault, a prominent Republican fundraiser and longtime supporter of Asian anti-Communists, representing the Nixon campaign, informed the South Vietnamese ambassador to the United States of the White House's plans to start negotiations before election day. Chennault suggested that South Vietnam's President Thieu should refuse to participate in the talks before the election, since a Nixon administration would show more sympathy for South Vietnam than would a government led by Humphrey.

In the final days of October three complex and interrelated sets of conversations went on simultaneously on three continents. In Saigon, President Thieu pondered ways to prevent the United States from stopping the bombing. He refused to attend a peace conference without explicit recognition of the South. In Washington, Johnson met at 2:30 A.M. on October 29 with his foreign policy advisers to discuss the announcement of a bombing halt. Harriman reported that the North would agree to meet on November 2 if the bombing stopped on October 30. Johnson and his advisers received word that Nixon was trying to prevent a bombing halt before the election. Eugene Rostow wrote his brother Walt that Nixon wanted matters to get worse in Vietnam. An informant in the Republican campaign told Eugene Rostow that "these difficulties would make it easier for Nixon to settle after January. Like Ike in 1953, he would be able to settle on terms which the president could not accept, blaming the deterioration of the situation between now and January or February on his predecessor." Johnson contemplated publicizing the connection between Thieu and Nixon. It "would rock the world if it were said he [Thieu] were conniving with the Republicans."[89]

Unwilling to give Humphrey an edge, Johnson ultimately decided not to make an issue of Nixon's dealing with the South. Ambassador Bunker's support of Thieu's refusal to go to Paris on November 2 forced Johnson to agree to delay the bombing halt. He also dropped insistence that the peace talks begin immediately after the bombing halt. He did not think it was "of world shaking importance" whether the talks occurred before or after November 5, election day. Not that he had great faith in a Nixon presidency. "Nixon will doublecross them after November 5," he predicted to his senior advisers.[90] In Paris, Harriman relayed word from the White House to the North Vietnamese that the United States wanted negotiations to begin within four days after the proclamation of a bombing halt. On October 31 Johnson announced the bombing halt and the commencement of negotiations on Wednesday after election day. Humphrey's campaign took off in the public opinion polls, but the momentum slowed on Sunday when Thieu once more said that South Vietnam would not participate. On election day Humphrey lost the election to Nixon by a scant 510,000 votes, and the Saigon leaders agreed to come to Paris. Illinois Republican Senator Charles Percy told Harriman that Nixon was certain that Humphrey would have won the election had the bombing halt and the negotiations been announced three days earlier than they had been.

By the end of 1968 most Americans wanted relief from the endless war in Vietnam, although they disagreed on the methods for doing so. The war had exacted a terrible cost on the terrain, the people, and the society of Vietnam. Hundreds of thousands were dead and as many as two million people were homeless. Successive governments of South Vietnam had proved corrupt and incapable of defending their citizens against the Communists without massive American intervention. The war became a tragedy for the Americans who fought there. About 37,000 lost their lives by the end of 1968, and that number would rise to 58,000 by the time the U.S. withdrew the last of its troops in 1973. The war deeply divided American society, opening enduring chasms between supporters and opponents of intervention. Officials' persistently unfounded public optimism and the failure of a variety of plans for winning the war left many people radically disillusioned with the government and institutions. What began as an intervention to bolster the American position in the Cold War, became by 1968 a major contributor to American dissatisfaction with the aims of post–World War ll foreign policy. Involvement in Vietnam also undermined the global political and economic standing of the United States. Public disappointment with the war helped Richard Nixon win the presidency. When Nixon and Henry Kissinger, his new national security adviser, took over in January 1969 they pleaded for patience, but they agreed "it was essential to reduce American casualties and get some of our troops coming home in order to retain the support of the American people."[91] It took them fully four years to arrange a cease-fire. They did so only by making Vietnam seem less important than American relations with the Soviet Union and China. In that way they followed the pattern of the Kennedy and Johnson administrations' plans for Vietnam. The blueprints always originated with something—be it the Cold War, domestic politics, various presidents desires to outshine their predecessors, the competition among policymakers—Americans considered more important than Vietnam.

NOTES

1. Frances Fitzgerald, *Fire in the Lake: The Vietnamese and the Americans in Vietnam* (New York, 1972), p. 7.

2. Walt W. Rostow oral history, Lyndon B. Johnson Library. (Hereafter LBJL). Lawrence Bassett and Stephen E. Pelz, "The Failed Search for Victory: Vietnam and the Politics of War," Thomas G. Paterson, ed. *Kennedy's Quest for Victory: American Foreign Policy, 1961–1963* (New York, 1989), p. 231.

3. Communist gains in Laos alarmed the Kennedy administration in 1961 and early 1962. In the spring of 1962 the U.S. participated fully in another peace conference in Geneva which led to a cease-fire and the creation of a neutral Laotian coalition government. In 1964 the U.S. commenced covert operations against the Communists in Laos. This so-called secret war continued until the end of the Vietnam war in 1975.

4. FRUS (1961–1963) 2: 571.

5. Quoted in George Herring, *America's Longest War: The United States and Vietnam, 1950–1975*, 2d ed. (New York, 1986), p. 88

6. Joint communique following visit of Lyndon B. Johnson to Vietnam. May 13, 1961. Foreign Office (FO) 371/160128. Public Records Office, London, England.

7. *FRUS* (1961–1963) 2: 575, 571.

8. *Washington Post*, January 3, 1963. *New York Times*, January 4, 1963.

9. Neil Sheehan, *A Bright Shining Lie: John Paul Vann and the American Experience in Vietnam* (New York: 1988), p. 282.

10. *FRUS* (1961–1963) 3: 61–62.

11. Ellen Hammer, *A Death in November: America in Vietnam 1963* (New York, 1987), p. 145.

12. Henry Cabot Lodge oral history interview. John F. Kennedy Library (JFKL).

13. *FRUS* (1961–1963) 3: 559.

14. Ibid., p. 629.

15. Bassett and Pelz, "The Failed Search for Victory," pp. 247–48.

16. Stanley Karnow, "The Edge of Chaos," *Saturday Evening Post*, September 28, 1963.

17. George Mc.T. Kahin to Frank Church, September 30, 1963. Series 2.2, Box 26. Frank Church papers. Boise State University.

18. Roger Hilsman to Secretary of State, September 16, 1963. Box 200. Vietnam Country file. National Security File. JFKL.

19. James N. Giglio, *The Presidency of John F. Kennedy* (Lawrence, Kansas, 1992), p. 251.

20. Central Intelligence Agency, Events and Developments in Vietnam, October 5–18, 1963. Box 200. NSF, Vietnam Country File. JFKL

21. *Pentagon Papers*, Gravel edition, 2: 257. "Checklist," Box 200, NSF, Vietnam Country File. JFKL.

22. "Suggested draft of Presidential letter" ND [October 1963]. Box 200, NSF, Vietnam Country Files. JFKL.

23. *FRUS* (1964–1968) 1: 9.

24. Ibid, p. 1.

25. Ibid., p. 15.

26. Italics in original. Ibid., pp. 8–9.

27. Ibid., pp. 155, 308.

28. George Mc.T. Kahin, *Intervention: How America Became Involved in Vietnam* (New York, 1986), p. 220.

29. *FRUS* (1964–1968) 1: 611, 664.

30. Ibid., p. 674.

31. Moyers to president, October 3, 1965. Box 8. President's Office File. Lyndon B. Johnson Library (LBJL).

32. Kahin, *Intervention*, pp. 226–27.

33. Dean Rusk oral history interview. LBJL.

34. Mansfield to President, December 9, 1964. Box 6, NSF name file. LBJL.

35. Public Broadcasting Service, "Vietnam: A History" Episode 6. "America Takes Over." (1983).

36. Kahin, *Intervention*, pp. 260–63.

37. Bundy to President, March 6, 1965. Bundy Papers, box 1. LBJL.

38. Ibid.

39. Goodwin to President, April 27, 1965. Box 5, President's Office File, LBJL.

40. McNamara to President, July 20, 1965. Box 8, Meetings on Vietnam. NSF. LBJL.

41. Ibid.

42. Meeting at cabinet room. Noon, July 22, 1965. Box 2, Notes of meetings, NSF. LBJL.

43. Jack Valenti to President. July 22, 1965. Box 12, President's Office File.

LBJL.

44. Kahin, *Intervention*, p. 373.

45. Meeting in cabinet room. Noon, July 22, 1965. Box 2, Notes of meetings. NSF, LBJL.

46. Kahin, *Intervention*, pp. 374–75.

47. Views of Clark Clifford on Vietnam, taken down by Jack Valenti. Camp David. 5 PM, July 25, 1955. Box 1, Reference file, Vietnam. LBJL.

48. Busby to president, July 21, 1965, 10PM. Box 3, Horace Busby Files, LBJL.

49. Kahin, *Intervention*, pp. 395–96.

50. Mike Mansfield to president, July 27, 1965. Box 6, NSF name file. LBJL.

51. Notes of telephone conversation. Secretary Fowler/Bill Moyers. November 18, 1965. LBJL.

52. Wallace Terry, *Bloods: An Oral History of Vietnam* (New York, 1984), p. 45

53. Andrew Krepenevich, *The Army and Vietnam* (Baltimore, 1986), p. 171.

54. Robert McNamara to president. October 14, 1966. Box 3, Papers of Paul Warnke, Files of John McNaughton. LBJL.

55. Richard N. Goodwin, *Remembering America: A Voice from the Sixties* (Boston, 1988), p. 392.

56. Handwritten note, advisory group meeting on Vietnam, March 25, 1968. Box 6, Walt Rostow files, NSF, LBJL.

57. Meeting of the president with Neil Sheehan, March 24, 1967. Box 1, George Christian Papers. LBJL.

58. Carl Marcy to J. William Fulbright, January 21, 1966. Record Group 46. Senate Committee on Foreign Relations Files. Carl Marcy files, 1966. National Archives.

59. Carl Marcy to J. William Fulbright, November 2, 1966. 48:3:16:3, J. William Fulbright papers. University of Arkansas Library.

60. Meeting with senior foreign policy advisers, April 3, 1968. Box 1, Tom Johnson's copyrighted notes of meetings. LBJL.

61. Harry McPherson to president. March 3, 1966. Box 52, Harry McPherson files. LBJL.

62. Memorandum of telephone conversation, Averell Harriman/Robert Kennedy. 6 PM, February 27, 1967. Box 520, Harriman Papers, Library of Congress.

63. Statement of Senator Robert F. Kennedy, March 21, 1967. 1968 campaign files. Box 5, speechwriters' files. Robert F. Kennedy papers, JFKL.

64. Rostow to president, March 15, 1967. Box 14, NSF, Walt Rostow memos to the president. LBJL.

65. McGeorge Bundy to president, May 4, 1967. Box 2. Papers of Paul Warnke. Vol III. McNaughton Drafts (1967 (1). LBJL.

66. Sidney Peck, "Some Reasons for a Massive Mobilization to End the War in Vietnam," No date, [April 1967]. Box 5. Student Mobilization Committee to End the War in Vietnam papers. State Historical Society of Wisconsin.

67. Melvin Small, *Johnson, Nixon and the Doves* (New Brunswick, N.J., 1988), p. 100.

68. Ibid, p. 112.

69. Notes of President's Wednesday night meeting. October 18, 1967. Box 1. Tom Johnson's notes of meetings. LBJL.

70. Ibid. Italics in original. George Ball oral history, LBJL.

71. Herring, *America's Longest War*, p. 184.

72. Meeting with senior advisers, December 5, 1967. Box 1, Tom Johnson's copyrighted notes of meetings. LBJL.

73. Meeting with Generals Wheeler and Abrams, March 26, 1968. Box 1, Tom Johnson's copyrighted notes of meetings. LBJL.

74. Clark Clifford, *Counsel to the President* (New York, 1991), p. 517.

75. CIA-DoD Briefing by General Dupuy and George Carver, March 28, 1968. Box 1, Tom Johnson's copyrighted Notes of meetings, LBJL.

76. *Public Papers of the President, Lyndon B. Johnson, 1968–1969* Vol.1 (Washington, 1970), p. 476.

77. Meeting with senior foreign policy advisers, April 2, 1968. Box 1, Tom Johnson's copyrighted notes of meetings. LBJL.

78. Memorandum of conversation, the president, Robert F. Kennedy and others. 10AM, April 3, 1968. Box 5, Walt Rostow Files, NSF. LBJL.

79. Memorandum for Secretary of State, April 9, 1968. Box 557, Harriman Papers, Library of Congress.

80. Ellsworth Bunker, "Vietnam Negotiations: Dangers and Opportunities." April 8, 1968. Box 95–96, Vietnam/NSF. LBJL.

81. Joint Chiefs of Staff to General Andrew Goodpaster, May 31, 1968. Box 3. Clark Clifford Papers, Southeast Asia: Cables. LBJL.

82. Averell Harriman," General Review of the Last Six Months, December 14, 1968. Box 562, Harriman Papers, Library of Congress.

83. Daniel Davidson and Richard Holbrooke to State Department, July 9, 1968. Box 558, Harriman Papers. Library of Congress.

84. Harriman, "General Review of the Last Six Months," Box 562, Harriman Papers, Library of Congress.

85. Averell Harriman, Memorandum for Personal files, August 22, 1968. Box 558. Library of Congress.

86. George Ball, Oral History, LBJL. Lewis Chester, Godfrey Hodgson, and Bruce Page, *An American Melodrama: The Preidential Campaign of 1968* (New York, 1969), p. 726.

87. Memorandum of conversation, Averell Harriman/Robert Shaplen. November 1, 1968 [Memo dated November 30, 1968]. Box 562, Harriman Papers, Library of Congress.

88. Notes of the President's meeting. October 22, 1968. Box 1, Tom Johnson's copyrighted notes of meetings. LBJL.

89. Notes of the President's Meeting. 2:30 AM. October 29, 1968. Box 1, Tom Johnson's notes of meetings. LBJL.

90. Notes on Tuesday Luncheon. October 29, 1968. Box 1, Tom Johnson's copyrighted notes of meetings. LBJL.

91. Memorandum of conversation, Harriman/William Rogers. January 21,

1969. Box 562, Harriman Papers. Library of Congress.

BIBLIOGRAPHY

Berman, Larry. *Lyndon Johnson's War* (New York, 1989).
——— *Planning a Tragedy: The Americanization of the Vietnam War* (New York, 1983).
Clifford, Clark. *Counsel to the President* (New York, 1991).
DeBenedetti, Charles with Charles Chatfield. *An American Ordeal: The Antiwar Movement of the Vietnam Era* (Syracuse, N.Y., 1991).
Hammer, Ellen. *A Death in November: America in Vietnam, 1963* (New York, 1987).
Herring, George. *America's Longest War: The United States and Vietnam, 1950–1975*, 2d ed. (New York, 1986).
Kahin, George McT. *Intervention: How America Became Involved in Vietnam* (New York, 1986).
Small, Melvin. *Johnson, Nixon and the Doves* (New Brunswick, N.J., 1988).
Smith, Ralph B. *An International History of the Vietnam War*, Vols. 2 and 3 (New York, 1983, 1991).

7

From Nonexistent to Almost Normal: U.S.-China Relations in the 1960s

•

ARTHUR WALDRON

Only a bold analyst indeed would have suggested, at the end of the 1960s, that the diplomacy between the United States and China during that decade had prepared the way for a dramatic breakthrough. Bold because, judged by what had gone before and what came after, the 1960s seem a period in which little happened of any consequence. Yet that analyst would have been correct.

The fifties, the era of the high Cold War and containment, had been marked by dramatic military confrontations in Korea and then the two Formosa Straits crises. The 1970s, the era of détente, would see reconciliation between China and the United States, first with Nixon's visit to Peking in 1972 and then with Carter's establishment of full diplomatic relations in 1979.

By comparison, the sixties seem uneventful. Theodore Sorenson records that President Kennedy "felt dissatisfied with his administration's failure to break new ground," and had been planning to reconsider China policy in his second term.[1] But when the Johnson administration did attempt a modest opening, as Kennedy might have done, China responded negatively. Only when Nixon came to office in 1969 did Chinese-American relations begin to develop, although the climax of the process came after the decade had ended.

Such apparent lack of achievement, however, is not the whole story. Although the 1960s were an often frustrating period in American-Chinese relations, they witnessed two crucial developments. First, Washington made clearer than it had in the 1950s its wish to improve relations with China, and second, at the very end of the decade, for both internal and external reasons, Peking decided to respond.

The Situation in 1960

When the 1960s began, the United States possessed only a few small pieces of the China puzzle. Our diplomatic relations were with the government of the Republic of China [ROC] in Taipei, on the island of Taiwan, some hundred miles off the coast of the Chinese mainland. That government held China's permanent seat in the United Nations Security Council throughout the decade, and almost until the end of the period the word "China" when used in official Washington also referred to that government. The government of the People's Republic of China [PRC] in Peking was not recognized by the United States, and was kept out of the United Nations largely through American-coordinated efforts. Its official name was never used; it was "Mainland China," "Communist China," or "Red China." American passports were not valid for travel there, nor could American tourists in such places as Hong Kong legally buy goods made on the mainland and bring them back to the United States.

The PRC's official posture toward the United States was at least equally distant, and became virulently hostile with the advent in mid-decade of the Cultural Revolution. As Ambassador [to Thailand] Kenneth T. Young put it in 1967, from the beginning of the decade "Peking . . . escalated its cult of hate inside China and rudely rebuffed with epithet and insult every American gesture of the President, the Vice-President, the Secretary of State, other American officials, and many private Americans."[2]

But the appearance of isolation and hostility was somewhat misleading. As some officials on both sides understood, better relations would clearly serve the interests of both, above all because they had a common adversary in the USSR. There were dangers to be avoided and positive opportunities to be grasped. For such reasons, secret American-PRC talks had been going on, first in Geneva and then in Warsaw, since 1955.[3] In fact, so great was the objective logic favoring it, that the lack of an improvement of relations is perhaps the most striking fact about the 1960s. Many writers have argued that the problem lay in Washington: that our China recognition policy and role in Vietnam, in particular, ruled out better relations.[4] Here the argument will be somewhat different, for a comparison of what the United States had been prepared to offer since the 1950s, and what the PRC accepted in the

1970s, suggests that American policy was far more consistent, and that of the PRC far more variable, than has been recognized.

Problems from the Past

A single incident brings together most of the key strands in American relations with China both before and during the 1960s: this is the exchange over policy toward the islands of Quemoy and Matsu between presidential candidates Richard Nixon and John Kennedy in their second televised debate in October 1960.

Quemoy and Matsu were reminders of an unhappy history, going back to the Second World War. The Republic of China had been created in 1912 when the last imperial dynasty, the Qing, abdicated. In 1937 the Japanese had invaded it, committing atrocities comparable to those of the Nazis in Europe. After the Japanese attack on Pearl Harbor in 1941 the United States had joined China in the common struggle, and had expected that a victorious China would, with Britain, the United States, and the Soviet Union, be one of the four great powers of the postwar world. It was to plan for this that the Chinese leader, Generalissimo Chiang Kai-shek, had attended the Cairo conference with Joseph Stalin, Winston Churchill, and Franklin Roosevelt in late 1943.

But like postwar Europe, postwar Asia emerged in a form unexpected by the United States. On the Chinese mainland, the communist armies of Mao Zedong defeated Chiang Kai-shek in a civil war that began in 1945. But even when Mao, victorious on the mainland of China, proclaimed his new state, the People's Republic of China in Peking in 1949, that civil war did not come to a complete end. Instead it moved offshore, where it remained a factor in 1960, as it is today. Instead of surrendering to the Communists, Chiang Kai-shek and two million of his followers had taken refuge in the offshore island of Taiwan, then widely known as Formosa, where they maintained the government of the Republic of China in existence. In addition to Taiwan, the ROC government also held the Pescadores Islands [Penghu] in the middle of the Taiwan Strait, Quemoy [Jinmen] and Matsu [Mazu] just off the coast of Fujian Province, and the Dachen and Nanjishan island groups off Zhejiang. From these offshore territories they vowed one day to liberate the rest of their country from Communism.

When Chiang was defeated on the Chinese mainland in 1949, the United States had initially seemed willing to write off the ROC refugee government and deal with the new administration of the

PRC. But Peking treated the American diplomats waiting at their posts on the mainland with great hostility, "beating up the Vice-Consul in Shanghai, imprisoning the consul and his staff in Mukden [Shenyang], confiscating consular property in Peking, and mishandling the American Ambassador in Nanking."[5] And when the Korean War began in 1950, and even more so when PRC troops nearly defeated American forces in the fighting there, the possibility of normal relations was ruled out for the time being. Instead, Washington moved to protect Taiwan: not, it should be stressed, to embrace Chiang Kai-shek's full claim to be the sole legitimate government of China, but at least to prevent the forced incorporation of more than ten million residents of Taiwan into the brutally administered PRC. Full diplomatic relations were maintained with the ROC, and a mutual defense treaty signed in 1954.

While estranging the United States from the PRC, the Korean war greatly strengthened the alliance between Peking and Moscow, first signed in February 1950, and this alliance, because of its global significance, came to preoccupy American strategy. Stalin had been cautious in his early dealings with the Chinese Communist regime, but he warmed considerably when the Chinese sacrificed more than half a million men to save North Korea. In the war's aftermath, cooperation grew between Moscow and Peking on every level: Soviet foreign aid paid for vast new factories and infrastructure projects that Soviet technicians helped design and construct; Soviet specialists assisted the Chinese in developing an up-to-date military capacity, even promising to share nuclear weapons technology. Joined together in the so-called Sino-Soviet bloc, the two largest states of Eurasia threatened to overawe the rest of the world.

The only hope was that the alliance would not last, and with deep cultural differences and a long and disputed border, China and the Soviet Union made an unlikely pair, as the United States had recognized from the start. In his letter of transmittal for his report on the Communist victory in China, the so-called China White Paper, Secretary of State Dean Acheson had foreseen a day when China would abandon its pro-Soviet alignment.[6] The Eisenhower administration had sought to hasten this process by every means available, punishing both partners for their alignment, while offering each rewards for independent behavior.[7] Indeed, as Gordon H. Chang notes, "at no time since 1949 . . . have the top policymakers of the United States ever assumed that communism was monolithic, that China was irretrievably 'lost' to the Soviet Union, or that the United States was not without [sic] means to encourage Sino-Soviet frictions, if not an eventual split."[8] And although no one realized it at the time, this effort had in fact been crowned with success in the confrontation over Quemoy and Matsu in 1958, known as the second Formosa Straits Crisis, about which Kennedy and Nixon sparred in October 1960.

The crisis began on August 23, 1958, with PRC artillery barrages against the two islands, which seemed designed to take them, and might well have succeeded, had not the United States come to the aid of the ROC. American forces initially assisted only in the perilous business of escorting supplies to the islands through the PRC naval and air attacks. But when the PRC extended its maritime claims to twelve miles from shore, a distance that would have encompassed areas in which American forces were operating, the United States became directly involved. Secretary of State John Foster Dulles announced that the United States would help defend Quemoy and Matsu against any attack by China. When word followed that the United States had emplaced artillery capable of firing nuclear shells on Quemoy, the PRC had little choice but to lower the level of confrontation dramatically.[9] This trip to the nuclear brink yielded a victory for the ROC and the United States, and one that was in fact far greater than was understood at the time, for as we shall see below, it strained the Sino-Soviet alliance beyond the breaking point. But it was nevertheless frightening. Many Americans believed that although the defense of Taiwan made sense, holding the ROC's offshore islands was not worth the nuclear risk. John Kennedy was one.

In the television debate Kennedy asserted that American defense in the area should not be focused on the offshore islands but rather on Taiwan itself. Richard Nixon denounced this as "woolly thinking"; Kennedy replied by calling the existing policy "trigger-happy," while further asserting that in fact Eisenhower himself had tried to persuade Chiang Kai-shek to withdraw from the islands.[10]

The issue may seem minor in retrospect, but in fact, rather as Berlin did in the West, it focused a whole series of issues. China was now divided, de facto, into two established states. Neither would recognize the other. Furthermore, they continued actually to fight over the offshore islands, the only places where each could reach the other. But perhaps if the geographical boundary could be made neater—if the ROC could leave the offshore islands—the active civil war could be brought to a close, and then what was called a "Two China" solution be imposed: one in which each state had diplomatic relations with other states and perhaps the other, representation in the U.N., with the permanent seat going to the PRC, and so forth. A related approach would be to recognize the PRC as "China," while substituting for the

ROC a regime democratically elected on the island, perhaps under UN auspices, to represent "Taiwan."

The United States had mentioned such policies publicly; so too, had the USSR. Before the Supreme Soviet in December 1957 Khrushchev had stated: "We say to the representatives of the western countries, and especially the United States . . . let us recognize the status quo . . . renounce any attempt to alter the existing situation by force."[11] And they might have worked, if the leading powers had imposed them the 1960s. But the powers did no such thing, because the policies were anathema to whichever China they supported, ROC and PRC alike.

Kennedy's position on the offshore islands was a sign that he favored such an approach. But Nixon's criticism did not amount to a repudiation of it; rather more to disagreement about tactics. For the two China solution has been the perennial American policy toward the PRC-ROC dilemma, and remains so today in practice, despite the one-China rhetoric of official relations. It goes back at least to 1955, when in a press conference President Eisenhower referred to two Chinas as one of the approaches being considered by the United States.[12] It appears always to have been a goal of that administration, although never achieved.

One China or Two?

The idea of "one China" had been identified as a problem even earlier: in 1953 Eisenhower's secretary of state John Foster Dulles pointed to insistence on China's territorial integrity as a main reason for failure of U.S. China policy. As he put it, "The territorial integrity of China became a shibboleth. We finally got a territorially integrated China— for whose benefit? The Communists."[13] The powerful pressure that the Eisenhower administration applied to the PRC, some of it through Taiwan, however, concealed the logic of the policy from many people, who imagined that Eisenhower and Nixon were simplemindedly and stubbornly supporting the ROC as the only China in the face of powerful imperatives to do otherwise.

The real shape of the Eisenhower policy was clear after the first Quemoy and Matsu crisis of 1954. When Yijiangshan island off Zhejiang fell following air and sea attacks in January 1955, the U.S. Congress reacted by giving Eisenhower authority to use U.S. forces for the defense of territories related to Taiwan, if he judged their protection "to be required or appropriate in assuring the defense of Formosa and the Pescadores."[14] But far from rushing to defend the islands off the

Zhejiang coast, the United States instead persuaded the ROC to with-draw from the Dachen Islands, and did nothing when the Nanjishan Islands were taken by the PRC a month later. As for the trip to the nuclear brink over Quemoy and Matsu in 1958, Dulles evidently hoped to follow it with bargaining "in the fullest meaning of Western negotiations," leading to ROC withdrawal from the offshore islands and possibly PRC diplomatic relations with the United States. But PRC frustrated his hopes by unilaterally ending the crisis without entering negotiations.[15]

The two China idea received renewed attention in November 1959, when a report commissioned by the U.S. Senate Committee on Foreign Relations, and partially authored by University of California professor Robert A. Scalapino, suggested initiatives toward the PRC including giving it the China seat in the U.N. Security Council.[16] A month later a prestigious study of foreign policy prepared for the Rockefeller Broth-ers Fund by Kennedy's future Secretary of State, Dean Rusk, and Adolphe A. Berle, Jr. called for reassessment of China policy. Rusk was certainly aware of the Sino-Soviet split, and favored the two China approach.[17]

The related approach, that Taiwan was distinct from China, and should be recognized independently, also received renewed attention as the 1960s began. Such was the argument set forth the January 1960 issue of *Foreign Affairs* by Adlai Stevenson, the two-time Democratic presidential nominee, who would serve Kennedy as ambassador to the United Nations. Stevenson advocated "acceptance of the right of the inhabitants of Formosa to determine their own destiny by a plebiscite supervised by the United Nations."[18] In an article in the April 1960 issue of the same journal, future Under Secretary of State Chester Bowles urged the formation of "an independent Sino-Formosan nation" predominantly Chinese in culture but Formosan in outlook. He further called for imaginative policies based on an acceptance of "two Chinas," not realizing that this had been the Eisenhower goal.[19]

A third approach, which favored conceding in principle the PRC's claim to Taiwan, while working in practice to maintain its autonomy and security, was put forward in January 1961 by Professor John Fair-bank of Harvard. He called for recognizing Chinese "suzerainty" over Taiwan, but giving the island the right to manage its own foreign affairs, and putting Peking in the Security Council, but giving Taiwan a separate seat in the General Assembly.[20]

Of course these policies were nuanced. Although they favored "unhooking the United States from Chiang Kai-shek, stranded on Tai-wan" none of these writers "favored jettisoning the Nationalists in order to improve relations with Beijing." Rather, they saw lack of contact with the PRC as "constrictive of American options and self-defeating." Indeed, many of these same writers regarded the PRC as possibly a more serious long-term threat to the United States than was the USSR, and would favor aligning with Moscow to counterbalance Peking, particularly after the PRC acquired nuclear weapons.[21]

And there were many in the United States opposed to all such approaches. They were represented best by the powerful "Committee of One Million," which supported single recognition of the ROC and isolation of the PRC, at least until Peking substantially changed its policies. Even allowing for this, however, it is remarkable how strong and broad a consensus was taking shape in favor of some form of two China policy. It is no exaggeration to suggest that the fundamental concepts that would frame the diplomatic breakthrough of the 1970s were already widely accepted in the United States in the 1950s, and they only grew stronger in the decade that followed.

Attempts at Change

Certainly it was clear from the start that the Kennedy administration was open to change. While reiterating American commitments to the ROC in his first news conference, on February 6, 1961, the new Secretary of State, Dean Rusk, also added that Washington was studying ways to bring Communist China into disarmament talks, noting that "it will not be easy to achieve any realistic or effective disarmament unless all those countries that are capable of producing . . . large armed forces are brought within the system."[22] Less than a month later, on March 7, 1961, talks resumed in Warsaw, with American Ambassador Jacob D. Beam renewing proposals first made in the Eisenhower administration for an exchange of journalists between the two countries, and the release of Americans imprisoned in Mainland China. His counterpart, Wang Bingnan, rejected all proposals until the United States withdrew its forces from Taiwan. The Warsaw talks did, however, lead in the 1960s to the repatriation of all but four of the seventy Americans imprisoned in the PRC, and permission for some Chinese stranded in the United States in 1949 to return home.[23]

Shortly after the resumption of the Warsaw talks, Kennedy met Khrushchev in Vienna. Knowing how concerned he was by developments in the PRC, the American president hoped to entice him with the bait of cooperation in dealing with China. To Kennedy's surprise, Khrushchev turned him down flat: Moscow's desire not further to alienate the PRC led it, logically enough, to stick close to Peking's line on Chinese questions.[24]

Another possible opening came in April 1961, when the U.N. General Assembly voted to admit together the Mongolian People's Republic and the newly independent (as of 1960) African state of Mauritania. Mongolia was a Soviet client state, over which the ROC had once claimed sovereignty. When it was first proposed for U.N. membership in 1955, the ROC had exercised its veto, hoping thereby to force Moscow to negotiate the issue with Taipei. But "linking admission of Mongolia to that of a new African state put the United States and Nationalist China [ROC] in a difficult position. If the Nationalists vetoed Mongolia this time, Mauritania would also be blocked, and enough African states might blame the Nationalists to tip the balance in favor of admitting Communist China [PRC] to the UN when it came up again in the fall."[25]

And at this time the United States was opposed to PRC entry into the U.N. When Ambassador John Kenneth Galbraith cabled Rusk from New Delhi urging that "subject to protecting the position of Taiwan and some possible revision of the membership of the Security Council" the will of the majority should be accepted and Peking admitted, Rusk responded, "To the extent that your position has any merit it has been fully considered and rejected."[26]

The Mongolia problem, however, was also an opportunity. As Chester Bowles and others realized, a gesture toward Mongolia could have many advantages: rewarding moderation in the USSR, signaling to other Communist powers Washington's willingness to do business, and showing other Asian countries that the U.S. was not rigidly linked to ROC policies. Nor need it stop with the United Nations: an embassy in Ulan Bator would be very useful. Feelers were extended, and the Mongolian response was favorable. Not so that from the United States, however: the Committee of One Million mobilized, and a vociferous campaign led the Kennedy administration to abandon the idea of recognition.[27] But the UN story ended differently. When ROC Vice President Chen Cheng visited Washington in August 1961, President Kennedy succeeded in pressuring him to prevent another ROC veto, and as a result the Mongolian People's Republic was admitted to the United Nations on October 25, 1961.[28]

Meanwhile, a crisis was brewing in the PRC. Although American intelligence was scarcely aware of the fact, 1961 was the worst year of a catastrophic human-made famine that claimed as many as thirty million lives.[29] For the ROC, this seemed the long awaited moment for the armed liberation of the mainland, and Taipei sought in 1961 and 1962 to win United States support for a landing of several divisions. Wanting no repeat of the Bay of Pigs, the administration distanced itself, but not completely: Kennedy was an enthusiast for guerrilla warfare, and the U.S. supplied aircraft and supplies used for ROC airdrops and amphibious operations against the PRC.[30] The PRC, however, began to concentrate large forces opposite Taiwan, whether for offensive or defensive purposes it was hard to tell. To defuse the situation the United States used the Warsaw channel on June 26, 1962 to assure Peking that Washington would not support any ROC attack on the mainland, while Kennedy told the press the next day that the United States would "take the action necessary to assure the defense of Formosa" provided for in the 1955 resolution.[31]

Then, beginning on October 20, 1962, the PRC unfolded a victorious attack on two areas along India's northern frontier, which it ended unilaterally on November 20 and followed with a partial withdrawal. The origins of the war are obscure, but it was in part a consequence of Peking's 1959 invasion and subjugation of Tibet, which India had deplored. Aksai Chin, one territory the PRC now occupied, lay on the only feasible land route between Tibet and the Chinese province of Xinjiang. But the war also had a larger psychological dimension. India and the PRC were natural rivals; the PRC attack was "a masterpiece of orchestrating military, political, and psychological instrumentalities," and while it elicited American assistance to India, it also demonstrated that India was weak and PRC strong. So in its aftermath President Kennedy pondered once again American relations with a China that had the world's largest population and would, if intelligence estimates were correct, soon have nuclear weapons as well. "It may take some years, perhaps a decade, before they become a full-fledged nuclear power," he told a press conference on August 1, 1963, "and we would like to take some steps now that would lessen that prospect that a future President might have to deal with."[32]

Kennedy deeply feared a nuclear-armed PRC, which he believed would become the "great menace on earth," willing to sacrifice hundreds of millions of its own people in nuclear war. This conviction led him to press for a test-ban treaty; it also led his administration to explore with the USSR cooperation against the PRC nuclear program, even including military options.[33] But it also made the quest for peaceful communications with Peking even more urgent.

Two important hints of an impending shift in American China policy came toward the end of 1963. In a November press conference, a week before he was assassinated, Kennedy indicated that the United States was not wedded to a policy of hostility toward the mainland

Chinese regime: if it expressed a willingness to coexist peacefully, the United States would reconsider its policies.[34] Behind the scenes, the administration was once again considering recognition of Mongolia, as well as bringing the PRC into the Geneva disarmament talks, and removing some restrictions on trade. No one expected immediate reciprocation from Peking, but all were concerned to get the message of American openness out. The American desire for progress was made very clear in the Warsaw talks.[35]

On December 13, 1963, the possibilities were spelled out more clearly in a speech at the Commonwealth Club, San Francisco, by Assistant Secretary of State for Far Eastern Affairs, Roger Hilsman. Hilsman, a Kennedy administration insider whose Asian experience had begun with the Office of Strategic Services (forerunner of the CIA) during World War II, had planned the speech before the President's assassination. And although the new president approved it for delivery without reading it, how it would fit with the policies of the Johnson administration was problematical.[36]

Hilsman began by refuting the common assertion that the United States was somehow ignoring China. After speaking of ties with "our ally, the Government of the Republic of China" and the "twelve million people in Taiwan" he turned to "the people on the mainland." "We are very much aware of them, and we have a deep friendship for them. Nor, finally, do we ignore the Communist leadership which has established itself on the mainland. We meet with them from time to time, as at the periodic talks between our Ambassadors in Warsaw. We should like to be less ignorant of them and for them to be less ignorant of us." And a few paragraphs later, Hilsman implicitly repudiated ideas of rolling back Communism in China, stating that "we have no reason to believe that there is a present likelihood that the Communist regime will be overthrown."[37]

Hoping to open up some sort of channel of communication with Peking, Hilsman noted that the United States had "been striving for years to arrange an exchange of correspondents; but we have been put off with the assertion that, so long as the 'principal issue'—which they define in terms of their absurd charge that we are 'occupying' Taiwan—is unresolved, there can be no progress on 'secondary issues.' "

Hilsman stressed America's desire for contact with the PRC. "If I may paraphrase a classic canon of our past, we pursue today towards Communist China a policy of the open door; we are determined to keep the door open to the possibility of change, and not to slam it shut against any developments which might advance our national good, serve the free world, and benefit the people of China."

On Taiwan Hilsman suggested some flexibility: he said "So long as Peking insists on the destruction of this relationship as the sine qua non for any basic improvement in relations between ourselves and Communist China, there can be no prospect for such an improvement." Note the word destruction: that does not rule out a whole variety of modifications. But Hilsman seemed reconciled to the lack of a Chinese response. As he noted sadly, and accurately, "The United States is the central figure in [PRC] demonology, and the target of a sustained fury of invective. After President Kennedy's assassination, while other nations—Communist and free—shared our grief, the Chinese Communist 'Daily Worker' [sic] published a cartoon of a man sprawled on the ground, with the caption 'Kennedy bites the dust.' If this speaks for the Chinese Communist leadership, I am confident that it does not speak for most Chinese."[38]

From the Great Leap Forward to French Recognition

Less than ten years later, comparable American initiatives would gradually elicit a matching PRC response. That they did not in the 1960s is a reflection not of American wishes or diplomacy, as is often argued, but rather of the state of internal PRC politics. And like the American situation described above, that in the PRC traced back to events in the year 1958.

The Great Leap Forward began in that year: it was an attempt, following the policies of Mao Zedong, to bring China to economic parity with the advanced nations through one vast transformation. Begun optimistically, it created, as we have seen, a terrible famine, worse than any China had suffered in the twentieth century, in which between fifteen and thirty million people perished unnecessarily. This tragic outcome had serious political consequences. Among the party leaders who knew the true history of the Leap, its failure discredited Mao Zedong, and attempts began, if not to remove him from power, at least to sideline him. These succeeded, at least partially, at the Lushan Plenum of 1959, which saw day to day management of PRC policy turned over to such relatively more steady figures as Liu Shaoqi, Zhou Enlai, and Deng Xiaoping.

But while the Leap was still on its upward trajectory in the summer of 1958, Peking had also begun its attacks on Quemoy and Matsu. When the United States backed up the ROC with nuclear threats, the PRC turned to the USSR for a countervailing menace. But Khrushchev declined, horrified that his country—then involved in trying to improve relations with the United States—was being drawn into a nuclear confrontation over a speck of PRC-claimed territory of which it had probably never heard. Mao, it seems, had never fully informed Moscow of his plans.[39] Rather than support the PRC, Khrushchev began to reduce military cooperation with his erratic ally, while urging Peking to accept the two-China solution that Dulles had made clear was on offer. Mao responded with great hostility, and the Sino-Soviet split, long sought by American policy, had become a reality.[40]

The strains with the Soviet Union were soon unmistakable: the USSR ended cooperation with PRC, withdrawing aid and experts, and by August 1960 Agence France Presse was reporting from Peking that the departure of Soviet technicians and their families had "increased at such a rate since the end of July that they are now coming to be spoken of openly in diplomatic circles in the Chinese capital as a veritable exodus."[41]

Freed of the Soviet alliance, the PRC was well placed to adopt a more independent policy, and it may puzzle some that rapprochement with the United States did not follow in short order. After all, during the high Cold War Peking had been somewhat forthcoming during the 1950s at Warsaw and other venues. But all progress ceased in 1960: while the Americans "sought a wide range of discussion and negotiations" the PRC, in Dean Rusk's words, kept "hanging up the phone"[42]—even though at this time ostensible moderates were in control in Peking. Indeed many of the same people who participated in the breakthrough of 1972 were running the PRC's foreign policy, but in the 1960s they consistently rebuffed U.S. overtures.

Such puzzlement is understandable, but it betrays a failure to grasp the diplomatic effects of the Sino-Soviet dispute at its early stages. The collapse of capitalism and victory of world revolution were, in those simpler days, still genuine articles of faith in both Moscow and Peking. For the PRC, the dispute was a split within, and not with, Communism. "Beijing saw Washington and Moscow moving toward a superpower détente that had threatening implications for China and the international Communist movement." The question was who should lead world revolution, and the answer would be found, both believed, in the newly independent countries of Africa and Asia, what today would be called the Third World.[43]

The American nuclear arsenal, rattled occasionally and with great effect by Eisenhower, had made any Communist breakthrough in Europe look unlikely. But those nuclear weapons would be of far less use in the sorts of anti-Western struggles to which Moscow and Peking now turned their attention: the wars of national liberation, which Mao

Zedong and his devoted military commander Lin Biao had long extolled, and to which Khrushchev had pledged Soviet support in 1961. From Vietnam to Ghana to Cuba, the two Communist powers competed to be better and more revolutionary friends. And in such a rivalry there could be little room on either side for genuine opening to the United States.

The bid for leadership of the international Communist movement would require that the PRC be military self-sufficient, including in nuclear forces. This had been an implicit goal of the Chinese Communists at least since the late 1940s, and Peking did not lose sight of this goal even when its alliance with the Soviet Union was reinforced following the Korean War. Soviet military aid greatly increased the strength of Chinese military industry in the 1950s, and laid critical foundations for the Chinese nuclear program. But when the USSR suggested joint Soviet-Chinese military forces, China demurred. And when the Soviets withdrew aid in 1960, considerable progress had already been made. It was enough, at least, to permit the Chinese to punctuate the 1960s with some dramatic demonstrations: October 16, 1964, when China exploded its first atomic bomb; October 27, 1966, when China successfully fired a ballistic missile with a live warhead, which exploded as planned on the test range (the only such test ever carried out by any country), and June 17, 1967, when China detonated its first hydrogen bomb.[44]

While the nuclear weapons program pushed forward, not all Chinese or Soviets had given up on their special relationship. Indeed, it was precisely the PRC's growing strength that led the USSR to stretch to accommodate it even as the split opened up. Talks between the two powers continued until Khrushchev was overthrown in October 1964, and even after. The final break did not come until 1965, when two visits by Kosygin failed to produce a communiqué, and the Soviet embassy in Peking became the target of demonstrations.

Even after the split was painfully evident, moreover, the PRC and USSR competed to support the military campaign of the Communist Democratic Republic of [North] Vietnam against the American-backed Republic of [South] Vietnam. Neither could very well cease to back the Communist north: to do so would be to admit collusion with the Americans. Yet this support undercut the PRC's interests in particular, drawing the United States into the conflict because it believed it was containing Chinese expansion, and at the same time making it impossible for Peking to align itself with the U.S. against Moscow, as its objective interests required. By the late 1960s, the American presence in Vietnam had become, in Peking's eyes, almost as much of a barrier to relations with Washington as was Taiwan, and it would remain so until immediate fear of the USSR overrode both.[45]

Integral to the PRC strategy of independence was entry into the international system neither through the patronage of the USSR, as it had done in the 1950s, nor through reconciliation with its ideological adversary the United States, as it would in the 1970s, but rather entirely on its own terms. The PRC might well have achieved this goal in the 1960s, had not its own internal politics cut the ground from under its diplomatic strategy.

To achieve this goal the PRC adopted in the early 1960s a strategy of promoting ties with nonaligned and newly independent states, and using their votes to enter the United Nations, whether the United States wanted it or not. Beginning in 1960 the diplomatic offensive began, as the leaders of the PRC stepped up their foreign travel. In April 1960 Premier Zhou Enlai was in Rangoon, New Delhi, and Kathmandu; in May he visited Phnom Penh and Hanoi, and then Mongolia; he kept up that pace in the years that followed. By 1961 Zhou's active diplomacy was beginning to break out of the initial group of countries with which China had either common borders or common interests; indeed out of the socialist bloc. In June 1961 President Sukarno of Indonesia visited China. Major agricultural sales were concluded between Australia and China and Canada and China. Tension over the PRC war with India in 1962 set back the approach a bit, but it rapidly recovered. In April 1963, Chinese President Liu Shaoqi, accompanied by Wang Guangmei, his beautiful, American-educated fifth wife, returned Sukarno's visit: this was the first time that the Communist Chinese head of state had visited a noncommunist country. Zhou Enlai established a foothold in Europe with a visit to Albania in 1964, and another to Africa. Air service to and from China expanded: the first flight by Pakistan International Airlines landed at Shanghai on April 29, 1964. Soothing noises were made toward the Soviet Union with the February 29, 1964 Chinese expression of willingness to take the treaties of 1858 and 1860, which made the Amur and Ussuri rivers the Sino-Russian border in the northeast, as a basis for settling the territorial dispute.

But the major diplomatic focus was Africa.[46] The Sino-African People's Friendship Association had been founded in Peking on April 12, 1960, and in the years that followed more and more of the new African states established relations with the PRC. This fact created many possible new channels for dealing with the United States, which, significantly enough, Peking refused to use. Thus Kennedy instructed his ambassador to Guinea, William Attwood, to attempt to make contact with the large PRC diplomatic contingent there—but had no success.

The PRC diplomats and the Americans used the same beach, and swam together nearly every day, but no American opening could elicit so much as a word from the Chinese, who acted as if Attwood and his associates simply were not there.[47]

But these moves were more than the cold shoulder. They manifested Peking's strategy, which was to establish itself at the head of world revolution by patronizing newly emerged African states and supporting armed insurgencies against South Africa and the Portuguese empire, while at the same time isolating the United States and the ROC by gradually winning over countries in between. The diplomatic harvest in Africa was spectacular: as the new year 1964 began, PRC Premier Zhou Enlai and Foreign Minister Chen Yi visited Tunisia, Ghana, Mali, Guinea, Ethiopia, and Somalia, to confirm existing relations. "Soon afterward fourteen African nations recognized Beijing, leaving only fifteen to continue their relations with Taipei."[48] But the road that began in Africa turned out to lead to the heart of Europe, as became clear on January 17, 1964 when Paris announced that it would establish diplomatic relations with Peking.

For the PRC, this was a major achievement, one that seemed to bring nearer a general European break with the United States over its unpopular China policy. And for France it made sense as well. The early 1960s had been stormy for Paris: Charles De Gaulle had decided to let Algeria go, a blow for which he tried to compensate with a renewal of nationalism in France proper, much to the distress of the United States. There had been the first French nuclear explosion in 1960, the veto of Britain's application to join the EEC in 1963, and the withdrawal from NATO commands in 1966. As it distanced herself from her Western allies, France needed China as a third balance point, between the United States and the USSR. De Gaulle couched the announcement in suitable language: "China, a great people, the most numerous people on the face of the earth, and a vast country; a State older than history, constantly determined to be independent, striving unceasingly to centralization, instinctively turned in on itself and contemptuous of foreigners, but aware and proud of a perennial immutability, such is the eternal China."[49]

France, however, was not about to burn its bridges to the West completely, and thus drove a hard bargain, one that was difficult for Peking to accept. For one thing, it made clear that recognition of the PRC did not imply a major break with the United States, in regard either to European or Asian policy. There would be no recognition of East Germany. Nor—and this made it difficult for Peking to swallow—did France break relations with Taipei.[50] Yet the PRC nevertheless accepted the French recognition, which suggests something about what sorts of bargains some in China might have been willing to strike thereafter. It was left to Taipei to complete the breach with Paris, withdrawing the ambassador, in a move later much regretted, on February 10, 1964.[51]

French China policy during this period is hedged with might-have-beens. The French model of recognition could well have been accepted by the United States: fundamentally, it was what Washington had been looking for since the end of the 1940s. Just as Tunisia and the African countries had prepared the way for France, so France would prepare the way for Washington. Initially, it looked as if this might happen.

Public and political opinion was increasingly ready. Thus on March 25, 1964, U.S. Senator J. William Fulbright, chairman of the Senate Foreign Affairs Committee, spoke in the Senate on "Old Myths and New Realities." This broadly critical assessment of American policy attempted to open new ground in dealing with China. While rejecting recognition of Peking "as long as the Peiping [the ROC name for Peking, which removes from the name the "king," meaning "capital"] regime maintains its attitude of implacable hostility toward the United States," Fulbright added significantly: "I do not believe, however, that this state of affairs is necessarily permanent. . . . Is it not possible that in time our relations with China will change again, if not to friendship, then perhaps to 'competitive coexistence.' It would therefore be an extremely useful thing if we could introduce an element of flexibility, or more precisely of the capacity to be flexible, into our relations with Communist China."[52]

In response, Secretary of State Rusk pointed to PRC aid to North Vietnam and refusal to renounce the use of force in the Taiwan strait as "realities" that stood in the way of better relations.[53] But that the American government was nevertheless attempting to develop a "capacity to be flexible" became clear during Rusk's visit to Taipei in April 1964. His statement omitted the previously standard mention of the ROC as "the only Chinese government which legally represents China," and did not oppose PRC membership in the United Nations, but rather only the turning over to the PRC of the ROC's seat. "This American attitude was unacceptable to the Republic of China and no joint communique was issued during Secretary Rusk's visit even though he held three meetings with high-level officials in Taipei. Relations between the United States and the Republic of China took a nosedive because of the change in the American policy toward Communist China."[54]

There was even flexibility implicit in President Johnson's seemingly hard line statement at about the same time: that "as long as the Communist Chinese pursue conflict and preach violence, there can be and will be no easing of relationships. . . . America must base our acts on present realities and not on future hopes. It is not we who must re-examine our view of China. It is the Chinese Communists who must re-examine their view of the world."[55]

October 16, 1964 witnessed the first detonation by the PRC of a nuclear weapon, which added great power status and fear of nuclear proliferation to reasons for the United States to deal with the PRC. On October 22 U.N. Secretary General U Thant called for disarmament talks to involve the United States, the USSR, Britain, France, and the PRC. The U.S. response was to state that existing channels for dialogue were open. Noting that the PRC would have to participate in negotia-tions "at some stage. . . if such agreements are to have any real mean-ing," the United States specified that "we have never precluded the participation of any country in disarmament negotiations."[56]

The United States was clearly on the diplomatic defensive, and the PRC close to a great diplomatic triumph, as was made very clear on November 17, 1965, when the UN Vote on seating the PRC was tied, for the first time, at 47–47. The PRC was winning more and more friends, and the ROC was helping them along by breaking relations with coun-tries that recognized Peking, even when they left diplomats in Taipei. The momentum was unmistakable. A year later, as will be seen, Peking would certainly have won, had not the whirlwind of the Cultural Rev-olution swept the carefully arranged diplomatic pieces entirely off the board.

Hints of the tempest to come were already in the air during what looked like the high point of France's briefly sweet relations with China, in August 1965, when André Malraux, the writer, then serving De Gaulle as a minister of state, visited Peking. Quite unwittingly, in the account in his *Anti-Memoirs*, Malraux discloses the basic problem that would leave De Gaulle's diplomatic initiatives stillborn. Malraux had been summoned to the Great Hall of the People on barely twenty-four hours notice, after returning from an excursion to Yanan. "As I enter the room I can distinguish the faces. I walk toward Liu Shao-ch'i [Shaoqi], since my letter is addressed to the President of the Republic. No one moves. "Mr. President, I have the honor of delivering to you this letter from the President of the French Republic, in which General de Gaulle empowers me to act as his spokesman with Chairman Mao Tse-tung [Mao Zedong] and yourself." When I reach the phrase which concerns Mao, I address it to him, and find myself in front of him, after handing over the letter, at the moment when the translation is com-pleted. His welcome is both cordial and curiously familiar." The discussion quickly turns to Mao, Yanan, and the history of the revolution. Liu Shaoqi never enters the conversation.[57]

So delighted was Malraux to be talking to Mao, whose prestige was then very high with the fashionable European intelligentsia, that he was utterly oblivious to the way the meeting embodied the problem that would overwhelm the promising start to French-Chinese relations: namely, Mao's irregular and extra-constitutional role, and the marginalization of Liu Shaoqi who, as we have seen, had traveled even to noncommunist Indonesia as Chinese head of state. Far from a beginning, Malraux's visit marked the conclusion, for the moment, of Zhou's remarkable diplomatic offensive, and coincided with the beginning of the Cultural Revolution.

As Jean Lacouture notes, De Gaulle's China policy failed to live up to expectations: "The consequences were less marked to begin with, more bitter later; when the embassy led by Lucien Paye, a former education minister, was at last bearing its first fruit two years later, the cultural revolution turned China into a witches' cauldron—which was not at all in tune with the peaceful, rational aims of the French head of state." And although De Gaulle dreamed to the end of his life of a trip to China, "it was Henry Kissinger and Richard Nixon, disciples in their own way of the general, who in 1972 were to collect the fruit of the operation begun eight years before in Paris."[58]

The Consequences of the Cultural Revolution in China

This promising set of diplomatic developments was doomed by the man whom Malraux idolized. Mao Zedong, it is clear, hated and mistrusted the officials at the Chinese helm during the early 1960s, and when he saw the opportunity, he turned China upside down in order to overthrow them.

In retrospect we can see that the Cultural Revolution, which began in late 1965 and ended under the menace of civil war in 1967, was Mao's final bid to take complete control of China and its destiny. His rivals for power and the men who had sidelined him after the catastrophe of the Great Leap would be driven out, many in fact dying horrible deaths. At the same time, China's whole culture and way of life would be transformed, to render impossible any attempt to reverse Mao's work. This second factor was more immediately visible at the time, and had a direct and disastrous effect on Chinese foreign policy.[59]

In the realm of rhetoric, September 1965 saw the publication of Defense Minister Lin Biao's essay *Long Live the Victory of People's War!*[60]

This manifesto reflected the belief of some in Peking that the next few years would likely see a string of Communist successes, in Vietnam most importantly, but also elsewhere in Southeast Asia and the world. It was a viewpoint that unsettled even those states inclined to support Peking. In Southeast Asia fear of Communism was added to tradition-al distrust of Chinese outside of China—the *huaqiao* or "sojourners"—to create a wave of anti-Chinese violence. As some of these overseas Chinese unwisely embraced the Cultural Revolution, they were caught in nationalistic anticommunist and anti-Chinese violence in Burma, Malaysia, and most bloodily, Indonesia, where an attempted coup, evi-dently backed by Peking, was crushed with much loss of life.[61] Chinese missions were sacked or closed; diplomats withdrew; Chinese resi-dents were killed. The gains of the early 1960s were lost in a flash.

The fire spread to Macao, where riots in December 1966 left the Por-tuguese administration as no more than a facade for Chinese Commu-nist control, and to Hong Kong, where a firm British reaction, and the clear opposition of the vast majority of the Chinese population, kept the Cultural Revolution from taking too great a toll. In Peking's new legation quarter, where the PRC had been building embassy structures before it knew who would occupy them, so fast had been the pace of recognition, foreigners once again felt themselves besieged as their pre-decessors had been in 1900. The thoroughfare outside the Soviet embassy was renamed "anti-revisionist street"; the British legation was put to the torch and the chargé beaten unconscious. In London three policemen, three Chinese, and a photographer were sent to hospital after PRC embassy employees, one wielding an axe, ran amok in the so-called Battle of Portland Place on August 29, 1967.[62] By dint of such madness, Peking lost its friends, confirmed its enemies, and generally cut itself off from diplomatic contacts, leaving itself with little more than Albania, Pakistan, and some African states.[63]

Continued United States Initiatives

Western politicians, however, did not entirely recognize the implica-tions of the Cultural Revolution, at least at the start. As a result, initia-tives to which another Chinese administration might have responded continued to be undertaken nonetheless. Assistant Secretary of State William P. Bundy made a speech on February 12, 1966 that signaled something of a new approach.[64] On March 8, 1966 the Senate Foreign Relations Committee began a series of hearings on United States China policy. The opinions voiced were what had been heard since the

1950s. Columbia University professor A. Doak Barnett urged recognition of the PRC as de facto government of the Chinese mainland, increased trade, and some formula to bring both the ROC and PRC into the United Nations. John Fairbank argued that containment was a blind alley, unless we added to it policies of constructive competition and international contact. On March 10, 1966 Secretary of State Dean Rusk outlined China policy to the House Subcommittee on the Far East, stating that "We expect China to become some day a great world power. Communist China is a major Asian power today. In the ordinary course of events, a peaceful China would be expected to have close relations—political, cultural, and economic—with the countries around its borders and with the United States. It is no part of the policy of the United States to block the peaceful attainment of these objectives."

After spelling out the policy differences that, he regretted, continued to divide the two countries, Rusk listed the avenues for exchange that the United States had already opened. "We have gradually expanded the categories of American citizens who may travel to Communist China. American libraries may freely purchase Chinese Communist publications. American citizens may send and receive mail from the mainland. We have in the past indicated that if the Chinese themselves were interested in purchasing grain we would consider such sales. We have indicated our willingness to allow Chinese Communist newspapermen to come to the United States. We are prepared to permit American universities to invite Chinese Communist scientists to visit their institutions." One can imagine any one of these openings turning into the so-called "ping-pong diplomacy" that preceded the Nixon visit. Furthermore, Rusk stressed the importance of the Warsaw ambassadorial talks, and stated a willingness to sit down "with Peiping and other interested countries to discuss the critical problems of disarmament and non-proliferation of nuclear weapons" noting that PRC had refused such overtures.[65]

Facing almost certain defeat in the United Nations, the United States was preparing major concessions there as well: no longer would entry of the PRC be opposed; the point would be to keep the ROC a member in some capacity. On April 19, Ambassador to the United Nations Arthur Goldberg set out the new conditions for allowing the PRC into the United Nations.[66]

With this plan went even more positive signals. At the White House, according to William Bundy, staffer James C. Thomson, Jr. seemed to take as "his sole mission in life" the insertion of positive phrases about the PRC in official speeches.[67] Secretary of Defense Robert McNamara would call for "bridge-building" to the Chinese Communists in a speech before the Newspaper Editors Association on May 18, 1966, and Vice President Hubert Humphrey would make the same call at West Point on June 8.[68]

President Lyndon Johnson underlined this approach with a speech to the American Alumni Council at White Sulphur Springs, West Virginia, and a nationwide telecast, on July 12, 1966. Like Rusk, he expressed a certain frustration at the unwillingness of the Chinese to respond to American initiatives. "For many years now, the United States has attempted in vain to persuade the Chinese Communists to agree to an exchange of newsmen as one of the first steps to increased understanding between our people. More recently, we have taken steps to permit American scholars, experts in medicine and public health, and other specialists, to travel to Communist China. And only today we, here in the Government, cleared a passport for a leading American businessman to exchange knowledge with Chinese mainland leaders in Red China."[69] There may have been Soviet encouragement of these initiatives; one of the Chinese rebuffs refers to "the Soviet revisionist leading clique's profuse nonsense" in connection with the U.S. initiatives.[70]

American public opinion was largely supportive of responsible opening to the PRC. The House of Representatives Foreign Affairs Committee held hearings on the PRC, which were published on May 20, 1966. And in December, the State Department formed a China study group consisting of a number of prominent American scholars of a variety of viewpoints. Also in 1966 private individuals formed the National Committee on United States-China Relations.[71]

These obvious United States initiatives stirred up a storm of protest in Taipei. Dean Rusk made two visits, on July 3 and December 7, 1966, to explain the United States position and presumably to try to win the ROC government over, to no avail.[72]

On Peking's side, however, not only were these initiatives ignored; they were actively rebuffed, both in public, and through the private Warsaw channel.[73] Zhou Enlai, now trimming his sails carefully to avoid being wrecked by the Cultural Revolution, responded to Rusk with a statement that although China did not want war with the United States, "should the United States impose a war on China, it can be said with certainty that once in China, the United States will not be able to pull out, however many men it may send over and whatever weapons it may use, nuclear weapons included."[74] A Chinese ambassadorial statement at the Sino-American talks on September 7, 1966 was equally harsh with Johnson: "Unreconciled to its failure, the U.S.

government is employing its counter-revolutionary dual tactics in every possible way in order to cover up its criminal acts of hostility against the Chinese people."[75] Peking's new rhetoric quickly scuttled the diplomatic achievements of the 1960s. At the U.N. "the Russians and everybody else didn't want the Chinese in," and PRC entry, virtually a sure thing a few months earlier, disappeared as an issue.[76]

Still, the United States did not entirely lose hope. The testing on June 17, 1967 of the first PRC hydrogen bomb strengthened the feeling in the United States that the PRC could not be ignored.[77] In summer 1967 Johnson made his most important overture to the PRC, through the Romanian Prime Minister, Ion Gheorghe Maurer. "He called on the President on June 26, just before going to mainland China. Johnson told Maurer that he wished neither war with China nor to change its form of government. He hoped to see Communist China join the society of nations. He believed the two countries should discuss the nonproliferation treaty and work out ground rules for avoiding nuclear war. He made it clear to Maurer that he was at liberty to express his view to other governments." But as W. W. Rostow adds, "The message was undoubtedly recorded in Peking, which had then not wholly emerged from the convulsion of the Cultural Revolution. It was a useful message to transmit; but there was not yet a political foundation for acting on it in Peking."[78]

And mindful of its treaty commitments, the United States continued to require that rapprochement with Peking not be at the real expense of Taipei. In a speech delivered on May 22, 1968 Under Secretary of State Nicholas Katzenbach "stressed that the United States government could not accept the demands of Communist China that it be admitted into the various international organizations and that the Republic of China be expelled."[79] The same point was made by Permanent Representative to the United Nations George Ball during a visit to Taipei in July 1968: the legal position of the ROC at the UN would be supported.[80]

The Johnson administration sought consistently "to project to the [PRC] the larger vision of an Asia in stable peace, concentrating its resources and talents on the great unfulfilled tasks of welfare and the building of a modern life for the people." And as early as January 1968 it was detecting signs that the fever of the Cultural Revolution was passing, and the Chinese foreign ministry was being recaptured by professionals. They understood that with a few more changes on the Chinese side, a breakthrough would be possible.[81] But it was to come too late for the Johnson administration. Through the first half of 1968 PRC signals were disappointing. Indeed, in May 1968 the PRC unilaterally suspended the Sino-American ambassadorial talks in Warsaw, saying "there was nothing to talk about" with U.S. representatives.[82]

What changed Peking's approach was a series of actions by the Soviet Union. Most important were the Warsaw Pact invasion of Czechoslovakia on August 20, 1968, and the outbreak of full-scale fighting at places along the Sino-Soviet border in the following year. Even so there was plenty of resistance in Peking to the logic of strategic alignment with the United States. Thus the initial reaction to the Czech invasion was to stick to revolutionary rhetoric and condemn alleged Soviet collusion with the United States: it was argued that American failure to protest the Czech invasion more vigorously reflected gratitude for Soviet efforts to help the United States reach a negotiated settlement at the Paris talks on Vietnam.[83] Only the fighting with the USSR finally jolted the PRC into considering how to deal with what was clearly a real Soviet threat.[84]

Facing a new situation within the Communist bloc, the PRC decided it had no choice but to take some steps toward an opening with the United States, in spite of Washington's positions on Taiwan and Southeast Asia. Most important was a call for renewal of the Warsaw talks after the Nixon administration took office.[85] The Nixon administration clearly signaled U.S. desire to improve relations with China. In 1967, Nixon had published an article, "Asia after Vietnam" in *Foreign Affairs* which indicated the sorts of policies he might pursue, and he was true to his word. In it he wrote that "Any American policy must come urgently to grips with the reality of China" although stipulating that this did not mean "rushing to grant recognition to Peiping, to admit it to the United Nations and to ply it with offers of trade."[86] On July 21, 1969 the Department of State issued new regulations permitting tourists abroad to purchase limited quantities of PRC produced goods, and allowed automatic validation of passports for travel to the PRC of various Americans, including members of Congress, journalists, and scholars.[87] A complete lifting of travel restrictions would follow less than two years later.[88] On September 18, 1969 Nixon called, before the U.N. General Assembly, for "the various communist powers" to come together on a number of issues, stressing that while the United States would not abandon its ties with the ROC, these would not be allowed to stand in the way of rapprochement with Peking.[89]

In September 1969 China issued an article on relations with the United States that could be read as marking a shift. In December 1969 China agreed to resume the ambassadorial talks in Warsaw, alternately at the U.S. and Chinese embassies in that city.[90] But the policy was not without internal opposition in China, which took the form of attacks on Liu Shaoqi.[91] Certainly the PRC did not rush to respond: the State Department validated more than a thousand American passports for travel to the PRC in 1970, but only three Americans received PRC visas. No Chinese even applied for entry to the United States.[92] It was these initiatives that reached fruition, three years later, in the Nixon visit.

American initiatives continued, however. In October 1969 Assistant Secretary of State Marshall Green made a statement to Subcommittee on Asian and Pacific Affairs of the House of Representatives carefully spelling out the difference between U.S. defense commitments to Taiwan under treaty, and the discretion to defend the offshore islands, given under the Formosa Resolution.[93] Nixon clearly signaled his willingness to change China policy in February 1971, when he used the term "People's Republic of China" for the first time.[94] Trade and travel restrictions were lessened. Relations with the ROC were cooled perceptibly. Foreign aid had ceased, because rapid economic growth had made it unnecessary, in 1965. Now the Seventh Fleet's patrols in the Taiwan Strait were ended. ROC commando raids were still taking a toll on the PRC—one in August 1969 had sunk three PRC gunboats at the mouth of the Min river (Fuzhou)—but pressure was now successfully brought on Taipei to end them, and a congressional proposal to supply phantom jets and three submarines to the ROC was vetoed.[95] In April 1971 a press officer at the State Department touched on the status of Taiwan under international law, which, to the great distress of both PRC and ROC, he stated was "an unsettled question subject to future international resolution."[96] This gave the United States great potential flexibility. An international resolution could mean an independent and sovereign Republic of China limited to Taiwan, a sovereign Taiwanese state, or recognition of PRC sovereignty over the territory, perhaps hedged with guarantees of the status quo for some time. In July 1971 Nixon's National Security Adviser, Henry Kissinger, made a secret trip to Peking to prepare the way for Nixon's visit, which came in February of the following year.

That visit has been thoroughly described elsewhere—the handshake, the trip to the Great Wall, the audience with Chairman Mao, the communiqués.[97] For the world's public, the breathless journalists accompanying the President, and even many members of the Nixon administration, it was thought of as a dramatic breakthrough made possible by a reversal of longstanding American policy.

Why the Breakthrough?

Our survey of the diplomacy of the 1960s should have made clear the error of such an assessment. Nixon's China policy differed scarcely if at all from those of his predecessors since Eisenhower, and one can imagine him, or any of the presidents who followed, making a comparable breakthrough, if only the global situation had been different. Nixon, it is important to remember, made no substantial modification in American policy toward the ROC: full diplomatic recognition, an American embassy, and a security treaty—all were in place after the Nixon visit and remained so, even as the American-PRC relationship developed, until 1979, when Jimmy Carter, seized with the diplomatic prospect of a PRC counterweight to the USSR and thus unwilling to wait any longer, dispensed with all of them as the price for full diplomatic relations with the PRC.

Even at the time of the Nixon visit the United States was at pains to assert its commitment to the security of the ROC. Thus a State Department spokesman stated in February 1972 that "The American position is that eventually the Red Chinese and the Nationalists must settle their own dispute. If and when such a settlement is made, there would be little reason for a U.S.- Taiwan security treaty. Until then it is needed."[98]

Furthermore, even Carter's action was not as dramatic as it seemed, for the reality of two Chinese regimes continued thereafter, with the United States continuing full dealings with the ROC (whose official title now became as thoroughly forbidden as that of the PRC once had been) through a sham "private" organization, the American Institute in Taiwan, created by Congress to serve as a de facto embassy.

The United States could have recognized the People's Republic of China early, as Britain did, and much retrospective diplomatic scenario-making has been devoted to what might have happened if we had. Clearly, some events would have turned out differently. But our consideration of the 1960s suggests that perhaps not as much as some have imagined.

The reason is that active international diplomacy required a commitment from China. There were always some in the Chinese government who favored it, Zhou Enlai being the most obvious example. But these men did not have unchallenged authority, and when others were calling the shots diplomatically, no amount of attempted rapprochement with China could get very far. The telling examples here are Britain and France. The first had recognized Peking from the start, and if China had wished, could have performed invaluable service in the 1950s as a channel for dealings with the United States, but it was never called upon. The second, France, was equally well situated in the 1960s, yet it too was not called upon. And there were direct U.S.-Chinese channels, most important in Warsaw, but through other routes as well. Given the number of possibilities, we must conclude that the reason American-Chinese relations seemed to develop so little in the 1960s were deeper than simply lack of contact. It was not etiquette, but refractory matters of national interest calculations, that kept the two countries apart.

It is tempting to see a sort of lost chance in China in the early 1960s. The Second Formosa Straits crisis of 1958, with its air and sea battles, artillery bombardments, and nuclear threats, might be thought to have foreclosed any future dealings with China, but in fact it did precisely the opposite. The trip to the nuclear brink during that crisis was the undoing of the Sino-Soviet alliance. Its dissolution was an objective precondition to any sort of U.S.-Chinese cooperation, and as Sino-Soviet relations slipped into passive, and then active, hostility, that precondition was reinforced. Yet as we have seen, it was only with the Warsaw Pact invasion of Czechoslovakia in 1968 that the Chinese finally began to court the United States, and then only half-heartedly.

Why? Because objective external circumstances had only limited weight in Chinese policy calculations. More important, for most of the 1960s, were the imperatives of ideological rivalry with the USSR, and the internal requirements of the power struggle within China, specifically of Mao Zedong's attempt to regain supreme control over state and party. No insurmountable obstacles blocked American-PRC rapprochement in the period 1958–1965, but by the same token, no strong incentives existed either. Only a very powerful new international challenge would move the configuration of Sino-American relations, which in the 1960s were anomalous, but scarcely intolerable. That move came when the growing power and belligerency of the Soviet Union caused China to look to the United States, and the stalemate in Vietnam created a powerful constituency in the United States for an approach to China.

Sino-American reconciliation, up to a point, came with the Nixon visit. But it is important to note that the solution was by no means clear and clean. The same problems that had bedeviled the relationship until the 1970s were still possible, at least potentially. In the 1950s and 1960s, Asian countries had feared China as a regional power: Korea, Vietnam, Indonesia, Malaysia, Singapore, the ROC, and others, all had very specific reasons to feel uncomfortable with a large and militarily strong PRC. The Sino-Soviet dispute, which gained heat during the 1960s, helped to solve this problem, by concentrating the PRC's security focus on her northern frontier, and providing a framework and a rationalization for her to work with the United States. In post-Communist Asia, however, a PRC untrammeled by a Soviet threat is becoming assertive once again, and the shadows of the security configuration of the 1950s are reappearing.

NOTES

The author is most grateful for research assistance to Erica Brindley, Princeton '93, and Alice K. Juda, reference librarian, U.S. Naval War College.

1. Theodore C. Sorenson, *Kennedy* (London, 1965), pp. 665–666, cited in Roderick MacFarquhar, ed. *Sino-American Relations, 1949–71* (New York, 1972), p. 182.

2. Kenneth T. Young, *Diplomacy and Power in Washington-Peking Dealings: 1953–1967* (Chicago, 1967), p. 27.

3. On the Warsaw talks, see Kenneth T. Young, *Negotiating with the Chinese Communists: The United States Experience, 1953–1967* (New York, 1968).

4. See for example Warren I. Cohen, *America's Response to China: An Interpretative History of Sino-American Relations*. Second edition (New York, 1980), pp. 230–238.

5. Young, *Diplomacy and Power*, p. 26. See also Beverley Hooper, *China Stands Up: Ending the Western Presence, 1948–1950* (Sydney, 1986).

6. *The China White Paper August 1949*. Reissued with the Original Letter of Transmittal to President Truman from Secretary of State Dean Acheson with a New Introduction by Lyman P. Van Slyke (Stanford: Stanford University Press, 1967) 2 vols. I:xvi.

7. See David Allan Mayers, *Cracking the Monolith: U.S. Policy Against the Sino-Soviet Alliance, 1949–1955* (Baton Rouge, 1986)

8. Gordon H. Chang, *Friends and Enemies: The United States, China, and the Soviet Union, 1948–1972* (Stanford, 1990), p. 3.

9. Edward E. Rice, *Mao's Way* (Berkeley, 1972), p. 155. See also Chang, 182–194; Thomas E. Stolper, *China, Taiwan, and the Offshore Islands, Together with an Implication for Outer Mongolia and Sino-Soviet relations* (Armonk, N.Y., 1985), pp. 117–131.

10. Kwan Ha Yim, ed. *China & the U.S. 1955–63* (New York, 1973), pp. 143–45.

11. Rice, p. 155.

12. *New York Times*, January 20, 1955, p. 12.

13. George McT. Kahin, *Intervention: How America Became Involved in Vietnam* (Garden City, N.Y.: Anchor Books, 1987), p. 68. See note 5: Dulles expressed such views to Hugh S. Cumming at least as early as 1953.

14. Colin Mackerras with the assistance of Robert Chan, *Modern China: a Chronology from 1842 to the Present* (San Francisco, 1982), p. 464.

15. Young, *Diplomacy and Power*, p. 19.

16. Conlon Associates, Ltd. *United States Foreign Policy: Asia*. Prepared at the request of the Committee on Foreign Relations, United States Senate (Washington, U.S. Government Printing Office, 1959). See Liu, *History of Sino-American Diplomatic Relations*, pp. 383–384.

17. Rockefeller Brothers Fund, *Prospect for America: the Rockefeller Panel reports*. . . (Garden City, N.Y., 1961); Chang, 219.

18. Adlai E. Stevenson, "Putting First Things First: A Democratic View" *For-*

eign Affairs 38, no. 2 (January 1960): 191–208. 19. Chester Bowles, "The 'China Problem' Reconsidered," *Foreign Affairs* 38 (April 1960): 476–486; see Chang, *Friends and Enemies*, pp. 218–219.

20. *Peking Review.* "A Brief Account of the US 'Two-Chinas' Plot," August 25, 1961 (Extract)" in MacFarquhar, *Sino-American Relations*, pp. 189–191.

21. Chang, *Friends and Enemies*, pp. 220–222.

22. Da Jen Liu, *A History of Sino-American Diplomatic Relations 1840–1974* (Taipei, 1978), pp. 385.

23. Young, *Diplomacy and Power*, p. 18; Liu, *History of Sino-American Diplomatic Relations*, pp. 385–386, 403.

24. Chang, *Friends and Enemies*, pp. 230–233.

25. Roger Hilsman, *To Move a Nation: The Politics of Foreign Policy in the Administration of John F. Kennedy* (Garden City, N.Y., 1967), p. 305.

26. John Kenneth Galbraith, *A Life in Our Times: Memoirs* (Boston, 1981), p. 405.

27. Hilsman, *To Move a Nation*, pp. 305–307.

28. Liu, *History of Sino-American Diplomatic Relations*, pp. 386–387, pp. 405–406; Arthur M. Schlesinger, Jr. *A Thousand Days; John F. Kennedy in the White House* (Boston, 1965), pp. 480–481; Hilsman, *To Move a Nation*, pp. 309–310.

29. For lack of intelligence, see Hilsman, *To Move a Nation*, pp. 315.

30. Chang, *Friends and Enemies*, p. 226.

31. Young, *Negotiating with the Chinese Communists*, pp. 250–52; Hilsman, *To Move a Nation*, pp. 317–319; Chang, *Friends and Enemies*, pp. 224–227; Liu, *History of Sino-American Diplomatic Relations*, pp. 402.

32. Hilsman, *To Move a Nation*, pp. 339.

33. Chang, *Friends and Enemies*, pp. 236–252.

34. *New York Times* November 15, 1963, p. 18; Hilsman, *To Move a Nation*, p. 349.

35. Hilsman, *To Move a Nation*, pp. 349; Young, *Negotiating*, pp. 255–263.

36. Hilsman, *To Move a Nation*, pp. 350–357.

37. "Assistant Secretary of State for Far Eastern Affairs Roger Hilsman's Speech on China Policy to the Commonwealth Club, San Francisco, December 13, 1963 (Extracts)" in MacFarquhar, *Sino-American Relations*, pp. 201–205.

38. MacFarquhar, *Sino-American Relations*, pp. 201–205.

39. Chang, *Friends and Enemies*, p. 188 note 28.

40. Richard Wich, *Sino-Soviet Crisis Politics: A Study of Political Change and Communication* (Cambridge, Mass: Council on East Asian Studies, Harvard University, 1980), pp. 12–13.

41. Mackerras, *Modern China*, p. 494.

42. Young, *Diplomacy and Power*, pp. 19–21.

43. Chang, *Friends and Enemies*, pp. 186, 213–217.

44. See John Wilson Lewis and Xue Litai, *China Builds the Bomb* (Stanford, 1988).

45. Chang, *Friends and Enemies*, p. 254–263; See also Allen S. Whiting, *The*

Chinese Calculus of Deterrence: India and Indochina (Ann Arbor, 1975).

46. For general treatments, see Bruce D. Larkin, *China and Africa 1949–1970: The Foreign Policy of the People's Republic of China* (Berkeley, 1971); Alaba Ogunsanwo, *China's Policy in Africa 1958–71* (Cambridge, 1974), and George T. Yu, *China's African Policy: A Study of Tanzania* (New York, 1975).

47. William Attwood, *The Reds and the Blacks: a Personal Adventure* (New York, 1967), p. 96 and passim.

48. Chang, *Friends and Enemies*, p. 261.

49. Quoted in Jean Lacouture, *De Gaulle: The Ruler, 1956–1970* Translated by Alan Sheridan (New York: Norton, 1992), p. 407.

50. *New York Times*, January 18, 1964, p. 1.

51. Liu, *History of Sino-American Diplomatic Relations*, p. 389.

52. Congressional Quarterly, Inc. *China and U.S. Far East Policy, 1945–1966* (Washington, D.C., 1967), pp. 136–137.

53. Liu, *History of Sino-American Diplomatic Relations*, p. 400.

54. Liu, *History of Sino-American Diplomatic Relations*, p. 390.

55. Liu, *History of Sino-American Diplomatic Relations*, p. 400.

56. Liu, *History of Sino-American Diplomatic Relations*, p. 391.

57. André Malraux, *Anti-Memoirs* Translated by Terence Kilmartin (New York, 1968), p. 356

58. Lacouture, *De Gaulle*, pp. 408, 586–87.

59. For a good analysis see Andrew Hall Wedeman, *The East Wind Subsides: Chinese Foreign Policy and the Origins of the Cultural Revolution* (Washington, D.C., 1988).

60. Chang, *Friends and Enemies*, p. 269.

61. See Wedeman, *East Wind Subsides*, pp. 183–208.

62. Rice, *Mao's Way*, pp. 377–379.

63. Robert G. Sutter, *China-Watch: Toward Sino-American Reconciliation*. With a foreword by Allen S. Whiting (Baltimore, 1978), p. 65.

64. Chang, *Friends and Enemies*, p. 272,

65. "Rusk's Statement Before the Subcommittee on the Far East and the Pacific of the House Committee on Foreign Affairs, March 16, 1966 (Extracts)" in MacFarquhar, *Sino-American Relations*, pp. 222–226; Liu, *History of Sino-American Diplomatic Relations*, p. 392–393.

66. Personal Statement by William P. Bundy, Lyndon Baines Johnson Library, pp. 21–24; Liu, *History of Sino-American Diplomatic Relations*, p. 395.

67. Bundy statement, p. 21.

68. *New York Times*, May 19, 1966, 11, and June 9, 1966, pp. 1, 4.

69. "Johnson's Speech to the American Alumni Council, July 12, 1966 (Extract)" in MacFarquhar, *Sino-American Relations*, pp. 229–230; *New York Times*, July 13, 1966; Liu, *History of Sino-American Diplomatic Relations*, p. 395.

70. "PRC Ambassador's Press Statement on the Sino-American Talks and the Text of His Main Statement at the 131st Meeting of the Talks, September 7, 1966 (Extracts)" in MacFarquhar, p. 231.

71. Liu, *History of Sino-American Diplomatic Relations*, p. 396.

72. Liu, *History of Sino-American Diplomatic Relations*, p. 396.

73. Young, *Negotiating*, pp. 276–298 has a summary.

74. "Chou En-lai's Four-Point Statement on China's Policy Toward the United States, April 10, 1966," in MacFarquhar, *Sino-American Relations*, pp. 226–227.

75. "PRC Ambassador's Press Statement on the Sino-American Talks and the Text of His Main Statement at the 131st Meeting of the Talks, September 7, 1966 (Extracts)" in MacFarquhar, *Sino-American Relations*, pp. 230–235.

76. Bundy statement, p. 23.

77. Liu, *History of Sino-American Diplomatic Relations*, p. 397.

78. W. W. Rostow, *The Diffusion of Power: An Essay in Recent History* (New York, 1972), p. 434.

79. Liu, *History of Sino-American Diplomatic Relations*, p. 398–399.

80. Liu, *History of Sino-American Diplomatic Relations*, p. 399.

81. Rostow, *The Diffusion of Power*, pp. 432–33.

82. Sutter, *China Watch*, p. 65.

83. Sutter, *China Watch*, p. 70.

84. Sutter, *China Watch*, p. 96–102.

85. Sutter, *China Watch*, p. 73.

86. Richard M. Nixon, "Asia After Viet Nam" *Foreign Affairs* 46 (October 1967): 111–125.

87. Liu, *History of Sino-American Diplomatic Relations*, p. 434.

88. Liu, *History of Sino-American Diplomatic Relations*, p. 435.

89. Liu, *History of Sino-American Diplomatic Relations*, p. 418.

90. Sutter, *China Watch*, p. 97–99.

91. Sutter, *China Watch*, p. 101.

92. Liu, *History of Sino-American Diplomatic Relations*, p. 435–436.

93. Liu, *History of Sino-American Diplomatic Relations*, p. 426.

94. Liu, *History of Sino-American Diplomatic Relations*, p. 419; *U.S. Foreign Policy for the 1970s: Building for Peace; a Report to the Congress by Richard Nixon, President of the United States, February 25, 1971* (Washington, D.C., 1971).

95. Liu, *History of Sino-American Diplomatic Relations*, p. 423.

96. Liu, *History of Sino-American Diplomatic Relations*, p. 429.

97. Henry Kissinger, *White House Years* (Boston, 1979), pp. 1049–1096.

98. Liu, *History of Sino-American Diplomatic Relations*, p. 432–433.

SUGGESTED READINGS

Chang, Gordon H. *Friends and Enemies: The United States, China, and the Soviet Union, 1948–1972*. Stanford, 1990.

Hilsman, Roger. *To Move a Nation: The Politics of Foreign Policy in the Administration of John F. Kennedy*. Garden City, 1967.

Lewis, John Wilson and Xue Litai. *China Builds the Bomb*. Stanford, 1988.

Rice, Edward E. *Mao's Way*. Berkeley, 1972.

Sutter, Robert G. *China-Watch: Toward Sino-American Reconciliation*. With a foreword by Allen S. Whiting. Baltimore, 1978.

Wedeman, Andrew Hall. *The East Wind Subsides: Chinese Foreign Policy and the Origins of the Cultural Revolution.* Washington, 1988.

Wich, Richard. *Sino-Soviet Crisis Politics: A Study of Political Change and Communication.* Cambridge, Mass, 1980.

Young, Kenneth T. *Negotiating with the Chinese Communists: The United States Experience, 1953–1967.* New York, 1968.

8

Altered States: The United States and Japan During the 1960s

•

MICHAEL SCHALLER

During the 1960s, Japan remained the closest and most important ally of the United States in Asia. While it continued to anchor American military strength in the Asia/Pacific region, in this period Japan also emerged as a major economic power. Although friendly relations prevailed between the two governments, large numbers of citizens in both countries began and ended the decade bitterly suspicious of the other nation's policies. Many Japanese feared that alliance with the United States would drag them into unwanted conflicts in Asia. In turn, many Americans resented what they saw as Japan's taking unfair advantage of "free" military security provided by the United States to enrich itself.

United States policy toward Japan had evolved dramatically since the surrender in Tokyo Bay on September 2, 1945. For nearly seven years American forces occupied the defeated nation and singlehandedly imposed a democratic political system. The original idea of punishing Japan and stripping its industry changed by 1948. Mounting occupation costs, the emerging Cold War and Communist revolution in China, and Washington's desire to find a regional ally led to the so-called Reverse Course. Occupation officials stressed recovery over reform and placed special emphasis on restoring Japan's economic viability. The outbreak of the Korean War in June 1950 not only heated up the Cold War, but also made Japan a critical asset in the American program of containing Communism in Asia. During the early 1950s, a flood of U.S. military orders rescued many failing Japanese companies and put the nation on the road to economic recovery.

The policies the Kennedy and Johnson administrations pursued toward Japan during the 1960s derived from the peace settlements that ended the American occupation in 1952. In exchange for American-provided security and economic assistance, Japan conceded to the United States dominance over its own foreign policy and use of military bases on its territory. Although the American-imposed postwar constitution banned all armed forces, in 1950 Washington ordered Tokyo to create a small army eventually called the "Self Defense Forces." Despite continual prodding, Japan's conservative leaders kept military spending to a minimum and barred any use of troops outside the country.

During the subsequent two decades, American policymakers viewed Japan through lenses crafted early in the Cold War. In their minds Japan's value lay chiefly in the bases it provided for U.S. forces deployed against China and the Soviet Union. American strategists also believed that Japan's large industrial infrastructure represented a prime Communist target that had to be denied America's adversaries. If China and the Soviet Union gained control over Japanese industry, the entire regional balance of power would shift in favor of the Communist bloc. In the early 1950s, as he supervised the writing of the peace settlement that ended the Occupation, diplomat and future Secretary of State John Foster Dulles questioned whether Japan could ever find a "satisfactory livelihood" without becoming dependent upon the "communist-dominated mainland of Asia." Unless the United States provided the needed economic alternative, the peace treaty would be a "failure" and Japan's loyalty uncertain. Dulles, like the generation of policymakers that succeeded him, remained convinced that the "future of the world depends largely on whether the Soviet Union will be able to get control over West Germany and Japan by means short of war."[1]

Beginning with the outbreak of the Korean War in June 1950, the United States compelled at least token Japanese rearmament and imposed a variety of barriers to Japanese trade with the Communist People's Republic of China (PRC). To compensate Tokyo for accepting these unpopular policies, the United States spent significant funds rehabilitating Japanese industry, made large military purchases in Japan, and agreed to accept a high level of imports despite protests by certain American manufacturers. In addition, from 1950 on, Presidents Truman, Eisenhower, Kennedy, and Johnson committed American power to blocking Communist expansion in Southeast Asia, a region considered important for Japan's economic well being.

Japanese business and political leaders appreciated these policies but often seemed to reverse their priority. Having lost their prewar dominion over much of Asia, they saw Western, especially American, markets as the key to the economic growth that alone could restore power and independence. Only the United States could provide the aid, technology, raw materials, and customers Japan desperately needed. Not only leftists, but also many conservatives in Japan doubted that either China or the Soviet Union posed much of a military threat. In addition, bitter memories of the Pacific War, appreciation of the "no-war" clause of the new constitution, and objection to the high cost of rearmament led successive prime ministers in Tokyo to stall American demands for increased military expenditures. In short, Japan's selective pacifism made political and economic sense for the nation.

The unequal nature of the defense agreement of the 1950s also generated wide discontent among Japanese. Even though the treaty compelled Japan to provide bases for U.S. forces to operate throughout Asia, it did not compel the United States to defend Japan. The pact had no termination date and contained no mechanism for consultation or amendment. Still, successive Japanese governments swallowed their doubts and followed Washington's lead in the Cold War, all in a calculated effort to assure economic assistance.

The United States reciprocated by providing various forms of aid during the 1950s. Perhaps the most helpful thing it did was to accept high levels of Japanese exports to assure its ally's economic stability and political support in containing Communist expansion in Asia. U.S. military operations in Korea and Vietnam were justified as struggles to protect Japan, and were conducted partly from bases in Japan and Okinawa. Securing Southeast Asia *for* Japan and securing Southeast Asia *from* facilities *in* Japan were two halves of the same walnut.

Partly because they feared that trade with the Communist bloc, especially China, would undermine Japan's loyalty to the West, Presidents Eisenhower, Kennedy, and Johnson battled with Congress to assure Japan unusually generous access to American markets.[2] Even when imports of textiles and consumer electronics injured American industry, Eisenhower, Kennedy, and Johnson resisted demands from domestic manufacturers, labor unions, and Congress to impose tighter import quotas.

As early as 1954 President Eisenhower framed the issue in talks before members of Congress and newspaper editors. It had become "absolutely mandatory to us" to ensure that Japan's industrial war making potential did not fall under Soviet control. But how were 85 million Japanese on a land area the size of California to survive? Eisenhower concluded that: "Japan cannot live, and Japan cannot remain in the free world unless something is done to allow her to make a living. Now if we will not give her any money, if we will not trade with her, if we will not allow her to trade with the Reds, if we will not try to defend in any way the Southeast Asia area where she has a partial trade opportunity, what is to happen to Japan? It is going to the Communists. None of these actions alone, he admitted, would save Japan, and "any one of them pursued to an extreme would ruin us." But, he told legislators, if we "didn't do a little of some of these things . . . we would lose Japan." Then the "U.S. would be out of the Pacific and it would become a Communist lake."[3]

When President John F. Kennedy took office in January 1961, few Americans perceived Japan as a particularly important country. Despite some lingering wartime bitterness, common views of Japan were probably shaped more by mass entertainment of the 1950s than by memories of the Pearl Harbor attack or bloody Pacific battles. The most popular American book then written on Japan, James Michener's *Sayonara* (1953—later a movie starring Marlon Brando) depicted the nation as a quaint land whose pliant women soothed occupying American soldiers. The popular series of "Godzilla" movies Japan exported in the later part of the decade entertained millions of young Americans who howled as fire breathing monsters ravaged Tokyo. Few among the audience recognized that the films ritually reenacted the air attacks inflicted upon Japanese cities by American planes a decade earlier.

Economic relations between the two nations were still in a formative stage. Americans considered Japan a relatively backward nation that filled marginal niches by exporting cheap, labor-intensive goods. These included tuna fish, toys, and women's so-called dollar blouses, named for their modest price and quality. Complaints from American manufacturers led Washington to impose some trade barriers and induced Tokyo to accept "voluntary" export quotas whereby Japan pledged not to permit high levels of textiles to enter the American market. Although the term "made in Japan" became a comic line in the 1950s, by 1959 the U.S. was already Japan's biggest customer and Japan was the second or third biggest American customer in several categories. Until about 1965 Japan ran a chronic trade deficit with the U.S. By 1969, however, Japan's growing trade surplus resulted in a huge transpacific dollar drain.[4]

The decade of the 1960s began on an especially sour diplomatic note. During the spring of 1960, tens of thousands of Japanese trade unionists, college students, intellectuals, and pacifists demonstrated in Tokyo against ratification of a treaty of "Mutual Cooperation and Security" with the United States. (This revised the security treaty written in 1951 and put into effect the next year.) Some objected to the high handed way Prime Minister Kishi Nobusuke pushed the revisions through the Diet. Others feared Japan would be drawn into conflict with China or the Soviet Union through an alliance with America. By June the protests grew so vociferous that President Eisenhower had to cancel a visit to Tokyo. Fears for his security peaked when anti-treaty activists surrounded an automobile carrying presidential Press Secretary James Hagerty, in Tokyo to survey the situation. A Marine helicopter had to swoop down and airlift him to the safety of the besieged embassy. State Department officials speculated that leftist mobs might soon control Tokyo and force cowering politicians to abandon the alliance with the United States.

Democratic politicians ridiculed the administration's handling of the crisis. Presidential candidate John F. Kennedy described the recent Soviet shoot down of the U-2 spy plane and the chaos in Japan as two of Eisenhower's biggest failures. Texas Senator Lyndon B. Johnson, rued that "Mr. Khrushchev's political ju-jitsu" in Japan seemed poised to toss American influence out of the country. Edwin O. Reischauer, Harvard professor and a leading academic expert on Japan, complained in a widely cited article that American insensitivity had led to a "broken dialogue" with Tokyo. James Reston, a senior reporter for the *New York Times*, warned that "at best, the United States has lost face; at worst it has lost Japan."

Yet, by 1964, these dramatic events had been almost completely forgotten. Within Japan, accelerated economic growth and expanded trade with America bolstered popular support for the ruling coalition of conservative businessmen and politicians which constituted the leadership of the Liberal Democratic Party (LDP). Public opinion surveys that year revealed that half of all Japanese, a post-1945 high, considered the U.S. the country they most admired, while only 4 percent indicated a dislike.

Within another five years, however, Japanese-American relations took a downward turn. By 1969, growing friction over trade, resentment at continued U.S. occupation of Okinawa, disagreement over how to deal with China, and, above all, the burgeoning war in Vietnam became focal points of conflict. By the time President Richard Nixon took office, only a fifth of Japanese described the U.S. as their favorite foreign country and some 13 percent bitterly condemned their former patron.

Even as Japan's economic growth surged during the 1960s, American views of its ally's vulnerability remained fairly constant. Within Japan, dissatisfaction with United States policies concerning Okinawa, China, and the Vietnam War increased dramatically. By the end of the decade, the military stalemate in Vietnam and America's relative economic decline forced the Nixon administration to reconsider nearly all its policies toward East and Southeast Asia.

Trade and Diplomacy

Shortly after taking office in January 1961, President John F. Kennedy told aides that among his greatest fears were the threat of nuclear war and America's growing balance of payments problem. The mounting pressure to devalue the dollar (whose value and predominant role in world trade had been set by international agreement at the end of World War II), along with the growth of Soviet and Chinese power in Asia, represented two symbols of waning American hegemony. Kennedy was the first modern president forced to adopt an economic strategy for an America in relative economic decline. No nation grew at a faster rate during the 1960s than Japan and no one's pattern of foreign trade affected the United States more dramatically.

In July 1960, soon after the revised security treaty took effect, Ikeda Hayato succeed Kishi as head of the ruling LDP in Japan and assumed the post of prime minister. Eager to repair the national consensus that had frayed so badly under Kishi, and hoping to deflect American pressure that Japan cooperate more actively against Communist movements in Asia, the Ikeda Cabinet emphasized domestic economic growth and foreign trade expansion. Bruised by the mass protests against the security treaty and worried about political challenges from organized labor and the Socialists, the LDP and its business allies resolved to raise wages and living standards. The resulting plan to double national income within ten years depended on a steady expansion of trade with Japan's biggest customer—the United States.

While Japanese leaders appreciated American protection, they placed an even higher value on the importance of a strong economic relationship with the United States. The preamble to the 1960 security treaty stressed that "mutual cooperation" referred not only to joint defense but also to the goal of encouraging "closer economic cooperation" between the two countries.

Like Ikeda, President Kennedy viewed expanded trade as an ideal method to overcome the bitter legacy of the security treaty riots. Although the United States was already running a trade deficit with Western Europe, in the early 1960s America still enjoyed a positive balance of trade with Japan. Expanded trade with Japan, Kennedy believed, would serve two purposes. Basically a supporter of the idea that tariff reductions would expand world trade and improve the economies of all capitalist nations, he favored doing away with barriers that impeded imports. At the same time, Kennedy hoped to encourage greater Japanese support for U.S. efforts to contain Chinese and Communist expansion in Southeast Asia. A program that minimized tariffs and quotas would, he hoped, achieve both these goals vis-à-vis Japan.

On June 20–21, 1961, Prime Minister Ikeda met with Kennedy and Secretary of State Dean Rusk in Washington. They agreed to convene annual meetings of a high level Joint Trade and Economic Affairs Committee composed of cabinet officials who would discuss ways to reduce trade barriers and friction. They also created three binational committees to discuss cooperation on cultural, educational, and scientific issues. The president and prime minister finessed their differences about the continued occupation of Okinawa by agreeing that both nations should increase economic aid to its inhabitants.

In spite of the American government's growing concern with Southeast Asian security, Kennedy rejected Ikeda's suggestion that the two nations cooperate in a major expansion of economic assistance to Southeast Asia. Ever since the early 1950s, in fact, Japanese leaders had proposed such schemes only to be rebuffed by Washington. American leaders proved far more willing to provide military than economic assistance to the region. In any case, the final summit communique confirmed the central importance of U.S.—Japan economic cooperation.[5]

The new joint economic committee met in Japan early in November 1961. Japanese delegates noted that they bought almost a billion dollars more goods from the U.S. each year than the U.S. purchased from Japan. This imbalance helped the American economy, which faced a large deficit in European trade. In consequence, the Japanese called on the U.S. to buy more of their products and resist calls for imposing textile quotas.

American delegates countered that Japanese calculations ignored the large sums spent by Washington to maintain military bases and personnel inside Japan. Furthermore, many American expenditures elsewhere in Asia actually went toward the purchase of Japanese goods and services. The U.S. cabinet secretaries also complained about Japanese restrictions on foreign imports and investment. If the United States were to maintain low tariffs which benefitted Japan, Tokyo ought to drop barriers on the import of foreign goods and capital.

The president interpreted this economic conference in the best possible light. At a press conference on November 9, Kennedy spoke of the emerging "American-Japanese partnership" in trade. Japan, he stressed, played a "key role in the economy of Asia and Free World economic objectives depend in a very important extent on her cooperation." He minimized the importance of the trade barriers imposed by Japan and disputed assertions that Japanese imports, especially textiles, hurt American industry.

Kennedy's views on textiles and trade found expression in the activities of George Ball, Under Secretary of State for Economic Affairs. To deflect demands by textile manufacturers, unions, and members of Congress, the president had appointed a "pro-industry" task force to consider the case for textile quotas. But Kennedy sympathized with the free trade argument and evinced great respect for Ball's opinions.

Ball ridiculed the American textile industry as technologically backward. Instead of trying to save it by imposing trade barriers on imports, Congress should allow it to whither away. Then, American capital could shift textile production to Third World countries (among which he still counted Japan) where they could take advantage of low labor rates. This would also encourage a shift in domestic investment to "capital intensive and knowledge intensive industries and services that befitted a nation with an advanced economy."[6]

Congressionally imposed quotas, favored by the industry, Ball argued, would "make a mockery of our concern for the Third World and our commitment to free trade." When industry spokesmen insisted that a large domestic textile base was "essential for national security," Ball mocked them by asking if they feared that "naked American soldiers would be easier to shoot than fully clothed enemies." In any case, studies proved that because Japan had accepted "voluntary" export restrictions, its textiles actually took a smaller share of the American market in the early 1960s than in the late 1950s.

To block the drive for quotas, Ball persuaded Kennedy to call for an international conference in Geneva in July 1961. Selected as a delegate, Ball first visited Hong Kong and Japan to discuss his ideas for nonquota restraints with industry groups. Ultimately, he devised a scheme that allowed importing nations, like the United States, to impose selective controls when specific categories of imported textiles "threatened to disrupt markets." This so-called orderly market procedure, Ball predicted, would allow the rate of imports to grow gradually without becoming too politically or economically disruptive.[7]

Despite calls in Congress to impose quotas (and one to make December 7 a holiday on which to annually condemn Japan), the president obtained his desired leeway to negotiate tariff reductions under the terms of the Trade Expansion Act of 1962. American trade negotiators reached an accord in February 1963 that actually lowered tariffs on many Japanese products, allowing more to enter this country.

Aside from their interest in free trade, Kennedy and his aides believed that Japan's strategic value in Asia outweighed any damages its exports might inflict on textiles and other "backward" sectors of the economy. At the same time, State Department studies cautioned that any trade restrictions that hampered Japanese economic growth would undermine the LDP and help the Socialist opposition, which favored a foreign policy of neutralism. From Washington's perspective, Japan still appeared weak and vulnerable, in need of trade assistance, not trade restrictions.[8]

Kennedy's actions to expand access to the American market delighted Japanese political and business leaders. During 1962 and 1963, the American government and Japan's Ministry of International Trade and Industry sponsored, with some fanfare, visits by Japanese engineers and industrialists to observe U.S. factories and advanced manufacturing processes. The sympathetic trade policy prompted Prime Minister Ikeda to extend an invitation for the president to visit Japan. In October 1963, a month before his death, Kennedy tentatively decided to travel to Tokyo early the next year.

The liberalization of American trade policy coincided with major Japanese economic initiatives. The Ikeda Cabinet committed substantial funds to modernizing the industrial base, giving special assistance to capital-intensive sectors of the economy and innovative technology. Easy credit and priority access to foreign exchange flowed to companies prepared to modernize the production of automotive products, electronics, petro-chemicals, and synthetic fibers. While aiding high technology, high value added export sectors, government planners phased out industries that depended on the export of high volumes of cheap labor goods, such as cotton blouses, which elicited howls of protest in foreign markets. This set the pattern for Japan's export strategy over the next decades.[9]

These policies helped Japan's real Gross National Product to expand at an average annual rate of 10 percent from 1960–65, double the U.S. rate. Japan's annual rate of export growth reached 17.5 percent, also more than double that of the U.S. The results for key industries were especially impressive. In 1960, Honda and Yamaha first entered the U.S. motorcycle market. Six years later, they sold 400,000 machines in America, about 85 percent of total U.S. sales. In 1964 Toyota shipped a mere 50 Corona sedans for test marketing in California. Less than a decade later the company sold a quarter of a million vehicles to Americans. The export surge radically altered the balance of Japanese-American trade. As shown in the accompanying tables, Tokyo's $452 million negative balance of 1960 became a $1 billion surplus in 1967 and a $1.5 billion surplus (on a total two-way exchange of $9 billion) by 1969 (tables 8.1 and 8.2).

TABLE 8.1
Japan's Trade with the United States
(in millions of dollars)

Year	Exports	Imports	Trade Balance
1950	181	421	-240
1955	456	774	-318
1960	1102	1554	-452
1965	2479	2366	93
1966	2969	2658	311
1967	3012	3212	-200
1968	4086	3527	559
1969	4958	4090	868
1970	5940	5560	380
1971	7495	4978	2517
1972*	8856	5848	3008

* The 1972 estimates are those of the Japanese ministry of finance, *Japan Times Weekly* 13 (February 1973): 9. American figures show a larger trade gap—projected at about $4300 million. *Japan Times Weekly* 13 (January 1973): 12, editorial. Statistical differences account for discrepencies.

Source: *Asahi Nenkan*, 1954–1973, passim.

TABLE 8.2
United States Trade with Japan
(in millions of dollars)

Year	Exports	Imports	Trade Balance
1965	2041	2401	-359
1968	2924	4044	-1120
1969	3462	4849	-1387

SOURCE: United States–Japan Trade Council, *United States and Japan: A Comparision of Trade and Economic Data*, Washington, D.C. 1969, table 6, and ibid., 1970, table 7. Statistical differences account for discrepencies.

Until the mid-1960s, the appearance of a chronic Japanese trade surplus appeared too novel to evoke much concern. In 1962 Tokyo agreed to repay $490 million of the roughly $2 billion in Occupation-era assistance. The Treasury and Defense departments pressed Tokyo to increase its purchase of U.S. military equipment and boost the level of its aid to Southeast Asia as methods of matching U.S. aid in the region, but neither tack was pushed very hard. Instead, administration spokesmen seemed pleased that Japan's growth made it still more dependent on the U.S. market, and, theoretically, more disposed to follow Washington's lead.

Improved relations during the first half of the 1960s stemmed not only from economic cooperation but also from personal diplomacy. President Kennedy's appointment of Edwin O. Reischauer as ambassador to Tokyo proved an extraordinarily deft move. A noted scholar fluent in the language and married to a Japanese woman, Reischauer had caught the eye of the educated public through a 1960 journal article that attributed the security treaty riots in part to inept American diplomacy.[10] Early in 1961, James C. Thompson, Jr., a former colleague of Reischauer's at Harvard, became an aide to Under Secretary of State Chester Bowles and suggested that the professor might be an ideal representative in Tokyo. Reischauer accepted the post Bowles offered him.

Given his lifelong interest in cultural diplomacy, the new ambassador saw a unique need and opportunity to restore what he called the "broken dialogue" between Americans and Japanese. This meant overcoming the "residues of racial prejudice, wartime hatreds and cultural unfamiliarity." Many Japanese, he knew, felt "helpless and resentful in their dependence on the United States." Washington, they feared, might drag them into a new war in Asia. By the same token, Reischauer felt that most Americans took Japan for granted as a Cold War ally.[11]

Reischauer used his forum as ambassador to tell Japan that the United States was not as aggressive or militaristic as widely depicted. Rather than endangering the region, America's military presence in Japan and the Western Pacific, he argued, helped stabilize Asia, protected Japan, and even restrained right wing Japanese who favored large-scale rearmament. Most Japanese, Reischauer concluded, saw the U.S. as "more powerful and domineering than it actually was, and Americans saw Japan as less cooperative and far less important than it was."

Nearly all Japanese considered Reischauer a vast improvement over his predecessor, Douglas MacArthur, II (nephew of the general), who had snubbed most Japanese outside the LDP leadership. The new ambassador made a point of meeting not only conservative politicians but also Socialist Diet members, labor activists, and other opposition groups. He and his wife Haru became popular figures on Japanese television. He spoke without interpreters, traveled widely, and held frequent and lively meetings with journalists.

Reischauer made the phrase "equal partnership" a hallmark of his tenure in Tokyo, working the concept into most speeches and official communications. It meant getting rid of the "occupation psychology" that persisted in Japan-U.S. relations and pressing Japanese to regard themselves as capable of playing an important role in world politics. President Kennedy adopted the phrase in his occasional references to Japan and the mass media in Tokyo soon referred to this as the "Kennedy-Reischauer offensive."

Nevertheless, the ambassador felt frustrated by what he considered the indifference of Kennedy and his inner circle to Japanese affairs. The president seemed intrigued by an aide's notion of a "New Pacific Community" in which Japan would play a major role but died before implementing the idea.[12] At the time and afterward, Reischauer voiced frustration that he could not get high officials to discuss Japan policy or even visit the country. Robert Kennedy, the Attorney General and brother of the president, proved the exception. He traveled to Japan in February 1962 en route to Indonesia. When student hecklers interrupted him at several university talks, he challenged them to impromptu debates and scored a public relations coup. Bobby Kennedy's visit, Reischauer recalled, raised his own status in Washington and won a bit more attention for the embassy.[13] Still, the lack of nearly any mention of Japan in the memoirs of those who served under Kennedy and Johnson is striking.

The sustained efforts by the ambassador and his staff to improve the American image yielded dramatic results. During 1960–61, demonstrators had besieged the embassy, while the diplomats inside denounced the protesters as Communists. Reischauer and the Japanese-speaking aides he recruited invited demonstrators into the embassy to discuss their grievances. By 1963, the Japanese media praised—while   the extreme left criticized—the success of the so-called Kennedy—Reischauer Offensive in improving the image of the United States.[14]

By 1963, Reischauer's initiatives and the steady growth of exports resulted in a dramatic improvement in Japanese-American relations. The death of President Kennedy evoked less concern in Japan, Reischauer recalled, than the uncertainty surrounding his successor. Most Japanese perceived Lyndon B. Johnson as crude and parochial, certainly a less cosmopolitan and sympathetic foreign leader than Kennedy. Johnson's growing fixation with the Vietnam War, and his indifference to most other questions in Asia including Japan, did little to improve his image.

The modest intimacy Reischauer enjoyed with the Kennedy brothers lapsed during the Johnson presidency. Secretary of State Dean Rusk had never liked Reischauer or supported his appointment to Tokyo. Kennedy's death removed the ambassador's friend in the White House. The new president also voiced suspicion of appointees considered especially close to Kennedy. Reischauer faced a personal tragedy as well when a deranged young Japanese man stabbed him in March 1964 as he left the embassy. Although the knife wounded him only slightly, a contaminated blood transfusion gave the diplomat a chronic hepatitis infection. During his long convalescence, Reischauer recalled with bitterness, neither the president nor secretary of state sent him a personal note.

Over the next two years, the ambassador found it increasingly difficult to defend American escalation of the war in Vietnam. He also objected to the refusal of the Johnson administration to reevaluate its frozen policy toward China. Frustrated by his inability to alter or defend his own government's actions, Reischauer resigned his post in July 1966. The president replaced him with U. Alexis Johnson, a career diplomat who had served on and off in Japan since the 1930s and who was by 1966 a high State Department official who vigorously supported the war in Vietnam.[15]

Less interested in "people to people" diplomacy than his predecessor, Johnson saw his main job as improving economic tensions and security (i.e. questions relating to Okinawa, China, rearmament, and Vietnam) relations. He believed that while Japan initially needed a protected market to speed recovery, its booming export market and growing trade surplus with the United States meant the time had come for Tokyo to change its economic policy. "In effect," Johnson complained, Japan was "treating [the U.S.] something like an underdeveloped country, purchasing agricultural products in return for its manufactured goods. American products that did penetrate Japanese customs found the domestic market very difficult to crack, with the Japanese shunning all foreign goods out of a deeply ingrained patriotic chauvinism."[16]

In September 1967 Foreign Minister Miki Takeo visited Washington to discuss the return of Okinawa and economic matters. U.S. military expenditures in Japan, Vietnam, and Southeast Asia resulted in at least a $1 billion per year "extra" flow of dollars into Japan, substantially worsening the U.S. trade deficit. American officials pressed him to agree to purchase several hundred million dollars more of American military equipment, to liberalize Japan's trade and investment policies, to sell more goods to Europe and less in the U.S., and to increase Japan's aid to Southeast Asia by contributing at least $200 million to a new Asian Development Bank. These initiatives, they hoped, would redress some of the growing trade imbalance.[17]

The administration made the point again in January 1968 when it sent Under Secretary of State for Political Affairs Eugene Rostow to Tokyo. That May Japan began eliminating some of the tariff barriers that blocked American exports, but this failed to stem Japan's growing trade surplus with the United States. By 1968, it topped $1 billion and within a year swelled by 50 percent.[18]

Although this economic hemorrhage angered Ambassador Johnson and prompted frequent calls for Japan to lower its formal and informal trade barriers, most officials in the embassy and in Washington focused their attention on security questions related to the widening war in Southeast Asia. Assuring Japanese government support for an unpopular war in Vietnam, rather than redressing trade problems, took first place in policy calculations. President Johnson's interest in Japan centered almost entirely on that nation's proximity to Vietnam and his determination to win expressions from Tokyo in support of the U.S. military effort there. From 1965 onward, policymakers viewed most questions concerning trade, Okinawa, and China in the light generated by the escalating conflict in Vietnam.

Okinawa

For some Japanese, the American Occupation continued long after the peace settlement of 1952. U.S. forces still occupied several small island chains that lay south of Japan, including the Bonin, Volcano, and Ryukyu islands. The island of Okinawa, at the heart of the Ryukyus, had a Japanese population of nearly one million and supported a network of U.S. military bases. Many Americans and Japanese remembered the island as the venue of one of the bloodiest battles of the Pacific War. After 1945, U.S. military planners first envisioned Okinawa as a base for controlling Japan and then, as the Cold War developed, for operations against China, the Soviet Union, or Southeast Asia.

In 1951, the Department of Defense blocked the return of Okinawa to Japan by arguing that it was vital for operations in Korea and the Pacific. The peace treaty did acknowledge Japan's "residual sovereignty" over Okinawa and the other occupied islands. By the 1960s, the military facilities on Okinawa constituted the largest American offensive base network in East Asia. They included facilities vital for communications, storage, repair, intelligence gathering, and conduct of the Vietnam War.

Most Japanese, seeing little direct threat from Communist forces in Asia, considered the extended occupation of Okinawa an unwanted reminder of defeat. While Eisenhower had rebuffed Tokyo's initial efforts to regain control of Okinawa, President Kennedy proved more sympathetic. In 1962 he reaffirmed Japan's legal claim for eventual recovery and established a commission to recommend reforms in the way the U.S. high commissioner, a military commander, ruled Okinawa. The panel suggested easing tensions with the local population by fostering economic progress and giving Japanese civilians a greater role in home rule. Kennedy supported these ideas and agreed with suggestions from Prime Minister Ikeda that Japan be permitted to extend economic assistance to the Ryukyus.

These proposals ran into resistance from both the Pentagon and General Paul Caraway, the Okinawa commander, who feared that any concessions would unravel the entire defense position in the region. The general, whom Ambassador Reischauer called a "rigid, bull-headed man," complained to Washington that the U.S. already overaccommodated Japan. Caraway declared that "the Japanese still cannot believe that the United States could have been so foolish as to set them up in business again and/or that the United States could be so timorous, really in asking that this country have a fair shake from Japan in the Western Pacific."

Effective American domination of the Pacific, Caraway argued, depended upon the ability to bring overwhelming military power to bear quickly at any point in the region. However, the 1960 security treaty required the U.S. to consult with Japan before bringing nuclear weapons onto American bases in Japan and before using those facilities to conduct military operations elsewhere in Asia, such as Vietnam. These restrictions did not apply to bases on Okinawa. Fearful that U.S. forces might soon be evicted from bases in Japan, the general complained that Ambassador Reischauer had entered a "conspiracy with the Japanese" to throw the American military out of the Ryukyus as well.[19]

The situation improved a bit when General Albert Watson replaced Caraway as high commissioner early in 1964. That April the embassy in Tokyo created a joint Japanese-American committee for economic aid to the Ryukyu islands. Clearly, though, progress required more pressure from Tokyo and more flexibility in Washington.

By the mid-1960s, both Socialists and the LDP endorsed the goal of recovering Japan's occupied territories. The Okinawans, who had been relatively complacent for a decade, showed new signs of restiveness as the beacon of Japan's prosperity shown more brightly. They hoped to share in their compatriots' economic boom and recover the large portion of the island used for bases. Although military officials disputed assertions that Okinawans resented foreign occupation, American diplomats concluded that "virtually all of them wanted ultimate reversion to Japan." Any serious civil disobedience would likely lead to violence and render the major air bases on Okinawa inoperative, not to mention placing bases in Japan proper in jeopardy.

McGeorge Bundy, who had served as Kennedy's national security adviser, stressed the importance of solving the Okinawa question in a message sent to Walt Rostow and President Johnson in May 1966. Bundy predicted that unless Japanese rule were restored soon, political pressure would build in Tokyo, turning the question from an irritant to a festering sore. The "desirable trade," Bundy asserted, would restore Japanese civil government "while insuring explicit Japanese acceptance of whatever military rights we need there. The trick here is that we need nuclear rights in Okinawa and it will be hard for the Japanese to grant them explicitly." Bundy suggested that if the president forcefully but quietly informed Tokyo of U.S. terms and showed real interest in returning Okinawa, a deal could be struck.[20]

When U. Alexis Johnson became ambassador in Tokyo, he recognized that the navy, army, marine, and air force facilities on Okinawa formed a "crucial ingredient in our Asian deterrent against Soviet, Chinese and especially North Korean aggression." Yet even a small incident on the island could play havoc with U.S.-Japan relations. In short, Washington must find a formula to restore Japanese sovereignty while retaining base rights. It required five years of arduous negotiations to achieve a solution.[21]

American military officials were uncomfortable about relinquishing any degree of control over Okinawa as long as the escalation in Vietnam continued. For example, in December 1965 Admiral U. S. Grant Sharp, commander of Pacific forces, said that "without Okinawa we couldn't continue fighting the Vietnam war." U.S. diplomats and civilian policymakers were more flexible, but hoped to tie any change in Okinawa to Japanese agreement to expand their own military power. These Americans expressed great irritation that Japanese did not worry very much about the Communist threat in Asia and were content to settle for protection under the U.S. nuclear umbrella. Far from expressing gratitude, most Japanese considered U.S. conventional bases in both Japan and Okinawa a nuisance, a humiliation, and a lightning rod that might draw them into a fight not of their own choosing. In short, the American presence proved a "source of small daily irritations and of large strategic risks."[22]

Ambassador Johnson favored returning Okinawa as a way of both assuaging Japanese sensibilities and forcing Tokyo to assume great regional responsibilities. Once Japan had to face up to protecting its outlying territory, Johnson predicted, it would force Japan to appreciate the protective role played by the U.S in the region. When Sato

Eisaku succeeded Ikeda as prime minister in November 1964, the Okinawa issue intensified. The new LDP leader followed Washington's lead on issues such as China and Vietnam, but took a more assertive line in favor of the so-called territorial question. The postwar era, and the nation's second class international status, the prime minister declared, would end only with the recovery of all Japanese territory. Sato came under additional political pressure in 1965 when, during a visit to Okinawa, islanders unpersuaded by his commitment to their cause chased the prime minister onto an American base.

The return of Okinawa, as predicted, blossomed into a major theme of Japanese politics, with all parties demanding reversion. The Socialists insisted that all American bases be removed from the Ryukyu islands. In contrast, the LDP would permit at least limited base operations provided Washington allowed Japan to assume political control over the islands.

President Johnson budged a little when he hosted Sato in Washington early in 1965. The two leaders released a communique stating that both recognized the importance of American bases in the Ryukyu and Bonin islands for the "security of the Far East." Sato expressed hope that Washington would return administrative control over the islands soon and that both nations would "promote the welfare" of the inhabitants. Acknowledging the deep concern of the Japanese, President Johnson stated that "he looked forward to the day when the security interests of the free world in the Far East will permit the realization of this desire."[23]

During 1966–67, Sato hoped that his profession of support for Johnson's policy in Vietnam would speed the return of Okinawa. In advance of the prime minister's November 1967 visit to Washington, mid-level officials explored the minimum terms acceptable to both sides. The Japanese wanted assurances that bases in Okinawa would operate more or less under provisions of the 1960 security treaty. This would require the United States to consult with Japan—in effect get permission—before introducing nuclear weapons or mounting operations from Okinawa against other countries such as Vietnam.

Even though most of President Johnson's civilian advisers favored reaching an accord over Okinawa and the Bonins, they hoped to use a settlement as a lever to move Tokyo into accepting a number of positions. For example, Defense Secretary Robert McNamara and Secretary of State Dean Rusk pressed Foreign Minister Miki to liberalize Japan's trade and investment policies and extend more aid to Southeast Asia to improve the atmosphere for a deal on Okinawa. President Johnson and members of the National Security Council hoped to link

Japan's desire for return of Okinawa and the Bonins to "our desire for Japanese cooperation in cutting our balance of payment problem . . . and the need for Japan to do more in economic aid to Southeast Asia."[24]

Johnson's advisers stuck to these points in briefing him for his November 1967 meeting with Sato. Since the prime minister cared so strongly about setting a date for the return of Okinawa, subordinates recommended that Johnson use this to achieve the "central objective" of getting Japan to "assume the larger political and economic responsibilities for Asian security we now expect and need from it." Johnson should insist upon Sato's making a public declaration of support for U.S. efforts in Vietnam, pledging to spend up to $500 million toward alleviating the American trade deficit with Japan, expanding aid to Southeast Asia, boosting Japanese defense expenditures, and "controlling pressures for Okinawa reversion" until needed security arrangements could be made.[25]

In the November 1967 meeting, Sato conveyed renewed verbal support for Vietnam policy along with a plea that the United States publicly pledge to set a target date for the quick return of Okinawa and the Bonins. The president countered that U.S. military bases there were so vital to current operation that an exact date could not be set. He did endorse the principle of a return "within a few years," which, in Japanese translations became "two or three years." The American side did not agree to restrict nuclear weapons from Okinawa bases nor did it pledge to consult Japan about force deployments. Sato, for his part, implied that bases on a Japanese-controlled Okinawa would still be available for the defense of South Korea and Taiwan.[26]

Both sides underestimated the complexity of returning even the tiny Bonin islands to Japan. Although the navy had only 65 men stationed there in 1967, Ambassador Johnson complained that the admirals resisted pulling out because they objected to "giving up anything, anywhere that might someday possibly be useful." When naval strategists asserted the Bonins might be useful if the U.S. lost access to Japan, Okinawa, Taiwan, and the Philippines, the ambassador retorted that in that case the Bonins would be irrelevant.

The status of the American flag on the memorial atop Iwo Jima presented another hurdle to negotiators. Many Americans recalled the stirring photograph of Marines unfurling the colors when they captured the island. Japanese negotiators insisted the flag must come down. A compromise, in 1968, permitted the U.S. to display a symbolic bronze flag in place of the cloth banner.

Okinawa proved more vexing. With the Vietnam War at full throttle, American officials were unwilling to terminate or even limit American base rights. The LDP would consider granting American forces base rights more generous than those in Japan proper, but could not escape the fact that Japanese political opinion demanded placing some restrictions on the Okinawan bases.

Privately, most U.S. officials were prepared to accept a ban on storing nuclear weapons on Okinawa since they could quickly be introduced following consultation with Japan. However, many expressed reluctance to accept restrictions on mounting military operations against third countries. Ambassador Johnson resigned himself to accepting both conditions since any future U.S. intervention in Asia would require enthusiastic Japanese support to succeed. Moreover, consultations would force Japan to assume more responsibility for regional security. As President Johnson's political fortunes waned during 1968, reaching a solution proved impossible. Following Richard Nixon's election and his decision to disengage from Vietnam, Okinawa's strategic value declined. In addition, the new administration did not want to raise problems that might jeopardize continuation of the U.S.-Japan Security Treaty. Under its terms, as of 1970 either party could cancel it with a year's notice.

A compromise also seemed more feasible late in 1968 after Prime Minister Sato replaced Foreign Minister Miki Takeo (who favored tight base restrictions, in part to curry favor with the electorate in his bid to become prime minister) with Aichi Kiichi. Aichi suggested to Americans that if Washington agreed to reversion by 1972, Tokyo would accept a gradual phase in of restrictions that would permit the U.S. flexibility in phasing out Vietnam War operations. When Nixon met Sato in 1969 they agreed to this timetable, with negotiations to clarify future American military rights.

The China Problem

The peace settlement Japan signed in 1951 did not lead immediately to the restoration of diplomatic and trade ties with most of its Asian neighbors. Southeast Asian nations insisted that Tokyo first pay reparations, while U.S. pressure blocked Japan from establishing normal relations with the Communist government in China. During the 1950s and 1960s, Japan gradually forged diplomatic and trade relations with most of Asia even though the region played a less important role in Japan's fortunes than it had before World War II.

Japanese reparations to Southeast Asia took the form of several billion dollars worth of grants, loans, technical advice, and investments. Since these were often tied to the purchase of Japanese goods, reparations helped assure Tokyo's future access to markets and raw materials. For example, Japan provided far more aid to resource-rich Indonesia and the Philippines than to resource poor South Vietnam and South Korea, despite the greater Communist threat to the latter countries. Although Japan's trade with Asian nations increased steadily between 1952 and 1969, its trade with the United States, Australia, and Western Europe increased even more rapidly.[27]

American treaty negotiators in 1951–52 imposed a virtual precondition that Japan sign a peace treaty with the Republic of China (Taiwan) rather than with the Communist People's Republic of China. A variety of U.S. laws, including the Battle Act, threatened economic retaliation against Japan (or any American ally) that engaged in unauthorized trade with Communist nations. The security pacts of 1951 and 1960 permitted American forces in Japan to defend not only Japanese territory but also South Korea and Taiwan from Chinese forces.

Despite American arm twisting, Tokyo gradually expanded its contacts and trade with the PRC. A sizable number of Japanese, including many in the LDP and business community, valued building bridges to China. They disparaged American views of a rock-solid Chinese-Soviet alliance and doubted that Beijing posed much of an expansionist threat. Moreover, expanded contacts with China, they believed, would give Tokyo a bit of independence from Washington and some trade options not dependent on America's tolerance. Of course, Americans fretted over just these possibilities.

During the 1950s and 1960s Tokyo forged something of a "two China policy" through its simultaneous links to both Taiwan and the PRC. The Japanese used the term "separation of politics and economics" to explain their pursuit of modest trade with China through informal channels. Meanwhile, Tokyo appeased Washington by voicing firm anticommunist sentiments even as it encouraged a series of private bilateral trade agreements with the Communist government in Beijing.

American officials never tired of warning Japan that trade with China would never amount to much. Whenever commerce did show signs of growth, these same officials cautioned that any deals with China had dangerous strings attached. During most of the 1950s and 1960s the U.S. government used various forms of pressure and prohibitions to inhibit Sino-Japanese trade. This tug of war proved a constant irritant to both sides (table 8.3).[28]

TABLE 8.3
Japan's Trade with China
(in millions of dollars)

Year	Amount
1952	16
1953	34
1954	60
1955	109
1956	151
1957	141
1958	105
1960	23
1961	48
1962	84
1963	137
1964	310
1965	470
1966	621
1967	558
1968	550
1969	625
1970	823

Source: MITI

From the beginning of his administration, President Kennedy worried about Japan's "soft" attitude toward China. Like his predecessor and his successor, Kennedy considered China the prime threat to U.S. interests in Asia and the force behind the region's insurgencies. Even when clear evidence surfaced in the 1960s that the Sino-Soviet alliance had fallen apart, American officials considered this proof that China had turned even more dangerous than the Soviet Union and certainly should not be rewarded with liberalized trade.[29]

When Kennedy first met Prime Minister Ikeda in 1961, he discussed China in terms designed to alarm the Japanese leader. At the second meeting of the U.S.—Japan Committee on Economic Affairs in December 1962 the president further ruffled the feathers of Japanese delegates by telling them that in addition to discussing bilateral economic issues they ought to cooperate in devising a plan to "contain Chinese Communist aggressiveness." That same month Under Secretary of State Averell Harriman told a Japanese newspaper that the American government would hesitate to open its market further to Japan unless Tokyo ceased its effort to improve ties with China. At a January 1963 meeting of Japanese and American security officials, U.S. delegates warned of the dangers posed by China's nuclear program (it tested an atomic bomb in November 1964) and urged Japan to extend more aid to South Vietnam and other nations resisting Communism.[30]

So long as American policymakers remained certain that they had to fight Communism in Vietnam in order to check Chinese expansion, they were determined to discourage any Japanese rapprochement with China. Nevertheless, so many elements in Japan shared the desire to expand economic and cultural contacts with Beijing that Prime Minister Ikeda had little choice but to resist American pressure. Defending Tokyo's policy of separating trade and politics, he explained that while he shared the U.S. dislike of Stalinism and opposed Communist expansion, this in no way justified isolating China or ignoring opportunities for beneficial trade and cultural exchange.

However, since Japanese officials recognized a need to mollify Washington's hard line, in 1961 Tokyo supported the American resolution in the UN that required a then unattainable two-thirds vote in the General Assembly for China to gain membership. In spite of Japan's support for the American position in the UN, in 1962 an ostensibly private Japanese delegation signed a trade agreement in Beijing expanding economic and cultural relations. In August 1963, Tokyo defied both U.S. and Taiwanese criticism by granting China $22 million in credits to build a synthetic textile plant.

By 1964 Japanese trade with the PRC passed the $300 million mark, compared with about $278 million with Taiwan. In 1965 China became Japan's fourth largest trading partner after the United States, Australia, and Canada. As China's trade with its new arch enemy, the Soviet Union, withered, Japan became China's largest trading partner. Starting in 1965, however, the Cultural Revolution severely disrupted China's economy, reducing Sino-Japanese trade, slowing the momentum to restore normal relations, and, in consequence, reducing Tokyo's friction with Washington.

During 1964 a number of factors brought China to the fore in U.S.-Japan relations. Early that year France recognized the PRC, leading many Japanese to worry that Tokyo would be left allied to Taiwan while most major nations dealt with Beijing. At the end of the year the PRC detonated its first nuclear device. Japanese once again pondered whether their alliance with the U.S. made them safer or a likely atomic target in case of a U.S.—China war. Finally, American military escalation in Vietnam raised the danger of Japan being pulled unwillingly into a regional conflict.

Still, Japan's leaders valued good relations with the U.S. over all other foreign ties. In January of 1964 Secretary of State Dean Rusk conferred with officials in Tokyo. Foreign Minister Ohira Masayoshi spoke of the "strong public support in Japan for coming to an understanding with Mainland China." Building economic and political bridges to China, he asserted, could blunt Chinese aggression. Rusk countered with references to China's aggression. The "U.S. could pull out of Southeast Asia," he declared and still survive." But "other Asian states could not." Japan should reflect on this fact instead of seeking American endorsement for its approaches to Beijing.[31]

During the summer of 1964 other American officials visited Tokyo to urge Japan to be wary of China and to give more aid to Southeast Asia. On July 11 Tokyo agreed to send $500,000 in medical aid to Saigon, agreed to trade terms which benefitted South Korea, and, on August 28, announced that it would grant permission for U.S. nuclear submarines to visit Japanese ports. Late in 1964, Sato Eisaku succeeded Ikeda as prime minister. More wary of China and more solicitous of Washington than his predecessor, Sato canceled several credit deals with China that Washington had condemned as "aid" rather than "trade," and curtailed talk of extending diplomatic recognition to the PRC. Washington nevertheless remained wary of Tokyo's aims.

In October 1964 Ambassador Reischauer launched harsh and uncharacteristic criticism of the reporting of the Vietnam War that appeared in the *Asahi Shimbun* and *Mainichi Shinbun*, two of Japan's largest circulation newspapers. Assistant Secretary of State William Bundy followed this up with a series of speeches attacking Japan's "dangerously mistaken views" of China. On December 22, *New York Times* journalist James Reston wrote a story critical of Japan for its inadequate assistance in Southeast Asia. The January 1966 issue of the influential journal *Foreign Affairs* (released in December 1965) featured an article by editor-in-chief Philip Quigg that reproached Japan for its behavior toward China, Vietnam, defense spending, and its attitude toward the United States.[32]

This chorus of criticism convinced Japanese business circles they must make a pro-American gesture or risk economic retaliation. Prodded by the LDP's major financial backers, Prime Minister Sato spoke out publicly about the threat posed by Chinese nuclear arms, canceled the visit of a Chinese trade delegation, and voiced renewed support for U.S. efforts in Southeast Asia.

China responded to Japan only indirectly. By this time the Cultural Revolution had turned on itself and, amidst massive economic and social dislocation, taken on an anti-foreign tone. This, along with the dramatic escalation of the Vietnam War beginning in February 1965, made moot any likelihood for improving diplomatic relations between

China and Japan. Perhaps in light of these impediments, Vice President Hubert Humphrey, during a January 1965 visit to Tokyo, told Japanese officials that "even if we don't like it," he knew Japan would try to increase trade with China. He added his personal observation that "Japanese trade with the mainland could be a positive factor" in reducing China's militant spirit.

LDP general secretary Miki Takeo eagerly seconded Humphrey's opinion. Nevertheless, many Japanese continued to resent Washington's inflexible China policy and its supercilious dismissal of Tokyo's efforts to reach out to the PRC. This made Washington's eventual unilateral rapprochement with China all the more galling to Japan.[33]

Ironically, the U.S., not Japan, finally took the lead in overturning the policy of isolating and containing China. In 1971–72, the military stalemate in Vietnam and mounting economic troubles impelled President Richard Nixon and National Security Adviser Henry Kissinger to resume contacts with China and abandon the effort to isolate Beijing. Japan, which had limited its China contacts at Washington's insistence, would add a new word to its language as a result of the secret American initiatives: "Nixon shocks."

The Impact of the Vietnam War

On May 23, 1961, Vice President Lyndon Johnson returned from a tour of Southeast Asia alarmed by what he saw as the growing threat posed by China and regional Communist movements to American interests. "The battle against Communism must be joined in Southeast Asia," he told President Kennedy, "with strength and determination . . . or the United States, inevitably, must surrender the Pacific and take up our defenses on our own shores." Unless mainland Southeast Asia resisted Communism, LBJ warned, the "island outposts—Philippines, Japan, Taiwan—have no security and the vast Pacific becomes a Red Sea."[34]

Apocalyptic visions of Japan's dependence on Southeast Asia stretched back more than a decade. In 1952 the Joint Chiefs of Staff had declared that Japan's reliability as an ally depended upon its "ability to retain access to her historic markets and sources of food and raw materials in Southeast Asia. Viewed in this context, United States objective with respect to Southeast Asia and United States objectives with respect to Japan would appear to be inseparably related . . . the loss of Southeast Asia to the Western World would almost inevitably force Japan into an eventual accommodation with the Communist-controlled areas in Asia."[35]

Arguments about the importance of Southeast Asia for Japan's future economic development became a virtual mantra chanted by American officials during the 1950s. For example, President Eisenhower lobbied Congress and the public to support intervention on behalf of the French in Indochina in the spring of 1954 largely on economic grounds. The president, in an April press conference, spoke of the rich mineral resources that would be sacrificed in Southeast Asia if Communist forces triumphed. Defeat in Indochina, while not vital in itself, would cause the remainder of mineral-rich Southeast Asia to "go over very quickly," like a "row of dominoes." Ultimately, this would compel Japan to gravitate "toward Communist areas in order to live." The "consequences of the loss" of Southeast Asia, Eisenhower warned, "are just incalculable to the free world." In a similar vein Secretary of State Dulles told the Cabinet that Americans had "no enthusiasm" for Japan's "cheap imitations of our own goods." Japan must instead cultivate markets in "underdeveloped areas like Southeast Asia."[36]

By the early 1960s rationales for intervening in Vietnam had proliferated. The region's immediate economic value for Japan diminished as Japanese products penetrated Western markets. Nevertheless, Japan remained the "superdomino" in American strategy, whose fall must be prevented at all cost. Thus, General Maxwell D. Taylor, Chairman of the Joint Chiefs, asserted in January 1964 that the loss of South Vietnam would influence the judgment of all non-Communist Asian nations, including Japan, "with respect to U.S. resolution and trustworthiness."[37]

Japan's involvement in the Vietnam War had several sources. The mutual security treaty of 1960 permitted the United States to use bases in Japan (in addition to those on Okinawa) as staging areas for military operations in Indochina. Japanese industry supplied at least $1 billion worth of military supplies and services annually to American forces in Indochina. Finally, American military activities in Southeast Asia resulted in several billion dollars worth of regional expenditures. Japanese exporters developed large new markets throughout the region by harvesting the dollars spent by the United States.

Honda Soichiro, whose automotive empire thrived without the financial assistance the Japanese government often provided to select industries, found a goldmine in the American war effort. During the 1960s, for example, sales of small Honda motorbikes to Saigon increased dramatically with the flow of dollars into South Vietnam. The profits from this niche market gave Honda a critical edge in expanding production facilities which soon produced larger motorcycles and cars for export to the United States.

Although the Japanese public divided on favoring an outright Communist victory in Vietnam, many felt great discomfort about their ties to the United States war effort. Many Japanese saw disturbing analogies between their own country's brutal campaign to dominate Southeast Asia during World War II and the American effort on behalf of its client regime in Vietnam. Some others considered the Vietnam War a proxy confrontation between the U.S. and China. Since most Japanese favored improving relations with Beijing, this increased their distaste for the war in Vietnam.

Antiwar sentiment proved strongest among intellectuals, the political left, and antinuclear activists who participated in the *Beheiren* movement. Large demonstrations against the war occurred regularly after 1965. As with the U.S. antiwar movement, protests peaked in the late-1960s and declined after 1970 when U.S. forces began leaving Vietnam. Many protesters recognized that Japan's disputes with Washington over trade, China policy, and Okinawa had links to the conflict in Southeast Asia. Nevertheless, the majority of Japanese voters who continued to cast their ballots for the conservative LDP did not consider the ruling party's support for the war sufficient cause to elect the antiwar Socialists.

The LDP leadership and the Japanese business community recognized their need to assure an uneasy public that Japan would avoid the moral and military costs of the war. At the same time, they recognized that alliance politics and business profits from military procurement required good relations with an American government anxious for Tokyo to endorse the war effort. As one Japanese journalist noted, "this country, like a magician, satisfied both its conscience and its purse" by protesting the war and profiting from it.[38]

Both Prime Ministers Ikeda and Sato (after November 1964) supported U.S. policy in Indochina. Following the August 1964 Gulf of Tonkin incident Japan authorized Japan-based U.S. forces to undertake noncombat actions without prior notification and, at Washington's request, sent medical teams and economic aid to Saigon. During the next seven years, despite the unpopularity of the Vietnam War among ordinary Japanese, Sato praised American policy and provided token economic assistance to South Vietnam. By adroitly balancing its rhetoric and policy, the Japanese government secured a large American market, muffled Washington's opposition to trade with China, and brought pressure on the Johnson administration to speed the reversion of Okinawa.

From 1965 on, when the U.S. escalated the air and land war in Indochina, opinion surveys showed that a majority of Japanese sympathized with the Viet Cong effort to unify Vietnam. Opposition by the press, intellectuals, and the loosely organized antiwar movement limited Sato's room to maneuver. Possibly, the conservative politicians welcomed these limits since they never tired of telling Washington that public opinion prevented them from aiding the American war effort more directly. In any event, Japan's straddle did not alienate Washington or impede the economic benefits accruing to Japanese business. As one Japanese intellectual, Royama Michio, put it: "Vietnam was a big fire, but it was a fire on the other side of the river. So Sato could ignore it, knowing that it was a secondary issue for most Japanese."[39]

When U.S. officials tried to prod Japan into offering more direct and material support for the war, their efforts often backfired. During 1965, State Department officials including Henry Cabot Lodge, William Bundy, and Walt Rostow all visited Tokyo to implore Japanese leaders to back American moves more enthusiastically. In Washington, George Ball and former Ambassador Douglas MacArthur II charged that Communist journalists had "infiltrated" Japan's major newspapers and spread disinformation about the true situation in Vietnam. Even Ambassador Reischauer, who harbored strong doubts about U.S. policies toward Vietnam and China and privately chided the State Department for its clumsy effort to shape Japanese opinion, waded into the controversy by accusing some journalists of acting as "Red mouthpieces."

When the American Air Force began unleashing B-52 strikes from bases in Okinawa, Vietnam became what Reischauer's deputy called "an all-consuming problem." By July 1966, the ambassador felt unable to continue to defend American policy to the Japanese and found President Johnson and Secretary of State Dean Rusk uninterested in his critique or advice on most aspects of policy. That month the president replaced Reischauer in Tokyo with a veteran "hawk," U. Alexis Johnson.[40]

Japan, the new ambassador asserted, "was vital to our effort in Vietnam." It provided "ports, repair and rebuild facilities, supply dumps, stopover points for aircraft, and hospitals for badly wounded soldiers." Japanese labor "did the great bulk of this for which we spent several billion dollars each year." Most Japanese politicians, he believed, "supported us strongly," despite public protests. "I felt it was my duty," Johnson explained, "to promote Japanese understanding and support of our involvement, both for its own sake and because it would encourage Japan to think more precisely about the kind of Southeast Asia it wished to see."[41]

Johnson had little interest in cultural diplomacy and instead used his post to prod the LDP to more aggressively support American actions in Vietnam. Even if Japan's constitution barred sending troops or military aid to Saigon, he urged Prime Minister Sato to expand economic aid. Although Tokyo did so, Johnson felt miffed that Japanese motivation stemmed more because they saw potential "attractive markets in that country" than from the inherent virtue of containing Communism. The ambassador arranged visits to Tokyo by Saigon embassy staff, General William Westmoreland (who commanded U.S. forces in Vietnam) and other "knowledgeable Americans."[42]

By early 1968 the ambassador believed most Japanese (or at least those who made policy) were "fairly relieved that the United States was willing to take on the dirty work of fighting Communism in Southeast Asia." But then the Tet Offensive and President Johnson's decision to not seek reelection undermined this achievement. The president's March 31 decision to reduce bombing in Vietnam, seek peace talks, and not stand for reelection, the ambassador believed, sent shockwaves through Japan. The LDP leadership concluded (correctly, it turned out) that these initiatives marked a major reversal of U.S. policy and a decision to abandon containment in Southeast Asia.

Both LDP and opposition politicians recognized that deescalation in Vietnam implied the beginning of a change in the U.S. attitude toward China. Even though détente with the PRC did not occur until President Richard Nixon's actions four years later, from 1968 on Tokyo suspected that Washington might reach a secret accommodation with Beijing leaving Japan out on a limb. Despite Ambassador Johnson's assurances that the American government would never "take such a radical step without including our most important Asian ally," this is precisely what happened in 1971.[43]

Although none of its forces fought in Indochina, the Japanese government played the role of silent partner to the U.S. war effort. As noted earlier, combat operations depended upon the bases, logistic, repair, and storage facilities in Japan. Bases on Okinawa, from which B-52 strikes could be launched, were especially vital.

Japanese industry provided a wide range of lethal and nonlethal supplies to American forces (chemicals, ships, uniforms, communications equipment) earning several billion dollars in the process. These special sales were particularly important since the profits generated went toward modernizing plants and developing new technology.[44]

American military procurement in Taiwan, South Korea, and throughout Southeast Asia pumped additional billions of dollars into the region. These nations, in turn, spent much of this money buying Japanese consumer goods. During this period Japanese business earned about $1 billion per year more in Southeast Asia than would have been the case without American military expenditures in the region. Japanese firms used their earnings to invest heavily in procuring new sources for raw materials. By the late 1960s Japan replaced the United States as the leading economic power in Southeast Asia, making Tokyo, in the words of one historian, "the chief beneficiary of the eight year war to save the Saigon regime."

As war production within the U.S. impinged upon the production of consumer goods, such as electronics, Japanese products filled the gap. Between 1965 and 1972, Japanese sales to the U.S. grew at an average annual rate of 21 percent, with much of this attributed to opportunities provided by the war. Imported consumer electronics and automobiles captured a growing share of the American market. As noted earlier, after 1965 the balance of trade shifted in Japan's favor with a vengeance.[45]

Prime Minister Sato adroitly balanced Washington's demands that Japan do more to support the Vietnam War effort against popular pressure that Tokyo distance itself from the American crusade. As with the conduct of China policy, Japan's leaders managed to separate politics from economics and, in the process, recovered Okinawa, vastly expanded sales to America, and reasserted economic dominance in Southeast Asia.

Conclusion

The American crusade in Vietnam, which reached its high point during the 1960s, provided the catalyst for the transformation of U.S.-Japan relations. Washington's fixation with containing China and drawing a line in Southeast Asia—inspired partly by concern over Japan's economic and military security—ultimately weakened the U.S. economy and its hegemony in the Asia/Pacific region. Simultaneously, American military expenditures provided a major boost to the Japanese economy through direct procurement and the flood of dollars circulating in Southeast Asia. Kennedy and Johnson's determination to secure Tokyo's nominal support for the Vietnam War obscured their understanding of Japan's economic transformation and the implications it held for the United States. By the time the Nixon administration recognized the folly of Vietnam and began to disengage, Japan's export drive was poised to sweep across the Pacific.

Along with the changing economic balance, Washington's détente with China that began in 1971 all but ended the Cold War in Asia. Thereafter, both Japanese and American leaders looked toward China as a trading partner and a barrier to Soviet expansion. Although the 1960 Security Treaty remained in force, it had largely lost its meaning. No longer America's client, Japan had emerged as an economic giant and potential rival of its former patron.

NOTES

1. "The Japanese Peace Treaty Problem," Minutes of the Council of Foreign Relations Meeting, October 23, 1950, John Foster Dulles Papers, Princeton University.

2. American economic policy toward Japan during the Occupation and the 1950s is discussed in Michael Schaller, *The American Occupation of Japan: The Origins of the Cold War in Asia* (New York, 1985), and William Borden, *The Pacific Alliance: United States Foreign Economic Policy and Japanese Trade Recovery, 1947–55* (Madison, WI, 1984); A concise discussion of the contradictions in the Eisenhower administration's China trade policy is found in Qing Simei, "The Eisenhower administration and Changes in Western Embargo Policy Against China," in Warren Cohen and Akira Iriye, eds., *The Great Powers in East Asia, 1953–60* (New York, 1990), pp. 121–42.

3. Remarks by Dwight D. Eisenhower before National Editorial Association, June 22, 1954, *FRUS* (1952–54) 14, pt.2: 1663; "Supplementary Notes" on Legislative Leadership Meeting, June 21, 1954, ibid, 1662.

4. Overall accounts of the 1960s period are found in the list of suggested readings at the end of this chapter.

5. U.S. Department of State, *Department of State Bulletin* 45, No. 1150 (July 10, 1961): 57–58.

6. George W. Ball, *The Past Has Another Pattern* (New York, 1982), pp. 188–92.

7. Ibid.

8. Maga, *JFK and the New Pacific Community*, p. 94.

9. For the most balanced analysis of Japanese economic planning and export success, see, Chalmers Johnson, *MITI and the Japanese Miracle: The Growth of Industrial Policy, 1925–1975* (Stanford, Ca., 1982).

10. Edwin O. Reischauer, "The Broken Dialogue with Japan," *Foreign Affairs*, 1960.

11. Edwin O. Reischauer, *My Life Between Japan and America* (New York, 1986), pp. 164–65.

12. For a discussion of this idea, see, Maga, *John F. Kennedy and the New Pacific Community*.

13. Reischauer, *My Life*, pp. 164–65, 197.

14. Ibid., 241, 256.

15. A general account of the Johnson administration's Japan policy can be found in the Department of State's "Administrative History, Vol. 1, Ch. 7, Japan," Lyndon B. Johnson Library; See also Department of State Policy on the Future of Japan, June 26, 1964, ibid.

16. U. Alexis Johnson, *The Right Hand of Power* (Englewood Cliffs, New Jersey, 1984), p. 444.

17. Henry Fowler for Johnson, August 31, 1967, Confidential File CO 141, Japan, box 10, Johnson Library; Robert McNamara for Johnson, August 30, 1967, ibid; Dean Rusk for Johnson, September 4, 1967, ibid; Memorandum of NSC Meeting of August 30, 1967, August 31, 1967, National Security Council File, NSC Meetings File, box 2, ibid; Memorandum of November 9, 1967,NSC Country File, Japan, memos, box 252, ibid.

18. Johnson, *Right Hand of Power*, pp. 487–88.

19. John Welfield, *An Empire in Eclipse: Japan in the Postwar American Alliance System* (London and Atlantic Highlands, N.J., 1988), p. 223; Reischauer, *My Life*, pp. 204–5.

20. McGeorge Bundy for Johnson, May 23, 1966, National Security File/Subject File, box 51, Johnson Library.

21. Johnson, *Right Hand of Power*, p. 448; Reischauer, *My Life*, p. 205.

22. Johnson, *Right Hand of Power*, pp. 451–52.

23. Joint Communique, *U.S. Department of State Bulletin* 52, No. 1336 (Feb. 1, 1965): 135.

24. Memorandum of NSC Meeting of August 30, 1967, August 31, 1967, National Security File, NSC Meetings File, box 2, LBJ Library.

25. Rusk for Johnson, November 10, 1967, NSC Country File, box 253, LBJ Library; "Talking Points" for Sato visit, no date, ibid.

26. Ibid., 482. Extensive briefing materials on Sato's 1965 and 1967 meetings with Johnson are located in National Security File, Country File, Japan, box 253, Johnson Library.

27. On Japanese relations with Southeast Asia during the 1950s and 1960s, see, Langdon, *Japan's Foreign Policy* and Welfield, *Empire in Eclipse*.

28. President Eisenhower, in both private councils and public forums, suggested that a modest amount of trade between Japan and China would help Tokyo's economy, reduce Japan's need to export to the United States, and soften up China's anticapitalist stance. However, despite some superficial relaxation in the U.S.-sponsored trade embargo on China, Washington totally banned Sino-American trade and limited the freedom of its allies to trade with China. Presidents Kennedy and Johnson were less flexible than Eisenhower on this issue.

29. For a discussion of U.S. China policy in this period, and Kennedy's perception of the China threat, see, Gordon H. Chang, *Friends and Enemies: China, the United States and the Soviet Union, 1948–1972* (Stanford, CA, 1990).

30. Welfield, *Empire in Eclipse*, p. 180; Reischauer, *My Life*, pp. 244—45.

31. Memoranda of Conversations between Rusk and Ohira, January 28, 1964, Country File, Japan, Vol. 1, Memos, box 250, National Security File, Johnson Library.

32. Welfield, *Empire in Eclipse*, pp. 186–94.

33. Ibid., 194–95; Memorandum of Conversation, January 13, 1965, NSC Country File, Japan, vol. 2, box 250, Johnson Library.

34. Johnson to Kennedy, memorandum on "Mission to Southeast Asia, India and Pakistan," May 23 1961, *The Pentagon Papers (New York Times Edition* (New York, 1971), pp. 127–30.

35. JCS to Secretary of Defense, July 28, 1952, *FRUS* (1952–1954) 14, pt 2: 1289–90.

36. *Dwight D. Eisenhower, Public Papers, 1954* (Washington, D.C., 1955), pp. 382–84; Dulles's remarks to the Cabinet on August 6, 1954 appear in two versions. See, *FRUS* (1952–54), 14 pt. 2: 1693–95, and Diary of James Hagerty, August 6, 1954, Hagerty Papers, box 1, Eisenhower Library.

37. General Maxwell D. Taylor to Robert McNamara, January 22, 1964, *Pentagon Papers (New York Times Edition)*, pp. 274–77.

38. Thomas Havens, *Fire Across the Sea: The Vietnam War and Japan, 1965–1975* (Princeton, N.J., 1987), pp. 6, 17; Welfield, *Empire In Eclipse*, p. 210.

39. Havens, *Fire Across the Sea*, pp. 51–52.

40. Reischauer, *My Life Between Japan and America*, pp. 285–90; Havens, *Fire Across the Sea*, pp. 41–42, 78–79; John K. Emmerson, *The Japanese Thread: A Life in the U.S. Foreign Service* (New York, 1978), p. 384.

41. Johnson, *Right Hand of Power*, p. 453.

42. Ibid., 498.

43. Ibid., 501.

44. See Treasury Department memorandum on "Economic Benefits to Japan Traceable to the Vietnam Conflict," November 9, 1967, NSC Country File, Japan, Japan Memo, Vol. 7, box 252 Johnson Library.

45. For a detailed discussion of the economic ramifications of the war, see Havens, *Fire Across the Sea*, pp. 88–96.

SUGGESTED READINGS

Barnet, Richard. J. *The Alliance: America, Europe, Japan, Makers of the Postwar World*. New York, 1983.

Buckley, Roger. *U.S.—Japan Alliance Diplomacy, 1945–1990*. New York, 1992.

Cohen, Warren, and Akira Iriye, eds. *The U.S. and Japan in the Postwar World*. Lexington, KY, 1989.

Havens, Thomas. *Fire Across the Sea: The Vietnam War and Japan*. Princeton, N.J., 1987.

Johnson, Sheila K. *The Japanese Through American Eyes*. Stanford, CA, 1988.

Johnson, U. Alexis with Jef Olivarius. *The Right Hand of Power*. Englewood Cliffs, N. J., 1984.

Langdon, F. C. *Japan's Foreign Policy*. Vancouver, 1973.

Maga, Timothy P. *John F. Kennedy and the New Pacific Community*. London, 1999.

Packard, George. *Protest in Tokyo: The Security Treaty Crisis of 1960*. Princeton, N.J., 1966.

Reischauer, Edwin O. *My Life Between Japan and America*. New York, 1986.

Welfield, John. *An Empire In Eclipse: Japan in the Postwar American Alliance System*. London, 1988.

9

A Fool's Errand:
America and the Middle East, 1961–1969

•

DOUGLAS LITTLE

The Sixties were a pivotal period in America's emerging relationship with the Middle East. The preceding decade and a half had been marked by unprecedented regional turmoil that defied the best efforts of the Truman and Eisenhower administrations to restore order. The discovery of rich new oil fields in Saudi Arabia and neighboring states had highlighted the growing economic importance of the Persian Gulf as early as 1945. The creation of Israel, the gradual erosion of British and French influence, and the rising tide of Arab nationalism soon generated chronic political instability that flared into military crisis at Suez in November 1956. And America's deepening commitment to containing Russia along the "northern tier" that stretched from Turkey through Iran to Pakistan helped make the Middle East a central arena of the Cold War by the late 1950s.

John F. Kennedy hoped to reshape U.S. policy in the Middle East by downplaying global considerations and focusing instead on such regional obstacles to peace as the smoldering Arab-Israeli conflict and the chronic economic underdevelopment that plagued much of the Muslim world. To nudge Egyptian President Gamal Abdel Nasser and Israeli Prime Minister David Ben Gurion toward peace, Kennedy would provide Egypt with shiploads of surplus wheat and would sell Israel surface-to-air missiles. To inoculate the region's oil-rich shiekdoms and monarchies against revolutionary change, the Kennedy administration would promote social reform and political modernization from Tripoli to Teheran. And to avoid driving the Muslim radicals into the Kremlin's orbit, Kennedy would resort to personal diplomacy predicated on even-handed treatment of both the Arab states and Israel. By late 1963, however, this bold plan for the Middle East had been derailed by bitter disputes between Arab radicals and conservatives and by a deepening conviction among the Israelis and their friends on Capitol Hill that Kennedy's rapprochement with Nasser was foolish in the extreme.

Lyndon Johnson shared these grave doubts about Kennedy's recent initiatives and took steps as early as the spring of 1964 to distance himself from Middle East policies he regarded as increasingly foolhardy. Troubled by Nasser's flirtation with the Kremlin and by his vocal support for anti-Western liberation movements from the banks of the River Jordan to the shores of the Red Sea, Johnson suspended U.S. wheat shipments to Egypt in 1965 and moved to isolate the Arab radicals. By the spring of 1967, America had clearly chosen sides in the Middle East, quietly aligning itself with both Israel and Nasser's conservative Muslim rivals. The June 1967 Six Day War and its aftermath confirmed Johnson's judgment that he had made the correct choice. The stunning Israeli military triumph over the Soviet-backed armies of Egypt and Syria suggested that Israel might well serve as a strategic asset in America's drive to hold back the tide of revolutionary nationalism that was sweeping the Third World. And the willingness of Iran and Saudi Arabia to keep their oil flowing west despite noisy calls from Arab radicals for embargoes and expropriation convinced Johnson that he had found two staunch allies to help shore up the security of the Persian Gulf as Britain prepared to liquidate its military bases there.

Although the "three pillars" approach to the Middle East that Lyndon Johnson passed along to his successor in January 1969 may have seemed wise in the short run, over the longer haul it looked more foolish than Kennedy's earlier even-handed initiative. The quasi-alliance Johnson cemented between Israel and the United States would gradually sour because neither side could agree whether Israel was to be America's partner or merely its proxy. And Johnson's efforts to isolate Nasser and the Arab radicals by beefing up Iran and Saudi Arabia would eventually backfire, polarizing the Muslim world and leaving first the Shah and then the House of Saud vulnerable to Islamic revolution and military aggression. For Johnson as for Kennedy before him, the perennial hope for an Arab-Israeli accommodation, the rigid Cold War logic of containment and counterrevolution, and the lure of Persian Gulf oil proved to be the will-o'-the-wisps that guided America on its fool's errand in the Middle East.

The Kennedy Years

As John F. Kennedy savored his triumph in one of America's closest and hardest-fought presidential elections in November 1960, the situation halfway around the world in the Middle East was quieter than at any time since World War II. In Cairo, Gamal Abdel Nasser, the Egyptian firebrand whose efforts to spread revolutionary nationalism throughout the Arab world had triggered confrontations with Israel, Great Britain, and the United States during the 1950s, was preoccupied with the challenge of governing the United Arab Republic (UAR), an unwieldy realm created in 1958 by Egypt's merger with Syria. Two hundred miles to the northeast, Prime Minister David Ben Gurion welcomed the relative calm along Israel's frontiers and devoted his attention to the upcoming trial of Adolf Eichmann, the notorious Nazi war criminal spirited out of Argentina earlier in the year by Israeli intelligence. Eleven hundred miles to the east in the Persian Gulf, the Shah of Iran, the Emir of Kuwait, and Saudi Arabia's King Saud encouraged multinational oil firms to build new pipelines, terminals, and refineries to speed the flow of Middle East crude that met three-quarters of Western Europe's petroleum needs and one-tenth of America's. Despite years of radical bluster from the Kremlin, only in Iraq, where Colonel Abdel Karim Qassim held sway with the support of local Communists, could Soviet premier Nikita Khrushchev claim a foothold in the Middle East.[1]

Eager to make the most of this propitious set of circumstances, Kennedy put together a foreign policy team well-versed in Middle Eastern affairs. Dean Rusk, the new Secretary of State, had become quite familiar with the Arab-Israeli conflict during the late 1940s, when he had assisted George Marshall in framing Palestine policy at Foggy Bottom. Phillips Talbot, Assistant Secretary of State for Near Eastern and South Asian affairs, was a university-trained orientalist who favored closer ties to the Arab world, as did John Badeau, whom Kennedy tapped as his new ambassador to Egypt. Although national security adviser McGeorge Bundy had no particular Middle Eastern expertise, National Security Council (NSC) staffer Robert Komer had monitored Arab affairs from his post at CIA headquarters during the late 1950s. White House counsel Myer Feldman, Kennedy's liaison with the American Jewish community, was well-connected with pro-Israeli groups in Washington such as the American Israel Public Affairs Committee (AIPAC), while Vice President Lyndon B. Johnson retained close ties with Israel's friends on Capitol Hill.[2]

Kennedy himself was no neophyte when it came to the Middle East. Two visits to Israel had left Congressman Kennedy with an abiding respect for Zionist pioneers like Ben Gurion, who were carving a Jewish state out of an extremely hostile political and geographic environment. Four years on the Foreign Relations Committee had left Senator Kennedy with grave doubts about the Eisenhower administration's tendency to write Nasser and other Arab nationalists off as mere Soviet stooges. And the overwhelming support candidate Kennedy received from American Jews during the extraordinarily tight 1960 election left him with renewed appreciation for the potential importance of Middle Eastern diplomacy in domestic political affairs. "Kennedy was the most knowledgeable man on the Middle East in the top echelon of his administration," Robert Komer recalled shortly after the tragedy in Dallas. "The President was his own Secretary of State in dealing with what we might loosely call Middle East affairs."[3]

Soviet gains elsewhere in the Third World had convinced the new president that there was little time to waste in the Middle East. Fidel Castro, Patrice Lumumba, and other left-wing nationalists had recently come to power in Latin America and Africa with the Kremlin's blessing, and just days before Kennedy entered the Oval Office Khrushchev had trumpeted Soviet support for wars of national liberation around the globe. Well aware that the UAR had been buying Russian arms for five years, Kennedy used personal diplomacy to signal Nasser early on that the New Frontier would embrace a "fair-minded and even-handed" approach to the Middle East.[4] Convinced that the road to regional stability ran through Cairo, Kennedy initiated a cordial correspondence with Nasser in which American economic aid for the UAR was implicitly linked to the Egyptian leader's willingness to tone down his anti-Israeli rhetoric. By mid-summer, Ambassador Badeau reported that Nasser was eager to place the Arab-Israeli confrontation "in the icebox" so that he might focus on more pressing matters closer to home like economic development and social reform. Syria's unexpected secession from the UAR in September 1961 constituted a serious blow to Nasser's prestige and prompted speculation in Cairo and other Arab capitals that the CIA had orchestrated events in Damascus. By delaying U.S. recognition of the new Syrian government and by continuing to hint that large amounts of American economic aid might soon be on the way to Egypt, however, the Kennedy administration managed to keep its rapprochement with Nasser on track during the autumn of 1961.[5]

Early in the New Year, JFK sent two high-ranking emissaries to Cairo to put the finishing touches on a three-year agreement to provide

Egypt with half a billion dollars in surplus American wheat under the auspices of Public Law 480 (PL-480), the Food for Peace Program. Chester Bowles, Kennedy's ambassador-at-large to the Third World, arrived in Cairo in mid-February 1962. Finding the Egyptians far more pragmatic and far less ideological than he had imagined, Bowles saw little danger that the UAR would gravitate into the Kremlin's orbit. Indeed, the real danger was that the United States might miss a unique opportunity to employ economic leverage to accelerate Egypt's tilt toward the West. "If Nasser can gradually be led to forsake the microphone for the bulldozer," Bowles cabled the White House at the end of his visit, "he may assume a key role in bringing the Middle East peacefully into our modern world."[6] Edward S. Mason, a Harvard specialist in international development who paid a visit to Cairo at Kennedy's request a month later, drew much the same conclusion. By fostering "effective economic cooperation with the UAR," Mason believed that the United States could prevent the spread of "political and social unrest" in the Arab world and avoid "increasing dependence on the Soviet Union which Nasser is currently loathe to see happen."[7] Kennedy accepted Bowles and Mason's recommendations and initialed the three-year PL-480 wheat deal on June 30, 1962.[8]

Closer relations between Washington and Cairo produced little joy in Israel. Unpersuaded that Nasser was seriously committed to an accommodation between Arab and Jew, Prime Minister Ben Gurion suspected that the Egyptians had placed their crusade against Israel on the back burner, not in the refrigerator. Ben Gurion shared his suspicions with Kennedy in May 1961 when the two men met at New York City's Waldorf Astoria. Kennedy replied that Israel must be more flexible in handling the plight of the 500,000 Palestinian refugees who huddled in squalid camps that dotted Jordan's strategically important West Bank.[9]

After reluctantly agreeing to cooperate with the United Nations in resolving the refugee question, Ben Gurion pressed for a quid pro quo. Claiming that the recent arrival of Soviet tanks and bombers in Cairo had created a dangerous military imbalance in the Middle East, Ben Gurion asked Kennedy to sell Israel several batteries of HAWK antiaircraft missiles. The president listened carefully, not least because he feared that in the absence of a conventional deterrent against Arab aggression, Israel might soon develop nuclear weapons. Six months earlier, during the waning days of the Eisenhower administration, the CIA had confirmed that Israel was building a large nuclear reactor at Dimona in the Negev desert capable of producing enough weapons-grade plutonium to build a small atomic bomb. Kennedy first learned of the "highly distressing" possibility of "atomic development in Israel" during a transition briefing in early December 1960.[10] Before leaving office, Eisenhower won grudging assurances that Israel would not seek nuclear weapons. But those assurances rang somewhat hollow during the spring of 1961 for Kennedy, who monitored Ben Gurion's quest for French medium-range bombers capable of carrying an atomic bomb with growing concern.[11] Although the minutes of his meeting with Ben Gurion at the Waldorf in May remain classified, Kennedy apparently insisted that the prime minister reaffirm his earlier pledge that the Dimona facility would be used only for peaceful purposes before the Pentagon began to review Israel's request for HAWK missiles.[12]

Convinced that an equitable solution to the Palestinian question would do more to ensure Israel's security than would U.S. arms, Kennedy quietly arranged for U.N. Secretary General Dag Hammarskjold to ask Joseph Johnson, head of the Carnegie Endowment for Peace, to develop a refugee resettlement plan. After shuttling among Middle Eastern nations for nearly a year, in July 1962 Johnson unveiled a scheme calling for the resettlement of up to 100,000 Palestinians inside Israel in exchange for Arab pledges to settle their differences with the Israelis peacefully. To win Israel's approval, the United States was prepared secretly to "provide financial help (plus a security guarantee)."[13] The reaction in Israel was predictable. Unwilling to accept what would amount to a "fifth column" inside the Jewish state, Ben Gurion and Foreign Minister Golda Meir insisted that bilateral U.S. military aid for Israel, not multilateral U.N. diplomatic initiatives with the Arabs, was the key to regional peace and stability.[14]

The Johnson Plan would almost certainly have been dead on arrival had not the Kennedy administration linked it to something the Israelis wanted badly—HAWK missiles. Kennedy sent Myer Feldman to Israel to inform Ben Gurion and Meir that the United States was prepared to sell them an antiaircraft system on favorable credit terms provided that the Israelis agreed to consider the refugee scheme and renewed their earlier pledge not to go nuclear. Once Israel agreed to review the Johnson Plan and to permit outside inspection of the Dimona reactor, Washington approved the HAWK sale in mid-September, just six weeks before the off-year Congressional elections.[15] Because Kennedy had taken pains to inform Nasser about the arms deal in advance, there was little anti-American invective in the Egyptian press. By the autumn of 1962, Kennedy had every reason to be pleased with the results of his Middle East initiative. Wheat for Egypt, weapons for Israel, and a liberal dose of his own legendary personal magic for both Nasser and Ben Gurion raised hopes in Washington for a comprehensive regional settlement before the end of Kennedy's first term.[16]

Before the year was out, however, Washington's even-handed policies were drawing heavy fire from Muslim conservatives who regarded the rapprochement with Cairo as shockingly naive. American relations with Iran, Saudi Arabia, and other traditional regimes in the Middle East had soured considerably after Kennedy signalled his support for political and social change. The Shah of Iran, for example, bitterly resented American calls for political liberalization after riots rocked Teheran in May 1961. Although he grudgingly agreed to trim his military spending in order to concentrate on "the task of building a strong anti-Communist society through social reform and economic development," the Shah reminded Kennedy and Rusk during an April 1962 visit to Washington that "we are not your stooges."[17] Saudi Arabia's King Saud and Libya's King Idris likewise bridled at U.S. pressure to liberalize their regimes. Preferring to use their oil revenues to reward loyal supporters or to purchase arms abroad, both monarchs were skeptical of American proposals for reform and questioned Kennedy's commitment to their security.[18]

Not surprisingly, rumors that Britain might scale back its presence East of Suez prompted the Shah and other Middle East autocrats to question whether America would be prepared to fill the ensuing vacuum. To be sure, Kennedy had stood firm in the face of Iraqi efforts to topple the Emir of Kuwait in July 1961 and supported a British show of force designed to signal continued Western support for the oil-rich regimes that rimmed the Persian Gulf.[19] But by mid-1962, many Muslim conservatives feared that America's rapprochement with Egypt and Kennedy's calls for change might spark revolutions of rising expectations from Tripoli to Teheran. Ominous events in Yemen, an archaic land at the southwest tip of the Arabian Peninsula, soon confirmed that such fears were not far-fetched. On September 26, Colonel Abdallah al-Sallal and other pro-Nasser Yemeni officers overthrew Imam Mohammad al-Badr, proclaimed a republic, and laid claim to disputed territory next door in Saudi Arabia and Britain's Aden protectorate. Bankrolled by the House of Saud and the British, al-Badr mounted a guerrilla war against the new republican regime. After Sallal requested Nasser's support in combating al-Badr's insurgents, the first contingent of what would become a 70,000-man Egyptian expeditionary force armed with tanks and planes left for Yemen in early October.[20]

Although the Saudi-Egyptian proxy war in Southwest Arabia was soon overshadowed by the Soviet-American confrontation in Cuba, Kennedy's Middle East experts worked hard to prevent the inter-Arab frictions from undermining U.S. policy in the region. Kennedy himself affirmed America's deep commitment to the territorial integrity of Saudi Arabia during Crown Prince Faisal's visit to Washington in October. But the White House also reaffirmed its rapprochement with Nasser by formally recognizing Sallal's Yemen Arab Republic (YAR) two months later.[21] Despite U.S. efforts at mediation, however, the crisis escalated in January 1963 after Egyptian MIGs struck at royalist base camps just across the Saudi frontier. Faisal, who was gradually wresting power from his older brother, King Saud, thundered that America had permitted Egypt "to take out a hunting license on Saudi Arabia" and hinted that he might revoke the huge petroleum concession held by the Arabian-American Oil Company (ARAMCO) unless Washington took a firm stand against the YAR and its friends in Cairo. Frustrated by Nasser's unwillingness to pull out of Yemen and worried by Faisal's bluster, in late February Kennedy agreed to station a squadron of F-100 jets plus several dozen green berets inside Saudi Arabia as part of Operation Hard Surface.[22]

Like the Saudis, the Israelis had always believed that Kennedy's trust in Nasser was misplaced. Egyptian intervention in Yemen deepened Ben Gurion and Meir's doubts about the Johnson Plan to resettle thousands of Arab refugees in Israel, as did Palestinian efforts to overthrow Jordan's King Hussein in January 1963. After military coups spearheaded by the Ba'ath, a pan-Arab socialist party with links to Nasser, brought radical anti-Israel regimes to power in Syria and Iraq later that winter, Israel scuttled the Johnson Plan and focused instead on building up its arsenal to combat Arab encirclement.[23] By mid-March the CIA worried that the wave of radicalism sweeping the Arab world might accelerate Israel's plans to develop a nuclear deterrent, with disastrous implications for American interests in the Middle East.[24]

Kennedy moved to prevent such an eventuality by distancing himself from Egypt, by reassuring Israel, and by seeking a regional arms limitation agreement. When pro-Nasser demonstrators nearly toppled King Hussein in April, Kennedy moved the Sixth Fleet into the Eastern Mediterranean and warned Egypt to stop meddling in Jordan. A few weeks later he reiterated America's longstanding commitment to the territorial integrity and independence of all states in the Middle East, including Israel.[25] And in June, Kennedy sent John J. McCloy, his special coordinator for disarmament, to Cairo to urge that Nasser begin disengaging from Yemen and that he curb Egypt's arms purchases from the Soviet Union.[26]

When McCloy returned empty-handed, Kennedy began to reconsider his entire even-handed approach to the Middle East. By early October, Kennedy was willing to give informal but explicit assurances to both Levi Eshkol, Ben Gurion's more moderate successor, and Crown Prince Faisal that the United States would provide military assistance in the event of an Egyptian attack on Israel or Saudi Arabia.[27] He also warned Nasser that unless UAR troops pulled out of Yemen and unless Arab radicals ceased their anti-Israel diatribes, irresistible pressure would mount on Capitol Hill to reverse Washington's rapprochement with Cairo. Kennedy's prophecy was fulfilled two weeks later when the Senate adopted Ernest Gruening's amendment to the 1963 foreign aid bill, banning Food for Peace shipments to any nation engaged in aggressive action against any country receiving U.S. economic or military assistance. Oil company lobbyists fearful that Nasser would use Yemen as a springboard for an all-out assault on Saudi Arabia had worked closely with friends of Israel to round up the votes necessary to cut off American aid for Egypt.[28] By the time Kennedy left for Dallas in November 1963, then, mounting inter-Arab friction in Yemen, growing concerns about Israel's nuclear capability, and congressional second-guessing about foreign aid had led him to shift away from his earlier even-handed Middle East policies and toward an approach based on closer relations with Israel and the Muslim conservatives. Lyndon B. Johnson would accelerate that shift.

Johnson Chooses Sides

Like most vice presidents, Lyndon Johnson had been overshadowed by the man in the White House. Although his role in shaping foreign policy during the Kennedy years was relatively limited, when he entered the Oval Office in late 1963 Johnson brought with him strong views and considerable knowledge about the Middle East. One of the most outspoken congressional supporters of the Jewish state from its inception in 1948 through 1960, Senator Johnson had been more sympathetic than his colleague from Massachusetts toward Israel in the aftermath of the 1956 Suez crisis.[29] Less tolerant of Third World nationalism than Kennedy, Vice President Johnson returned from an August 1962 visit to Iran, Lebanon, and Turkey convinced that America must do more to prevent "communist expansion to the oil of the Middle East" by reversing Soviet inroads in Egypt and elsewhere in the "chaotic Arab world."[30]

President Johnson surrounded himself with friends and advisers who shared his own more pro-Israel and anti-Soviet attitudes toward the Middle East. He selected Minnesota Senator Hubert H. Humphrey, a vocal supporter of Israel, as his running mate in 1964, named Arthur Goldberg, an ardent Zionist, as U.S. ambassador to the United Nations in 1965, and appointed the avowedly pro-Israel Rostow brothers to key posts in 1966—Walt as Bundy's successor as national security adviser and Eugene as Under Secretary of State. Johnson's "kitchen cabinet" included Supreme Court Justice Abe Fortas, a staunch friend of Israel, and other prominent members of the American Jewish community, including Democratic party fundraisers Abe Feinberg and Arthur Krim. AIPAC's Isaiah "Si" Kenen was a frequent visitor to the White House, as was Ephraim "Eppie" Evron, Israel's deputy chief of mission in Washington. Even such Kennedy holdovers as Rusk, Talbot, and Komer had begun to have second thoughts about the even-handed policies they had helped design a few years earlier.[31] Worried by growing Soviet support for wars of national liberation in the Middle East and elsewhere in the Third World, the Johnson administration would work hard to convert Israel and other pro-Western states into strategic assets.

Nasser's encouragement for the anti-Israel crusade waged by West Bank Palestinians, his calls for revolutionary change among the sheikdoms and monarchies of the Arab East, and his support for a variety of pro-Soviet liberation movements helped bring Egypt's relations with America to the breaking point during 1964. Just two months after Kennedy's death, Nasser unveiled plans to create a Palestine Liberation Organization (PLO) whose chief objective was to be the destruction of Israel.[32] Worse still, during the spring of 1964, Egypt secretly began to funnel aid to Marxist rebels who sought to sabotage Britain's plans to convert its Aden protectorate into an independent pro-Western South Arabian Federation.[33] The Kremlin's hand in all this loomed larger in May, when Soviet premier Nikita Khrushchev echoed Nasser's support for the PLO and called for the "liquidation of foreign military bases in Libya, Oman, Cyprus, [and] Aden."[34] By the end of the summer, the CIA saw Nasser "intensifying his drive to remove the remaining vestiges of colonialism in the Arab world," while the State Department worried that his support for the fledgling PLO might "provoke pre-emptive action by Israel."[35] The gloom in Washington deepened in September after Nasser vowed to drive Zionism and Western imperialism from the Middle East. To "prevent Israel from consolidating the status quo," he promised the PLO a multi-million dollar subsidy for a "Palestine Army to be trained in Sinai and [the] Gaza Strip."[36]

Pressure had been building among Israel's friends on Capitol Hill for months for Johnson to invoke the Gruening amendment and cut off all PL-480 wheat shipments to Egypt. As late as September 1964 the White House remained reluctant to cancel the UAR's Food for Peace allotment because in the past the Egyptians had responded to American economic pressure by moving closer to the Soviets. But Nasser's unwillingness to halt plans to buy guided missiles from the Kremlin and his vitriolic attacks on U.S. intervention in the Congolese civil war later that fall tested the limits of Johnson's patience. After pro-Nasser students burned the United States Information Agency offices in Cairo to the ground on November 26, Johnson summoned the Egyptian ambassador to the White House and exploded: "How can I ask Congress for wheat for you when you burn down our library?" When Egyptian MIGs downed an unarmed American cargo plane that had strayed into UAR airspace three weeks later, killing its two-man crew, Washington hinted that there would be no further U.S. aid until Cairo made amends. Outraged by what he regarded as a crude attempt at diplomatic blackmail, Nasser told a huge crowd gathered on the banks of the Suez Canal on December 23 that "those who do not accept our behavior can go and drink from the sea." Lest Johnson miss the point, Nasser added: "And if the Mediterranean is not enough to slake their thirsts, . . . they can carry on with the Red Sea."[37]

American relations with Egypt and other radical Arab states deteriorated rapidly during the following eighteen months. Nasser's refusal to implement a U.S.-backed disengagement plan in Yemen rekindled suspicions in Washington and Riyadh that he had designs on the entire Arabian Peninsula. So did his clandestine aid to radical groups like FLOSY (the Front for the Liberation of South Yemen) and PFLOAG (the Popular Front for the Liberation of the Occupied Arab Gulf), whose guerrillas launched hundreds of raids against British installations in Aden and Oman during the late 1960s.[38] Equally unsettling was Nasser's bitter denunciation of America's escalating military involvement in Vietnam and his well-publicized decision to allow the Viet Cong to open an information bureau in Cairo in April 1965. Worse still was his promise to help finance a PLO campaign of "Arab revolutionary action" against Israel later that spring.[39]

Inspired by Nasser's strident rhetoric, Yasser Arafat and other PLO radicals formed Fatah, a paramilitary group that by mid-1965 was staging hit-and-run raids inside Israel from bases on the West Bank. Eight months later a "radical military clique" including Colonel Hafez al-Assad staged a bloody coup in Syria, embraced the Palestinian cause, and established "close ties with the Communist bloc." Adopting a "vitriolic anti-Western posture," by late 1966 the new regime in Damascus was calling for the swift destruction of Israel and permitting Fatah commandoes to mount attacks on the Jewish state from sanctuaries in the Golan Heights.[40]

The rising tide of Arab radicalism merely confirmed Israel's judgment that Kennedy's earlier rapprochement with Nasser had been misguided and highlighted the necessity of consummating the special relationship between Israel and America that Lyndon Johnson was rumored to favor. "You have lost a very great friend," the new president told an Israeli diplomat shortly after Kennedy's death. "But you have found a better one."[41] The Israelis wasted little time ascertaining whether Johnson meant what he said. Pointing out that Kennedy had promised that the United States would preserve the military balance in the Middle East, Israeli Prime Minister Levi Eshkol requested American M-48 battle tanks and A-4 Skyhawk jet fighters in early 1964 to offset recent Soviet arms deliveries to Nasser.[42]

Nevertheless, many in Washington questioned whether Israel really needed such sophisticated weaponry. The Pentagon, for example, saw no numerical imbalance between the Arab and Israeli arsenals and suspected that Eshkol sought to drive a wedge between Egypt and America in order to upgrade Israel's "tactical offensive capabilities." The State Department agreed and urged Johnson not to sell Israel tanks or planes but rather to launch a new round of regional arms limitations talks instead.[43] Top U.S. officials realized, however, that "Israel is at least putting itself in a position to go nuclear" and that failure to obtain conventional arms would probably accelerate its quest for atomic weapons.[44] As a result, although Johnson told Eshkol in June 1964 that the United States could not provide tanks or planes, he promised to help Israel obtain military hardware from West Germany or France provided the Jewish state pledged "not to lend itself to escalation of the Near East arms race through acquisition of missiles or nuclear weapons."[45]

The White House worked for eight months to arrange a three- cornered arms deal calling for the United States to ship 250 new M-48s to West Germany, which in turn would transfer 250 older tanks from its own arsenal to Israel. Once news of the arrangement leaked to the press, however, West German Chancellor Ludwig Erhard backed out in early 1965, prompting Israel to renew its request to purchase tanks directly from the United States.[46] U.S. officials balked, and tensions mounted in February after Eshkol learned that America was considering arms sales to Jordan, whose military policies were influenced increasingly by King Hussein's half-million Palestinian subjects bent on the destruction of Israel. Eager to resolve the problem, Johnson sent diplomatic troubleshooter Averell Harriman and NSC Middle East expert Robert Komer to Israel in late February. Eshkol and his cabinet refused to acquiesce in U.S. arms sales to Jordan unless the Johnson administration provided comparable weapons to Israel. Worse still, the Israelis evidently hinted that they were prepared to develop a nuclear deterrent against Arab aggression.[47] Harriman and Komer returned to Washington in early March carrying a wish list that included not only 250 M-48 tanks and two squadrons of A-4 Skyhawk jet fighters but also 75 B-66 medium-range bombers that, according to the Pentagon, were "capable of carrying an Israeli developed nuclear weapon."[48]

Determined to "keep up pressure on Israel not to go nuclear," Secretary of State Dean Rusk recommended that Johnson approve the sale of M-48 tanks to Israel in April 1965. Lest the Israelis forget the major reason for this relatively more accommodating American policy on arms sales, however, Rusk reminded them on April 21 that "we continue unalterably opposed to [the] proliferation [of] nuclear weapons."[49] No sooner was the tank deal completed than Israel moved to upgrade its air force by requesting supersonic F-4 Phantom jets capable of carrying atomic bombs. Once again Washington urged the Israelis to seek aircraft in Bonn and Paris, and once again they came up empty-handed.[50] To avoid another lengthy round of haggling during an election year, Johnson approved the sale of 48 slower A-4 Skyhawks on March 23, 1966. Although the Skyhawk deal sparked protests throughout the Arab world, top U.S. officials believed this was a small price to pay for curbing the "threat of nuclear proliferation." As the State Department put it in a mid-April message to Nasser, "denial of conventional weapons to Israel when threats [are] being voiced and arms [are] being built up by [the] other side would strengthen the position of those in Israel who advocate the development of [a] nuclear option."[51]

The Johnson administration hoped to limit the fallout from its tank and plane sales to Israel by cultivating closer ties with pro-Western conservative regimes in the Muslim world. Johnson had already taken the first steps in this direction by agreeing to sell Jordan 250 M-48 tanks in the spring of 1965. The CIA, of course, had secretly been bankrolling King Hussein for nearly a decade, hoping thereby to ensure that he would continue to pursue a relatively benign policy toward Israel.[52] By February 1965, however, top U.S. officials were convinced that unless the Johnson administration provided Hussein with tanks, "Jordan would receive an uncontrolled supply of Soviet arms, the King's position would be undermined, and Jordan would very likely fall under Soviet-Nasser influence."[53] A year later LBJ authorized the sale of two squadrons of A-4 Skyhawks to Hussein, whom he now regarded as a "firm and reliable friend."[54] Further evidence of U.S. support for Jordan came after a bloody Israeli retaliatory raid against Palestinian commandoes at the West Bank village of Samu in November 1966. Eager to prevent Hussein from drifting into Nasser's camp, Johnson sent the king a secret message condemning Israel's attack on Samu and pledging to support the territorial integrity of Jordan.[55]

While some American policymakers struggled to prevent events in Jordan from transforming an Arab-Israeli cold peace into a hot war, others pondered how best to shore up the sagging Western position in the Persian Gulf. Britain's deepening financial woes forced Whitehall reluctantly to announce the abandonment of its huge naval base at Aden in February 1966 and the liquidation of the rest of its military installations east of Suez a year later.[56] Having tried unsuccessfully to persuade the British to reconsider, the Johnson administration scrambled to prevent a vacuum in a region whose strategic and economic importance was growing rapidly. By the mid-1960s, Saudi Arabia, Iran, and their smaller neighbors were exporting 3.5 billion barrels of petroleum annually, one-third of the Free World's output. Although the United States still received less than 10 percent of its oil from the Middle East, skyrocketing domestic consumption meant that American imports were bound to increase. Moreover, nearly three-quarters of Western Europe's petroleum imports continued to originate in the Persian Gulf, while Japan relied on Saudi and Iranian crude to meet almost all its energy needs. No longer able to rely on a string of British protectorates stretching from Bahrein to Aden to safeguard the flow of oil, U.S. officials sought to establish an over-the-horizon presence by acquiring a naval base at Diego Garcia in the Indian Ocean. Because there was no enthusiasm for having American GI's replace the departing British Tommies in the Persian Gulf, however, Washington gravitated toward the creation of regional proxies.[57]

Among those most eager to replace Britain as guardian of the gulf was the Shah of Iran, who hoped to use his burgeoning oil revenues to purchase American arms and recapture the glory of the ancient Persian empire. Iranian-American relations had begun to improve in the months following Kennedy's death. Gambling that Johnson would be less interested in social reform than in the security of the Persian Gulf and its oil, as early as 1964 the Shah moved to position himself as America's most likely Muslim partner. In short order, he signed an accord with the United States that granted Americans extraterritorial privileges in Iran in exchange for a $200 million military aid package. After the agreement prompted fiery protests by Islamic fundamentalists like the Ayatollah Ruhallah Khomeini and left-wing nationalists like the Mujahadeen i-Khalq, the Shah unleashed his secret police, the dreaded SAVAK, to restore order with Washington's blessing.[58]

By early 1966, the Iranian monarch made no secret that he was willing to assume Britain's mantle in the Persian Gulf and to supply Israel with all the oil it needed, provided the United States permitted Iran to purchase jet aircraft and other sophisticated weaponry. Pleased by Iran's emergence as a regional power, top U.S. officials nevertheless worried that the Shah's proposed military spending spree would divert resources away from economic development and destabilize his regime. As a result, the Johnson administration adopted what U. S. Ambassador Armin Meyer termed a "papa knows best attitude" and insisted that the Shah scale back his arms request. The Shah refused, holding out instead for another $200 million arms package including supersonic F-4 Phantoms and hinting darkly that should he come up empty-handed in Washington, he might be forced to turn to Moscow.[59] Unwilling to risk opening the door to fresh Kremlin inroads in the region, the White House changed course in August 1966 and adopted policies aimed, in the words of national security adviser Walt Rostow, at "keeping the Shah from going overboard." Before the year was out, Lyndon Johnson had approved a multi-million dollar arms deal and opened wide America's arsenal for its new found Iranian proxy.[60]

The Shah's Iran was by no means the only conservative Muslim regime eager to cooperate with the United States in stabilizing the situation in the Persian Gulf. Since the early 1960s, Saudi Arabia, the largest and most thinly populated of the Arab oil states, had been seeking sophisticated weapons and other concrete signs of American support for its territorial integrity. The Johnson administration was quick to oblige newly crowned King Faisal, who had finally wrested the Saudi throne from his ailing brother Saud in a March 1964 palace coup. Nine months later, for example, a contingent from the U.S. Army Corps of Engineers arrived in Saudi Arabia to supervise the construction of a network of roads and military installations essential for the desert kingdom's internal security.[61] When Faisal sought to upgrade his air force in April 1965, White House advisers thought it wise to "help him buy US planes" in order to "protect our billion dollar oil investment." And after Egyptian jets based in Yemen strafed targets inside Saudi Arabia later that year, Washington agreed to sell Riyadh ten batteries of HAWK surface-to-air missiles.[62]

A tacit Saudi-American alliance blossomed during 1966. Early in the new year U.S. officials encouraged King Faisal to pursue plans for an "Islamic Pact" among traditional Middle Eastern regimes determined to combat Nasser's brand of revolutionary nationalism. When Faisal visited the White House in June 1966, LBJ personally reaffirmed earlier American pledges to protect the territorial integrity of Saudi Arabia. Johnson also promised to work with Faisal "to fill the gap the British will leave in South Arabia and the Persian Gulf."[63] To be sure, the King did not receive the tanks he evidently sought in Washington, but three months later Lyndon Johnson did approve the sale of $100 million worth of nonlethal military equipment—mostly trucks and jeeps—to the House of Saud. As a result, when the war in Yemen heated up again in late 1966, the broad outlines of a Saudi-American partnership had begun to emerge, a partnership based on a common desire to contain the tide of radical Arab nationalism that with Nasser's help seemed to be sweeping out of Southwest Arabia toward the Persian Gulf.[64] Like Israel's Levi Eshkol and the Shah of Iran, King Faisal was emerging as one of America's staunchest allies in a very troubled part of the world.

The Six Day War

By the autumn of 1966, top U.S. officials had begun to worry that growing ideological polarization in the Middle East might easily ignite the smoldering Arab-Israeli conflict into full-blown military conflagration. In September, Johnson himself commissioned a special report that "revealed a pattern of serious Soviet advances" in the Arab world, particularly in Egypt, Iraq, and Syria, where pressure for a showdown with Israel was mounting rapidly.[65] As the year drew to a close, Radio Cairo was beaming fiery calls for the liberation of Palestine onto the West Bank, Iraqi pilots were learning to fly Soviet MIGs, and Syrian leaders were encouraging Yasser Arafat's Fatah to step up its raids on Israeli villages.[66]

Increasingly preoccupied with America's widening war in Vietnam, Johnson drew analogies between the Viet Cong and Fatah and between the pro-Soviet regimes in Hanoi and Damascus. "A radical new government in Syria increased terrorist raids against Israel . . . in flagrant violation of international law," Johnson recalled in his memoirs. "Every state," he added with an eye to North Vietnam, "is as responsible legally for irregular forces of armed bands attacking a neighbor as it is for attacks made by its own army."[67] American officials held out hope in early 1967 that the resumption of U.S. Food for Peace shipments to Egypt might prompt Cairo to rein in its more radical friends in Damascus. Some Israeli diplomats privately agreed that shipping Egypt modest amounts of surplus wheat was a small price to pay to "keep [American] relations with Nasser open and not leave the field to the Soviets" or their friends in Syria. According to Walt Rostow, Nasser was certain to interpret the rejection of his latest bid for American grain as a sign that "we're out to get him," and he would "make plenty of trouble" in return, from North Africa and the West Bank.[68] When State Department officials floated the possibility of a $100 million wheat package on Capitol Hill in March, however, Republicans critical of "foreign aid give-aways" joined forces with AIPAC to torpedo the proposal. Predictably, Nasser moved closer to Syria and Fatah and stepped up his attacks on American imperialism in Vietnam.[69]

Nasser's latest anti-Western outbursts merely highlighted the parallels between the conflicts in the Middle East and Southeast Asia, parallels that the Israelis had been drawing for months. In February 1967 Eshkol requested 200 M-113 armored personnel carriers to prevent PLO guerrillas from infiltrating into Israel from the Golan Heights and the West Bank. The State Department initially rejected Eshkol's latest arms request, not only because Israel seemed to be treating its relationship with Washington as "a One-Way Street" but also because of concern at Foggy Bottom that the Israelis were "not entirely leveling with us" about the Dimona reactor. While the State Department sought to link the M-113s to a "more tangible quid pro quo" regarding "nuclear proliferation," Palestinian commandoes based in Syria escalated their raids on Israel.[70] Determined to short-circuit this powerful current of revolutionary Arab nationalism before it could ignite a war for the liberation of "occupied Palestine," Israel struck back at Fatah and their friends in Damascus. After Israeli jets bombed PLO base camps just inside Syria and downed six Syrian MIG's over the Golan Heights on April 7, 1967, Nasser warned Israel not to attack Damascus.[71]

The diplomatic witch's brew simmering in the Middle East that spring finally boiled over in early May. Claiming that Israel had mobilized twelve divisions for an assault on the Golan Heights, the Kremlin advised Nasser on May 13 that he might soon have to come to the aid of Syria. The Israelis denied that they had moved troops to the Syrian frontier and dismissed Moscow's allegations as a blend of misinformation and disinformation, a verdict borne out by recent scholarship. Nasser, however, accepted the Soviet warning at face value and ordered Egyptian troops to prepare for a showdown with Israel.[72]

Seeking to prevent a full-scale war, Johnson asked Harold Saunders, who had recently succeeded Komer as the Middle East expert on the NSC staff, to undertake a fact-finding mission to the region. Although the Israelis were well aware of Johnson's "personal desire to maintain a warm relationship," they told Saunders that they must have concrete

American help in combating "Arab terrorism," which they termed "the greatest threat to their security today." When Saunders crossed the Jordan River from Israel to the West Bank, angry Palestinian refugees made no secret that they supported "the Fatah terrorist group [that] sends its saboteurs into Israel." This confirmed that "the 'war of national liberation' as a technique has come to the Middle East," not merely inside Israel and Jordan but also far to the south in Aden, where pro-Nasser guerrillas battled pro-Western sheiks backed by U.K. commandoes. Having heard Johnson insist "that he will not tolerate this brand of aggression" in Southeast Asia, his Israeli and British friends now wondered: "How can he stand against terrorist attackers in Vietnam and not in Israel or South Arabia?"[73]

Moreover, Saunders doubted that Israel would accept the Johnson administration's new nuclear nonproliferation treaty (NPT) unless America stood firm against Nasser and the Arab radicals. "Before signing an NPT," Eshkol would insist that Washington and Moscow "keep the lid on the Arab arms inventory while the conventional balance is still in Israel's favor," something few believed the Kremlin would do. "What this adds up to," Saunders observed grimly, "is great pressure on us to join in a confrontation with Nasser and prediction that US will lose its stature in the area if we refuse and fail to stop him, the USSR and the liberation armies." It would be nearly impossible, Saunders predicted in mid-May, for America to resist the temptation "to conclude with our friends that Nasser is a lost cause and throw in the sponge on trying to deal with him."[74]

Before the month was out, the United States would do just that. Responding to fresh reports from Moscow and Damascus that Israel was about to strike Syria, Nasser sent troops across the Sinai on May 17 to replace the U.N. Emergency Force that had patrolled the no-man's-land between Egypt and Israel for a decade. "Some pretty militant public threats from Israel by Eshkol and others" had persuaded top U.S. officials that "the Soviet advice to the Syrians that the Israelis were planning to attack was not far off." As a result, Johnson warned Eshkol on May 18 that Israel must "not put a match to this fuse."[75] Relieved by Israeli assurances that they did "not intend any military action," during the next forty-eight hours the White House pressed the Kremlin to use its influence among the Arabs "in the cause of moderation" and urged U.N. Secretary General U Thant to renew his efforts to secure a peaceful resolution of the Middle East crisis. As late as May 21, Johnson believed that if Israel continued "to display steady nerves," hostilities could be averted.[76] The next day, however, Nasser escalated the crisis by prohibiting Israeli vessels from using the Straits of Tiran that connected the Gulf of Aqaba with the Red Sea. Reminding Johnson that President Eisenhower had pledged a decade earlier to keep the straits open to Israeli shipping, Eshkol let it be known that his government would regard Nasser's closure of the international waterway as an act of war.[77]

While the Johnson administration scrambled to prevent Eshkol from taking preemptive action on May 23, an avalanche of letters and telegrams urging that Washington unleash Israel swamped the White House mailroom. Abe Feinberg, Arthur Krim, and other influential friends of Israel privately pressed their case inside the Oval Office.[78] Johnson went on national television to denounce Nasser's action as "illegal and potentially disastrous to the cause of peace." He signalled America's continued support for Israel by releasing the long-awaited M-113 armored personnel carriers. And he urged the Israelis to be patient while he organized a multinational flotilla to challenge the Egyptian blockade.[79]

The mood at the NSC meeting that Johnson convened the next day to review America's options, however, was very grim. "The issue in the Middle East today," the State Department explained in a background paper, "is whether Nasser, the radical states and their Soviet backers are going to dominate the area." In early May, "we expected South Arabia to provide the test," but the current Arab-Israeli flareup had "brought the test sooner than we expected." With Britain scaling back its presence east of Suez and with Egypt and Russia sponsoring the PLO, FLOSY, and other Arab liberation movements, some expected America to "back down as a major power" in the Middle East. To prevent the erosion of U.S. credibility in the region, the State Department recommended quiet encouragement for Israel, Iran, and Saudi Arabia.[80] The most pressing item on the NSC's agenda was how to prevent such quiet encouragement from prompting an Israeli preemptive strike on Egypt that could easily escalate into a superpower confrontation. Secretary of State Rusk had little faith that U Thant could act swiftly or forcefully enough to prevent war. Secretary of the Treasury Henry Fowler doubted whether proposed economic sanctions against Egypt would "hold the Israelis off" for more than a few days. And no one believed that the multinational "Red Sea Regatta" Johnson had proposed the previous day would ever materialize.

According to General Earle Wheeler, Chairman of the Joint Chiefs of Staff, the presence of Egyptian submarines and attack planes in the Red Sea made it "harder to open the Gulf of Aqaba than we first thought." Although key portions of the NSC minutes have been "sanitized," some U.S. officials evidently feared that Israel was prepared to use "unconventional weapons" against Nasser's forces. Even without going nuclear, however, Wheeler was certain that "the Israelis can hold their own." CIA director Richard Helms agreed and warned that the biggest danger America faced was being "fully blackballed in the Arab world as Israel's supporter."[81]

Despite the Johnson administration's faith in Israel's military invulnerability, pressure continued to build inside Eshkol's cabinet for a preemptive strike against Egypt. On May 26, Foreign Minister Abba Eban arrived in Washington with the news that unless the Straits of Tiran were reopened very soon, Eshkol would unleash the Israeli military. Johnson played for time, counseling patience while the United States worked with Britain, the Netherlands, and other maritime powers to organize a multilateral naval squadron to break Nasser's blockade. He also cautioned the Israelis against acting precipitously. "Israel would not be alone," Johnson told Eban, "unless it acted alone." Although Eban promised to relay Johnson's views to Eshkol, the president was pessimistic about prospects for peace. "I failed," he told Eugene Rostow after the Israeli diplomat had departed. "They're going to go."[82]

For the next week, the White House worked nonstop to preserve peace. Johnson cabled Soviet premier Alexei Kosygin to urge the Kremlin to apprise Nasser of just how explosive the situation had become. He exhorted U.N. Secretary General U Thant to redouble his efforts to find a compromise between Arab and Jew.[83] And he asked Robert Anderson, a Texas businessman and diplomatic troubleshooter who had served as Eisenhower's secret Middle East emissary during the mid-1950s, to fly to Cairo to discuss opening a private back-channel between Nasser and the White House. Anderson reported on June 2 that the Egyptian leader had promised not to attack Israel and actually seemed quite eager for a negotiated settlement. Hinting that he might be willing to refer the dispute over the Straits of Tiran to the World Court, Nasser agreed to send Vice President Zakaria Mohieddin to Washington for secret talks before the week was out.[84]

But early on the morning of June 5, Israeli jets streaked across the Nile delta and destroyed Nasser's air force while it was still on the runway. When the guns fell silent six days later, Israel controlled not only Gaza and the Sinai but also the Golan Heights and the West Bank. In retrospect, the rationale behind Israel's surprise attack seems clear. On May 30, King Hussein had flown to Cairo, where he and Nasser announced an alliance between Jordan and Egypt, thus confronting Israeli military planners with the specter of a two-front war. More important, once the Israelis learned that Vice President Mohieddin

would visit Washington, they suspected an American diplomatic doublecross that might leave Nasser in control of the Straits of Tiran and
Israel bottled up in the Gulf of Aqaba. Israeli ambassador Avraham
Harman raised these concerns with State Department officials on June
2, prompting Secretary of State Rusk to recall Johnson's earlier warning
that Israel must not act alone. But when Harman discussed the Middle
East crisis with Abe Fortas a few hours later, those cautionary words
seemed far less categorical. According to Fortas, Johnson believed that
"Rusk will fiddle while Israel burns." Lest the Israeli diplomat miss the
point, Fortas added: "If you're going to save yourself, do it yourself."[85]
Israel did just that three days later.

Although Johnson evidently signalled his acquiescence in an Israeli
first strike at the last moment, he soon had good reason to worry that
the splendid little war would spiral into a superpower confrontation.
Moments after the fighting erupted on June 5, Dean Rusk had flashed
word to Soviet Foreign Minister Andrei Gromyko that the United
States was working for a ceasefire under U.N. auspices.[86] Once Israeli
armor rolled across the Sinai on June 6 and into the West Bank the next
day, Washington expected Israel to halt its offensive. Meanwhile, Johnson had moved to prevent any unintended escalation of the war by
establishing an NSC "Special Committee" modeled on the one
Kennedy had employed during the 1962 Cuban missile crisis and headed by McGeorge Bundy, temporarily on leave from his new post at the
Ford Foundation. Buoyed by signs of a serious Soviet falling out with
Egypt, Bundy's group accurately predicted that the Kremlin would
grudgingly accept an American proposal for an Arab-Israeli ceasefire
in place on June 8.[87]

Before the shooting stopped, however, Israel wished to settle one
last score with Syria, which had taken Nasser's advice and stayed out
of the war. Well aware that the Israelis had long coveted the Golan
Heights that towered over the Sea of Galilee, the Pentagon apparently
instructed the U.S.S. *Liberty*, a lightly armed intelligence ship stationed
off the Sinai coast, to monitor Israeli military activities along the Syrian
frontier. Just after noon on June 8, three waves of Israeli planes and tor-
pedo boats attacked the surveillance vessel, ripping huge holes in its
hull and leaving 34 sailors dead and another 171 wounded. While the
Liberty limped back to port, Israel apologized for what it termed a tragic case of mistaken identity, an explanation many in Washington found
hard to believe.[88] Dean Rusk, for example, called the attack "literally
incomprehensible," while Clark Clifford, a senior member of Bundy's
Special Committee and a longtime friend of Israel, snapped that it was
"inconceivable it was [an] accident."[89] In any case, just fifteen hours

after the first rockets destroyed the *Liberty*'s eavesdropping equipment and just eight hours after the ceasefire was supposed to have gone into effect, Israel launched a lightning assault on Syria which brought Israeli troops within sight of Damascus. The CIA believed that this move was "aimed at overthrowing the left-wing Baathist party which the Israelis blame for starting the entire Middle East crisis."[90]

Few in Washington expected Moscow to stand aside while Israel accomplished its goal. "The Soviets [had] hinted," Dean Rusk recalled in his memoirs, "that if the Israelis attacked Syria, they would intervene with their own forces."[91] Not surprisingly, the White House-to-Kremlin "Hot Line" lit up three times on June 10 with messages indicating that Soviet military action was imminent. Johnson moved swiftly to forestall such an eventuality. First, he sent word to Eshkol that he expected an effective ceasefire "without delay." Then he moved elements of the U.S. Sixth Fleet from Athens to the Eastern Mediterranean, where "Soviet submarines monitoring the Fleet's operations would report immediately to Moscow." In the end, Israel halted its offensive, Russia edged away from intervention, and "everyone relaxed a bit as it became clear that the fighting was petering out."[92]

Yet the lessons were clear. First, America's special relationship with Israel and Russia's special relationship with Nasser and the Arab radicals had brought the two superpowers perilously close to the brink of war. To prevent a replay, Lyndon Johnson and Soviet premier Alexei Kosygin would open a dialogue on the Middle East during their mini-summit at Glassboro, New Jersey in late June. Second, America's interests in the region were certain to be targeted by resurgent Arab revolutionary nationalists bent on avenging the recent military debacle. With the United States increasingly overextended in Southeast Asia and with the Soviet Union angling to rebuild its influence among the Arabs in the wake of the Six Day War, closer relations with Israel and with Nasser's chief Muslim rivals in Riyadh and Teheran seemed the course most likely to provide the Johnson administration with the strategic assets it needed to promote American objectives in the Middle East.

Three Pillars

A more sharply defined American approach to the Middle East based on three pillars—Saudi Arabia, Iran, and Israel—had begun to take shape shortly after the guns fell silent in June 1967. Assuaging Saudi anger over U.S. acquiescence in Israel's preemptive war was absolutely essential if ARAMCO and other U.S. firms were to retain their petroleum concessions in the Arab world. Led by the House of Saud, the Arabs had imposed an embargo on all oil shipments to America and Britain on June 6. A week later, Persian Gulf petroleum exports had plummeted sixty percent, the American-owned Trans-Arabian Pipeline that carried Saudi crude to the Eastern Mediterranean had been dynamited, and left-wing oil workers had shut down refineries from Baghdad to Beirut. U.S. and U.K. officials managed to lessen the impact of the embargo by convening an "Emergency Oil Supply Committee" to help Standard Oil of New Jersey, British Petroleum, and other multinational giants divert Western Hemisphere crude to Western Europe.[93] What finally killed the embargo, however, was growing friction between the conservative Arabs who controlled oil production and the radical Arabs who brandished the oil weapon. Convinced that "restrictions on oil export are harming the Arab producers more than the boycotted nations," the Saudis permitted ARAMCO to resume operations in late June. By August, Arab oil exports were actually slightly higher than four months earlier while Saudi relations with Egypt had soured appreciably.[94]

The inter-Arab friction generated by the abortive embargo permitted the Johnson administration to drive a wedge between Riyadh and Cairo. The time had come, McGeorge Bundy told the president in early June, to show "sympathy for good Arabs as against bad Arabs."[95] Walt Rostow agreed, and recommended some "hand-holding" for Arab moderates like Jordan's King Hussein and the Emir of Kuwait, both of whom soon received quiet thanks from Johnson for their refusal to follow Nasser's lead in severing relations with the United States.[96] King Faisal received much more than that during the next three months. Grateful that the Saudis had lifted their oil boycott, Johnson authorized the Pentagon to provide the House of Saud with a $25 million package of nonlethal military equipment including four C-130 transport aircraft on June 30. Seven weeks later the State Department agreed to expedite the export licenses the Saudis required to purchase another $50 million worth of HAWK missiles from the Raytheon company.[97] Although the Shah of Iran may not have been a good Arab, or even an Arab at all, the Johnson administration certainly regarded his refusal to embargo oil shipments to Israel and the United States during the Six Day War as a Persian sign of good faith that, like Faisal's, was well worth rewarding. During the last half of 1967, Washington stepped up its economic aid for Iran and encouraged the Shah to work closely with Saudi Arabia in planning for regional defense.[98]

Such Saudi-Iranian cooperation took on added significance in early 1968 with the news that Britain would definitely liquidate its entire presence in the Persian Gulf within three years. As a National Security Council staff study put it shortly after the devaluation of the pound sterling in November 1967, "Britain no longer has the will, or can afford, to play a major security role in the Middle East."[99] The best way to "fill the gap left by the British," Walt Rostow told President Johnson on January 16, was greater American support for the "rich and increasingly confident" regimes in Teheran and Riyadh. In short, Rostow explained, "we should give them both encouragement and sell them arms."[100] Johnson evidently agreed, for within a few days the president approved Faisal's request for more weaponry including F-86 jets armed with Sidewinder missiles and promised the Shah that the Pentagon would ship him military hardware that had been back-ordered for months.[101]

The emerging American partnership with Saudi Arabia and Iran might shore up Western access to Persian Gulf oil, but it would do little to resolve an even more explosive regional problem, the deepening Arab-Israeli confrontation. Here Washington hoped to cement a special relationship with Israel that could convert the Jewish state into America's third pillar in the Middle East. To be sure, Israel's territorial ambitions and its emerging nuclear capability threatened to exacerbate tensions with its Arab neighbors in the wake of the Six Day War. But the Johnson administration believed that the overwhelming Israeli military triumph would make Israel supremely confident of its own security, more likely to forego its territorial ambitions, and less likely to build atomic bombs.[102] Shortly after the shooting stopped in June 1967, however, Foreign Minister Abba Eban informed Dean Rusk that Israel intended to keep much of the territory it had seized from Egypt and Syria and most of Jordan's West Bank. Nor was Eban willing to offer any categorical assurances regarding nuclear nonproliferation. "Don't you be the first power to introduce nuclear weapons into the Middle East," Rusk snapped after a nasty exchange over the Dimona reactor. "No," Eban retorted. "But we won't be the second."[103]

Top U.S. officials continued to wrestle with how best to handle Israel throughout the summer of 1967. Acquiescing in Israel's seizure of East Jerusalem, the West Bank, and the Golan Heights, Rusk told the NSC Special Committee on June 14, could "create a revanchism for the rest of the 20th c[entury]." Even worse, many in Washington feared that a lengthy territorial stalemate would "probably increase pressure favoring going nuclear in both Israel and the Arab states."[104] In light of these concerns, President Johnson placed the Middle East at the top of the agenda during his hastily scheduled summit meeting with Soviet Premier Alexei Kosygin at Glassboro, New Jersey in late June.

Unless America could persuade Israel "to withdraw its forces back to the original [prewar] armistice line," Kosygin warned Johnson, "hostilities were certain to break out again." Likening the Arab-Israeli dispute to a family disagreement between younger siblings, Johnson maintained that "it was up to the older brothers to provide proper guidance." This meant, he continued, Soviet-American agreement to work through the United Nations to resolve the territorial question plus fresh efforts by Washington and Moscow to achieve regional arms limitation. Although Kosygin refused to discuss arms limitation until the Kremlin was able to redress the military imbalance created by Israel's destruction of Egypt's arsenal in the Six Day War, he did pledge to cooperate with Johnson in arranging a U.N.-backed territorial settlement.[105]

By early autumn, the elements of a "peace for land" compromise had begun to take shape at U.N. headquarters in New York City. In exchange for Arab acknowledgment of both Israel's right to exist and its right to use the Straits of Tiran, the Israelis would return those areas they had seized from their neighbors in June. Because this fell considerably short of the formal settlement complete with peace treaties and diplomatic recognition that the Israelis desired, however, they balked at restoring the prewar status quo and insisted that some territorial adjustments were necessary to ensure their security. As a result, before the U.N. Security Council adopted Resolution 242 on November 22 calling for "withdrawal of Israeli armed forces from all territories occupied in the recent conflict," the United States arranged to have the word "all" stricken, creating enough ambiguity to permit Israel to stake a claim to parts of the West Bank and the Golan Heights.[106]

Having thus demonstrated America's commitment to Israeli security, Washington was disappointed by Israel's unwillingness to comply speedily with Resolution 242. Nor were American policymakers happy about rumors that Israel was secretly pursuing its nuclear option at Dimona. On the eve of Levi Eshkol's visit to the LBJ Ranch outside Austin, Texas in January 1968, Middle East expert Harold Saunders recommended that the president remind his guest that the Israeli-American relationship must be a two-way street. "We can't tie ourselves to a 'Fortress Israel,' " Saunders explained, especially if the Jewish state "decides to build nuclear weapons."[107] Although key documents detailing Johnson's conversations with Eshkol remain classified, the president evidently pressed hard for Israeli pledges to avoid "permanent moves in [the] occupied lands" and to forego development of "Nuclear Weapons and Missiles." Unimpressed by the prime minister's assurances on either front, Johnson tabled Eshkol's request for 50

F-4 Phantom jets until Israel clarified its positions on Resolution 242 and nonproliferation.[108]

By the spring of 1968, many in Washington worried that Israeli backtracking from the U.N. peace-for-land formula would strain American relations with Muslim conservatives and permit the Kremlin to rebuild its influence among the Arab radicals. Under increasing fire from Nasser for being American stooges, the Saudis wrapped themselves in the shroud of Arab nationalism, stepped up their anti-Israeli rhetoric, and fired on Iranian drilling rigs in a dispute over offshore oil rights in the Persian Gulf. Determined to prevent the Saudi-Iranian skirmish from derailing American plans for "greater regional economic and political cooperation among the Gulf states" in the wake of Britain's withdrawal, the Johnson administration moved quickly to mediate the dispute. Before the spring was out, both the Shah and Crown Prince Khalid, Faisal's heir apparent, would visit the White House to discuss the importance of Saudi-Iranian cooperation for the security of the Persian Gulf. Better relations between Teheran and Riyadh were of the "greatest importance," State Department officials explained in June 1968, not merely "in assuring stability in [the] Gulf after British withdrawal" but also in "preventing opportunity for radical Arab exploitation or successful communist lodgement."[109]

Throughout the first half of 1968 the Johnson administration had detected ominous signs that Moscow was stepping up its activities in the Arab world. In January, the CIA reported that the Arab Nationalist Movement, a militant Palestinian organization headed by George Habash, had won "Soviet backing" for its guerrilla war against Israel and for its plans to subvert pro-Western Muslim regimes from Libya to Kuwait.[110] At an NSC meeting a month later, Johnson learned that the Russians were seeking to "improve the military facilities available to them" in the Middle East.[111] By June the CIA confirmed that the Soviets had recently acquired intelligence installations in Egypt "greater than they ever dreamed of two years ago."[112] Before the summer was out, anti-Western Ba'athist radicals eager for closer ties between Iraq and the Soviet Union had seized power in Baghdad in a bloody coup masterminded by thirty-one year old Saddam Hussein.[113] By October, growing Soviet influence in Syria sparked much speculation in Washington about a possible alliance between Damascus and Moscow.[114] Even more worrisome was the situation in Jordan, where Ambassador Harrison Symmes reported that a "rather feckless" King Hussein was doing nothing to prevent the PLO from receiving clandestine shipments of Soviet weapons for use in its increasingly bloody attacks against Israeli military and civilian targets on the West Bank and inside Israel.[115]

The Kremlin's decision to redouble its military and diplomatic support for the Arab radicals during 1968 encouraged the White House increasingly to regard Israel as a strategic counterweight that must have an arsenal second to none in the Middle East. The Israelis had worked hard throughout the spring to position themselves alongside Iran and Saudi Arabia as America's "third pillar" in the region. High-ranking Israeli officials warned U.S. policymakers in February that unless the Jewish state received F-4 Phantom jets and other sophisticated U.S. military hardware, Moscow would gain the upper hand in the Middle East.[116] Four months later, Menachim Begin, a minister without portfolio in Eshkol's coalition cabinet, visited Washington to urge the Johnson administration to sell Israel the weapons it needed to offset recent Soviet inroads in the Arab world.[117] General Yitzhak Rabin, whom Eshkol had recently tapped as Israel's new ambassador to the United States, reminded Dean Rusk in September that America's longstanding commitment to preserve the Arab-Israeli military balance served Washington's interests in the region as well as Israel's.[118]

Nagging doubts about Israel's territorial and nuclear ambitions, however, left many in Washington somewhat reluctant to cement a special relationship. Well into the fall, top U.S. officials insisted that Israel must take concrete steps to implement Resolution 242 and ratify the NPT before the White House would authorize the sale of the F-4 Phantoms Eshkol had requested in January. With the PLO escalating its operations and with the 1968 presidential election looming, however, pro-Israeli pressure groups on Capitol Hill and Main Street lobbied hard for the release of the supersonic jets on Israel's wish list. Although Johnson had renounced his own plans for a second term in March, Abe Feinberg and other influential friends of Israel insisted that selling the Jewish state Phantoms might provide just enough swing votes to keep California and New York in the Democratic column in what was expected to be an extraordinarily close election in November. In early October, AIPAC persuaded seventy U.S. senators to sign an open letter urging the president to provide Israel with F-4s as soon as possible.[119] After receiving fresh assurances that Israel accepted the peace-for-land principles outlined in U.N. Resolution 242 and that Israel would not be the first nation to introduce nuclear weapons into the Middle East, Johnson informed Eshkol in late November that the Israelis would soon receive the Phantom jets they had long coveted.[120]

By the time Lyndon Johnson handed the Oval Office over to Richard Nixon and returned home to the banks of the Padernales in January 1969, then, he and his advisers regarded Israel—and Iran and Saudi Arabia too—as strategic assets essential to the containment of Soviet influence in the Muslim world. This meant opening wide the door of America's conventional arsenal to the Israelis both to ensure that they outgunned the Arab radicals and to discourage them from going nuclear. It meant placing a higher premium on military security and political stability than on social reform in Iran, Saudi Arabia, and other oil-rich states threatened by revolutionary change. It meant terminating American efforts to woo Nasser with surplus wheat, technical assistance, and personal diplomacy. But despite AIPAC and oil industry support for the new three pillars approach, it did not mean that the Johnson administration had succumbed to interest group politicking. Rather, when it came to the Middle East, strategic concerns like nuclear nonproliferation and secure access to Persian Gulf petroleum were at least as important in shaping Johnson's policies as domestic political considerations.

Not long after Johnson returned to the Lone Star State, however, his quest for regional stability began to unravel. From the Suez Canal to the banks of the River Jordan, Arab and Israeli forces waged an escalating "war of attrition." From Tripoli to Teheran, the Organization of Petroleum Exporting Countries (OPEC) was beginning to challenge western control of Middle East oil. And from Radio Cairo came word that several thousand Soviet military advisers were on their way to Egypt, where they would help Nasser rebuild the war machine Israel had crippled in June 1967. Bedeviled by intractable Arab-Israeli tensions, increasingly polarized by Soviet-American rivalry, soon to be enriched by growing oil revenues, the Middle East was rapidly becoming a battleground where East confronted West and North confronted South. In the long run, then, Johnson's Middle East policies were no more successful than Kennedy's. A quarter century after Big Daddy from the Padernales left office, a nuclear-armed Israel sits atop a Palestinian powderkeg on the West Bank, radical regimes in Baghdad and Teheran threaten western access to Persian Gulf oil, and 50,000 U.S. troops stand guard in Saudi Arabia to prevent the House of Saud from going the way of Iran's Pahlavi dynasty. Will the end of the Cold War, the start of Israeli-Palestinian peace talks, and changing patterns of American petroleum consumption tempt new fools to undertake an old errand on the outside chance the world may call them genius?

NOTES

1. For a contemporary optimistic look at prospects for peace and stability in the Middle East, see Jules Davids, "The United States and the Middle East: 1955–1960," *Middle Eastern Affairs* 12 (May 1961): 130–140.

2. Douglas Little, "From Even-Handed to Empty-Handed: Seeking Order in the Middle East," in Thomas G. Paterson, ed., *Kennedy's Quest for Victory: American Foreign Policy 1961–1963* (New York, 1989), pp. 159–160; Warren I. Cohen, *Dean Rusk* (Totowa, NJ, 1980), pp. 16–31; John S. Badeau, *The Middle East Remembered* (Washington, DC, 1983), 169–185; and Phillips Talbot to author, August 26, 1985.

3. Robert Komer Oral History, JFKL, pp. 1, 5. On Kennedy's prepresidential attitudes toward the Middle East, see John F. Kennedy, *The Strategy of Peace* (New York, 1960), pp. 106–123, 217–219, and Little, "From Even-Handed to Empty-Handed," pp. 157–159.

4. JFK to Nasser, n.d., appended to Rusk to Badeau, tel. 18 April 1963, JFKL, POF:CO, Box 127, "UAR Security—1963."

5. Rusk to JFK, May 5, 1961, with undated enclosures, JFKL, POF:CO, Box 127, "UAR Security—1961"; National Security Action Memorandum 105, "Policy toward Egypt and Syria," Oct. 16, 1961, JFKL, NSF: Meetings & Memos, Box 332, "NSAM 105."

6. "Action Program for the United Arab Republic," 10 Jan. 1962, and Bowles to JFK, Rusk, & Fowler, Feb. 1962, both in JFKL, POF:CO, Box 127, "UAR Security—1962."

7. Mason to JFK, March 22, 1962, JFKL, POF: Departments & Agencies, Box 88, "State Department—1962;" Mason, "Report on Mission to the UAR," n.d. (March 21, 1962), JFKL, POF:CO, Box 127, "UAR Security—1962."

8. William J. Burns, *Economic Aid and American Policy toward Egypt, 1955–1981* (Albany, NY, 1985), pp. 133–134.

9. State Department cirtel, June 2, 1961, JFKL, NSF:CO, Box 119, "Israel—1961"; Mordechai Gazit, *President Kennedy's Policies toward the Arab States and Israel* (Syracuse, NY, 1983), pp. 38–41. Gazit was deputy chief of mission at the Israeli Embassy in Washington during the early 1960s.

10. JFK quoted in "Memo for the Record," Dec. 6, 1960, DDEL, AWF: Transition Series, Box 1, "Memos of the Staff re Change of Administration." For a sanitized CIA assessment of the Dimona reactor, see "Minutes of the 470th NSC Meeting," Dec. 8, 1960, *FRUS* (1958–60) 13: 391–392.

11. On the background to the Dimona reactor, see Seymour Hersh, *The Samson Option: Israel's Nuclear Arsenal and American Foreign Policy* (New York, 1991), pp. 47–81, and George Quester, "Nuclear Weapons & Israel," *Middle East Journal* 37 (1983): 548–549.

12. Gazit, *Kennedy's Policy toward the Arab States & Israel*, 38–41; Gazit to author, 27 Feb. 1989.

13. State Department memcon, "The Johnson Plan," n.d. (Aug. 1962), *Declassified Documents Reference System, 1991,* (New Carrollton, MD, 1991), item #1435 (hereafter *DDRS* for the appropriate year); Steven L. Spiegel, *The Other Arab-Israeli Conflict: Making America's Middle East Policy from Truman to Reagan* (Chicago, 1985), pp. 110–112; Herbert Parmet, *JFK: The Presidency of John F. Kennedy* (New York, 1983), pp. 228–231; Little, "From Even-Handed to Empty-Handed," pp. 164–166.

14. "Problems of U.S.-Israel Relations," July 6, 1962, JFKL, NSF:CO, Box 118, "Israel—1962."

15. Talbot to Feldman, Aug. 9, 1962; Feldman to JFK, Aug. 10, 1962; JFK to Ben Gurion, Aug. 15, 1962; and Feldman to JFK and Rusk, Aug. 19, 1962, all in JFKL, NSF:CO, Box 119, "Israel Security—1962." On the inspection of the Dimona reactor, see McGeorge Bundy, *Danger and Survival: Choices About the Bomb in the First Fifty Years* (New York, 1988), p. 510.

16. Douglas Little, "The New Frontier on the Nile: JFK, Nasser, and Arab Nationalism," *Journal of American History* 75 (September 1988): 509–511.

17. Memcon of Kennedy-Shah meeting, April 13, 1962, and memcon of Rusk-Shah meeting, April 13, 1962, JFKL, NSF:CO, Box 116/117, "Iran—Shah's Visit."

18. Rusk to JFK, "Libya, June 1962: U.S. Objectives" and Komer to JFK, Oct. 16, 1962 , JFKL, POF:CO, Box 121a, "Libya—1962"; Rusk to JFK, "U.S. Economic Assistance to Saudi Arabia," n.d. (early Oct. 1962), JFKL, NSF:CO, Box 158, "Saudi Arabia Security—1962"; Little, "From Even-Handed to Empty-Handed," pp. 167–169.

19. On Iraq and Kuwait, see Komer to Bundy, "Notes for Tuesday Lunch," Jan. 9, 1961, JFKL, NSF: Meetings & Memoranda, Box 321, "Staff Memos—Komer 1961"; Battle to Bundy, March 7, 1961, *DDRS*, 1982, item 345.

20. State Department, "Developments in Yemen," n.d. (early Oct. 1962), JFKL, NSF:CO, Box 158, "Saudi Arabia—Faysal Briefing Book"; John S. Badeau, *The American Approach to the Arab World* (New York, 1968), pp. 130–132.

21. William Brubeck to Bundy, "Elements of United States Policy toward the UAR," Dec. 11, 1962, JFKL, POF:CO, Box 127, "UAR Security—1962"; Little, "New Frontier on the Nile," pp. 513–517.

22. Parker Hart Oral History, JFKL, pp. 18, 61–62; Bundy, "National Security Action Memorandum 227: Decisions Taken at the President's Meeting on the Yemen Crisis," Feb. 27, 1963, JFKL, POF:CO, Box 123b, "Saudi Arabia—1961–1963"; Little, "New Frontier on the Nile," pp. 517–519.

23. Komer to Bundy, March 6, 1963, JFKL, NSF: Meetings & Memoranda, Box 322, "Staff Memos—Komer 1963"; State Department memcon, "Middle East Tour d'Horizon," April 2, 1963, JFKL, NSF:CO, Box 119, "Israel Security—1963."

24. CIA, "Consequences of Israel Acquisition of Nuclear Capability," March 6, 1963, JFKL, NSF:CO, Box 119, "Israel Security—1963."

25. Benjamin Read to Bundy, May 13, 1963, and Talbot to Rusk, May 14, 1963, JKL, NSF:CO, Box 119, "Israel Security—1963." See also Douglas Little, "The Making of a Special Relationship: The United States and Israel, 1957–1968," *International Journal of Middle East Studies*, 25 (November 1993): 569–571.

26. Burns, *Economic Aid & American Policy toward Egypt*, pp. 141–143; remarks by Hermann Eilts at the New England Historical Association Meeting, 21 Oct. 1989, Smith College, Northampton, MA.

27. "United States Security Assistance for Israel, 11 Sept. 1963, JFKL,

NSF:CO, Box 119, "Israel Security—1963"; Komer to JFK, 7 Oct. 1963, JFKL, POF:CO, Box 123b, "Saudi Arabia Security—1963"; Komer to the author, June 23, 1987.

28. Mohamed Heikal, *The Cairo Documents: The Inside Story of Nasser's Relationship with World Leaders, Rebels, and Statesmen* (Garden City, NY, 1973); pp. 222–223; Rusk, cirtel. Nov. 8, 1963, JFKL, POF:CO, Box 127, "UAR Security— 1963"; Burns, *Economic Aid & American Policy toward Egypt*, pp. 143–148.

29. Louis Gomolak, "Prologue: LBJ's Foreign Affairs Background, 1908–1948," Ph.D. Dissertation, (University of Texas-Austin, 1989), pp. 30–35, 44–51, 94–96; Thomas M. Gaskin, "Senate Majority Leader Lyndon B. Johnson: The Formosa and Middle East Resolutions," in Bernard J. Firestone and Robert C. Vogt, eds., *Lyndon Baines Johnson and the Uses of Power* (New York, 1988), pp. 250–253; I. L. Kenen, *Israel's Defense Line: Her Friends and Foes in Washington* (Buffalo, NY, 1981), pp. 148–153.

30. LBJ to JFK, Sept. 10, 1962, LBJL, Vice Presidential Security Files, Box 10, "Middle East Memos." For a fuller discussion of LBJ's vice presidential attitudes toward the Middle East, see Douglas Little, "Choosing Sides: Lyndon Johnson and the Middle East," (forthcoming in Robert Divine, editor, *The Johnson Years: Volume Three* [Lawrence, KN, 1993]).

31. On pro-Israel sentiment among LBJ's advisers and friends, see Spiegel, *Other Arab-Israeli Conflict*, pp. 128–129; Kenen, *Israel's Defense Line*, pp. 148–153; and Edward Tivnan, *The Lobby: Jewish Political Power and American Foreign Policy* (New York, 1987), pp. 59–60.

32. Read to Bundy, Feb. 12, 1964, LBJL, NSF:CO, Box 159, "UAR—Vol. 1."

33. Badeau to Rusk, tel. May 10, 1964, LBJL, NSF:CO, Box 158, "UAR—Vol. 1."

34. Badeau to Rusk, tel. May 25, 1964, LBJL, NSF:CO, Box 158, "UAR—Vol 1."

35. CIA, "Nasir's Arab Policy: The Latest Phase," Aug. 28, 1964, and State Department, "Major Issues in U.S.-U.A.R. Relations," n.d. (Aug. 1964), both in LBJL, NSF:CO, Box 159, "UAR—Vol. 2."

36. William O. Boswell (Cairo) to Rusk, tel. Sept. 12, 1964, LBJL, NSF:CO, Box 159, "UAR—Vol 2."

37. Heikal, *Cairo Documents*, p. 229; Burns, *Economic Aid & American Policy toward Egypt*, pp. 158–160.

38. On FLOSY and PFLOAG, see J. B. Kelly, *Arabia, the Gulf, and the West* (New York, 1980), pp. 26–41, 136–150.

39. CIA, NIE 36.1–65, "Problems & Prospects for the United Arab Republic," 31 March 1965, LBJL, NSF: NIE File, Box 6; Talbot to Rusk, 22 April 1965, LBJL, NSF:CO, Box 139, "Israel—Vol. 4"; Raed to Bundy, June 5, 1965, LBJL, NSF:CO, Box 159, "UAR—Vol. 4."

40. On Nasser, FATAH, and the PLO, see William Quandt, Fuad Jabber, and Amy Mosely Lesch, *The Politics of Palestinian Nationalism* (Berkeley, CA, 1973), pp. 55–58, and Alan Hart, *Arafat: A Political Biography* (New York, 1989), pp. 160–178. On Syria, see CIA, "Syria under the Baath," May 20, 1966, and CIA,

"Syria: A Center of Instability," March 24, 1967, LBJL, NSF:CO, Box 156, "Syria—Vol. 1."

41. Kenen, *Israel's Defense Line*, p. 173.

42. Komer to LBJ, 29 Jan. 1964, LBJL, NSF:CO, Box 139, "Israel—Vol. 1"; Komer to LBJ, Feb. 18, 1964, LBJL, NSF: Name File, Box 6, "Komer Memos— Vol. 1."

43. Rear Admiral J. W. Davis (JCS) to Robert McNamara, Jan. 18, 1964, LBJL, NSF:CO, Box 145, "Israel—Tanks, Vol. 1"; Dean Rusk to LBJ, Feb. 25, 1964, LBJL, NSF:CO, Box 158, "UAR Memos, Vol 1"; and McGeorge Bundy to LBJ, May 12, 1964, LBJL, Memos to the President Files, Box 1.

44. Komer to LBJ, May 28, 1964, LBJL, NSF:Files of McGeorge Bundy, Box 19, "Memos & Meetings with the President, Vol. 1."

45. "Quid Pro Quo of Visit," May 28, 1964; George Ball to LBJ, n.d. (late May 1964); and Rusk, "Assessment Eshkol Visit," cirtel. June 26, 1964, all in University Publications of America, *Lyndon B. Johnson National Security Files: Israel*, microfilm edition (Fredrickton, MD, 1982), reel 3, frames 27–31, 85–88, 101–103, (hereafter cited as *LBJ-NSF: Israel*).

46. Assistant Secretary of Defense John McNaughton to Komer, July 15, 1964, *DDRS, 1988*, item 3237; "Recommendations for Near East Arms," n.d., attached to George Ball to LBJ, n.d. (probably late Feb. 1965), LBJL, NSF:CO, Box 116, "Near East—Vol. 1."

47. State Department memcons, Feb. 25 and 26, 1965, LBJL, NSF:CO, Box 145, "Israel—Harriman Mission."

48. Deputy Assistant Secretary of Defense for International Security Affairs Peter Solbert to McGeorge Bundy, March 8, 1965, *LBJ-NSF: Israel*, reel 3, frames 150–156.

49. Rusk to Lucius Battle (Cairo), tel. March 18, 1965, "Countries: UAR," Box 159, NSF, LBJL; and Rusk to Phillips Talbot (Tel Aviv), tel. April 21, 1965, *LBJ-NSF: Israel*, reel 1, frames 239–244.

50. Komer memcon, Oct. 18, 1965, LBJL, NSF: Name File, Box 6, "Komer Memos—Vol. 2"; Komer to LBJ, Jan. 18, 1966, and Rusk to Barbour, Feb. 3, 1966, LBJL, NSF:CO, Box 139, "Israel—Vol. 5."

51. DOS to Ambassador Lucius Battle (Cairo), tel. April 11, 1966, LBJL, NSF:CO, Box 159, "UAR—Vol. 4"; Benjamin Read to Walt Rostow, April 30, 1966, LBJL, NSF:CO, Box 139, "Israel—Vol. 5."

52. On CIA support for Hussein, see *Washington Post*, Feb. 18, 1977, 1:1; and Wilbur Crane Eveland, *Ropes of Sand: America's Failure in the Middle East* (New York, 1980), p. 191.

53. State Department memcon, Feb. 25, 1965, LBJL, NSF:CO, Box 145, "Israel—Harriman Mission."

54. LBJ to Hussein, n.d. (probably late March 1966), LBJL, NSF:CO, Box 139, "Israel—Vol. 5"; LBJ to Hussein, May 4, 1966, *DDRS, 1991*, item 468.

55. Uriel Dann, *King Hussein and the Challenge of Arab Radicalism: Jordan, 1955–1967* (New York, 1989), p. 155.

56. Glen Balfour-Paul, *The End of Empire in the Middle East: Britain's Relin-

quishment of Power in Her Last Three Arab Dependencies (New York, 1991), p. 84; Karl Pieragostini, *Britain, Aden and South Arabia* (New York, 1991), pp. 108, 167; Frank Brenchley, *Britain and the Middle East: An Economic History 1945–1987* (London, 1989), pp. 165–167; Denis Healey, *The Time of My Life* (New York, 1990), pp. 278–281.

57. On Persian Gulf Oil, see CIA, NIE 36–66, "The Eastern Arab World," Feb. 17, 1966, LBJL, NSF: NIE Files, Box 6. On Diego Garcia, see William Stivers, *America's Confrontation with Revolutionary Change in the Middle East, 1948–1983* (New York, 1986), pp. 49–57.

58. On LBJ and the Shah, see James Bill, *The Eagle and the Lion: The Tragedy of American-Iranian Relations* (New Haven, CT, 1988), pp. 154–182, and Barry Rubin, *Paved with Good Intentions: The American Experience and Iran* (New York, 1980), pp. 115–123.

59. CIA, NIE 34–66, "Iran," March 24, 1966, LBJL, NSF: NIE File, Box 6; Rostow to LBJ, May 5, 12 and 23, 1966, *DDRS, 1991*, items 452–454; Armin Meyer to LBJ, tel. May 23, 1966, LBJL, NSF:CO, Box 136, "Iran—Vol. 2."

60. Walt Rostow to LBJ, Aug. 10, 1966, LBJL, NSF:CO, Box 136, Iran—Vol. 2." See also Rubin, *Paved with Good Intentions*, pp. 115–123, and Bill, *The Eagle and the Lion*, pp. 154–182.

61. Komer to LBJ, April 15, 1965, LBJL, NSF:CO, Box 155, "Saudi Arabia—Vol. 1."

62. McNaughton to Komer, April 7, 1965; Komer to LBJ, April 15, 1965; and State Department Background Papers, "Future Prospects for Yemen" and "U.S. Involvement in the Yemen Problem," Feb. 20–25, 1966, LBJL, NSF:CO, Box 155, "Saudi Arabia—Vol. 1."

63. Walt Rostow to LBJ, June 20 and 22, 1966, LBJL, NSF:CO, Box 155, "Saudi Arabia—Faisal Trip." On the proposed Islamic Pact, see John L. Esposito, *The Islamic Threat: Myth or Reality* (New York, 1992), p. 74.

64. Nadav Safran, *Saudi Arabia: The Ceaseless Quest for Security* (Cambridge, MA, 1985), pp. 119, 121–122, 198, 200–201.

65. Lyndon B. Johnson, *The Vantage Point: Perspectives of the Presidency, 1963–1969* (New York, 1971), p. 288.

66. CIA, "Syria's Radical Future," Oct. 10, 1966, LBJL, NSF:CO, Box 156, "Syria—Vol. 1"; Rostow to LBJ, Nov. 8, 1966, and LBJ to J. William Fulbright, draft letter, Nov. 8, 1966, *DDRS, 1991*, item 152.

67. Johnson, *The Vantage Point*, p. 279.

68. Rostow to LBJ, Feb. 14, 1967, LBJL, NSF:CO, Box 160, "UAR—vol. 5."

69. On Nasser and the PLO, see Benjamin Read to McGeorge Bundy, June 5, 1965, "Countries: UAR," Box 159, NSF, LBJL. On Nasser and Vietnam, see Mohammed Heikal, *The Cairo Documents* (Garden City, NY, 1972), pp. 307–312.

70. Barbour to Rusk, tel. Feb. 1, 1967; State Department Background Paper, "U.S.-Israel Relations," Feb. 8, 1967, LBJL, NSF:CO, Box 140, "Israel—Vol. 6"; Harold Saunders, "Terrorist Origins of the Present Crisis," n.d. (mid-June 1967), LBJL, NSF: NSC History File, Box 17, "Middle East Crisis—Vol. 1."

71. On Nasser's reaction to the Syrian-Israeli dogfight, see Donald Neff,

Warriors for Jerusalem: The Six Days that Changed the Middle East (New York, 1984), pp. 57–58, and Spiegel, *Other Arab-Israeli Conflict*, pp. 136–137.

72. For first-hand assessments of the significance of the Soviet warning, see Mohammed Heikal, *Sphinx and Commissar: The Rise and Fall of Soviet Influence in the Arab World* (London, 1978), pp. 174–175, and Abba Eban, *Personal Witness: Israel Through My Eyes* (New York, 1992), pp. 353–354. For scholarly assessments of Moscow's motives and the fallout in Cairo, see L. Carl Brown, "Nasser and the June 1967 War: Plan or Improvisation?" in S. Seikaly, R. Baalbaki, and P. Dodd, editors, *Quest for Understanding: Arabic and Islamic Studies in Memory of Malcolm H. Kerr* (Beirut, 1991), pp. 119–123, and Richard Parker, "The June 1967 War: Some Mysteries Explored," *Middle East Journal*, 46 (Spring 1992): 178–184.

73. Harold Saunders, "The President's Stake in the Middle East," May 16, 1967, LBJL, NSF: Name File, Box 7, "Saunders Memos."

74. Ibid.

75. Saunders, "Terrorist Origins of the Present Crisis," n.d. (mid-June 1967), LBJL, NSF: NSC History Files, Box 17, "Middle East Crisis—Vol. 1"; Rostow to LBJ, May 17, (two memos) and LBJ to Eshkol, May 18, 1967, LBJL, NSF: Memos to the President File, Box 16, "Rostow—Vol. 28."

76. Barbour to Rusk, tel. May 18, 1967, quoted in Neff, *Warriors for Jerusalem*, p. 172; Rostow memcon, May 19, 1967, LBJL, NSF: Rostow Files, Box 1, "Meetings with the President Jan/June 1967"; LBJ to Kosygin, n.d., enclosed in Rusk to AmEmbassy Moscow, tel. 19 May 1967, LBJL, NSF: NSC History Files, Box 17, "Middle East Crisis—Vol. 1"; LBJ to Eshkol, May 21, 1967, LBJL, NSF: Memos to the President File, Box 16, "Rostow—Vol. 22."

77. Johnson, *Vantage Point*, p. 290; LBJ to Nasser, May 22, 1967, LBJL, NSF: Memos to the President File, Box 16, "Rostow—Vol. 22."

78. Johnson, *Vantage Point*, pp. 290–293. On the influx of pro–Israel letters and telegrams, see Rostow to Marvin Watson, May 24, 1967; Rostow memo, June 5, 1967; and Wilbur Jenkins to William Hopkins, June 15, 1967, all in LBJL, NSF: NSC History Files, Box 19, "Middle East Crisis—Vol. 6."

79. LBJ statement, May 23, 1967, *Public Papers of the Presidents, Lyndon B. Johnson 1967*, 1: 561–563; "Israeli Aid Package," n.d., attached to Saunders to Lois, May 23, 1967, LBJL, NSF:CO, Box 145, "Israel—Aid."

80. Rostow to LBJ, May 23, 1967, and State Department, "Future of South Arabia," n.d. (mid-May 1967), LBJL, Meeting Notes File, Box 1, "Briefing Papers NSC Meeting."

81. Minutes of the NSC Meeting, May 24, 1967, LBJL, NSF: NSC Meetings File, Box 2.

82. Rusk to LBJ, May 26, 1967, LBJL, NSF:CO, Box 143, "Israel—Vol. 12"; State Department Historical Office, "US Policy and Diplomacy in the Middle East Crisis, May 15-June 10, 1967," Jan. 10, 1969, LBJL, NSF: NSC History Files, Box 20, "Middle East Crisis—Vol. 9"; Eugene Rostow Oral History, LBJL, pp. 17–18.

83. Nathaniel Davis (USUN) to Rostow, May 27, 1967, LBJL, NSF: NSC His-

tory Files, Box 20, "Middle East Crisis—Vol. 8"; Rusk to Gromyko, May 29, 1967, enclosed in Rostow to LBJ, May 29, 1969, LBJL, NSF: Memos to the President File, Box 16, "Rostow—Vol. 29."

84. Anderson to LBJ, tel. June 2, 1967, LBJL, NSF: NSC History Files, Box 18, "Middle East Crisis—Vol. 3."

85. William Quandt, "Lyndon Johnson and the June 1967 War: What Color Was the Light?," *Middle East Journal*, 46 (Spring 1992): 216–222. Fortas is quoted on p. 221.

86. Rusk to Gromyko, tel. June 5, 1967, Dean Rusk Papers, Lot File 72D 192, Box 927, U.S. Department of State.

87. Saunders, "Minutes of the NSC Special Committee Meeting," June 8, 1967, and Bundy to Tom Johnson, June 9, 1967, LBJL, NSF: NSC History Files, Box 19, "Middle East Crisis—Vol. 7." For more on the Special Committee, see John Prados, *Keepers of the Keys: A History of the National Security Council from Truman to Bush* (New York, 1991), pp. 180–183.

88. Neff, *Warriors for Jerusalem*, pp. 246–263; James Ennes, *Assault on the Liberty* (New York, 1979), passim; and Carl Marcy to Bourke Hickenlooper, Aug. and 25, 1967, Foreign Relations Committee Files: Countries, Box 152, "Near East," Bourke Hickenlooper Papers, Herbert Hoover Presidential Library, West Branch, Iowa.

89. Saunders, "Minutes of the NSC Special Committee," June 9, 1967, LBJL, NSF: NSC History Files, Box 19, "Middle East Crisis—Vol. 7."

90. CIA, "Arab-Israeli Situation Report," June 9, 1967, LBJL, NSF: NSC History Files, Box 21, "Middle East Crisis—Vol. 11."

91. Dean Rusk, *As I Saw It* (New York, 1990), p. 386.

92. Saunders, "Hot Line Meeting June 10, 1967," Oct. 22, 1968, LBJL, NSF: NSC History Files, Box 19, "Middle East Crisis—Vol. 7."

93. Daniel Yergin, *The Prize: The Epic Quest for Oil, Money & Power* (New York, 1991), p. 555–557; State Department Activities Report, June 6, 1967, LBJL, President's Appointments File, Box 66, "Diary Backup, May-June 1967"; CIA, "Arab-Israeli Situation Reports, June 11, 12 and 13, 1967, LBJL, NSF: NSC History Files, Box 21, "Middle East Crisis—Vol. 11."

94. CIA, "Arab-Israeli Situation Reports," June 18 and July 3, 1967, LBJL, NSF: NSC History Files, Box 21, "Middle East Crisis—Vol. 11"; Yergin, *The Prize*, p. 558.

95. Bundy to LBJ, June 9, 1967, LBJL, NSF: NSC History Files, Box 21, "Middle East Crisis—Vol. 7."

96. Rostow to LBJ, June 14, 1967, LBJL, NSF: Memos to the President File, Box 17, "Rostow—Vol. 31."

97. Saunders to Walt Rostow, Aug. 11, 1967, and DOS to Eilts (Riyadh), tel. Aug. 11, 1967, LBJL, NSF:CO, Box 155, "Saudi Arabia—Vol. 2."

98. Meyer to DOS, tel. Dec. 7, 1967, LBJL, NSF:CO, Box 136, "Iran—Vol. 2."

99. "NSC Paper on the United Kingdom," n.d. (probably March 1968), *DDRS 1990*, item 319.

100. Rusk to Eilts, tel. Jan. 12, 1968, LBJL, NSF:CO, Box 155, "Saudi Arabia—

Vol. 2"; Rostow to LBJ, Jan. 16, 1968, LBJL, NSF: Name File, Box 7, "Rostow Memos."

101. Rusk to LBJ, "Release of Arms for Saudi Arabia," Jan. 19, 1968, LBJL, NSF:CO, Box 155, "Saudi Arabia—Vol. 2"; Meyer to Rusk, tel. Feb. 9, 1968, and Eugene Rostow to Meyer, tel. March 8, 1968, LBJL, NSF:CO, Box 136, "Iran—Vol. 2."

102. CIA, "Israeli Objectives in the Current Crisis," June 6, 1967, LBJL, NSF:CO, Box 116, "Middle East Crisis—Vol. 4"; Barbour to Rusk, tel. June 13, 1967, LBJL, NSF: NSC History Files, Box 18, "Middle East Crisis—Vol. 5."

103. Rusk and Eban are quoted in Thomas J. Schoenbaum, *Waging Peace and War: Dean Rusk in the Truman, Kennedy, and Johnson Years* (New York, 1988), p. 463. Schoenbaum based his account on extensive interviews with Dean Rusk.

104. Saunders, "Minutes of the NSC Special Committee," June 13 and 14, 1967, LBJL, NSF: NSC History Files, Box 19, "Middle East Crisis—Vol. 7."

105. State Department memcons, June 23 and 25, 1967, LBJL, NSF:CO, Addendum, "USSR (Glassboro Memcons)."

106. On Resolution 242, see Gideon Gera, "Israel and the June 1967 War: 25 Years Later," *Middle East Journal*, (Spring 1992): 233–235.

107. Saunders to Rostow, Dec. 29, 1967, LBJL, NSF:CO, Box 144, "Israel—Eshkol Visit 1968."

108. Rostow to LBJ, "The Issues for Eshkol," Jan. 5, 1968; Rostow to LBJ, "Talking Points for Prime Minister Eshkol," Jan. 5, 1968; and "Notes of Johnson-Eshkol Meeting," Jan. 7–8, 1968, all in LBJL, NSF:CO, Box 144, "Israel—Eshkol Visit 1968."

109. Rusk to Meyer, June 12, 1968, LBJL, NSF:CO, Box 136, "Iran—Vol. 2"; State Department cirtel, June 18, 1968, and "Briefing Paper," n.d., attached to Read to Rostow, June 22, 1968, LBJL, NSF:CO, Box 155, "Saudi Arabia—Vol. 2."

110. CIA, "The Arab Nationalists Movement," Jan. 19, 1968, LBJL, NSF:CO, Box 160, "UAR—Vol. 6."

111. Minutes of the NSC Meeting, Feb. 26, 1968, LBJL, NSF: NSC Meetings File, Box 2.

112. Donald Bergus (Cairo) to Rusk, tel. June 15, 1968, LBJL, NSF:CO, Box 160, "UAR—Vol. 6."

113. For a discussion of the July Ba'athist coup in Baghdad, see Marion Farouk-Sluglett and Peter Sluglett, *Iraq Since 1958: From Revolution to Dictatorship* (London, 1987), pp. 107–126.

114. John W. Foster to Rostow, "The Situation in Syria," Oct. 28, 1968, LBJL, NSF:CO, Box 156, "Syria—Vol. 1."

115. Harrison Symmes Oral History, Lauinger Library, Georgetown University, Washington, DC.

116. Minutes of the NSC Meeting, Feb. 26, 1968, LBJL, NSF: NSC Meetings File, Box 2.

117. Saunders memcon, June 17, 1968, LBJL, NSF:CO, Box 142, "Israel—Vol. 10."

118. Rusk to Parker Hart, tel. Sept. 19, 1968, LBJL, NSF:CO, Box 142, "Israel—Vol. 10."

119. John Rielly to Hubert Humphrey, May 10, 1968, Vice Presidential Files: Coded Files, Box 960, "Miscellaneous Countries—Israel 1968," Hubert H. Humphrey Papers, Minnesota Historical Society, St. Paul, Minnesota; Hersh, *Samson Option*, pp. 188–190; Spiegel, *Other Arab-Israeli Conflict*, pp. 161–163; Rostow to LBJ, Oct. 8, 1968, LBJL, NSF:CO, Box 142, "Israel—Vol. 10."

120. Paul Warnke, "Negotiations with Israel: F-4 & Advanced Weapons," Nov. 4, 1968, and Warnke to Rabin, Nov. 25, 1968, LBJL, NSF:CO, Box 142, "Israel—Vol. 10"; Warnke to author, Sept. 12, 1989.

SUGGESTED READINGS

Bill, James A. *The Eagle and the Lion: The Tragedy of American-Iranian Relations* New Haven, 1988.

Burns, William J. *Economic Aid and American Policy Toward Egypt 1955–1981* Albany, 1985.

Gazit, Mordechai. *President Kennedy's Policies Toward the Arab States and Israel* Tel Aviv, 1983.

Neff, Donald. *Warriors for Jerusalem* New York, 1984.

Safran, Nadav. *Saudi Arabia: The Ceaseless Quest for Security* Cambridge, 1985.

Schoenbaum, David. *The United States and the State of Israel* Oxford, 1993.

Spiegel, Steven. *The Other Arab-Israeli Conflict* Chicago, 1985.

Yergin, Daniel. *The Prize* New York, 1991.

10

The Black Revolt: The United States and Africa in the 1960s

•

GERALD E. THOMAS

The 1960s offered the United States an unprecedented opportunity to change its previously indifferent approach to the problems of black Africa—a challenge the Kennedy and Johnson administrations did not shirk. This chapter will examine the general U.S. foreign policy towards Africa during the 1960s and will follow the conduct of American policy toward specific high interest countries during that period. The American domestic racial situation will also be addressed since these events were part of the transatlantic black revolt of the 1960s. The two major segments of the black revolt—in Africa and in the U.S.— strengthened each other with pride and political support during that decade. They also demonstrated the difficulty that the U.S. government had in dealing directly and effectively with black rights and concerns, whether in America or in Africa.

The era seemed to offer to blacks—both in Africa and the United States—hope of finally gaining political freedom and economic opportunity after centuries of white oppression. In Africa this process began dramatically in 1957 with the independence of Ghana. It accelerated at the beginning of the 1960s when, in September and October of the year 1960 alone, seventeen new black African nations gained their freedom. With the glaring exception of southern Africa, many more former black African colonies gained their independence in the 1960s.[1] In the Belgian Congo, unrest and political violence in 1959–60 frightened the Belgians, many of whom had thought that they would stay as de facto rulers of the Congo indefinitely. However, shocked by the crisis of 1959, they soon abandoned the Congo.[2] By 1960, the French government had also loosened the bonds of colonialism even as it attracted most of the former French colonies into a newly formed French Union of Africa with strong economic and military ties to France. The British move toward decolonization was dramatized when British Prime Minister Harold Macmillan told the South African parliament that, "The winds of change are blowing through this continent."[3]

Among blacks in America a new, quietly defiant attitude had appeared even before 1960, partially triggered by empathy with and pride in the accelerating black African struggle for freedom. It was dramatized when, on December 1, 1955, a quiet, ladylike black seamstress, Rosa Parks, was arrested in Montgomery, Alabama for refusing to move to the back of a bus as local custom required. The arrest of Mrs. Parks, a college graduate and church worker, inflamed the blacks of Montgomery and led to a black boycott of Montgomery city buses. This boycott was organized by the Montgomery Improvement Association, led by the Reverend Martin Luther King, who based his struggle on the nonviolent principles of Gandhi and of Christianity. In a dramatic victory in December 1956, the Supreme Court declared Alabama's state and local segregation laws to be unconstitutional. King went on to lead the Southern Christian Leadership conference, based in Atlanta, which he dedicated to fighting for civil rights by peaceful means.[4]

The year 1960 marked a major expansion of the so-called "Negro Revolt" in America when, on February 1, 1960 four students from the black Agricultural and Technical College in Greensboro, North Carolina, began the "sit-in" movement. The sit-ins were reinforced by organizations like the interracial Congress of Racial Equality (CORE), which had been founded in 1942 and had conducted earlier Freedom Rides to test segregation laws. The sit-in movement, although joined by CORE, the NAACP, and the Urban League, and other organizations, remained primarily a student movement and also led to the formation of the Student Non-Violent Coordinating Committee (SNICK) in Atlanta. The sit-ins galvanized a newly militant combination of blacks and liberal white supporters, who were determined to destroy the system of American segregation once and for all. Starting in 1964, CORE instituted the Freedom Ride movement, which challenged travel segregation throughout the South. By the mid- 1960s, blacks found themselves able to eat and travel throughout the South in relative safety.[5]

On April 3, 1963, against the implied plea by the ever cautious (on racial matters) President Kennedy that blacks should not have to "take to the streets" to gain their rights, King led anti-segregation demonstrations in Birmingham, Alabama, one of the bastions of Southern segregation and oppression. During the months of May and June 1963, there were demonstrations in many cities around the United States. These were instrumental in hastening Kennedy's submission of a civil rights program to Congress. They ultimately led to the March on Washington on August 28, 1963, when King gave his famous "I have a dream" speech to the assembled crowd at the Lincoln Memorial. Supporters included a vast array of prominent persons, including union leaders, major Christian church groups, the American Jewish Congress, and many others. In spite of such support, Kennedy's Civil Rights program and the accompanying ratification by Congress of the Twenty-Fourth Amendment outlawing the poll tax were not accomplished until the summer of 1964, even with the strong support of President Lyndon Johnson. The Civil Rights Act forbade discrimination in most places of public accommodation, protected voting, education, and the use of public facilities, and established a federal Equal Employment Opportunity Commission. In addition it extended the term of the Commission on Civil Rights to January 1968.[6]

The notorious "white backlash" which followed the passage of the 1964 Civil Rights Act underscored the resistance of white America as a whole to the basic idea of true equality for blacks. During 1965 there were continuing black protest demonstrations, including the bloody, yet effective march from Selma to Montgomery, Alabama, by white and black marchers, led by Martin Luther King. The 1965 Voting Rights Act suspended literacy tests and other such devices which had prevented blacks from voting in the South. It further established the use of federal examiners to ensure compliance.with the law.[7]

The 1960s saw new mutual support between black Africans and American blacks in many areas of activity. The empathy and pride each felt for the trials and valor of the other seemed to feed back and fuel their simultaneous freedom struggles. Black Americans, ranging from the Black Muslims and Malcolm X to Dr. King, attempted to support the aspirations of Africans insofar as they were able. This interaction was dramatized during Malcolm's several trips to Africa, which demonstrated the pride Africans took in the progress of black Americans and the reciprocal pride black Americans took in African history and progress. The Black Muslim movement, which first blossomed in the early 1930s, and burgeoned after World War II, offered to blacks a new, proudly defiant organization dedicated to the attainment of full civil rights. Other militant organizations arose, including the Black Panther Party, which was founded in Oakland, California in 1966. These new groups seemed to threaten the white power structure with slogans like "black power" and by blacks' increased willingness to risk confrontations with the police and authorities.[8] Black American support for Africa at times embarrassed Kennedy, especially when his African policies were assailed by black leaders. For example, Martin Luther King criticized Kennedy before the American Negro Leadership Conference on Africa, and was barely dissuaded by members of the administration from publicly attacking Kennedy's relations with South Africa before the U.N.[9]

Black-led organizations like the NAACP joined with white liberal organizations, including the AFL-CIO, the American Committee on Africa, and with dignitaries including Eleanor Roosevelt, the Reverend James Pike, and the historian Arnold Toynbee, to criticize U.S. support of the ruling whites in South Africa and elsewhere on the continent. Such pressures, combined with black American demands for increased U.S. sensitivity to the needs and aspirations of black Africans, were strengthened by the U.S. fear that even the perception of American support for continued white rule over black Africa might weaken America's own position in black Africa. This was critical in view of the supposedly always lurking specter of Soviet Cold War competition. These combined pressures helped to foster the limited change in the previous U.S. "hands off" attitude toward African affairs. Vice President Richard Nixon's trip to Ghana in March 1957 offers an example of this improved American attitude. In a speech, Nixon called for America to support decolonization and to offer economic aid to new black African nations. Nixon said that racial discrimination in America was interfering with U.S. diplomacy in Africa. With Nixon's backing, a separate African Bureau was established in the State Department.[10]

Other organizations of black Americans also attempted to influence U.S. policy toward Africa. In 1962, the American Negro Leadership conference (ANLCA) was organized by more than one hundred prominent black leaders, including dignitaries like Martin Luther King, A. Philip Randolph, head of the Brotherhood of Sleeping Car Porters, and Whitney Young of the Urban League. In 1964 this group asked President Lyndon Johnson to take a stand against apartheid in South Africa and to take measures against the apartheid government, including the prohibition of further U.S. investments there and endorsing a UN oil embargo against South Africa. Johnson paid little attention to the pleading of the group, and after a failed attempt by the ANLCA to mediate in the Nigerian civil war, it drifted out of existence.[11]

The new American involvement in Africa was dramatically underscored when postindependence violence erupted in the Congo in 1959. The Belgians, seeing the handwriting of black independence on the wall, precipitously abandoned the Belgian Congo in 1960, taking with them virtually all of their supporting personnel and their technical and

administrative structure. They had made virtually no attempt to educate, train, and prepare the people of the Congo for independence. In
addressing the resulting armed chaos in the Congo, the Eisenhower
administration evolved a foreign policy toward the Congo, later
applied to other emerging black African states, which Henry F. Jackson
has referred to as "the Congo Syndrome." The United States would not
"allow" the new nations the option of remaining neutral in the Cold
War. Rather, they were seen being either friends of the United States in
its struggle against Russia and Communism, or they were considered
to be virtual "enemies."[12]

In practice this resulted in the U.S. backing, or at least tolerating, a
series of often unsavory "strong men." America attempted to tie these
leaders to American policy through bilateral treaties and agreements,
which in theory would ensure new allies in its Cold War contest. While
Jackson's "Congo Syndrome" theory cannot be applied precisely, or
proved in many African cases, it has remained valid in the Congo, now
Zaire. There, Mobutu Sese Seko, still in power and still corrupt, has
shown that, at least in his case, mutual agreements with the U.S. have
worked more to Mobutu's advantage than to the long-term advantage
and reputation of the United States or the Congo.[13]

By the time he left office in 1961, President Dwight D. Eisenhower
was looked upon by most blacks with well-founded suspicion. Eisenhower had a conservative, generally negative attitude toward the
rights of black Americans, which had been underscored by his opposition to integrating the U.S. armed forces during and following World
War II. This mindset carried over into his attitudes toward black
Africans. He thus naturally considered that the Africans' demands for
self-rule and freedom were excessive. Throughout most of his presidency, the negative effects of his attitude were exacerbated by the
Manichean approach of his pious, Calvinistic, first Secretary of State,
John Foster Dulles. Dulles's Cold War fears intensified his myopic
world view, and made him adamant that no Third World nation had
the right to chose the path of neutrality between the East and the West
in the Cold War. To Dulles, such nations were either committed friends
and client states, or they were considered to be in the enemy camp.[14]
Eisenhower's image was not helped by the fact that he was extremely
uncomfortable conversing or dealing with blacks, including black
African leaders and diplomats. Especially during his first term Eisenhower, Dulles, and most of their foreign policy team were openly sympathetic with the white regimes. They feared the black surge for freedom, and Eisenhower went so far as to call it "a torrent overturning
everything in its path" in his memoirs.[15]

Thus, the election of John F. Kennedy as President of the United States brought a surge of hope both to black Americans and to Africans. His reputation was based on a series of well-publicized actions by then Senator Kennedy in the late 1950s and early 1960s. As early as July 1957, Kennedy criticized the Eisenhower regime's attempts to remain friendly with both the European powers and their former colonies, and he faulted Eisenhower's failure to back global self-determination. Kennedy called for U.S. backing for international efforts to recognize Algerian independence from France. He had been appointed to head the new subcommittee on Africa which was established by the Senate Foreign Relations Committee. Few noted at the time that Kennedy allowed his work on the subcommittee to languish because of lack of personal interest and support. From 1957 through the 1960 election campaign Kennedy kept up a barrage of criticism against the neglect of black Africa by Eisenhower and Nixon. Yet Kennedy knew that his own record of supporting black causes in the Congress was decidedly weak. He thus made it a point during the 1960 presidential campaign to refer to Africa 479 times in speeches made during three months of campaigning. As a result of Kennedy's positive and relatively liberal image, he gained the support of the great majority of American blacks, whose support made the key difference in a number of key states to bring about Kennedy's 1960 presidential victory.[16]

To the satisfaction of both black Americans and Africans, Kennedy appeared to make an unalterable commitment toward self-determination and majority rule in Africa when he appointed several prominent liberals to head key international and African-oriented posts in the U.S. Department of State. He appointed Chester Bowles as Under Secretary of State and former Governor of Michigan, G. Mennen "Soapy" Williams to be Assistant Secretary of State for African Affairs. He also appointed Adlai Stevenson as U.S. Ambassador to the United Nations. It appeared to blacks that these appointments offered hope for a more equitable U.S. foreign policy toward black Africa. Kennedy also appointed ambassadors, some of them black, to the emerging black nations. Additionally, he appointed many more blacks to high positions in the federal government than had any of his predecessors.[17] Further, Kennedy's naturally friendly and gracious style helped him immensely in dealing with visiting African leaders. The fact that, unlike Eisenhower, he was willing to sit down and meet with blacks as equals made a positive impression on African leaders.

Kennedy's sending of thousands of volunteers from his new Peace Corps to African nations to aid them in country-building helped enhance his reputation with Africans. For example, he sent hundreds of Peace Corps volunteer secondary school teachers to Ethiopia. In a very effective public relations move, Kennedy put the Peace Corps itself under the leadership of his brother-in-law, Sargent Shriver.[18]

The group started in 1961 with five hundred volunteer teachers and advisers in eight nations. By 1963 there were seven thousand Peace Corps workers in forty-four nations. By 1966 there were more than 15,000 Peace Corps volunteers overseas. There were some growing pains for the Peace Corps, including some poorly prepared or psychologically unsuitable individuals. Additionally, there were at times Communist accusations—untrue then and now—that the Peace Corps was CIA connected. Overall, however, there is no doubt that the Peace Corps improved America's image in the Third World and Africa.

On most issues concerning Africa, however, as time progressed Kennedy paid less heed to the views of liberals. As was often his style, he had been somewhat disingenuous in his appointments of obvious liberals to high positions. The political reality was that Kennedy had not given them any key cabinet positions or truly powerful jobs such as Secretary of State. Even though Adlai Stevenson was the American UN ambassador, Kennedy somewhat downplayed that UN post while Stevenson occupied it.[19]

The advisers upon whom Kennedy ultimately relied, and thus the most powerful players in the administration's foreign policy team, were those whom he considered to be "tough thinkers." Most of them had a Europe-centered and Cold War dominated view of the world. These "Europeanists," or "realists," included George Ball, who soon replaced Bowles as Under Secretary of State for Economic Affairs, former Secretary of State Dean Acheson, Secretary of Defense Robert McNamara, MIT professor Walt Rostow, Presidential adviser McGeorge Bundy, and Chairman of the Joint Chiefs of Staff General Maxwell Taylor. Most of these men had little interest in Africa.[20]

Although the two opposing camps of "Africanists" versus Europe-oriented "realists" made many of the Kennedy administration's decisions on African policy seem to be tests of strength, in reality, the "Africanists" never had a chance. Kennedy distrusted those he considered to be "soft" thinkers as much as he did the cautious career diplomats in the State Department. Additionally, he was deeply involved in non-African crises, including the Bay of Pigs, the Berlin confrontation, and the Cuban missile crisis. Thus, within two years, the "Africanists" had been effectively upstaged by the "realists" on most issues concerning Africa.[21]

Upon taking office, Lyndon Johnson followed Kennedy's policies toward Africa to a large extent. Like Kennedy, Johnson appointed many blacks to high positions. While he kept most of Kennedy's Africa team, both liberal and conservative, he became rapidly enmeshed in the Vietnam morass, in addressing America's own problems, and facing emerging European and Middle East crises, like the 1967 Arab-Israeli War. Thus, his personal attention to Africa, never strong, weakened progressively during his tenure as President. For example, by the end of his first year as president, John F. Kennedy had more than doubled American financial aid to Africa over that of the Eisenhower administration, to a total of almost $500 million. This included loans and guarantees, "food for peace" shipments, and Import-Export bank financing guarantees.

In contrast, Johnson, stung by Africans' criticism of U.S. policies in the Congo and of the American voting record in the UN, lowered U.S. aid to African nations (calculated as a percentage of American GNP).[22] Also, as with the Kennedy administration, conservative voices, buttressed by bureaucrats in the State and Defense departments, argued against the "risk" of helping black Africans gain their freedom and instead opted for cooperation with the ruling whites.[23] However, Johnson's attitude toward Africa, even when distracted, was vastly more favorable than that of his successor, Richard Nixon. When he entered the presidency, Nixon soon replaced Johnson's group with his own conservative team, the most important of whom was the Europeanist, Henry Kissinger. Kissinger's attraction to powerful (Western) nations, and his negative, almost supercilious posture toward black Africans and the new (weak) black African states boded ill for Africa's future. Under Nixon and Kissinger, many negative U.S. policy assumptions and attitudes toward black Africa soon reemerged, which closely resembled those of the early Eisenhower administration.

With the preceding overview in mind, and to gain further insight into the conduct of U.S. foreign policy toward Africa in the 1960s, we will examine American dealings with selected nations with which American policy was most involved, or which were considered to be of greatest importance to U.S. interests at that time. There were, of course, many nations, especially the smaller ones, which were never in the line of significant U.S. foreign policy interest. Further, it must be remembered that black Africa never occupied center stage in American diplomacy, especially after the formation of NATO, and the onset of the Cold War.[24]

These nations can be divided into three groups. First, those that had been independent throughout the colonial period, and that had longstanding diplomatic ties to the United States. Second, newly independent states with no history of diplomatic relations to the United States and where U.S. foreign policy was being worked out for the first time. Third, white-dominated states that resisted African demands for freedom and majority rule.

Previously Independent States

Liberia

The United States played a vital role in the birth of Liberia, which was founded in the early 1820s by agents of the American Colonization Society, primarily as a haven for freed American slaves. Since Liberia's earliest days, the relations of the United States with that small nation have been at times intimate, yet often "unofficial." The United States government, fitfully, and not always to the advantage of the Liberians, acted as a distant "big brother." However, the U.S. at least supported the continued independence of Liberia. This unofficial protection continued even through financial scandals in the nineteenth and early twentieth centuries. It survived scandals in the late 1920s and early 1930s involving alleged slave trading in indigenous Africans by the ruling descendants of the original American slave-immigrants.[25] At that time, the Americo-Liberian ruling oligarchy, pampered, greedy and averse to laboring on their own behalf, had found ways to sell the labor, and with it the virtual freedom, of indigenous blacks to outside interests and nations, such as the Spanish cocoa growers on the pest-hole island of Fernando Po. Only after international investigations and pressures in the early 1930s did the ruling Americo-Liberian ruling class address itself to shutting down this trade.[26]

U.S. relations with Liberia, in addition to the historic connection, were both economic and strategic. In 1926, the Firestone Rubber Company entered into an agreement with the corrupt and always cash-starved Liberian government to lease up to a million acres of land for 99 years at the ridiculously low price of 6 cents per acre. This was accompanied by Liberian "assurance" of an available labor force to work in the projected Firestone rubber plantations. The terms of the agreement would prove to be hugely profitable and beneficial to Firestone and the United States. Although many Liberians did obtain jobs with Firestone, these were usually low-paying, dead-end jobs, working under grueling conditions. While the Firestone agreement did build up the country in many ways, and did at least offer low wage employment to many Liberians, the agreement benefitted mainly the Liberian ruling class. The dominance of white American employees lasted well into the 1970s.[27]

During the Second World War, Liberia's iron and rubber resources, and its air and harbor facilities, made it almost indispensable to the U.S. war effort in Africa. In 1941 Pan American Airways received the right to operate in Liberia and, with the help of Firestone, Roberts Field was made into one of the finest airfields in the world. Liberia, although technically "neutral" until 1944, as early as 1942 allowed the United States to construct bases and also allowed American troops to enter the country. An agreement was made between the two governments that the U.S. would build a new port in Monrovia to handle the shipping of war goods and raw materials through the port. After signing a lend-lease agreement with the U.S. in 1943, Liberia finally declared war in January, 1944.[28] By the middle 1960s, Liberia was enjoying mild prosperity, due mainly to the income from rubber and iron ore production. Another source of national wealth was the practice of American and other national shipping companies using the Liberian flag as a "flag of convenience" to register their ships. This practice allowed non-Liberian companies and ships to circumvent international safety regulations, to pay lower salaries to their crews, and to save on such items as maintenance, safety standards, and fees. By 1965 ships under Liberian "flags of convenience" had higher total deadweight tonnage than the combined U.S. and British merchant fleets. As late as 1986, a third of the Liberian commercial fleet consisted of American-owned tankers and bulk carriers and at least 75 percent of American ships flew the Liberian flag.[29]

In 1944, on first gaining office, President William Tubman had announced an "open door" policy which encouraged foreign investment in Liberia. At that time Firestone was the only significant foreign company in Liberia. Tubman's Open Door policy worked so well that, by the early 1960s, there were 25 large foreign companies operating in Liberia, primarily in mining and agricultural production. On the negative side, however, as had long been the custom in Liberia, most of the profits went to the tiny Americo-Liberian oligarchy. In the 1950s Liberia's economy expanded at a rate faster than most countries in the world. The gross domestic product multiplied, and there was a huge increase in government receipts. However, this growth has since been termed "growth without development." The great expansion in exports and trade, mostly in primary commodities, resulted in little structural change to foster complementary economic growth. Worse, it did little to force the institutional change which was necessary to permit the distribution of wealth throughout the nation.[30]

Following World War II Liberia and the United States maintained their close cooperation. After the war, the U.S. continued to be Liberia's chief trading partner. In addition to the military agreements signed in 1951 and 1959, Liberia permitted the United States to install a large Voice of America facility in the country. On July 8, 1959, an agreement of cooperation was signed in Washington, D.C. between Liberia and the United States, which pledged the U.S. to continue to assist in the promotion of Liberia's economic development and in the preservation of Liberia's independence and integrity. It further stated that in the event of aggression or its threat the two governments would immediately determine what action might be appropriate for the defense of Liberia.[31]

In the 1960s Tubman was well aware that Liberia and Liberians were by no means admired or even fully accepted by many Africans and thus tried to be more active in supporting other new African nations. For example, in 1960, together with Ethiopia, Liberia was co-sponsor of a suit, ultimately unsuccessful, brought before the International Court of Justice at the Hague to declare the continued South African occupation of Namibia illegal.

By 1960 the U.S. had provided Liberia with more than $50 million in aid. This included support for road building, schools, communications, and for health and other public facilities. American foreign aid in the year 1962 alone granted funds that were equal to one-third of the Liberian government revenue for that year. Liberia received an estimated $60 million from 1963 to 1968. In addition, during the period 1962–63 alone, there were approximately 350 foreigners in Liberia, including the Peace Corps and others working on social and economic programs.[32]

At times in the 1960s President Tubman had been embarrassed by strikes and demonstrations by the poorly paid and often mistreated workers in mines and agricultural plantations, and by protests by students at the University of Liberia. He managed to conciliate plantation workers who marched on his mansion in 1961, but he dealt strictly with several attempted military coups during the 1960s. Politically, President Tubman had opened up his government to indigenous Liberians somewhat by his "unification" policy which was designed to bring more indigenous Liberians into the government and the political mainstream. However, in reality he virtually ruled Liberia through an interlocking, family-dominated political and business apparatus. He was "unopposed" for election in 1971 and he died peacefully in office the same year and was succeeded by President William Tolbert. At that time Liberia was one of the few African

nations not to have undergone a violent overthrow of its government—a record that was gruesomely overturned in April, 1980, when
Tolbert's government was overthrown by Liberian soldiers and he
was murdered.[33]

Ethiopia

Following its liberation from Italian control in 1941, Ethiopia fell under
the control of British military and police units and "advisers." Additionally, the British, after World War II, took control of British Somaliland, Italian Somaliland, Eritrea, and essentially the whole Horn of
Africa. Shortly after the British left Ethiopia in 1953, the United States
signed a mutual defense agreement with the government of Emperor
Haile Selassie. The most important element was a 25 year U.S. lease for
the former British World War II communications station at Kagnew,
near Asmara. The United States agreed to provide arms and military
training to Ethiopia, and an American Military Advisor Group
(MAAG) was attached to the Ministry of Defense to assist Ethiopia to
develop a self-defense capability and the capacity to aid in the defense
of the region if required. This not only improved Selassie's ability to
ensure stability and order within his own country, but also increased
his military capability vis-à-vis his neighbors.[34]

The communications station at Kagnew, which cost the U.S. $160
million, infused about $4 to $6 million annually into the Ethiopian
economy. By 1973 the U.S. had provided more than $210 million in mil-
itary assistance to Ethiopia and more than $277 million in economic
aid. Also, the United States made Ethiopia into a major trading partner.
This support was especially important to Ethiopia since warlike Somalia gained independence in 1960, and there was armed rebellion in
Eritrea from 1961 to 1962. Ethiopia was the main African recipient of
American and British aid between 1950 and 1982.[35] On the negative
side of the relationship, Ethiopia continued to resent any U.S. aid to
Ethiopia's rival, Somalia. For instance, even before the independence of
Somalia, late in January 1959, the Ethiopian government become angry
at U.S. support for a British proposal to unite British Somalia with former Italian Somalia. Haile Selassie, in protest, took that excuse to visit
the Soviet Union. His trip not only resulted in financial aid—the Soviets gave him 400 million rubles of credits—but also led to a countering
U.S. arms assistance agreement in 1960.[36] The generally positive U.S.-
Ethiopian relationship continued into the 1970s and was ended only by
the overthrow of Haile Selassie in 1974 by leftist army officers led by
Lieutenant Colonel Mengistu Haile Mariam. Soon after Mengistu's

takeover, Ethiopian foreign policy turned sharply away from the West, and became supported by and supportive of the Soviet bloc.[37]

Newly Independent States

The Congo

President John F. Kennedy inherited an immediate African political headache from the Eisenhower administration with the bloody crisis in the mineral-rich Belgian Congo. The Congo was to be the African nation that would command most of Kennedy's attention during his presidency.[38] It began to boil politically in 1957 when several new parties began clamoring for independence. One of the most effective groups, the National Congolese Movement (MNC) had as members several future Congolese leaders, including Cyrille Adoula and party president, Patrice Lumumba. In January 1958, apprehensive over growing black political agitation, the Belgian authorities prohibited speeches by Joseph Kasavubu and other leaders. This action angered the Congolese further. The ensuing rioting in Leopoldville on January 15, 1959 cost the lives of at least 52 Congolese and led to the imprisonment of Kasavubu and others. On July 13, 1959, the Belgian government announced a plan for allowing political change and calling for elections to municipal and provincial bodies for late 1959. While most Belgians thought the plan too generous, Africans rejected it as too little and too late. Factions multiplied, headed by men like Lumumba, Kasavubu, and Moise Tshombe. Elections, held in December 1959, were inconclusive, but led to a Round Table meeting in Belgium on January 20, 1960, which agreed that the Congo would be given independence in six months. On June 25, 1960, Belgium announced the independence of the Congo, with Kasavubu as the elected President of the Congo and Lumumba as his appointed Prime Minister. A few days later, on June 30, 1960, a revolt of the ill treated Congolese troops against their Belgian officers threw the country into civil war.

The first impact of the civil war was the increased pace of evacuation of remaining Belgian administrators, technicians, and other trained support personnel. Their departure left the Congo stripped of expertise in virtually every field at a time when it was most needed. The Belgians, apparently convinced before 1959 that they would remain in control of the Congo forever, had done little to prepare the huge country for independence. For example, there were just over a dozen Congolese college graduates at the time of independence. To ameliorate the chaos caused by the military revolt, Prime Minister Lumumba appointed one of his supporters, Colonel Joseph Mobutu, to replace the insensitive and stubborn Belgian General Emile Janssens, and he elevated many Congolese noncommissioned officers to officer status.

Almost immediately troubles increased when the mineral-rich province of Katanga attempted to secede as a separate state, under the leadership of the former provincial governor, Tshombe, who was backed by Belgian mining interests.[39] The situation worsened when the Belgians, ostensibly to protect some remaining Belgian nationals, sent troops back into the Congo. At this point Lumumba, fearing an attempt by the Belgians to reinstate their rule over the Congo asked the United Nations for help. Regrettably, the UN troops, none from the Great Powers, were forbidden by Secretary General Dag Hammarskjold to be involved in "internal squabbles" or from supporting "factions." This, in effect, elevated the rebels to equal status, if only as a faction, and it tied the hands of UN troops. The Secretary General's order therefore actually accelerated the process of dissolution. Lumumba then turned to the Soviet Union for support. Soviet Premier Nikita Khrushchev not only gave Lumumba diplomatic support in the UN and sent military supplies, but he also offered "volunteer" troops. To make matters worse, Kasavubu and Lumumba started feuding, and within two months each was trying to remove the other from his post.

To terminate the increasingly confused and incendiary situation, and the continued feuding between Lumumba and President Kasavubu, Mobutu suspended all political activity. He subsequently, in effect, ruled the Congo from September 1960 until February 1961. Parliament was not convened until August, 1961. However, Mobutu did not regain control of the northeast region of the Congo, and Antoine Gizenga, a protégé of Prime Minister Lumumba, installed what he called the only legitimate government at Stanleyville (now Kisangani). Following his arrest by Leopoldville authorities, Lumumba had been living in Leopoldville under the protection of the UN. However, after an unsuccessful attempt to join his supporters in Stanleyville, he was captured by Mobutu's forces and delivered to his enemies in Katanga, who murdered him in mid-January. Whether, as many thought, his murder had been arranged by the CIA in conjunction with Tshombe and his Belgian backers or not, the American agency received the blame from Africans and the Third World.[40] Khrushchev ranted against the West in the United Nations and gave his support to Gizenga. It appeared that events in the Congo reinforced the leftist convictions of some African nations, including Ghana and Guinea, which were already moving into the Marxist orbit.[41]

Following the death of Lumumba, rather than backing Tshombe, who had been the favorite of many in the Eisenhower administration and of many European and Belgian interests, the U.S. backed, at first, the reticent black labor leader Cyrille Adoula, over Gizenga. Adoula's coalition government had been elected by the parliament in the summer of 1961. The UN also changed its original mandate, which had limited its troops to self-defense, and authorized UN troops to use force if necessary to prevent chaos. At the request of the Adoula government the UN undertook to control Tshombe and to crush Gizenga's secessionist movement. The American Ambassador, Edward Gullion, advised Kennedy that unless Tshombe was brought under control and Katanga brought back into line, there was little chance for peace in that country. Gizenga's forces were finally defeated by UN and Congolese troops in January 1962. It took the UN until January, 1963 to defeat Tshombe's mercenaries in a bloody finale and to bring Katanga back into the fold.[42]

In November, 1963, when Lyndon Johnson became President of the United States following Kennedy's assassination, he inherited the still-simmering Congo crisis, along with the Africa team headed by G. Mennen Williams. Under Williams's positive influence the U.S. continued a pattern of UN voting that at least made the African states feel that the U.S. still recognized black rights and aspirations.[43]

The UN had scheduled the removal of its remaining forces from the Congo by June 1964. However, during that year a revolt spread in the Eastern Congo. By the time of Johnson's election for a full term in November, 1964, a full rebellion was underway against President Kasavubu. To help handle the situation Kasavubu unexpectedly recalled Moise Tshombe, a man still reviled by most African leaders, to serve as his Premier. Soon an odd, U.S. and Western-backed mix including white mercenaries, Congolese troops under General Mobutu, and Cuban exiles flying CIA-furnished American aircraft, were in operation against the rebels. The U.S. involvement in the operation became more and more apparent and unpalatable to Africans. In November 1964, President Johnson allowed U.S. pilots and American military aircraft to fly Belgian paratroops into Stanleyville, the center of the revolt, for the avowed purpose of rescuing hundreds of white hostages. This action resulted in the deaths of hundreds of rebels, and many of their leaders. Not only the rebels, but also most Africans were angered by what many of them considered to have been a transparent U.S. and Western plot.[44] Additionally friction also arose between the U.S. and some European nations, France and Belgium in particular, over the competition between private investors of those nations for what were treated by them as the spoils of the Congo. David N. Gibbs has stressed the impact of international business competition and conflict on events in the Congo.[45] The following year Kasavubu tried to dismiss Tshombe. Once again, as in 1960, a political deadlock ensued between the head of government and the head of state, as Kasavubu's faction and Tshombe's supporters faced off. Once again, on November 24, 1965, Mobutu took over the government. Kasavubu retired to a non-political status, and Tshombe went into exile in Spain.[46]

For the rest of the 1960s and to the present day, the venal and corrupt Mobutu, tacitly backed by the U.S., came to enjoy virtually unlimited personal power over the Congo. He proceeded to strip the country, which he renamed Zaire, of its wealth by squandering a great deal of its mineral and agricultural riches on projects such as palaces, unneeded highways, monuments and stadiums. These excesses, in addition to Mobutu's penchant for overseas bank accounts and properties, ultimately crippled the economy of Zaire.[47]

Ghana

When he became the first President of Ghana in 1957, Kwame Nkrumah profited from the fact that the United States government hoped to use his American education and connections and his prestige to enhance U.S. credibility with black Africans. In 1956, the Eisenhower administration belatedly realized that it had lost credibility in the Third World, and especially in Africa, after it precipitously withdrew previously promised support for the Aswan Dam project of Egypt's President Gamal Abdul Nasser. This prompted Eisenhower, somewhat reluctantly, to agree to support Nkrumah's huge Volta Dam hydroelectric and aluminum smelting project. However, Nkrumah and his Convention People's Party advocated a vague, African form of ill-defined socialism, and he kept up a steady attack on the United States and its policies. His increasingly shrill criticism led Eisenhower to delay approval of the U.S. government loan guarantees that were necessary to allow private investors to finance the project. U.S.-Ghana relations worsened further after September 1960 when Eisenhower and his then Secretary of State, Christian Herter, refused to receive Nkrumah, who was on a visit to the UN.

Thus, by the time President John F. Kennedy's new ambassador arrived in Ghana in January 1961, relations were so sour that the Ghanaian cabinet debated whether to receive the new ambassador or not. The death of Lumumba in the Congo especially enraged Nkrumah to the extent that he paid a well-publicized visit to the Soviet Union.[48]

In an attempt to win Nkrumah's support, President Kennedy, in spite of advice to the contrary, impetuously promised Nkrumah that he would support the Volta Dam project. To Kennedy's consternation, this generous and one-sided gesture seemed to have no positive effect on Nkrumah's policies or statements. On the contrary, Nkrumah, apparently no longer constrained by any apprehension that he might lose the American loan guarantees, went so far as to tour the Soviet bloc countries and Communist China, criticizing the U.S., predicting the end of colonialism, and demanding disarmament. This would have meant at that time unilateral disarmament of the West.

When Kennedy, upset at Nkrumah's ingratitude and agitation, hinted at withdrawing U.S. support, Nkrumah threatened to publish Kennedy's broken promise as one more example of American duplicity and non-support for African aspirations. Thus having put himself in an untenable position, Kennedy was forced reluctantly to agree to $96 million in loan guarantees to support the Volta Dam project.[49]

At the time of independence, Ghana was the leading world exporter of cocoa, and enjoyed a gross domestic product comparable to that of South Korea. It produced 10 percent of the world's gold supply, and it had impressive resources in bauxite, diamonds, manganese, and agricultural and forest products. The country enjoyed a flourishing export trade, a high literacy rate, and a trained cadre of educated personnel. Yet, within a few years Nkrumah had alienated his own people and squandered his nation's resources, its credit, and its future. Unnecessarily, he mortgaged its natural wealth under a mountain of debt largely incurred because of grandiose "ego" projects. By 1966, he had nationalized much of Ghana's agricultural and mineral output, and had driven the country to virtual bankruptcy.[50] Even after turning to the Soviet bloc in a desperate search for economic and political support, Nkrumah drove Ghana further into economic disaster.

By 1965 Nkrumah had turned Ghana into a one-party police state, with agents throughout Ghana to report on those who were possibly disloyal to him. He used Ghana's Preventive Detention Act of 1958 to imprison opponents for as long as five years without trial. The show elections held in 1965 only served to emphasize how thoroughly he had destroyed any meaningful democratic process in Ghana.

At the founding conference of the new Organization of Africa Unity, which convened in Addis Ababa on May 22, 1963, Nkrumah peppered the meetings with demands that the African nations unite quickly in a political union "along the lines of the USA or the USSR." Nkrumah's demands were buttressed by his writings, including his book, *Africa Must Unite*.[51] However, his dictatorial actions within Ghana, plus the feeling among many African leaders that his version of Pan-Africanism involved the necessary condition that he be leader of such a confederation helped to doom his version of pan-Africanism from the start.

Opposition to Nkrumah's ego-driven insistence on his version of Pan-Africanism increased to the point that during the first Assembly of the OAU Heads of State in Cairo in July 1964 Nkrumah's persistence led Julius Nyerere of Tanganyika to tear up his prepared speech and publicly chastise Nkrumah. By the time he was ousted in 1966 Nkrumah had lost the respect of black Africa and of his own people. To add to his final troubles, Ghana by 1966 was gripped in a fierce recession caused mainly by the 75 percent drop in world cocoa prices. He was toppled on February 24, 1966 and succeeded by General Joseph Ankrah, and the National Liberation Council (NLC). The military men promised to settle the foreign debt and somehow to gain solvency for the country. They failed. They were followed in 1969 by Dr. Kofi Busia, who also was unable to solve Ghana's economic troubles. Unemployment deepened and the slide in Ghana's balance of payments continued. There followed a series of military regimes, each of which failed in turn to rectify the political and economic troubles of the country.[52]

Nigeria

During the 1960s the U.S. generally enjoyed good relations with Nigeria. This was vital in view of Nigeria's huge population—the largest in Africa—and its mineral resources, including plentiful supplies of sweet, crude oil.[53] The Eisenhower administration dealt with Nigeria only in the context of seeing U.S. "vital interests." In contrast, the approach of the Kennedy and Johnson administrations was broader, less Cold War oriented, and more humanitarian than either the Eisenhower administration or the succeeding Nixon regime. The Democratic administrations of the 1960s hoped to see a more liberal, democratic, and peaceful Nigeria, which would serve as a regional good example of democratic government, economic progress, and stability. With these ends in mind, the Kennedy and Johnson administrations, in the years 1960–62 alone, proffered grants and loans totalling more than $200 million.

In spite of difficulties over the years, including the bloody civil war of the mid-1960s, Nigeria fulfilled those earlier American foreign policy hopes in that it has been notably careful not to interfere militarily or politically in the affairs of its neighbors. This has been partly due to a relatively enlightened attitude on the part of Nigeria's ruling groups and partly out of a practical realization of the delicacy of the ethnic and political balances within Nigeria itself, which could make military or political adventures beyond Nigeria's borders dangerous for the future of Nigeria.[54]

When Nigeria first gained its freedom from Britain on October 1, 1960, it was headed by Sir Abubakar Tafawa Baleewa, who served as both Prime Minister and Minister of Foreign Affairs. Dr. Nnamdi Azkiwe became President after first replacing the former British Governor-General. However, in reality Nigeria was a precariously held-together mixture of a Muslim North and a Christian South, with three main ethnic and religious groupings. On January 15, 1966, after more than five years of political bickering, young Ibo officers assassinated the Muslim Prime Minister, who was a Northerner, and several other key ministers. The government was taken over by a predominantly Eastern Ibo group, headed by Major-General Johnson Aguyie Ironsi. After six months of attempted military rule, General Ironsi and many Ibo officers were murdered in a military coup, followed by bloody anti-Ibo riots in the north. The leader of the Northerners was a young, Christian Lieutenant Colonel, Yakubu Gowon. Gowon set about to mend ethnic and religious fences, but before he had time to take any significant measures, the Ibo military commander of the eastern region, Lieutenant Colonel Chukwumega Odemegwu Ojukwu, on May 30, 1967 declared his region's independence as the Republic of Biafra.[55] Fighting soon broke out, and for almost three years following Ojukwu's precipitous declaration, Ibos and others allied with them fought against Nigerian government troops in a bloody war estimated to have cost more than 600,000 lives and untold material destruction.

During that time, many Americans were won over by the Ibos, their admiration goaded by the almost daily coverage by the American press of the war, usually on the side of the underdog Ibos with their almost suicidal determination and bravery.[56] Sympathizers encouraged the American government to side with the Ibos, or as least to become involved as a major peacemaker. This resulted in a strange mix of bedfellows backing the Ibo separation cause, including such diverse individuals as the liberal Senator Eugene McCarthy and the conservative Richard Nixon. Additionally, the Roman Catholic Church, including Pope Paul, took a deep and active interest in the cause of the Ibos, many of whom were Catholic.[57]

President Johnson had less personal interest in African affairs than President Kennedy. Further, Johnson was increasingly ensnared in the Vietnam war. Thus, he resisted becoming enmeshed in the Biafran civil war, although a few African nations, including Zambia, the Ivory Coast, and Gabon, came out in support of Biafran independence and Tanzania actually recognized Biafra. To further complicate matters, Britain and the Soviet Union supported the federal government, while the French supported the breakaway Ibo state of Biafra. At the close of the 1960s, President Nixon, like Johnson before him, and for similar reasons, also avoided entanglement, although humanitarian pressures forced the Nixon administration to add to the relatively large aid program which had been established by the Johnson administration to help the suffering Ibos.[58]

Finally, in January 1970, federal forces, led by General Gowon, overcame Ibo resistance. Gowon took immediate steps to heal the wounds of war. He pardoned all participants on the Ibo side with the exception of Ojukwu, who fled to the Ivory Coast. Gowon became head of a postwar federal military government which tried to reconcile the former warring parties. Many Easterners and Ibos were taken back into the military and government. A new twelve-state structure was finally instituted to replace the politically troublesome former system of three main regions. Regrettably, the army, swollen to more than 250,000 men, posed a problem of demobilization. Jobs and civilian resources would have to be found for a huge number of veterans if the army were demobilized to any significant extent. The "solution" the military government chose was simply to stay in power, with the rationale of "restructuring and reforming" the government. Gowon and his government, while they continued dealing with Britain and the United States, remained cool toward them, since Lyndon Johnson, increasingly preoccupied with the Vietnam war, and wary of entanglement in the Nigerian civil war, withheld military arms support from Gowon in 1967 when Gowon's central government desperately needed arms. However, U.S. trade, private investment, economic aid, and contacts continued, although on a lessened scale. Additionally, many thousands of Nigerians emigrated to the United States, and tens of thousands attended American colleges and universities.[59] In spite of these interactions and Nigeria's undeniable actual and potential power and potential importance, Robert B. Shepard has pointed out that, both under the relatively selfish "vital interest" approach of the Eisenhower and Nixon regimes, and under the more humanitarian and "liberal international" approach of the Kennedy and Johnson years, each American administration treated Nigeria as being only marginal to American foreign policy interests.[60]

Kenya

The earliest significant American contact with the emerging government of Kenya was between labor unions in the late 1950s. The American Federation of Labor-Congress of Industrial Organizations (AFL-CIO), gave limited financial support to the Kenya Federation of Labor, headed by the young Luo, Tom Mboya. Also in the late 1950s, Senator Jack Kennedy gained the gratitude and respect of Kenyans as the result of his part in instituting the so-called Kennedy airlifts. He had arranged with the Kennedy Foundation to pay the air fares of Kenyan students who had scholarships to study in the United States. Kennedy's reputation was further enhanced when, after independence in 1963, he raised the level of the consulate in Kenya to ambassadorial status and the U.S. became a major source of aid to Kenya. This assistance included loans, grants, technical, educational, and agricultural assistance.[61]

Additionally, the first Peace Corps volunteers arrived in Kenya in 1965 and soon were conducting one of the larger Peace Corps operations. These U.S. actions to promote good will were considered especially important at that time for Kenyan-American relations, since President Jomo Kenyatta's left-leaning Luo political foe, Oginga Odinga constantly criticized Kenyatta's dealings with the U.S. Odinga's influence moved the Kenyatta government to take a more critical stance toward the U.S. and toward American African policies during the mid-1960s. This was especially apparent during the Congo crisis when the Kenyans, like most African governments, were incensed at what they thought was American collaboration with the white oppressors of the Congo.[62]

From his high posts in the Kenyatta government, first as Minister of Home Affairs and then as Vice President, Odinga continued to attack America and to seek Communist bloc support. He arranged for unofficial arms shipments from the People's Republic of China and for scholarships, financial aid, and grants to send Kenyan students to study in the Soviet Union and China. Odinga overplayed his hand, however, when, in September, 1965, Kenyan students from the Soviet-built Lumumba institute were arrested after seizing Kenyatta's KANU party headquarters and demanding the resignation of the Western-oriented Tom Mboya from his post as KANU Secretary General.

By the late 1960s, the exposure of Odinga's schemes by the government, the overplaying by the Communists of their limited hand, together with Kenyatta's innate distrust of Communism combined to improve U.S.-Kenyan intergovernmental relations. The Kenyatta government expelled 10 Communist diplomats in 1967 for being too involved in Kenyan politics, while Kenyatta's supporters in parliament published press reports that Odinga and his people were Communist agents.[63]

Luckily for American interests in Kenya, the dynamic young Luo politician and Kenyatta supporter Tom Mboya acted as a highly effective counter force against Odinga's scheming. Mboya transcended his narrow ethnic loyalties to grow as a genuine national leader in Kenya and as a friend of the United States. On April 14, 1969, after a second group of Soviet diplomats were expelled, Odinga resigned from KANU. Within a few days, he accepted the presidency of the new Kenya People's Union (KPU)—an organization which was to last only three years. Soon, Tom Mboya was mysteriously assassinated, the KPU was banned, and many of its leaders, including Odinga, were detained.[64]

With the fall of Odinga from political power the attitude of the Kenyan government relaxed into a more positive stance toward the United States for the rest of the 1960s. Although Great Britain remained the major source of aid to Kenyans, the U.S. was also a strong source of real and potential income from tourism, financial activity and technical expertise.[65]

Tanzania

When Tanzania became independent on December 9, 1961, President Julius Nyerere had too few trained Tanzanians to operate his government and social infrastructure effectively. Partly out of necessity, and partly following his goal of creating an African socialist state in Tanzania, Nyerere gradually allowed his TANU party to carry virtually the entire load of administering Tanzania. Unnoticed by his admirers, especially in the socialist world and the Scandinavian countries, Nyerere, in spite of his humble manner, soon developed a de facto one-party state, with an unpleasant, but little known, readiness to detain and imprison his political opponents.

Nyerere embarked on a series of grandiose socialist schemes, including his favorite, the so called Ujamaa ("familyhood") scheme, in which he moved tens of thousands Tanzanian small farmers from their farms and onto large collectives for the purpose of providing them with better education and health care. Health care and education did improve and the economic growth rate in the 1960s held at about 5 percent annually. Regrettably, however, Nyerere and his socialist advisers neglected to answer the question of how those peasants, once taken from their farms and homes, were to feed and support themselves. Ultimately, in spite of his obvious good intentions Nyerere can be said to have virtually singlehandedly kept Tanzania from the progress and prosperity which its neighbor Kenya enjoyed, using similar resources and population base but under a relatively free enterprise system.[66]

In the international arena, under Nyerere's leadership, Tanzania, more or less successfully, managed to maintain neutrality and to avoid Cold War entanglements. Nyerere has been a consistent opponent of white domination of southern and South Africa. In addition, he remained a supporter of a kind of federal pan-Africanism, and has been a consistent supporter of regional organizations like the Organization of African Unity (OAU).

Tanzania began receiving American aid shortly after independence in 1961. This aid included a $10 million gift to help with education and communications. It also included humanitarian aid and long-term loans. After the droughts and subsequent floods in the winter of 1961–62, the U.S. provided large quantities of emergency food—some of it air-dropped—to the Tanzanians. During the 1970s, Tanzania—constantly in financial difficulty because of Nyerere's "African Socialist" mismanagement—became the largest recipient of American aid south of the Sahara. Although it continued to be a leading African per capita recipient of aid from other nations, including Western, Soviet bloc, Communist Chinese, and Scandinavian, Nyerere's version of socialism left the Tanzanian economy a shambles.[67]

Somalia

American relations with Somalia have fluctuated over the past three decades, often more in response to Somali-Ethiopian relations than to anything that the U.S. might or might not do. Further, U.S.-Somali relations have been complicated by Somali irredentism, which has led Somalia's leaders over the years to covet territory in adjacent Kenya, Ethiopia, and Djibouti, which was occupied by ethnic Somalis. It should be noted that even after independence on June 26, 1960, Italian political and economic influence remained strong in Somalia. The Italians sponsored Somalia's associate membership in the EEC, which opened Western markets for Somali exports. In addition, Italy continued as an important source of aid and technical assistance.

The United States was the second largest supplier of nonmilitary aid to Somalia in the 1960s. Much of this was in the form of grants, including scholarships for Somali students to study at American universities. Additionally, hundreds of American Peace Corps members, mainly teachers, worked in Somalia, as well as in Ethiopia during the 1960s.

The Somalis, although they considered Communism to be against their Islamic faith, nevertheless asked Russia for arms they had been unable to obtain from the West. The Soviets gave $32 million to help equip the growing Somalia army. This aid, plus the training of more than 800 Somali officers in the Soviet Union, gave the Soviets a power-ful influence in the Somali military.

The Somalis had never been reconciled, however, to the large amount of American military and other aid going to their rival, Ethiopia. This was of great importance to the Somalis, whose backing of irredentist Somali guerrillas in the Ogaden region had resulted in open warfare with Ethiopia in 1964. A lessening of tension between Somalia and its neighbors in 1967 temporarily lessened the tensions in those disputed areas. As a result, in 1968 and 1969, with the easing of local tensions, Somali-U.S.relations improved to the extent that Vice President Hubert Humphrey visited Mogadishu and Prime Minister Egal visited Washington twice.

After the military coup in October 1969, in which leftist Major General Mohamed Siad Barre and his Supreme Military Council (SRC) came to power, the Soviets again were very forthcoming with military equipment and advisers. Somalia soon took a hostile attitude toward the U.S., which still supported Ethiopia in numerous ways. Somalia also feared U.S. participation in a possible counter coup and resented what it saw as continued U.S. support of South Africa. By the end of the decade Somali-U.S. relations were so strained that the Somalis expelled the Peace Corps Program and five employees of the U.S. Agency for International Development and the State Department in April 1970 for "counterrevolutionary activities." Further, when the Somalis refused to end their practice of allowing the Somali flag to be used as a flag of convenience for ships carrying cargoes to North Vietnam, the United States announced that it would halt all aid within a year.[68]

White-Ruled States

Rhodesia

In 1953, the British government united the Crown Colony of Northern Rhodesia, the protectorate of Nyasaland, and the self-governing colony of Southern Rhodesia into the Central African Federation, primarily to strengthen whites by combining markets, resources, and military and police forces for greater strength and stability. Black Africans opposed the Federation, resenting their token economic benefits and political representation. In 1963, the Federation collapsed. Northern Rhodesia became independent Zambia, under Kenneth Kaunda, and Nyasaland gained its independence as Malawi, under the leadership of the American-educated physician, Dr. Hastings Banda. Southern Rhodesia, where the ruling whites were determined to fight to maintain their hegemony over the huge black majority, reverted to its previous semi-independent status as a self-governing colony.

On November 11, 1965 Rhodesia's Prime Minister, Ian Smith, leader of the ruling white minority and his Rhodesian Front Party, declared independence from British control rather than agreeing to move toward black freedom and majority rule. The British government, under pressure from other members of the Commonwealth, chose to oppose Smith's initiative. The United States was already at least ostensibly committed to majority rule in Africa. Thus, Johnson was ready to support the British in the diplomatic lead, in their unaccustomed role of protecting the rights of black Africans against whites.[69] The situation on the ground was further complicated by the fact that the newly independent nation of Zambia was landlocked and 95 percent of its imports and exports went through Rhodesia; thus a British UN blockade of Rhodesia could possibly destroy Zambia's economy. It was at this time that Zambia, turned down by America for support in building a blockade-evading railway through Tanzania, turned to Communist China for help. The Chinese agreed, and soon sent materials, necessary equipment, and thousands of laborers, technicians, and engineers, to build the so-called Tan Zamm railroad—a task that was to take eight years.[70]

Smith's announcement of his Unilateral Declaration of Independence (UDI) faced President Lyndon Johnson with a unique foreign policy situation. In other major political problems in Africa, such as the crises in the Congo, Angola, and South Africa, Johnson had essentially inherited and continued Kennedy's policies. However, events now forced him to create a brand new policy for the unique Rhodesian situation: how to deal with breakaway, white-dominated Rhodesia following UDI. In this case Great Britain had the lead. Although Britain was much weaker than the U.S. in the post-World War II world, Britain maintained political oversight over Rhodesia. Also, the U.S. had deferred to the authority of the UN in the Rhodesian situation far more than it had in any other similar situation in Africa. However, many Americans and Europeans empathized with the whites' fears of being submerged by Rhodesia's blacks, over whom the whites had ruled since the turn of the century. Various conservative business interests in the U.S. and the West supported Smith. Additionally, a powerful pro-Rhodesian, racist lobby sprang up in the United States, backed by conservative American organizations like the Young Americans for Freedom, the Liberty Lobby, and the John Birch Society.[71] On the other side of the question, by 1965, American blacks, more aggressive than ever before in attempting to influence policy on African matters, demanded that the United States recognize the blacks' right to self-rule in Rhode-sia.[72] After failed talks with Smith in December 1966, British Prime Minister Harold Wilson felt it necessary to ask for tighter, mandatory sanctions. Many conservative American businessmen and political leaders, especially from the U.S. South, backed the cause of the whites, whom they saw as "patriots" defending their "freedom" from the British (and from the blacks).

In 1967, Britain and the U.S. joined in tighter sanctions, to the fury of the American right wing, led by Dean Acheson and others. Acheson viciously attacked American UN ambassador Arthur Goldberg over the policy. Goldberg gave Acheson as good as he got in a spirited defense of the tough new U.S. action. This led Acheson into continued attacks on Goldberg, America's sanctions policy, and Wilson through the remainder of the Johnson administration.[73]

Meanwhile, during the 1960s, the black Rhodesian resistance move-ment was growing stronger and more determined. The Zimbabwe African Peoples Union (ZAPU), was formed under Joshua Nkomo in 1961, and the Zimbabwe African National Union (ZANU), led by the Reverend Ndabanangini Sithole and Robert Mugabe, in August 1963. These fledgling organizations were attempting guerrilla attacks by the mid-1960s. They would slowly expand and be heard from devastating-ly more than a decade later.[74] Once Johnson announced on March 31, 1968 that he would not run for reelection, U.S.-African policy making virtually ground to a halt. Although the United States did continue to cooperate in sanctions which had been imposed in 1965 against Rhode-sia, no one expected the weak measures to have much effect.

Even as it entered office in 1968, the Nixon administration was guid-ed by the pro-white assumptions of National Security Study Memo-randum 39 (NSSM39) with its "Option 2" declaration that "the whites are here to stay" [in power] forever in southern Africa. Nixon's nation-al security adviser, Henry Kissinger, made no secret of his disdain for blacks and his consistent lack of interest in the problems of black Africans in the white-dominated nations of southern Africa. "Option 2" was officially endorsed in January, 1970, and Nixon and Kissinger proceeded to "tilt" toward and to develop a policy of "communication" with the white ruled regimes, including Rhodesia.

The unfortunate culmination of this new U.S. approach to foreign policy toward Rhodesia was a dramatic and successful right wing American attack to weaken the sanctions against Rhodesia. This was accomplished by the notorious Byrd amendment, which called for relaxation of the sanctions on the grounds of American security requirements for Rhodesian chrome and other defense-related metals.

The Nixon administration, although it did not formally sponsor the Byrd amendment, did not oppose its passage and, in fact, failed to support the efforts of the State Department to defeat it.[75]

In judging the record of the Western nations toward Rhodesia in the 1960s, it must be concluded that U.S., British and UN policies failed, insofar as they were meant to force or to encourage the white regimes to grant freedom to their black populations. The U.S. followed its habit of trying to seek a "middle ground" to accommodate both whites and blacks. This made it virtually impossible to put real pressure for change in Rhodesia at that time.[76]

South Africa

In its dealings with the white dominated black nations of southern Africa, and especially with South Africa, the United States broke sharply with the "Congo Syndrome" style of supporting local dictators whom the U.S. hoped to control in a comfortable, predictable "Cold War" framework. The vital difference was that the rulers of the black nations of southern Africa were whites. Those ruling groups often had potent military power, and political and economic backing overseas, as well as within their borders. Thus, it would have been difficult for the United States or the Western nations to force them to give freedom to their black majorities, even had the Western nations desired to do so. Additionally, many Americans in the 1960s were subtly or often openly racist, and they looked with frustrated amusement, contempt, and some status-threatened fear at the efforts of black Americans to gain their rights. They just as easily discounted and ignored the humanity and the rights of black Africans. Consequently, they often supported, both emotionally and politically, the white ruling oligarchies. Thus the United States, with regard to these white controlled states, continued the de facto "whites first" stance that Eisenhower and his administration had followed.[77]

To understand the ramifications of Kennedy's dealings with South Africa, we should look briefly at the record of the preceding Truman and Eisenhower administrations. The Truman administration, caught up in the Cold War, and believing in the necessity to contain Communism, cooperated with the South African government in many ways. This cooperation continued even after the National Party's election victory and the subsequent rise of stringent apartheid and racial oppression.

During the Korean War, America had sought a maximum number of allies, or so-called international "flags" of nations who would join UN forces in the war against the North Koreans and Communist Chinese. America thus welcomed the several small detachments of troops and aircraft which the South African government sent to join the UN forces in Korea. A grateful America collaborated with South Africa even after that time in scientific and military matters. The American United Nations voting record in not supporting anti-apartheid votes was underscored at the end of Truman's administration when in December 1952 the United States abstained on a General Assembly resolution calling for South Africa to do away with apartheid and to establish a commission to study racial issues.[78]

The Eisenhower administration, in turn, cooperated even more fully on most matters with South Africa. The racist oppression in South Africa did not particularly bother Eisenhower. Like others before and after him, Eisenhower easily took up the Cold War rationalizations for continued close U.S.-South Africa interaction.

The Eisenhower administration collaborated with South Africa so closely that it participated in joint naval exercises in October 1959. Additionally, intelligence and military cooperation remained very close. A temporary hitch in relations occurred after the Sharpeville massacre of unarmed African demonstrators on March 11, 1960. The United States joined in a Security Council resolution on April 1, 1960 that blamed the South African government for the shootings, and called for South Africa to institute measures to promote equality. However within a few months, in September 1960, the United States signed an agreement with South Africa to establish three NASA tracking stations in that country. Further, within a year after Sharpeville, American banks lifted the temporary freeze on South African credit and investments imposed after the massacre. This marked the start of the South African economic boom of that decade.[79]

The inauguration of John F. Kennedy, and his appointment of liberals to several important posts in the State Department, seemed to hint at a more humane approach toward helping the blacks of South Africa. On July 4, 1963, for example, black South Africans were invited to the American Embassy for the first time, leading South African officials to boycott the reception. Although such gestures were more numerous in the Kennedy administration and the rhetoric against apartheid was somewhat stronger, scientific and military cooperation continued. This cooperation included joint naval exercises off Durban in 1961. While the U.S. gave "neither encouragement nor discouragement" to investment and trade with South Africa, both burgeoned after the lifting of economic restrictions in the early 1960s. Investors were attracted by the mineral and natural wealth of the country, and especially by the huge profits inherent in being able to utilize the output of semi-enslaved black labor.

The Kennedy administration affected periodic, dramatic posturing in support of black South African aspirations. In reality, however, Kennedy, like Eisenhower before him, in spite of his stronger rhetoric, rationalized continued close dealings with the white regimes of southern Africa. He continued to cooperate with the South African government in many ways, including allowing continued U.S. investment in that country. Kennedy's larger interests were in the Cold War and in the situations in Europe, the Middle East, and Vietnam. It appeared better to him in the short run to leave Africa quiescent. He thus continued Eisenhower's deferential approach toward ruling white regimes. From that time to the mid 1970s, American administrations, with the Cold War always in mind, rationalized tolerating apartheid because of the supposed absolute "need" for South Africa's strategic minerals, and the usefulness of South African bases for protection of sea lines of communication into the Indian Ocean. They emphasized the "need" for the U.S. to maintain missile tracking stations in South Africa and they used other convenient rationalizations to justify industrial and military cooperation.[80]

The American "tilt toward the whites" remained the norm in spite of initial hopeful words and political moves by President Kennedy in the first months following his inauguration. It continued despite the hypocritical U.S. habit of periodically "deploring" or "condemning" apartheid, while at the same time cooperating with South Africa in many vital activities. In the words of Thomas Karis, "For two decades, since Eisenhower's second term, U.S. policy toward South Africa has been an ambivalent mixture: rhetorical abhorrence of apartheid, sorrowful slaps on the wrist, and wishful thinking that contact and business with the ruling whites would somehow produce 'trickle down' economic and political reform and thus avoid violent revolution."[81]

In 1962 the U.S. Defense Department concluded an agreement for a space-tracking facility in South Africa. Although the agreement also called for U.S. sales of arms to South Africa, pressure in the UN, especially by the Soviet Union, led the U.S. to declare a unilateral embargo against sales of arms to South Africa after the end of 1963. However, U.S. laxness in enforcing the restrictions of the arms embargo, and the fact that South Africa had by that time developed a highly sophisticated arms industry of its own, made the gesture almost meaningless.[82]

On taking office in November 1963, Lyndon Johnson inherited the members of John F. Kennedy's African policy team, both "Africanists" and "Europeanists." He also inherited the dual mode of dealing with the South African government—verbal condemnation of apartheid and real life cooperation with South Africa. Naval cooperation did ultimately end, following the insistence of the government of South Africa that a scheduled visit by the American aircraft carrier *Franklin Delano Roosevelt* in February 1967 would have to be under segregated conditions. The American Negro Leadership Conference on Africa and others, including some members of Congress, opposed the visit if it was to be on a segregated basis. Ultimately no recreational shore leave was granted, and that ended visits by U.S. naval ships to South Africa. Johnson also continued to "enforce" the embargo on U.S. arms to South Africa as weakly as Kennedy had done. As before, lenient interpretation of what should be considered to be arms which could be used to enforce apartheid made it a weak enforcement instrument. After the South African government cracked down on the African National Congress (ANC) and their freedom conspirators in a raid at Rivonia in 1963, there was a political hiatus and relative "peace" in that country. This fitted nicely with President Johnson's desire to concentrate on other problems. These included his increasing involvement in Vietnam, and in the Middle East after the 1967 Arab Israeli War, and his desire to deal with America's own internal racial turmoil.

On December 4, 1963, shortly after Johnson's assuming the presidency, the Security Council unanimously appointed a small group of distinguished diplomats, headed by the Swedish diplomat Alva Myrdal as chairperson, to study the South African situation. The group issued its report on April 20, 1964, noting that South Africa was on the verge of "an explosion" and calling for a national convention in South Africa, to include both the Progressive Federal Party and the Zulu Inkatha party of Chief Gatsha Buthelezi. It proposed amnesty for opposition leaders, including Nelson Mandela, and proposed a study of how effective sanctions, especially on oil imports, might be in pressuring South Africa to change. The U.S. refused to go along with strict sanctions since, as Adlai Stevenson stated, South Africa was not yet a "threat to the peace." American and Western opposition to the idea ultimately made the Myrdal report virtually useless.[83]

In effect, the Johnson administration left the American South Africa relationship much as it had been for the previous decade. This meant combining rhetorical denunciation with more subtle, de facto economic and military cooperation under the guise of "neither encouraging nor discouraging" the growing investment by American companies in highly profitable South African enterprises.[84]

The foregoing review of American foreign policy toward the nations of

Africa in the 1960s shows a record of success, failures, and mixed out-comes in dealing with various African nations. The Eisenhower admin-istration began the 1960s with a tentative approach based mainly on the fears and racist assumptions of both President Dwight D. Eisenhower and his long serving Secretary of State, John Foster Dulles. The Kennedy administration at first thrilled blacks worldwide with the apparent fairness and dynamism of John F. Kennedy, and his seeming ability to understand the black victims' viewpoint in the African polit-ical context. In the event, this promise was to prove more or less still-born. In the final analysis, Kennedy's approach proved to be not too different than that of Eisenhower before him.

The same must be said for the administration of President Lyndon Johnson, who ended his only full term as a defeated and broken man due mainly to his immersion in the self-defeating and profitless Viet-nam tangle.

In sum, the American record at the end of the decade is mixed. In the Congo, the brutal and corrupt Joseph Mobutu, backed by the United States, still ruled the nation with an iron hand. In Angola, the Ameri-can government continued the modus vivendi with the Salazar and Caetano dictatorships, so long as Portugal allowed the United States to use the Azores air bases. Liberian President William Tubman died peacefully in office in 1971, a privilege that would not be allowed to his successor, William Tolbert. In Ghana, Kwame Nkrumah had long since been deposed in disgrace and there followed a succession of brutal and inept military regimes.

Nigeria was especially important because of its huge physical size, strategic location, large population, and mineral resources, including high grade oil. By the end of the 1960s Nigeria was in the hands of a succession of military governments which maintained an ongoing trade and investment relationship with the United States.

In Kenya, Jomo Kenyatta and his KANU party had taken tight, vir-tually one-party control by the end of the 1960s. Kenya and the United States enjoyed a reciprocally profitable and fairly stable relationship, with the United States using Kenya's port and tourist facilities and agricultural products like coffee and tea, while Kenya received aid and assistance from America in many areas of activity. Tanzania, like Kenya received large amounts of American aid of different kinds. Nev-ertheless, Nyerere managed to remain on his eccentric but independent "African socialist" course, more or less staying out of any bloc's or nation's grasp, while at the same time receiving aid and charity from virtually every potential donor in the world.

Ethiopia at the end of the 1960s appeared to be in a stable, friendly mode in its relations with the United States. Ethiopia was also a large recipient of American financial aid and military assistance. It seemed to be firmly under the control of Emperor Haile Selassie and his brutal, inept, and class-ridden regime. Ethiopia's foe, Somalia, had been taken over in 1969 by Major General Mohamed Siad Barre. By the end of the decade Barre and the U.S. were on poor terms, exacerbated by Somalia's allowing the use of its flag on ships transporting material to North Vietnam.

As to the two "pariah states" of Rhodesia and South Africa at the end of the 1960s, the arrival of the Nixon-Kissinger team seemed to undermine the already desperate plight of the blacks of those two countries, since hope of moral or political support from the United States virtually vanished with Nixon's arrival.

Assistant Secretary of State G. Mennen Williams left government in mid-1966 after having served both the Kennedy and the Johnson administrations for much of the decade. He oversaw much of American foreign policy making toward black Africa during most of the 1960s, and was in a position to monitor policy making closely for the rest of the decade. In 1969, he published his memoir, *Africa for the Africans*. In that book he looked back on the African record of the Kennedy-Johnson years. His statements on the American foreign policy aims of those years and his views of the outcome of those aims and approaches offer a good final vantage point from which to view the decade.

Williams listed the five major points of American policy toward Africa during the Kennedy and Johnson administrations, plus one overriding factor—the necessity to contain Communism. These five points were as follows: First, and most important, the U.S backed the principle of self determination, including nonalignment in Africa. Second, the U.S. looked primarily to the Africans to solve their own problems, including the establishment of joint, regional African organizations such as the OAU. Third, America hoped to help raise the African standard of living by the use of aid and trade, including governmental and private sources. Fourth, the U.S. discouraged arms build ups in the new African nations beyond that required for security and self-defense. Finally, the U.S. hoped to remind other Western nations of their continued responsibilities toward Africa. The American effort to contain Communism remained the overriding interest.

The actual performance of the Kennedy and Johnson administrations and the subsequent events leave a mixed record, and not one that recognized the human rights of black Africans in South and southern Africa to any commendable extent. Presidents Kennedy and Johnson were very similar in their approach to African policy. Like Eisenhower before them and Nixon following, their primary consideration was always the Cold War, Europe, and the Middle East, and to a growing extent, especially for Lyndon Johnson, the war in Vietnam. Both John Kennedy and Lyndon Johnson were wealthy, powerful men who prided themselves in being realistic "hard thinkers" and who were used to success and to getting what they wanted, in both their personal and their political lives. Each in turn thought that he would put a realistic but "tough minded" slant on America's African foreign policy. Each saw himself as conducting a victorious struggle against Soviet expansionism, especially in Vietnam. They paid too little attention to the massive changes that had come about in the world of the 1960s. The United States was no longer the world's only wealthy and powerful nation. The Europeans were bothered by the American obsession with Vietnam and they often were uncooperative in supporting what they considered to be the U.S. folly. Further, they resented U.S. interference in their African affairs.[85]

In dealing with black-led nations all U.S. administrations sought those leaders whom they could control, or at least count on for support of American foreign policy. This did not often turn out to be the case. This of course reflected the historical mode of Western dealings with the Third World and with black African nations. To its credit, the United States did attempt to aid African nations economically and with other support, such as the Peace Corps, and gained much general good will by these efforts.

In contrast, in dealing with the white-dominated regimes of southern Africa, the U.S. tried to work within an impossible middle ground that would satisfy both black and white in Africa. There was simply no way simultaneously to satisfy the white determination to maintain control over the blacks and yet to tell the world that this was a just or necessary course of action.[86] Within the American government and State Department, in questions concerning Africa, there was conflict and tension between two major groups. On one side were usually conservatives and racists, who tended to support white regimes. On the opposing side were usually liberals and blacks, who supported freedom and independence for blacks in Africa. By the end of the 1960s the hopes of the early part of the decade had faded under the pressure of white resistance and, too often, of black African poor performance or corruption of one form or another.

Thus, notwithstanding the positive outlook of G. Mennen Williams, the 1960s, insofar as black freedom and progress in Africa is concerned, can be said to have come in like a lion but gone out like a lamb. The one undeniably positive note during the decade was that the great majority of formerly colonized black nations had indeed gained their freedom from immediate European political domination. However, the hopes of many of these new nations had waned by the end of the decade. Most had gained independence with too few educated and trained indigenous personnel to run their governmental and administrative machinery. Many of them also faced destructive opposition of embittered whites, whether within their countries or overseas. The maneuvering of both Communist and Western and Soviet bloc nations who were playing their own Cold War games at the expense of the Africans added extra complications. Also, Western economic adventurers attempted to profit from the mineral and other wealth of the region, also often at the expense of the Africans. Further, black Africans had been repelled by what they had been allowed to experience of the benefits of Western political democracy and the free market economic system. Usually, they had experienced these systems only through their own eyes as victims of colonial oppression. Understandably, if not entirely logically, many of them threw out the twin babies of political freedom and a free market economy with the dirty bath water of white colonial racism. These burgeoning populations too often literally "ate up" any economic surplus. Their own resources for self-help were limited, although they formed the OAU, which at least offered them at times a united, and thus more powerful, voice in the UN, and which did help to stabilize African boundaries. The OAU, however, offered little prospect of significant help in the economic or military sphere.

Thus, they naturally turned to Russia, China, and the Marxist and socialist systems for military, economic, and political support. Many of them attempted to establish local variations of Marxism or socialism. Ironically, although the Communist motivation for supporting independence movements in the Third World and Africa was, at best, opportunistic and self-serving, it is undeniable that the military equipment and advisers, including at times troops, which they provided were often unobtainable from the Western nations or the United States. Yet they often were provided by Soviet bloc, Communist Chinese and by surrogates like Cuba, at low or no cost to the receiving nation. This aid was often instrumental, and in some cases indispensable, in helping many Third World and African countries obtain their freedom and independence. In addition to their basic motive of furthering their own ideological aims and Cold War ambitions, the Soviets, although "white" and often demonstrably racist, nevertheless did not have the historic baggage, and political inhibitions carried by many Western leaders that made them reluctant to support Africans against whites.[87]

In the economic sphere, however, Soviet and Communist aid,

although initially welcome, often proved to be counterproductive. In nations like Tanzania and Ghana, most of the new socialist and Communist inspired economic schemes soon faltered, and ultimately failed, often due to incompetence or corruption on the part of the new African governments. They also suffered from relying on African versions of Marxism, or "African" socialism. Ironically, it now appears that these Marxist systems of demand performance suffer from insuperable, internal contradictions and inefficiencies that ultimately combine to make any Communist type of economic and political system inefficient and ultimately unworkable.[88]

As if to underscore the problems of the new African states, even before the end of the 1960s a series of military coups toppled one head of government after another, as the combined effects of overpopulation, poor administration, greed, and tribal competition became felt. These revolts replaced many of the heroes of African independence. The first, and most disappointing, was the coup against the highly respected, gentle, and democratic Sylvanus Olympio of Togo. Olympio was deposed by the military and murdered on January 13, 1963. On November 25, 1965, Colonel Joseph Mobutu seized control of the Congo in a bloodless coup. These coups were followed by others: in Dahomey in December 1965, and in the Central African Republic and in Upper Volta in January 1966. Then followed a series of military takeovers in Nigeria in 1966. On February 24, 1966, the increasingly dictatorial Kwame Nkrumah, while on an overseas trip, was himself deposed. In 1968 the government of Mali was overthrown. In Burundi, in 1969, the king was overthrown by his son, who was himself removed by the prime minister. Thus, before the end of the 1960s black Africans had ample reason to be concerned for their future.[89]

For blacks in the United States, the exciting, hopeful start of the 1960s also turned out to be largely illusory. In spite of technical advances in legally ordained civil and voting rights, blacks found themselves in a poor economic and social position and still segregated and discriminated against in virtually every area of activity in America. They were still victims of de facto segregation which was as oppressive as had been the previous de jure discrimination against them. In August 1965, the Watts area of Los Angeles erupted in a race riot that was followed by other large riots over the United States during the next several years. In 1966 there were more than 40 riots and in 1967 there were about 150 major disturbances, 75 of which were considered to be major riots. The worst two were in Newark, New Jersey and Detroit, Michigan. Following the Detroit riot, President Johnson appointed a commission headed by Governor Otto Kerner of Illinois. Kerner's

National Advisory Commission on Civil Rights stated in its report that, "Our nation is moving toward two societies, one black, one white— separate and unequal."[90]

If one judges the diplomatic record of the United States in Africa during the 1960s as that of just another powerful, Western white nation looking out solely for its own interests and its short-range economic and political interests, then the record is, if nothing else, typical of great power dealings with Africa. If, however, one judges the American record as that of a nation which in recent history had loudly proclaimed support for human rights, individual freedom, and national self-determination, then the record of the United States in Africa in the 1960s leaves much to be desired.[91]

One must look back on the 1960s as a decade of lost opportunity for America and the West to "do the right thing" regarding the most basic human rights of the oppressed black populations of South and southern Africa. In the long run this would have been the proper thing to do for the long-term interests of the United States, since the black populations of almost every one of those countries were destined to control those nations in the future. However, the Kennedy and Johnson administrations, like their Republican counterparts and their European allies too often ignored the human and civil rights of Africans. The resultant resentments and pressures built up in the African populations until they exploded in the bloody freedom struggles of the 1970s.

NOTES

1. Arthur M. Schlesinger, Jr., *A Thousand Days: John F. Kennedy in the White House* (Cambridge, 1965), p. 552; Sanford Ungar, *Africa: The People and Politics of an Emerging Continent* (New York, 1986), p. 58.

2. Stephen R. Weissman, *American Foreign Policy in the Congo 1960–1964* (Ithaca, 1974), p. 23.

3. David Lamb, *The Africans* (New York, 1982), pp. 138–39; Basil Davidson, *Africa in History: Themes and Outlines* (New York, 1991), pp. 325–37; Thomas J. Noer, *Cold War and Black Liberation: The United States and White Rule in Africa, 1948–1968* (Columbia, 1985), pp. 56, 129.

4. Taylor Branch, *Parting the Waters: America in the King Years 1954–63* (New York, 1988), pp. 128–205; Benjamin Quarles, *The Negro in the Making of America* (London, 1969), pp. 250–51; Louis Lomax, *The Negro Revolt* (New York, 1963), pp. 16–17, 92.

5. Quarles, *The Negro in the Making of America*, pp. 252–55; Branch, *Parting the Waters*, pp. 412–49; Mary Frances Berry and John Blassingame, *Long Memory: The Black Experience in America* (New York, 1982), pp. 383–84.

6. Quarles, *The Negro in the Making of America*, pp. 250–70.

7. Berry and Blassingame, *Long Memory*, pp. 384–85; David Garrow, *Bearing the Cross: Martin Luther King, Jr. and the Southern Christian Leadership Conference* (New York, 1986); John Hope Franklin and Alfred A. Moss, Jr., *From Slavery to Freedom: A History of Black Americans* (New York, 1988), pp. 439–40, 443–61.

8. Berry and Blassingame, *Long Memory*, pp. 418–22; Stokely Carmichael and Charles Hamilton, *Black Power: The Politics of Liberation in America* (New York, 1967).

9. Malcolm X, *The Autobiography of Malcolm X* (New York, 1965), pp. 317–63; C. Eric Lincoln, *The Black Muslims in America* (Boston, 1961), pp. 98–134, 248–55; Franklin and Moss, Jr., *From Slavery to Freedom: A History of Black Americans*, pp. 461–63, 482–85.

10. Noer, *Cold War and Black Liberation*, pp. 48–59.

11. Henry F. Jackson, *From the Congo to Soweto: U.S. Foreign Policy Toward Africa Since 1960* (New York, 1982), pp. 145–47.

12. Richard D. Mahoney, *JFK: Ordeal in Africa*, (New York, 1983),p 19; Jackson, *From the Congo to Soweto*, pp. 18–19, 42–45; Schlesinger, *A Thousand Days*, pp. 298–99, 506–9.

13. Jackson, *From the Congo to Soweto*, pp. 21–25, 42; Elise Forbes Pachter, *Our Man in Kinshasha: U.S. Relations With Mobutu, 1970–1983. Patron-Client Relations in the International Sphere*, pp. ii-iii).

14. Schlesinger, *A Thousand Days*, pp. 506–7; Noer, *Cold War and Black Liberation*, pp. 34–40, 44–45, 52–56.

15. Weissman, *American Foreign Policy in the Congo 1960–1964*, pp. 43–50; Mahoney, *JFK: Ordeal in Africa*, pp. 34–35; Noer, *Cold War and Black Liberation*, pp. 41–44; William Minter, *King Solomon's Mines Revisited: Western Interests and the Burdened History of Southern Africa* (New York, 1986), p. 110.

16. Schlesinger, *A Thousand Days*, 554; Franklin and Moss, Jr., *From Slavery to Freedom*, pp. 440–41; Mahoney, *JFK: Ordeal in Africa*, pp. 25–30, 33; Thomas J. Noer, "The New Frontier and African Neutralism: Kennedy, Nkrumah, and the Volta River Project," *Diplomatic History*, 7 (Winter, 1984): 61.

17. Franklin and Moss, Jr., *From Slavery to Freedom*, pp. 441–43.

18. Gerard T. Rice, *The Bold Experiment: JFK's Peace Corps* (South Bend, 1985), pp. ix-xi, 16–18.

19. Noer, *Cold War and Black Liberation*, pp. 61–64.

20. Tom Wicker, *JFK and LBJ: The Influence of Personality Upon Politics* (New York, 1968), pp. 249–50; Robert Schulzinger, *American Diplomacy in the Twentieth Century* (New York, 1990), pp. 260–62.

21. Noer, *Cold War and Black Liberation*, pp. 65–67; Thomas G. Paterson, ed., *Kennedy's Quest for Victory: American Foreign Policy, 1961–1963* (New York, 1989), pp. 16–19.

22. Ungar, *Africa: People and Politics*, pp. 60, 66–68.

23. Anthony Lake, *The Tar Baby Option: American Policy Toward Southern Rhodesia* (New York, 1976), pp. 609–70, 75–77).

24. Noer, *Cold War and Black Liberation*, pp. ix-x, 1–3, 238–42.

25. Charles S. Johnson, *Bitter Canaan: The Story of the Negro Republic* (New

Brunswick, NJ, 1987); J. Gus Liebenow, *Liberia: The Evolution of Privilege* (Ithaca, 1969).

26. Johnson, *Bitter Canaan*, pp. xii, xx, xiv, 180–97.

27. D. Elwood Dunn, *The Foreign Policy of Liberia During the Tubman Era, 1944–71* (London, 1979), pp. 22–27; Ungar, *Africa: People and Politics*, pp. 97–98; Johnson, *Bitter Canaan*, introduction, xv-xxi, 136–42.

28. Ungar, *Africa: People and Politics*, pp. 102; Johnson, *Bitter Canaan*, 126; Harold D. Nelson, ed., *Liberia: A Country Study* (Washington, D.C., 1985), pp. 50–55; Robert A. Smith, *The American Foreign Policy in Liberia, 1822–1971*, (Monrovia, Liberia, 1972), pp. 67–72.

29. Ungar, *Africa: People and Politics*, p. 98; Nelson, ed., *Liberia: A Country Study*, pp. 47–59.

30. Robert W. Clower, et al., *Growth Without Development: An Economic Survey of Liberia* (Evanston, 1966), pp. v-vii; Dunn, *The Foreign Policy of Liberia During the Tubman Era*, p. 39.

31. Dunn, *The Foreign Policy of Liberia During the Tubman Era*, 57; *U.S. Department of State Bulletin*, 41, No. 1058 (October 5, 1959): 490–91.

32. Jackson, *From the Congo to Soweto*, 50; Nelson, ed., *Liberia: A Country Study*, pp. 47–61; Clower, ed., *Growth Without Development: An Economic Survey of Liberia*, p. 361.

33. Ungar, *Africa: People and Politics*, pp. 87–89, 93–96, 100; Nelson, ed., *Liberia: A Country Study*, pp. 5; Europa Publications Limited, *Africa South of the Sahara: 1986* (London, 1985), p. 591.

34. John H. Spencer, *Ethiopia, The Horn of Africa and U.S. Policy* (Cambridge, 1976), pp. 22–23.

35. Jackson, *From the Congo to Soweto*, p. 222.

36. Spencer, *Ethiopia, The Horn of Africa and U.S. Policy*, pp. 26–27.

37. Harold D. Nelson and Irving Kaplan, eds., *Ethiopia: A Country Study* (Washington D.C., 1981), pp. 45–52.

38. Schlesinger, *A Thousand Days*, p. 574.

39. Schlesinger, *A Thousand Days*, pp. 574–75; Mahoney, *JFK: Ordeal in Africa*, p. 36.

40. Mahoney, *JFK: Ordeal in Africa*, pp. 41, 47–48, 54–70; Weissman, *American Foreign Policy in the Congo*, pp. 95–96, 108–9, 137–38; Jackson, *From the Congo to Soweto*, pp. 36–37.

41. Schlesinger, *A Thousand Days*, pp. 552; Noer, *Cold War and Black Liberation*, pp. 138–39.

42. Schlesinger, *A Thousand Days*, pp. 576–577; Peter Duignan and L. H. Gann, *The United States and Africa: A History* (New York, 1987), pp. 317–18; Lamb, *The Africans*, pp. 43–44; John W. Spanier, *American Foreign Policy Since World War II* (New York, 1968), pp. 198–202; Europa Publications Limited, *Africa South of the Sahara: 1986* (London, 1985), pp. 1010–11.

43. Ungar, *Africa: People and Politics*, 66; Lamb, *The Africans*, pp. 45–46.

44. William Attwood, *The Reds and the Blacks: A Personal Adventure* (New York, 1967), pp. 191–236; Fred E. Wagoner, *Dragon Rouge: The Rescue of Hostages*

in the Congo (Washington, D.C., 1980), pp. 1–4, 121–89, 197–204.

45. David N. Gibbs, *The Political Economy of Third World Intervention: Mines, Money, and U.S. Policy in the Congo Crisis* (Chicago, 1991), pp. 1–36, 101, 159–60, 202–5.

46. Ungar, *Africa: People and Politics*, pp. 66–67; G. Mennen Williams, *Africa for the Africans* (Grand Rapids, 1967), pp. 86–103; Roger Hilsman, *To Move a Nation: The Politics of Foreign Policy in the Administration of John F. Kennedy* (New York, 1967), pp. 233–71.

47. Davidson, *Africa in History: Themes and Outlines*, 365; Ungar, *Africa: People and Politics*, pp. 62–65; Schlesinger, *A Thousand Days*, pp. 576–77; Duignan and Gann, *The United States and Africa: A History*, pp. 317–318; Lamb, *The Africans*, pp. 43–46; Gibbs, *The Political Economy of Third World Intervention: Mines, Money, and U.S. Policy in the Congo Crisis*, p. 2.

48. Schlesinger, *A Thousand Days*, p. 570.

49. Schlesinger, *A Thousand Days*, pp. 571–72; Noer, "The New Frontier and African Neutralism: Kennedy, Nkrumah, and the Volta River Project," *Diplomatic History*, 8: 61–80; Kwame Nkrumah, *Africa Must Unite* (New York, 1970), pp. 114–17.

50. Lamb, *The Africans*, pp. 286–87.

51. Nkrumah, *Africa Must Unite*, pp. 132–72, 205–22.

52. Ungar, *Africa: People and Politics*, pp. 390–95; Irving Kaplan, et al., (Washington, D.C., 1971), pp. 253–67.

53. Jackson, *From the Congo to Soweto*, pp. 146, 169–76.

54. Robert B. Shepard, *Nigeria, Africa, and the United States: From Kennedy to Reagan* (Bloomington, 1991), pp. 1–5; Duignan and Gann, *The United States and Africa*, p. 317; Bassey E. Ate, *Decolonization and Dependence: The Development of Nigerian-U.S. Relations, 1960–1984* (Boulder, 1987), pp. 1–2.

55. John de St. Jorre, *The Brothers' War: Biafra and Nigeria* (Boston, 1972), pp. 29–102.

56. de St. Jorre, *The Brothers' War*, p. 18.

57. Roger Morris, *Uncertain Greatness: Henry Kissinger and American Foreign Policy* (New York, 1979), pp. 120–30; de St. Jorre, *The Brothers' War*, 272–73; John J. Stremlau, *The International Politics of the Nigerian Civil War 1967–1970* (Princeton, 1977), pp. 118–27.

58. Shepard, *Nigeria, Africa, and the United States: From Kennedy to Reagan*, pp. 6, 34.

59. Lamb, *The Africans*, pp. 307–10; Ungar, *Africa: People and Politics*, pp. 126–28; Europa Publications Limited, *Africa South of the Sahara: 1986*, pp. 726–29; Stremlau, *The International Politics of the Nigerian Civil War 1967–1970*, pp. 62–66; Ate, *Decolonization and Dependence*, pp. 3–4, 71–76, 158–61.

60. Robert B. Shepard, *Nigeria, Africa, and the United States: From Kennedy to Reagan* (Bloomington, 1991), pp. 6, 34, 36–39, 41–43.

61. Mahoney, *JFK: Ordeal in Africa*, pp. 31–33.

62. Irving Kaplan, et al., *Area Handbook for Kenya* (Washington, D.C., 1976, pp. 40–45; Attwood, *The Reds and the Blacks: A Personal Adventure*, 193–95,

197–205, 215–28.

63. Attwood, *The Reds and the Blacks: A Personal Adventure*, 263–67; Kaplan, et al., *Area Handbook for Kenya*, pp. 45–48.

64. Attwood, *The Reds and the Blacks*, pp. 263–67; Kaplan, et al., *Area Handbook for Kenya*, pp. 47–48; Ungar, *Africa: People and Politics*, pp. 171–72; Tom Mboya, *The Challenge of Nationhood: A Collection of Speeches and Writings by Tom Mboya* (New York, 1970), foreword by Jomo Kenyatta.

65. Attwood, *The Reds and the Blacks*, pp. 237–70; Kaplan, et al., *Area Handbook for Kenya*, pp. 245–50; Harold D. Nelson, ed., *Kenya: A Country Study* (Washington, D.C., 1984), pp. 35–41.

66. Lamb, *The Africans*, pp. 64–69; Ungar, *Africa: People and Politics*, 407–16.

67. Lamb, *The Africans*, pp. 67–69; Duignan and Gann, *The United States and Africa: A History*, pp. 318–23; Irving Kaplan, ed., *Tanzania* (Washington, D.C., 1978), pp. 121–25.

68. Harold D. Nelson and Irving Kaplan, eds., *Ethiopia: A Country Study* (Washington D.C., 1981), pp. 220–24, 236–39; Irving Kaplan, et al., *Area Handbook for Somalia* (Washington, D.C., 1977), pp. 171–77, 185–91.

69. Noer, *Cold War and Black Liberation*, pp. 188–90.

70. Noer, *Cold War and Black Liberation*, pp. 192–93.

71. Noer, *Cold War and Black Liberation*, pp. 85–86, 222–25, 229–31, 234; Ungar, *Africa: People and Politics*, pp. 321–22.

72. Noer, *Cold War and Black Liberation*, pp. 187, 207, 228.

73. Douglas Brinkley and G. E. Thomas, "Dean Acheson's Opposition to African Liberation," *Trans-Africa Forum* 5, (Summer 1988), 70–72; Noer, *Cold War and Black Liberation*, pp. 229–30; Lake, *The Tar Baby Option*, pp. 112–16.

74. Noer, *Cold War and Black Liberation*, pp. 235, 237.

75. Noer, *Cold War and Black Liberation, 1948–1968*, pp. 238–50.

76. Noer, *Cold War and Black Liberation*, 237.

77. Brinkley and Thomas, "Dean Acheson's Opposition to African Liberation," *Trans-Africa Forum*, pp. 5, 63–81.

78. Thomas Karis, "United States Policy Toward South Africa," in *South Africa, the Continuing Crisis*, Gwendolyn M. Carter and Patrick O'Meara, eds., 2nd edition (Bloomington, 1982), pp. 321–22.

79. Study Commission on U.S. Policy Toward Southern Africa, *Time Running Out (The Report of the Study Commission on U.S. Policy Toward Southern Africa)* (Berkeley, 1981), pp. 346–48; Thomas J. Noer, "New Frontiers and Old Priorities in Africa," in Thomas G. Paterson, ed., *Kennedy's Quest for Victory: American Foreign Policy, 1961–1963* (New York, 1989), pp. 255–60; Karis, "United States Policy Toward South Africa," in *South Africa, the Continuing Crisis*, Carter and O'Meara, eds., 322–25, 329–30.

80. William J. Foltz, "Africa in Great Power Strategy," in W. J. Foltz and Henry Bienen, eds., *Arms and the African: Military Influences on Africa's International Relations* (New Haven, 1985), pp. 2–8, 19–20; Noer, "New Frontiers and Old Priorities in Africa," in Paterson, ed., *Kennedy's Quest for Victory*, pp. 275–78.

81. Karis, "United States Policy Toward South Africa," in *South Africa, the*

Continuing Crisis, Carter and O'Meara, eds., p. 314; Study Commission on U.S. Policy Toward Southern Africa, *Time Running Out,* p. 347.

82. Karis, "United States Policy Toward South Africa," in *South Africa, the Continuing Crisis,* Carter and O'Meara, eds., 325–28.

83. Karis, "United States Policy Toward South Africa," in *South Africa, the Continuing Crisis,* Carter and O'Meara, eds., 331–32.

84. Study Commission on U.S. Policy Toward Southern Africa, *Time Running Out,* pp. 349–50; Karis, "United States Policy Toward South Africa," in *South Africa, the Continuing Crisis,* Carter and O'Meara, eds., 329–33.

85. Schulzinger, *American Diplomacy in the Twentieth Century,* p. 259, 289–90; Thomas G. Paterson, ed., *Kennedy's Quest for Victory: American Foreign Policy, 1961–1963* (New York, 1989), pp. 3–23.

86. Mohamed A. El Khawas and Barry Cohen, eds., *National Security Study Memorandum 39: The Kissinger Study of Southern Africa* (Nottingham, 1975), pp. 5–6.

87. Foltz, "Africa in Great Power Strategy," in W. J. Foltz and Henry Bienen, eds., *Arms and the African: Military Influences on Africa's International Relations* (New Haven, 1985); Louis George Sarris, "Soviet Military Policy and Arms Activities in Sub-Saharan Africa," in ibid., pp. 12–16; Louis George Sarris, "Soviet Military Policy and Arms Activities," in ibid., pp. 29, 31–53; Davidson, *Africa in History: Themes and Outlines,* pp. 351–57, 362–63.

88. Lamb, *The Africans,* pp. 186–88; Williams, *Africa for the Africans,* 33–39.

89. Williams, *Africa for the Africans,* pp. 40–48; Kaplan, et al., *Area Handbook for Kenya,* p. 263.

90. Quarles, *The Negro in the Making of America,* pp. 270–75; *Report of the National Advisory Commission on Civil Disorders* (New York, 1968), p. 1.

91. Lake, *The Tar Baby Option,* pp. 3–4.

REFERENCES

Ate, Bassey E. *Decolonization and Dependence: The Development of Nigerian-U.S. Relations, 1960–1984.* Boulder, 1987.

Clower, Robert W., et.al. *Growth Without Development: An Economic Survey of Liberia.* Evanston, IL, 1966.

Duignan, Peter, and L.H. Gann. *The United States and Africa: A History.* New York, 1987.

Jackson, Henry F. *From the Congo to Soweto: U.S. Foreign Policy Toward Africa Since 1960.* New York, 1982.

Mahoney, Richard D. *JFK: Ordeal in Africa.* New York, 1983.

Noer, Thomas J. *Cold War and Black Liberation: The United States and White Rule in Africa, 1948–1968.* Columbia, MO, 1985.

Ungar, Sanford. *Africa: The People and Politics of an Emerging Continent.* New York, 1986.

Weissman, Stephen R. *American Foreign Policy in the Congo 1960–1964.* Ithaca, 1974.

Index